ESSAYS ON INTERNATIONAL CRIMINAL JUSTICE

Crimes of atrocity have profound and long-lasting effects on any society. The difference between triggering and preventing these tragic crimes often amounts to the choice between national potential preserved or destroyed. It is also important to recognise that they are not inevitable: the commission of these crimes requires a collective effort, an organisational context and long planning and preparation. Thus, the idea of strengthening preventative action has taken on greater relevance, and is now encompassed in the emerging notion of 'responsibility to prevent'. International courts and tribunals contribute to this effort by ending impunity for past crimes. Focusing investigations and prosecution on the highest leadership maximises the impact of this contribution. The ICC has an additional preventative mandate which is fulfilled by its timely intervention in the form of preliminary examinations. Moreover, when atrocity crimes are triggered, its complementarity regime incentivises states to stop violence and comply with their duties to investigate and prosecute, thus strengthening the rule of law at the national level. The new role granted to victims by the Rome Statute is key to the ICC's successful fulfilment of these functions. This new book of essays, which includes the author's unpublished inaugural lecture at Utrecht University, examines these issues and places particular emphasis on the additional preventative mandate of the ICC, the ICC complementarity regime, the new role granted to victims and the prosecution of the highest leadership through the notion of indirect perpetration.

Essays on International Criminal Justice

Hector Olasolo

IBEROAMERICAN INSTITUTE OF THE HAGUE
IIH
FOR PEACE, HUMAN RIGHTS AND INTERNATIONAL JUSTICE

• HART •
PUBLISHING

OXFORD AND PORTLAND, OREGON
2012

Published in the United Kingdom by Hart Publishing Ltd
16C Worcester Place, Oxford, OX1 2JW
Telephone: +44 (0)1865 517530
Fax: +44 (0)1865 510710
E-mail: mail@hartpub.co.uk
Website: http://www.hartpub.co.uk

Published in North America (US and Canada) by
Hart Publishing
c/o International Specialized Book Services
920 NE 58th Avenue, Suite 300
Portland, OR 97213-3786
USA
Tel: +1 503 287 3093 or toll-free: (1) 800 944 6190
Fax: +1 503 280 8832
E-mail: orders@isbs.com
Website: http://www.isbs.com

British Library Cataloguing in Publication Data
Data Available

ISBN: 978-1-84113-052-1

Typeset by Hope Services, Abingdon
Printed and bound in Great Britain by
CPI Group (UK) Ltd, Croydon, CRO 4YY

ACKNOWLEDGMENTS

To those who after having tried everything, and despite my deep resistance, have been the only ones to give me the strength necessary to face each day the power of the addiction and the affliction of the illness, and move forward with my restoration process: to God the Father and his Son Jesus Christ.

To Dilia Paola Gómez Patiño for making a true act of faith by staying at my side and trusting that my healing was possible even under the worst circumstances.

To my parents Valentin and Mercedes for not ceasing in three decades despite my continuous rejection of their efforts in offering me this marvellous gift that they themselves received thirty-three years ago.

To Nadime Patiño for her beauty, kindness, care and prayers in the Kennedy neighbourhood south of Bogota (Colombia).

To my brothers and sisters of the Neo-catechumenal communities of the parishes of St Agnes in the Hague, San Mateo in Bogota and Carmelitas in Logroño that have offered me support and spiritual and personal guidance.

To the music of St Roberto Belarmino Church in the Kennedy neighbourhood of south of Bogota and of San Pablo in Logroño (Spain) that permitted my ears to pay attention to the Word.

To the millions of human beings who have been, and continue to be as of the writing of these lines, victims of international crimes by the continuing wars for political, economic, military and cultural power, they are the ones who really deserve recognition, and it is to them whom I publically apologise for the enormous limitations that are still present today in international criminal law in providing them effective material support.

To those, who, as my teacher, boss and friend, Judge of the International Criminal Court Sylvia H Steiner, have a vital commitment to international criminal law that is not of an exclusively formal nature, but, despite all obstacles, aims at offering greater effective material protection.

And to Michelle Coleman, Enrique Carnero-Rojo, Alejandro Kiss and Lachezar Yanev for their invaluable help in so many aspects of the preparation of this *book*.

SUMMARY CONTENTS

CONTENTS

TABLE OF ABBREVIATIONS

AC	Appeals Chamber
AMIS	African Union Mission in Sudan
ARK	Autonomous Region of Krajina
Art./s.	Article/s.
AUC	*Autodefensas Unidas de Colombia*
CAR	Central African Republic
CCrP	Code of Criminal Procedure of Spain
Court	International Criminal Court
DRC	Democratic Republic of Congo
ECCC	Extraordinary Chambers of the Courts of Cambodia
ECHR	European Court of Human Rights
Ed	editor
FNI	*Front des Nationalistes et Intégrationnistes*
FPLC	*Patriotic Front for the Liberation of Congo*
FRPI	*Forces de Résistance Patriotique d'Ituri*
HAC	Humanitarian Affairs Commission of Sudan
IACtHR	Inter-American Court of Human Rights
IACHR	Inter-American Convention on Human Rights
ICC	International Criminal Court
ICC-OTP	Prosecutors Office of the International Criminal Court
ICCPR	International Covenant on Civil and Political Rights
ICC Statute	Rome Statute of the International Criminal Court (17 Jul 1998)
ICISS	International Commission on Intervention and State Sovereignty
ICTR	International Criminal Tribunal for Rwanda
ICTY	International Criminal Tribunal for the former Yugoslavia
JCE	Joint Criminal Enterprise
JEM	Justice and Equality Movement
LLM	Master of Laws Programme
MGS Haskanita	Military Group Site Haskanita (Sector 8)
MLC	*Mouvement pour la Libération du Congo*
NATO	North Atlantic Treaty Organization
NGO	Non-governmental Organization
NISS	National Intelligence and Security Service of Sudan
No	Number

OLCICC	Spanish Organic Law 18/2003 of 10 December 2003 on Cooperation with the International Criminal Court
OLJP	Spanish Organic Law 6/1985 of the Judicial Power
OTP	Office of the Prosecutor
para	paragraph
PTC	ICC Pre-Trial Chamber
PTC I	ICC Pre-Trial Chamber I
PTC II	ICC Pre-Trial Chamber II
PTC III	ICC Pre-Trial Chamber III
RegC	ICC Regulations of the Court
Res	Resolution
RPE	ICC Rules of Procedure and Evidence
RPP	Relevant Physical Perpetrators
SLM/A	Sudan Liberation Movement/Army
TC	ICC Trial Chamber
TC I	ICC Trial Chamber I
TC II	ICC Trial Chamber II
tr	Translator
TRC	Truth and Reconciliation Commission
UN	United Nations
UN Basic Principles	United Nations Basic Principles and Guidelines on the Right to Remedy and Reparation for Victims of Gross Violations of International Humanitarian Law
UNCHR	United Nations Commission on Human Rights
UNGA	United Nations General Assembly
UNSC	United Nations Security Council
UNSG	United Nations Secretary-General
UPC/RP	*Union des Patriotes Congolais pour la Reconciliation et la Paix*
UPDF	Uganda People's Defence Force
US	The United States of America
Utrecht Legal Clinic	Utrecht Law Faculty Clinical Programme on Conflict, Human Rights and International Justice
Vol	Volume
Waki Commission	Commission of Inquiry into the Post Election Violence in Kenya

TABLE OF CASES

European Court of Human Rights

Extraordinary Chambers in the Courts of Cambodia

Inter-American Court of Human Rights

International Criminal Court

International Criminal Tribunal for the former Yugoslavia

Special Court for Sierra Leone

Special Tribunal for Lebanon

Argentina

Australia

Colombia

THE AUTHOR

Professor Hector Olasolo was born in Madrid in 1972 and completed his primary and secondary studies in Logroño (La Rioja). In 1990 he attended the University of Salamanca, where he completed his undergraduate education 1996. Between 1997 and 2002 he completed research stays at Harvard, Columbia and Bolonia Universities. In New York, between January 1999 and June 2002, he served as a legal advisor to the Spanish delegation to the Preparatory Commission for the International Criminal Court at the United Nations. In 2002 he completed his Master's degree at Columbia University, where he was appointed as a Kent Scholar and taught as a Teaching Fellow at the Human Rights Institute. In February 2002, he received a special award doctorate from the University of Salamanca.

From July 2002 to August 2004, Professor Olasolo worked in the legal advisory and appellate sections of the Office of the Prosecutor of the International Criminal Tribunal for the former Yugoslavia. He was appointed as legal officer of the Pre-Trial Division of the International Criminal Court in August 2004 and from September 2005 also held a senior honorary lecturer position at Utrecht University. On 1 February 2009, he was appointed Professor of International Criminal Law and International Criminal Procedure at Utrecht Univeristy's Willem Pompe Insitute, and on 31 May 2011, he became the first Chairman of the Ibero-American Institute of The Hague for Peace, Human Rights and International Justice, positions in which he currently serves.

In addition to being the director of the Utrecht Law School Clinical Programme on Conflict, Human Rights and International Justice (www.uu.nl/legalclinic), which since 2009 provides pro bono legal services to Hague-based international courts and tribunals, Professor Olasolo teaches courses on international criminal law and procedure at the bachelor and master levels, including a moot-court type course specifically focused on the International Criminal Court (www.uu.nl/h.olasolo).

For the last ten years, Professor Olasolo has actively participated in training programmes for legal actors (judges, prosecutors, defence attorneys, victims' representatives, police and military personnel) in criminal, international and processes relating to the prosecution of international crimes, and for that he has spent periods of time in such diverse countries as Germany, Argentina, Canada, Chile, Colombia, Spain, the United States, the Netherlands, Italy, Mexico, Nicaragua, Peru, Serbia, Switzerland, Uruguay and Venezuela.[1]

[1] For more information regarding Professor Hector Olasolo Alonso see: www.uu.nl/h.olasolo.

Professor Olasolo, who is currently a member of the academic committee of the International Association of Criminal Law, has published several books in English and Spanish including: *Corte Penal Internacional: ¿Dónde Investigar?* (Tirant lo Blanch, 2003); *The Triggering Procedure of the International Criminal Court* (Martinus Nijhoff/Brill Publishers, 2005); *Ataques contra Personas y Bienes Civiles y Ataques Desproporcionados* (Tirant lo Blanch, 2007); *Terrorismo Internacional y Conflicto Armado* (with Professor Pérez Cepeda) Tirant lo Blanch 2008); *Unlawful Attacks in Combat Operations* (Martinus Nijhoff/Brill Publishers, 2008), *The Criminal Liability of Political and Military Leaders as Principals of International Crimes* (Hart Publishing, 2009); *Ensayos sobre la Corte Penal Internacional* (Universidad Javeriana/Dyke, 2009); *Estudios de Derecho Penal Internacional* (INACIPE, México DF 2010); *Ensayos de Derecho Penal y Procesal Internacional* (Tirant lo Blanch, Valencia, 2011) and *Formas de Imputación de los Dirigentes en Derecho Penal Internacional* (Temis/Universidades Sergio Arboleda y El Rosario, Bogotá, 2011).

He has also published around fifty articles in English and Spanish in prestigious law journals, including: *The American Journal of International Law*; *The Journal of International Criminal Justice*; *Criminal Law Forum*; *International Criminal Law Review*; *Leiden Journal of International Law*; *Revue Internationale de Droit Penale*; *IBCCrim* (Brazil); *Casación Penal* (Argentina); *Poder Judicial* (Spain); *La Ley* (Spain); *Revista Penal* (Spain); *Criminet* (Spain); *Indret* (Spain); *Revista de Derecho Publico* (Colombia); *Legis* (Colombia); *Iter Criminis* (Mexico); *Revista de la Universidad Central de Caracas* (Venezuela) and *Revista Global* (Dominican Republic).

The present volume presents a collection of studies, including the recent inaugural lecture of Professor Hector Olasolo as Chair of International Criminal Law and International Criminal Procedure at the University of Utrecht, delivered on 18 October 2010 at the *Aula* of the Academic Building of Utrecht University. The studies deal with various current issues in each of areas that make up the discipline of international criminal law: criminal law, procedural law, international cooperation and judicial assistance, and criminal policy.

FOREWORD

THE LAW IN THE TWENTY-FIRST CENTURY

Writing a foreword to Professor Hector Olasolo's new book on international justice is part of the ongoing dialogue we have had since he was appointed to Utrecht University.

I first encountered Professor Olasolo when, shortly after the International Criminal Court began its work, he joined the Chambers as legal officer of Judge Sylvia Steiner. She was the single judge in the first pre-trial proceedings of the Court. In those days, our conversations were brief and usually occurred at unconventional hours when we would meet at the doors of the Court. When I was leaving late in the evening, he would be returning to work. Hector used to come to the court house at eleven at night to take advantage of the quietness to prepare his arguments. Hector's remarkable diligence and dedication was acknowledged by this institution in which his career was born and developed.

Since his transition to the academic field, our dialogue revolved around substantive issues of the International Criminal Court. As an academic, Professor Olasolo retains his conviction in the need to strengthen international criminal law, and in particular the International Criminal Court as an institution through which a strong international justice system can be attained. Like few others, Professor Olasolo has transformed his knowledge of the internal functioning of the International Criminal Court's into theoretical knowledge. He uses his experience at the Court in order to identify and analyse the major theoretical challenges faced by the innovative system of justice created by the Rome Statute.

The majority of academic works on the Rome Statute focus on the Court's level of compliance with the fundamental guarantees established by states: the principles of legality and culpability, the presumption of innocence, due process of law. Such scrutiny is welcome. The International Criminal Court is in the process of building its foundation which must be solid. Academic scrutiny ensures technical control and will, with time, consolidate the different views of authors influenced by their own national legal traditions. This process of academic discussion and synthesis is fundamental because it distils the criminal procedure mechanisms that the Court implements and will make them universal.

At the same time, it is necessary to analyse the less classical aspects of the system created in Rome. Criminal jurisdiction, like currency and the flag of a state, constitutes one of the principal elements of national sovereignty. The existence of the International Criminal Court with the capacity to investigate and prosecute the heads of state of States Parties constitutes both a confirmation and a departure from the principles of Westphalia. It is a departure from the traditional forms of international relations, accepted by the sovereign states that have signed the treaty. Therefore it is not a revolution, but rather an evolution from one legal system to another that is substantially different. Legal academia of the twenty-first century must analyse this new legal system that has a universal aspiration and does not pertain to a single government but helps to coordinate multiple national governments.

This departure reflects a new world, a new demand from all of the world's citizens. The citizens of the twenty-first century, forming part of different communities, are citizens of a city like Tripoli, a country like Libya; they belong to regional groups like the Arab League and the African Union. They are also part of the United Nations. They are using new technologies to request respect for their rights from local, national, regional and global leaders. The Rome Statute is following this new trend; it created an institutional framework to protect the rights of any citizen under the jurisdiction of the Court. Its creation modifies the dynamic of the national, regional and global institutions without changing their rules. Academia must develop these different perspectives and distinguish which questions are to be resolved at the local level by a mayor, who corresponds to the prime minister, and which call for regional or global resolution.

In this sense, the work that Professor Olasolo presents to us in this volume follows this innovative approach. In his inaugural lecture, as a professor at Utrecht University, he addresses the fundamental question of the preventative role of the International Criminal Court. That is the mission established by the States Parties in the preamble of the Rome Statute: 'to put an end to impunity for the perpetrators of these crimes and thus to contribute to the prevention of such crimes'.

Professor Olasolo addresses this issue by analysing the preventative effects of the Court's actions, not only by means of a final sentence, but through timely intervention, during the phase, of the investigation or even during the preliminary examination of a situation.

After eight years' experience as Prosecutor of the Court, in which we have conducted several preliminary examinations, I am pleased that the inaugural lecture of Professor Olasolo addresses this issue. It is a pioneering, in-depth and rigorous analysis of the possibilities that the procedural framework of the Rome Statute and the Rules of Procedure and Evidence provide to the International Criminal Court. It can help the Office of the Prosecutor, to develop, in an effective manner, legal actions aimed at preventing crimes against humanity, war crimes or genocide.

The preventative role of the International Criminal Court is of tremendous relevance; it requires theoretical discussions and factual analysis of its impact, and can make the difference between life and death for the people of Darfur or Ivory Coast.

The book carries this lesson. It contains a different and innovative aspect of the issue. It is accompanied by a collection of chapters of the highest quality about the latest developments in a number of issues concerning substantiv criminal procedure, criminal policy, international cooperation anc tance, and international relations, in which the author demonstr parative character and multidisciplinary nature of his legal ec research.

The work of Professor Olasolo breaks new ground in the academic field of international criminal law, as an analysis of the system as a whole. I therefore wish to express my congratulations for this work.

Luis Moreno Ocampo
Prosecutor, International Criminal Court

The Hague, 27 April 2011

PRELIMINARY REFLECTIONS

THE PREVENTATIVE ROLE OF THE INTERNATIONAL CRIMINAL COURT

Scholars and commentators frequently state that the adoption of the Treaty of Rome for the establishment of a permanent International Criminal Court in July 1998 marked a historic milestone in the development of International Human Rights Law, International Humanitarian Law and in particular, International Criminal Law. Nevertheless, the interpretation of the penal provisions encompassed in the Statute has been difficult.

The Court has achieved considerable progress since it become operational in March 2003. However, these advances have faced manifold challenges: (inter alia) the lack of timely political will of the States Parties in enforcing the warrants of arrest issued by the Court; the complex nature of international criminal law, which is still in the making and lacks a general theory; and the different legal backgrounds and training of judges.

Professor Hector Olasolo has in recent years written thought-provoking essays which provide theoretical and practical problems arising from the interpretation and application of the Rome Statue in situations and cases thus far before the Court. In each one of the chapters compiled in this publication the author delves into the doctrine, offering his vision on the scope of the ICC provisions, while contrasting them with national legislation and critically examining the most recent jurisprudence of the Pre-Trial, Trial and Appeals Chambers of the ICC.

As a young scholar, Professor Hector Olasolo is already a known and respected author of books, essays and articles in which he continually explores the panorama of international criminal law, what he has referred to as a passionate calling. This passion, coupled with his professional experience in international criminal tribunals – including his work as a Legal Officer at the International Criminal Court – have led him to offer us with this collection of chapters, some of them unpublished until now. His compilation provides an enormous source of easy reference to students, academia and legal actors in the field of international law.

A look at the titles compiled in this volume demonstrates the present challenges to international criminal justice. The range of the themes examined is broad in scope. Issues covered by this publication include, inter alia: the criteria for admissibility of situations and cases; the application of such criteria to national jurisdictions; the right of victims to participate in proceedings; the complexity in defining concepts such as indirect perpetration and co-perpetration in international criminal law; and the need for the amendment of national legislations in order to enable cooperation with the Court. In all these, Professor Olasolo provides important academic and practical contributions that no doubt will fuel expert debate and hopefully assist in the creation of a body of national and international criminal law jurisprudence that is more consistent with the values and principles of the Rome Statute. One chapter in this volume that particularly caught my attention and motivated me to share some reflections is 'The Role of the International Criminal Court in Preventing Atrocity Crimes through Timely Intervention: From the Humanitarian Intervention Doctrine and *Ex Post* Facto Judicial Institutions to the Notion of Responsibility to Protect and the Preventative Role of the International Criminal Court'. It is noteworthy to mention that this chapter was first delivered by Professor Olasolo on 18 October 2010 during his inaugural lecture as Professor of International Law and International Criminal Procedure at the prestigious University of Utrecht in the Netherlands.

It is widely acknowledged that the entry into force of the Rome Statute and the subsequent establishment of the International Criminal Court were significant steps towards ending impunity for the commission of international crimes and thus, to promote peace and reconciliation. 'There will be no peace without justice' was the motto that was coined and incessantly repeated to provide legitimacy for the Court's mandate. I personally support this guiding principle.

Looking back at history – from the Nuremberg to the Tokyo tribunals to the 1993 and 1994 atrocities and genocide that took place in the former Republic of Yugoslavia and Rwanda respectively – the international community has recognised the need to set up an effective mechanism to prosecute and thereby deter the commission of future atrocities. The *Ad hoc* Tribunals for the former Yugoslavia and Rwanda (ICTY and ICTR correspondingly) were created to put an end to impunity for crimes already committed and no special attention was given to the plight of victims. Nevertheless, these tribunals were essential since they drew the attention of the international community to the need for the creation of a permanent judicial body. Their jurisprudence served as a basis for drafting the Rome Statute. In particular, the *Ad hoc* Tribunals were responsible for defining crimes of sexual violence as war crimes and crimes against humanity, which later led to the inclusion of these crimes within the Rome Statute. The *Ad hoc* Tribunals have therefore been relevant in the development of modern international criminal law. However, what has not yet been evaluated – and it does not yet seem possible – is the importance they played in fighting impunity at the international level and their role in achieving equality, peace and reconciliation in the territories of the former Yugoslavia and Rwanda.

These questions are also applicable to the International Criminal Court and its role in achieving peace, which cannot be limited only to its judicial function or to the prosecution of important political or military leaders around the world for crimes already committed. Professor Olasolo explores this possibility (ethical and categorical imperative, I would say), that the International Criminal Court also has a crucial function in its global responsibility to protect victims before their fundamental rights are violated.

The long-standing doctrine of humanitarian intervention was abandoned for different reasons ranging from global geopolitics and international real-politik. In 2005, the international community renewed its commitment and agreement to act through the United Nations as part of its 'responsibility to protect' civilians from atrocities when their governments fail to do so (World Summit, 14–16 September 2005).

In his chapter, Professor Olasolo clearly exposes the fundamentals of international law that enshrine the responsibility to protect, while emphasising that prevention is a natural role that must be fulfilled by the Court as part of its mandate. He provides an original perspective on how a series of preventive actions and timely intervention can be offered by the ICC to the international community in order to prevent the commission of international crimes.

From section III and until the end of the chapter, he portrays distinct scenarios of the two dimensions of the Court's preventive mandate: general prevention and timely intervention. 'Atrocious crimes are not inevitable', says Professor Olasolo. This is an affirmation that I share and that draws from a profound confidence in the mission of the Court. The ICC can intervene with concrete warnings to future atrocities (section IV) and during the commission of such crimes (section V).

As I write this commentary, atrocities which could have been prevented are ongoing in different parts of the world. Some of these situations have been referred to the Court by the United Nations Security Council for investigation by the ICC Prosecutor. These ongoing similar situations around the world could provide a historic opportunity for the ICC to open these new perspectives within the preventive mandate of the International Criminal Court. This would undoubtedly make the ICC a unique institution, to become a judicial mechanism that integrates three fundamental areas of international law (criminal, humanitarian, human rights) effective in protecting life, liberty, and freedom of all human beings. A court that fulfils its mandate as clearly provided for at the second paragraph of the preamble of the Rome Statute which reads '[m]indful that during this century millions of children, women and men (who) have been victims of unimaginable atrocities that deeply shock the conscience of humanity'.

One day, this will become possible through cooperation between the ICC and the international community and efforts of scholars like Professor Olasolo, whose contribution prompts debate among those interested in international criminal justice. I thank him for his efforts in renewing our conviction and commitment to the International Criminal Court and in a universal system of criminal justice that protects humanity against serious crimes.

Elizabeth Odio Benito
Judge and Former Vice-President, International Criminal Court

The Hague, May 2011

INTRODUCTION TO *ESSAYS ON INTERNATIONAL CRIMINAL JUSTICE*

This collection, written by a brilliant and prolific scholar and practitioner of international criminal justice, is an insightful and important contribution to the existing literature. Authored by an individual steeped in the jurisprudence of the *Ad hoc* Tribunals, as well as the legal traditions of Spain and much of the Spanish speaking world, the book serves as a bridge from the world of the *Ad hoc* Tribunals to the new world of the International Criminal Court (ICC) as well as from the International Criminal Court to national legal systems, particularly Spain and Colombia. The chapters it contains take as their premise the central role of the International Criminal Court in the system of international criminal justice that developed over the past two decades since the fall of the Berlin wall, but places the current operations of the ICC in historical and juridical context.

Each chapter in this collection is copiously footnoted and thoroughly researched, making it an important reference tool for scholars and practitioners in the field. Additionally and importantly, the chapters explore, without polemic, areas of controversy and dissent and thoughtfully and scrupulously set forth arguments for and against particular doctrinal choices. Where Professor Olasolo inserts his own views, as he properly does, those are clearly and forthrightly labelled as such. Well written and concise, the chapter address some of the most interesting current issues in the practice of the ICC: the question of complementarity before the Court itself (chapters 2 and 3); its application before national legal systems (chapters 4 and 5); forms of joint and indirect perpetration (chapters 6 and 7); the role of victims in criminal proceedings before the ICC (chapter 8) and finally, the role of legal clinics in continental Western Europe, and more particularly the operation and establishment of the Utrecht Legal Clinic on Conflict, Human Rights and International Justice (chapter 9).

The scholar will find much of interest and importance in the chapters on doctrine and its application, particularly in the extraordinarily helpful analysis of the Court's early case law as well as the jurisprudence of the ICTY. Professor Olasolo's experience as not only a scholar but practitioner of international criminal law is evident in his creative thinking about what kinds of preparatory acts might give rise to liability in the ICC for attempt, for example, and in thoughtfully analysing the relationship between national measures of transitional justice such as conditional amnesties and the admissibility criteria of the ICC Statute. His careful analysis of the text of the ICC Statute as well as its ancillary instruments, combined with his thorough knowledge of the law and his participation in the

Statute's negotiation as a member of the Spanish delegation, make his analyses particularly cogent and rigorous.

Finally, this book is obviously of tremendous current value. As this introduction was being written, the Security Council unanimously adopted Resolution 1970, which, among other things, referred the situation in Libya to the International Criminal Court, demonstrating the international community's belief in the Court's preventive value (as well as its possible punitive effect). This kind of role for the Court was identified in the first chapter of this collection, on 'The Role of the International Criminal Court in Preventing Atrocity Crimes through Timely Intervention', which thoughtfully and presciently analyses the relationship between the 'responsibility to protect' doctrine and the operations of the Court.

Books such as this are long in the making and represent a tremendous effort on the part of their authors. This book – representing the fruit of Professor Olasolo's thinking over several years – is no exception. It is a superb contribution not only to the literature on the International Criminal Court, but to the operations of international criminal justice itself. Containing constructive criticisms as well as imaginative thinking about how the ICC might respond in future cases, it demonstrates not only the author's ability as a legal scholar, but his commitment to a world in which the commission of atrocity crimes becomes less and less frequent, and their prevention and punishment becomes increasingly effective.

Leila Nadya Sadat

Henry H Oberschelp Professor of Law and Director, Whitney R Harris World Law Institute,

Washington University School of Law; Alexis de Tocqueville Distinguished Fulbright Chair,

Université de Cergy-Pontoise

Paris, Spring 2011

1

The Role of the International Criminal Court in Preventing Atrocity Crimes Through Timely Intervention*

'[T]he brutal legacy of the twentieth century speaks bitterly' of the collective inadequacies of international institutions and 'the profound failure of individual States to live up to their most basic and compelling responsibilities'.[1] Given the profound and long-lasting costs to a society of engaging in atrocity crimes,[2] strengthening preventative action becomes of utmost relevance.[3] This is emphasised by the emerging notion of 'responsibility to protect'.[4] In this chapter I will address the role of the International Criminal Court (ICC) in implementing the notion of responsibility to protect through means other than ending impunity for past crimes.

I Humanitarian Intervention Doctrine and Responsibility to Protect

The 1990s saw the establishment, by the United Nations (UN), or with the direct involvement of the United Nations, of several international tribunals with

* Inaugural Lecture of Professor Hector Olasolo as Chair of International Criminal Law and International Criminal Procedure at the University of Utrecht. It was delivered on 18 October 2010 at the *Aula* of the Academic Building of the University of Utrecht. The author thanks Gordon Brandt and Margaret Wichmann for their research on legislation, case law and doctrine. The views expressed herein are those of the author alone and do not necessarily reflect the views of the International Criminal Court (ICC), the ICTY, the United Nations in general or the Spanish Government.

[1] United Nations General Assembly (UNGA) 'Implementing the Responsibility to Protect: Report of the Secretary-General' (12 January 2009) UN Doc A/63/677 paras 5, 6.

[2] In this chapter, the term 'atrocity crimes' includes the following crimes: genocide, crimes against humanity including ethnic cleansing and war crimes. See in this regard, D Scheffer, 'Atrocity Crimes Framing the Responsibility to Protect' (2007–08) 40 *Case Western Reserve Journal of International Law* 111, 117. See also D Scheffer, 'Genocide and Atrocity Crimes' (2006) 1 *Genocide Studies and Prevention* 229, 238–39.

[3] As UNGA, 'On Responsibility to Protect' (above n 1) highlights at para 32, '[t]he difference between the two paths can amount to the choice between national potential preserved or destroyed'.

[4] ibid at 2, paras 1–10.

jurisdiction over atrocity crimes that had already taken place.[5] These tribunals were characterised by their primacy over national jurisdictions, their temporary nature and the limitation of their jurisdiction to a specific crisis situation, such as the breakup of the former Yugoslavia or the Rwandan genocide.[6] As explained by Leila Sadat and Michael Scharf, they were part of a broader post-conflict UN strategy and their primary goal was to facilitate reconciliation.[7]

Extending the basis for judicial intervention, while perpetuating a global system that tolerated atrocity crimes through inaction, was unsustainable.[8] As a consequence, the 1990s also saw the greatest development of the humanitarian intervention doctrine, and its application to situations such as those in Somalia in 1993 and Kosovo in 1999.[9] This doctrine is based on the understanding of sovereignty as responsibility, which can be traced back to Francisco de Vitoria and Bartolomé de las Casas. Their ideas led to the 1542 New Laws of the Indies, which abolished native slavery for the first time in European colonial history.[10] In the

[5] A Cassese, 'From Nuremberg to Rome: International Military Tribunals to the International Criminal Court' in A Cassese, P Gaeta and JRWD Jones (eds), *The Rome Statute of the International Criminal Court: A Commentary* vol I (Oxford, Oxford University Press, 2002) 10–17.

[6] R Cryer, H Friman, D Robinson and E Wilmshurst, *An Introduction to International Criminal Law and Procedure* (Cambridge, Cambridge University Press, 2007) 102–17.

[7] L Sadat, 'The Legacy of the ICTY: The International Criminal Court' (2003) 37 *New England Law Review* 1073; V Morris and M Scharf, *An Insider's Guide to the International Criminal Tribunal for the Former Yugoslavia* vol I (Irvington-on-Hudson, Transnational Publishers, 1995) 17–36. See also United Nations Security Council (UNSC), 'Report of the Secretary-General Pursuant to Paragraph 2 of the Security Council Resolution 808 (1993)' (3 May 1993) UN Doc S/25704; UNSC, 'Report of the Secretary-General Pursuant to Paragraph 5 of Security Council Resolution 955 (1994)' (13 February 1995) UN Doc S/1995/134.

[8] International Commission on Intervention and State Sovereignty (ICISS), 'The Responsibility to Protect' (Ottawa, International Development Research Centre, 2001). See also Scheffer, 'Atrocity Crimes' (above n 2) at 117.

[9] See generally A Hehir, *Humanitarian Intervention: An Introduction* (London, Palgrave Macmillan, 2010). For a specific account of humanitarian intervention in Kosovo, see ibid at 201–20. For a specific account of humanitarian intervention in Somalia see F Teson, *Humanitarian Intervention: An Inquiry into Law and Morality* 3rd edn (Ardsley, Transnational Publishers, 2005) 298.

[10] The ideas of Francisco de Vitoria (1483/86–1546) and Bartolomé de las Casas (1485–1566) led to the approval of the 'New Laws of the Indies for the Good Treatment and Preservation of the Indians'. The New Laws, which abolished native slavery for the first time in European colonial history, were passed to prevent the exploitation of the Indigenous peoples of the Americas by large scale landowners (*Encomenderos*) by strictly limiting their power and dominion. Francisco de Vitoria extrapolated his ideas of legitimate sovereign power to society at the international level. For him, not only relations between states ought to respect the rights of all, but there was also a common good of the world that was superior to the good of each state. As a result, relations between states had to pass from being justified by force to being justified by law and justice. See the translation of those extracts of Vitoria's works *De Indis* (1532) and *De Jure belli Hispanorum in barbaros* (1532) contained in his posthumous work F de Vitoria, *Relectiones Theologicae* (1557), reprinted in 1917 with the edition of JB Scott (New York, London, Oceana Publications, 1917). They were reprinted again by the Carnegie Institution of Washington in 1964 with the edition of Ernest Nys, who highlighted his influence over Hugo Grotius. See also B De las Casas, *Brevísima relación de la destrucción de las Indias* (1542), translated by N Griffin, *A Short Account of the Destruction of the Indies* (London, Penguin Classics, 1999). This is a translated version of the 1542 De las Casas work.

After the approval of the 1542 New Laws, a debate concerning the treatment of natives of the Indies was held in the Spanish city of Valladolid in 1550 and 1551. It opposed two main positions. On the one hand, Bartolomé de las Casas, Dominican and Bishop of Chiapas, argued that natives of the Indies were free men in the natural order and deserved the same treatment as others, according to Catholic theology.

early seventeenth century, Jesuit Francisco Suarez, leading representative of the School of Salamanca,[11] underscored that political power originates in the consensus of free wills, and that men are thus entitled to disobey even to the point of deposing an unjust government.[12] Subsequently, Hugo Grotius,[13] John Locke,[14] and the contract theorists of the eighteenth century, developed the notion of sovereignty as responsibility so as to shape it into its current form.

Based on this premise, the humanitarian intervention doctrine, formulated for the first time by Hersch Lauterpacht in the immediate aftermath of the Second World War,[15] justifies a right of armed intervention into a state that is unwilling or unable to protect its own population against atrocity crimes.[16] According to its

On the other hand, fellow Dominican Juan Ginés Sepúlveda insisted the Indians were natural slaves, and therefore reducing them to slavery or serfdom was consistent with Catholic theology and natural law. The New Laws were kept after the triumph of De las Casas' position. See A Losada, *The Controversy between Sepúlveda and Las Casas in the Junta of Valladolid* (DeKalb, Northern Illinois University Press, 1971) 280–82. See also B Keen, *The Legacy of Bartolomé de Las Casas* (Boulder, Westview Press, 1998) 57–69; DA Brading, *The First America: The Spanish Monarchy, Creole Patriots, and the Liberal State 1492–1867* (Cambridge, Cambridge University Press, 1991) 80–88; A Padgen, *The Fall of Natural Man: The American Indian and the Origins of Comparative Ethnology* (Cambridge, Cambridge University Press, 1982) 109; J Crow, *The Epic of Latin America* 4th edn (Berkeley, University of California Press, 1992).

[11] The leading members of the School of Salamanca were Francisco de Vitoria (1486–1546), Domingo de Soto (1494–1560), Martín de Azpilicueta (1493–1586), Tomás de Mercado (1525–75) and Francisco Suarez (1548–1617).

[12] See in particular F Suárez, 'Defensio Fidei Catholicae adversus Anglicanae sectae errores (The Defence of the Catholic Faith against the Errors of the Anglican)' (1613) in F Suárez, *Selections from Three Works of Francisco Suárez, S.J.: De legibus, ac deo legislatore, 1612; Defensio fidei catholicae, et apostolicae adversus anglicanae sectae errores, 1613; De triplici virtute theologica, fide, spe, et charitate, 1621* trans GL Williams and H Davis (London, Clarendon Press, 1944) 647–728.

[13] This understanding is reflected in Grotius's conception of things that are public and common to all men. See H Grotius, *De Mare Liberum* (1609) trans R Magoffin (New York, Oxford University Press 1916) 22–44; H Grotius, *Dejure Belli AC Pacis* book II (1625) trans F Kelsey (Gloucestershire, Clarendon Press 1925) ch 2; see generally H Lauterpacht, 'The Grotian Tradition in International Law' in *British Yearbook of International Law* (London, Oxford University Press, 1946) 1, 27.

[14] See, eg, J Locke, 'The Second Treatise of Government' (1690) in P Laslet (ed), *Two Treatises of Government* 3rd edn (Cambridge, Cambridge University Press, 1988) 265.

[15] H Lauterpacht (ed), *Oppenheim's International Law: A Treatise* 6th edn (London, Longmans Green and Company, 1947) 280. See also P Jessup, *A Modern Law of Nations* (New York, The Macmillan Company, 1948) 172–74; I Brownlie, 'Humanitarian Intervention' in J Moore (ed), *Law and Civil War in the Modern World* (Baltimore, Johns Hopkins University Press, 1974) 217; I Brownlie, 'The Principle of Non-Use of Force in Contemporary International Law' in W Butler (ed), *The Non-Use of Force in International Law* (Dordrecht, Martinus Nijhoff, 1989) 17.

[16] According to its supporters, 'humanitarian intervention [is] the proportionate transboundary help, including forcible help, provided by governments to individuals in another state who are being denied basic human rights and who themselves would be rationally willing to revolt against their oppressive government'. See Teson, *Humanitarian Intervention* (above n 9) at 5. See also BF Burmester, 'On Humanitarian Intervention: The New World Order and Wars to Preserve Human Rights' (1994) 1 *Utah Law Review* 269; J Delbruck, 'A Fresh Look at Humanitarian Intervention under the Authority of the United Nations' (1992) 67 *Indiana Law Journal* 887, 897–901; R Gordon, 'Humanitarian Intervention by the United Nations: Iraq, Somalia, and Haiti' (1996) 31 *Texas International Law Journal* 43, 44–46; R Lillich, 'Forcible Self Help under International Law'(1980) 62 *Readings in International Law from the Naval War College Review* 129, 134; J Nafziger, 'Self-Determination and Humanitarian Intervention in a Community of Power' (1991) 20 *Denver Journal of International Law and Policy* 9, 21–26. For these authors, humanitarian intervention was not unlawful under art 2(4) of the UN Charter because (i) it does not violate the territorial integrity of a state, since the purpose of such intervention is not to gain territory or alter an existing border; and (ii) it does not violate the political independence of states

supporters, humanitarian intervention by the United Nations, or by states with or without UN authorisation, is consistent with the principles of sovereignty and territorial integrity embraced in the UN Charter. Such principles, they argued, aim to protect the citizens of states rather than states as entities.[17] As a result, they cannot apply in favour of states that perpetrate or otherwise fail to prevent atrocity crimes.

Nevertheless, the humanitarian intervention doctrine has been progressively abandoned in the last decade for several reasons.[18] First, it failed to provide precise criteria to define those circumstances giving rise to the alleged right to armed intervention.[19] Secondly, it did not receive broad consensus as many argued that the UN Charter's prohibition on the use of force admits of no exception for humanitarian intervention.[20] Thirdly, as the notion of humanitarian intervention was limited to reaction to actual atrocity crimes, it left states with no other option than to choose between two undesirable choices: (i) standing by in the face of mounting civilian deaths; or (ii) deploying military force to protect the threatened populations.[21]

With the loss of support for the humanitarian intervention doctrine and the structural limitations of ex post facto judicial institutions, there was a need to identify new effective mechanisms for preventing atrocity crimes. The notion of responsibility to protect, endorsed by the UN General Assembly at the 2005

because it does not seek to subject the recalcitrant state to the political domination of the intervening state. Moreover, it was in consonance with the Charter's goals of promoting human rights and self-determination. See in particular R Lillich, 'Forcible Self-Help by States to Protect Human Rights' (1967) 53 *Iowa Law Review* 325, 332–38; R Lillich, 'Humanitarian Intervention: A Reply to Ian Brownlie and a Plea for Constructive Alternatives' in JN Moore (ed), *Law and Civil War in the Modern World* (Baltimore, Johns Hopkins University Press, 1974) 229; R Lillich, 'Intervention to Protect Human Rights' (1969) 15 *McGill Law Journal* 205; JN Moore, 'Toward an Applied Theory for the Regulation of Intervention' in JN Moore (ed), *Law and Civil War in the Modern World* (Baltimore, Johns Hopkins University Press, 1974) 3, 24–25; W Reisman, 'Sovereignty and Human Rights in Contemporary International Law' (1990) 84 *American Journal of International Law* 866.

[17] Lillich, 'Forcible Self-Help' (above n 16) at 332–38; Lillich, 'Humanitarian Intervention' (above n 16) at 229; Lillich, 'Intervention' (above n 16); Moore, 'Toward an Applied Theory' (above n 16) at 24–25; Reisman, 'Sovereignty' (above n 16).

[18] The theoretical debates over humanitarian intervention are summarised in S Murphy, *Humanitarian Intervention: The United Nations in an Evolving World Order* (Washington, DC, PAIL Institute, 1996) 202–12; O Ramsbotham and T Woodhouse, *Humanitarian Intervention in Contemporary Conflict: A Reconceptualization* (Cambridge, Polity Press, 1991) 33–65; D Richemond, 'Normativity in International Law: The Case of Unilateral Humanitarian Intervention' (2003) 6 *Yale Human Rights and Development Law Journal* 45, 48–49.

[19] See generally R Zacklin, 'Beyond Kosovo: The United Nations and Humanitarian Intervention' in LC Vorah, F Pocar, Y Fetherstone, O Fourney, C Graham, J Hocking and N Robson (eds), *Man's Inhumanity to Man* (The Hague, Kluwer Law International, 2003) 935; T Franck, 'Legality and Legitimacy in Humanitarian Intervention' in T Nardin and MS Williams (eds), *Humanitarian Intervention* (New York, New York University Press, 2006) 143.

[20] M Akehurst, 'Humanitarian Intervention' in H Bull (ed), *World Politics* (Oxford, Clarendon Press, 1984) 95, 104–07; I Brownlie, *International Law and the Use of Force by States* (Oxford, Clarendon Press, 1963) 338–42. See also N Ronzitti, *Rescuing Nationals Abroad through Military Coercion and Intervention on Grounds of Humanity* (Dordrecht, Martinus Nijhoff Publishing, 1985).

[21] UNGA, 'On Responsibility to Protect' (above n 1) paras 5–6. Moreover, as highlighted by the ICISS, 'external military intervention for humanitarian protection purposes has been controversial both when it has happened – as in Somalia, Bosnia and Herzegovina and Kosovo – and when it has failed to happen, as in Rwanda'. See ICISS, 'Responsibility to Protect' (above n 8) at 7.

World Summit,[22] reaffirmed by the UN Security Council in 2006,[23] and further elaborated on by the UN Secretary-General in 2009, aims at fulfilling this role.[24]

Like the humanitarian intervention doctrine, the notion of responsibility to protect is based on the understanding of sovereignty as responsibility. Nevertheless, it has several distinctive features, which, as Carsten Stahn has pointed out,[25] have secured its broad acceptance in a short period of time. First, it addresses the dilemma of intervention from the perspective of those suffering atrocity crimes rather than from the perspective of those asserting a right to intervention.[26]

Second, it does not limit responsibility and intervention to reaction to actual atrocity crimes. On the contrary, the notion of responsibility to protect constitutes a holistic approach to address crisis situations[27] based on the premise that an

[22] In response to Kofi Annan's question at the 2000 Millennium address, the Canadian Government established an ICISS, which, under the chairmanship of Gareth Evans and Mohamed Sahnoun, left aside the controversial doctrine of humanitarian intervention to focus on the new emerging notion of responsibility to protect. ICISS, 'Responsibility to Protect' (above n 8) was issued in December 2001. For an insider account of the work of the Commission and the ideas that shaped it, see G Evans, *The Responsibility to Protect: Ending Mass Atrocity Crimes Once and for All* (Washington, DC, Brookings Institution Press, 2008). See also A Bellamy, *A Responsibility to Protect: the Global Effort to End Mass Atrocities* (Cambridge, Polity Press, 2009); R Thakur, *The United Nations, Peace and Security: From Collective Security to the Responsibility to Protect* (Cambridge, Cambridge University Press, 2006) 245–86; R Thakur, 'Outlook: Intervention, Sovereignty and the Responsibility to Protect Experience from ICISS' (2002) 33 *Security Dialogue* 323; T Weiss and D Hubert, *The Responsibility to Protect: Research, Bibliography and Background* (Ottawa, International Development Research Centre, 2001). The notion of responsibility to protect was subsequently endorsed by the UN Secretary-General's (UNSG) High-Level Panel on Threats, Challenges and Change (see UNSG's High-Level Panel on Threats, Challenges and Change, 'A More Secure World: Our Shared Responsibility' (2 December 2004) UN Doc A/59/565 paras 65–66). On 16 September 2005, the UN General Assembly in the framework of the 2005 World Summit approved, by consensus, the concept of responsibility to protect in relation to atrocity crimes. (UNGA '2005 World Summit Outcome' (24 October 2005) UN Doc Res A/Res/60/1 paras 138–39. The General Assembly adopted the Summit Outcome in its resolution. Ibid at para 138.

[23] In para 4 of UNSC Resolution (Res) 1674 (2006) (28 April 2006) UN Doc S/Res/1674, on the protection of civilians in armed conflict, the Security Council reaffirmed the provisions of paras 138 and 139 of the Summit Outcome regarding the responsibility to protect populations from genocide, war crimes, ethnic cleansing and crimes against humanity. In the second preambular paragraph of UNSC Res 1706 (2006) (31 August 2006) UN Doc S/Res/1706 on the crisis in Darfur, the Council recalled its earlier reaffirmation of those provisions.

[24] UNGA, 'On Responsibility to Protect' (above n 1). See also C Joyner, 'The Responsibility to Protect: Humanitarian Concern and the Lawfulness of Armed Intervention' (2007) 47 *Virginia Journal of International Law* 693, 709.

[25] C Stahn, 'Responsibility to Protect: Political Rhetoric or Emerging Legal Norm?' (2007) 101 *American Journal of International Law* 99, 101, 118.

[26] ibid at 103.

[27] The need for a multi-phased vision of international engagement became evident during the multidimensional UN peacekeeping of the 1990s. Secretary-General Boutros-Ghali developed a tripartite conception of peacemaking, which distinguished peace-preventative diplomacy, peace-making and 'post-conflict peace building' in his Agenda for Peace. See UNSG, 'An Agenda for Peace-Preventative Diplomacy, Peacemaking, and Peace-Keeping' (17 June 1992) UN Doc A/47/277-S/24111 para 5. Some aspects of this distinction were subsequently developed in other reports. See for instance, (i) the Brahimi Report, which emphasised the continuous engagement from preventive action to peace building (UNGA and UNSC, 'Report of the Panel on United Nations Peace Operations' (21 August 2000) UN Doc A/55/305-S/2000/809), and (ii) the 2001 UN Secretary General Report, 'No Exit without Strategy', which put the emphasis on post-intervention responsibility (UNSC, 'No Exit without Strategy: Security Council Decision-making and the Closure or Transition of United Nations Peacekeeping Operations' (20 April 2001) UN Doc S/2001/394 para 26).

effective response requires a continuing intervention that starts with the adoption of preventative measures.[28] Only if such measures fail, reaction to actual atrocity crimes will be needed.[29] Moreover, the determination of the most appropriate mechanisms for reaction, including military intervention, must be driven by the need to subsequently fulfil the commitment to build a long-lasting peace, and promote good governance, rule of law and sustainable development.[30]

Third, the notion of responsibility to protect is based on a complementarity approach with three main pillars. According to Pillar I, states whose populations may be at risk have the primary responsibility to protect them from the incitement and commission of atrocity crimes.[31] When states concerned are unable to do so because of capacity deficits or lack of territorial control, third states, as well as the international community at large, must support and assist them under Pillar II.[32] If assistance measures are of no use because of the unwillingness of national leadership or the great deficit of national capacity, responsibility devolves to the international community to take timely and decisive action under Pillar III,[33] including armed intervention in extreme circumstances.[34]

As a result, the notion of responsibility to protect can be said to place a particular emphasis on prevention.[35] This has led, in turn, to a shift in the focus of the debate from the criteria under which military intervention, with or without UN authorisation, may be justified, or even required, to the timely implementation of effective preventative measures.

[28] UNGA, 'On Responsibility to Protect' (above n 1) paras 1–10.

[29] ibid.

[30] ibid.

[31] See UNGA Res A/Res/60/1 (above n 22) para 138: 'Each individual State has the responsibility to protect its populations from genocide, war crimes, ethnic cleansing and crimes against humanity. This responsibility entails the prevention of such crimes, including their incitement, through appropriate and necessary means. We [States] accept that responsibility and will act in accordance with it'. As UNGA, 'On Responsibility to Protect' (above n 1) para 18 has explained, Pillar I rests on long-standing obligations under international law, according to which responsibility for the prevention of violations of human rights lies with the national protection system of each state. See also N Jayawickrama, *The Judicial Application of Human Rights Law: National, Regional and International Jurisprudence* (Cambridge, Cambridge University Press, 2003) 46–50; B Ramcharan, 'The National Responsibility to Protect Human Rights' (2009) 39 *Hong Kong Law Journal* 361, 369–74.

[32] See UNGA Res A/Res/60/1 (above n 22) para 139: (i) We [States] also intend to commit ourselves, as necessary and appropriate, to helping States build capacity to protect their populations from genocide, war crimes, ethnic cleansing and crimes against humanity and to assisting those which are under stress before crises and conflicts break out'; and (ii) 'The international community, through the United Nations, also has the responsibility to use appropriate diplomatic, humanitarian and other peaceful means, in accordance with Chapters VI and VIII of the Charter, to help to protect populations from genocide, war crimes, ethnic cleansing and crimes against humanity'. Moreover, according to para 140 of the same resolution: 'We [States] fully support the mission of the Special Adviser of the Secretary-General on the Prevention of Genocide'.

[33] UNGA Res A/Res/60/1 (above n 22) para 139: 'In this context, we are prepared to take collective action, in a timely and decisive manner, through the Security Council, in accordance with the Charter, including Chapter VII, on a case-by-case basis and in cooperation with relevant regional organizations as appropriate, should peaceful means be inadequate and national authorities are manifestly failing to protect their populations from genocide, war crimes, ethnic cleansing and crimes against humanity'.

[34] UNGA, 'On Responsibility to Protect' (above n 1) paras 40, 50, 56.

[35] ibid at paras 1–2.

II The Two Dimensions of the ICC's Preventative Mandate: General Prevention and Timely Intervention

As the twenty-first century has witnessed a change in focus from the humanitarian intervention doctrine to the notion of responsibility to protect, it has also experienced a shift from ex post facto judicial institutions to the establishment and consolidation of a permanent International Criminal Court. As Cherif Bassiouni has underlined,[36] the ICC represents a rather different approach to the adjudication of atrocity crimes because it: (i) has been created through an international treaty by the States Parties; (ii) constitutes an independent international organisation of a permanent nature[37]; and (iii) is not part of a broader post-conflict UN strategy.[38]

In particular, the ICC has been established with a view to act over situations of atrocity crimes that take place after 1 July 2002[39] in the territory of any of its 114 States Parties,[40] and even outside such territory when there is a substantial involvement of their nationals[41] or a UN Security Council's referral.[42] Furthermore, the ICC operates on the basis of a complementarity regime, according to which it can only exercise its jurisdiction when states are inactive, or are unwilling or unable to genuinely carry out their own national proceedings.[43]

There is a clear connection between the notion of responsibility to protect and the ICC's mandate as both have their focus on future situations of atrocity crimes,[44] and are based on the primary responsibility of the states concerned. Indeed, last year, UN Secretary-General Ban Ki-moon referred to the ICC Statute as 'one of the key instruments relating to the responsibility to protect'.[45]

[36] MC Bassiouni, 'The Making of the International Criminal Court' in MC Bassiouni (ed), *International Criminal Law* vol 3, 3rd edn (Leiden, Martinus Nijhoff Publishers, 2008) 117–53.

[37] United Nations General Assembly (UNGA), 'Rome Statute of the International Criminal Court' (17 July 1998) UN Doc A/Conf.183/9, arts 1, 4 [hereinafter ICC Statute].

[38] The ICC has its own political and financial organs, which include an Assembly of States Parties, as well as a Bureau and a Secretariat of the Assembly, and a Budget and Finance Committee (See art 112 ICC Statute; Assembly of States Parties, 'ICC Financial Regulations and Rules,' ICC-ASP/7/5 (21 November 2008). Moreover, as provided for in art 4 ICC Statute, it has international legal personality, and the necessary legal capacity for the exercise of its functions and the fulfilment of its purposes.

[39] See art 11 ICC Statute.

[40] See art 12 ICC Statute.

[41] ibid.

[42] See arts 12, 13(b) ICC Statute.

[43] See para 10 of the Preamble ICC Statute; arts 1, 17 ICC Statute. See also *Prosecutor v Germain Katanga and Mathieu Ngudjolo Chui* (Judgment on the Appeal of Mr Germain Katanga against the Oral Decision of Trial Chamber II of 12 June 2009 on the Admissibility of the Case) ICC-01-04-01/07-1497 (25 September 2009).

[44] The notion of responsibility to protect is confined to four specific crimes (genocide, crimes against humanity, war crimes and ethnic cleansing), which, along with the crime of aggression, also constitute the jurisdiction *ratione materiae* of the ICC. (Art 5 ICC Statute). Nevertheless, it is important to highlight that the International Commission on Intervention and State Sovereignty envisioned the notion of responsibility to protect as having a significantly wider scope (See ICISS, 'Responsibility to Protect' (above n 8)). On the controversy about the potential for a wider scope for the notion of responsibility to protect, see Scheffer, 'Atrocity Crimes' (above n 2) at 113–16.

[45] UNGA, 'On Responsibility to Protect' (above n 1) para 19.

In this regard, it must be noted that the ICC shares with ex post facto judicial institutions a commitment to ending impunity as a means to promote: (i) positive general prevention, consisting of upholding the application of international criminal law and reinforcing the core societal values protected therein; and (ii) negative general prevention or deterrence, resulting from sending the message to the world's leadership that those engaging in atrocity crimes will not get away with them.[46] Such commitment is fulfilled by combining judicial proceedings with a number of external relations, outreach and public information activities.[47] The ICC's efforts on general prevention may assist UN officials and other stakeholders to emphasise, under Pillars II and III of the notion of responsibility to protect, both the costs of engaging in atrocity crimes and the benefits of abandonment.[48]

Nevertheless, unlike ex post facto judicial institutions, the ICC's preventative mandate has a second dimension. It consists of timely intervention into situations where there are tangible threats of future atrocity crimes, or where atrocity crimes are already taking place. It is mainly discharged by the ICC Prosecutor through his preliminary examinations and investigations, and may cover a broad range of situations as shown by: (i) the 9000 communications received to date by the Prosecutor from individuals located in more than 140 countries;[49] and (ii) the variety of geographical locations in which preliminary examinations or investigations have been started since 2003: Afghanistan, Central African Republic, Colombia, Darfur, Democratic Republic of Congo, Georgia, Guinea, Iraq, Ivory Coast, Kenya, Palestine, Uganda and Venezuela.[50]

As the notion of responsibility to protect places the emphasis on prevention through timely intervention, the ICC's timely intervention can make a unique contribution to discharging the responsibility of the international community under Pillars II and III of this notion.

III The ICC's Timely Intervention as a Result of Tangible Threats of Future Atrocity Crimes

Atrocity crimes are not unavoidable. They take long planning and preparation, as they require a 'collective effort' and an 'organisational context'.[51] Moreover, there

[46] Cryer et al, *An Introduction to International Criminal Law* (above n 6) at 22–39.

[47] ICC, 'Outreach': www.icc-cpi.int/Menus/ICC/Structure+of+the+Court/Outreach.

[48] UNGA, 'On Responsibility to Protect' (above n 1) paras 19, 53.

[49] To date the ICC Prosecutor has received 8733 individual communications. See ICC, 'Communications, Referrals, and Preliminary Examinations': www.icc-cpi.int/Menus/ICC/Structure+of+the+Court/Office+of+the+Prosecutor/Comm+and+Ref/Communications+and+ Referrals. htm.

[50] ibid.

[51] K Ambos, 'Epilogue: Future Developments of International Criminal Law in Relation to the Responsibility of Superiors for International Crimes' in H Olasolo, *The Criminal Responsibility of Senior Political and Military Leaders as Principals to International Crimes* (Oxford, Hart Publishing, 2009) 333.

is usually sufficient information about impending atrocity crimes, which, regrettably, is ignored or minimised by high-level national and international decision makers with competing political agendas.[52] Hence, statutory provisions on planning, preparation, incitement and attempt are of the utmost relevance for the effectiveness of preventative efforts through timely intervention. It may thus come as no surprise that, except for the definition of genocide which has always been taken verbatim from the 1948 Genocide Convention,[53] the approach taken by the ICC Statute is rather different from that taken by the statutes of the ex post facto judicial institutions. In the latter, as William Schabas has explained, provisions on planning, preparation, incitement and attempt would simply have been superfluous and were not included.[54]

Article 25 of the ICC Statute provides for liability for attempt in relation to all atrocity crimes (not just genocide), and attaches such liability to 'action that commences the execution of a crime by means of a substantial step'.[55] Although this definition requires more than just planning, the question arises as to where to draw the line between mere preparatory acts, and conduct amounting to a substantial step for the execution of atrocity crimes.[56] Neither the ICC Statute nor the case law of international tribunals provides guidance on this matter.[57] Some national systems, such as Germany's, have taken a more restrictive approach and require a direct movement towards the completion of the crime.[58] Others, such as the United States (US), favour a broader conception by attaching liability for attempt to possess, collect, or fabricate the means of the crime or to track the victims of the crime.[59]

As a result, should the ICC case law embrace a less restrictive approach, liability for attempt may encompass situations such as that which occurred in Rwanda, where for 16 consecutive months starting in January 1993, more than half a million machetes were imported and distributed, along with firearms and grenades, under the guise of a self-defence programme.[60]

[52] UNGA, 'On Responsibility to Protect' (above n 1) para 6.

[53] Genocide is the only exception as its definition, including the references to conspiracy, incitement and attempt, has been taken verbatim by the statutes of ex post facto judicial institutions, such as the ICTY, the ICTR and the Special Court for Sierra Leone, from the language of the 1948 Convention for the Prevention and Punishment of the Crime of Genocide, which expressly criminalises in its art 3 conspiracy to commit genocide, direct and public incitement to commit genocide and attempt to commit genocide. See also JD Ohlin, 'Attempt to Commit Genocide' in P Gaeta (ed), *The UN Genocide Convention: A Commentary* (Oxford, Oxford University Press, 2009) 183; A Eser, 'Individual Criminal Responsibility' in Cassese, Gaeta and Jones (eds), *The Rome Statute of the International Criminal Court* (above n 5) at 807; K Ambos, 'Article 25 Individual Criminal Responsibility' in O Triffterer (ed), *Commentary on the Rome Statute of the International Criminal Court* 2nd edn (Oxford, Munich, Hart Publishing and Verlag CH Beck, 2008) 764.

[54] WA Schabas, *Genocide in International Law* (Cambridge, Cambridge University Press, 2000) 281.

[55] See art 25(3)(f) ICC Statute.

[56] Ohlin, 'Attempt to Commit Genocide' (above n 53) at 178.

[57] ibid at 178, 182–84.

[58] See StGB § 22 (Germany). See also Eser, 'Individual Criminal Responsibility' (above n 53) at 812.

[59] See United States Model Penal Code § 5.01(1)(c). See also GP Fletcher, *Rethinking Criminal Law*, 2nd edn (New York, Oxford University Press, 2000) 180.

[60] *Prosecutor v Nahimana et al* (Judgment and Sentence) ICTR-99-52-T (3 December 2003) para 113.

Article 25 of the ICC Statute also attaches criminal liability to acts of 'public and direct incitement to commit genocide'.[61] Despite its limitation to the crime of genocide, its scope of application may be significant in situations like that in Rwanda where, starting in 1991, the media systematically incited Hutus to perpetrate violence against Tutsis,[62] or like that in Cambodia, where for years, the radio of the Khmer Rouge urged listeners to 'purify' the 'masses of the people' of Cambodia.[63]

With regard to the crime of aggression, the definition approved in June 2010 at the first ICC Review Conference, attaches criminal liability to the 'planning' and 'preparation' of an act of aggression.[64] This brings the ICC Statute more in line with most national systems, in which criminal liability can arise as a result of agreeing to commit a crime, participating in the design of a criminal plan or contributing to establish the necessary conditions for its execution.[65] Indeed, if today it is broadly accepted at the national level that criminal liability arises for such preparatory acts, there is no justification to say otherwise at the international level in relation to offences with the magnitude and gravity of atrocity crimes.[66]

[61] Regardless of whether genocide actually takes place. See in this regard *Prosecutor v Akayesu* (Judgment) ICTR-96-4-T (2 September 1998) para 561. See also JD Ohlin, 'Incitement and Conspiracy to Commit Genocide' in P Gaeta (ed), *The UN Genocide Convention: A Commentary* (Oxford, Oxford University Press, 2009) 192–95. See in particular art 25(3)(e) ICC Statute. In this particular area, the ICC Statute is somewhat more restrictive than the Genocide Convention, as well as than the statutes of the other international and internationalised courts and tribunals, which, although limited to the crime of genocide, provided the notion of 'conspiracy'.

[62] *Prosecutor v Nahimana et al* (Judgment) ICTR-99-52-A (28 November 2007) paras 41, 45. See also JP Chrétien, *Rwanda: Les Medias du Génocide* 2nd edn (Paris, Karthala/Reporters sans Frontiers, 2002). In particular, despite several reports during those critical months by the United Nations Assistance Mission in Rwanda and the Special Rapporteur on extrajudicial, arbitrary or summary executions on the incendiary programming of Radio *des Mille Collines*, there was no attempt by the international community to jam such broadcasts. See the UNSC, 'Report of the Secretary-General on the Situation in Rwanda' (31 May 1994) UN Doc S/1994/640, para 11; UNSG, 'Letter dated 15 December 1999 From the Secretary-General addressed to the President of the Security Council' (16 December 1999) UN Doc S/1999/1257, enclosure, annex I; UN Commission for Human Rights (UNCHR), 'Report of the Special Rapporteur on Extrajudicial, Arbitrary or Summary Executions, Mr BW Ndiaye, on his Mission to Rwanda from 8 to 17 April 1993' (11 August 1993) E/CN.4/1994/7/Add.1.

[63] British Broadcasting Corporation, 'Summary of World Broadcasts' FE/5813/A3/2 (15 May 1978).

[64] See Assembly of States Parties, 'Amendments to the Rome Statute of the International Criminal Court' Resolution RC/Res. 6 (11 June 2010) Annex I, art 8 bis, para 1.

[65] The extension of the scope of criminal law at the national level to criminalise this type of conduct, regardless of whether the commission of the crime is subsequently completed or even started, has been, to an important extent, utilised to confront situations in which a plurality of persons acting in a concerted manner resort systematically to criminal conduct to achieve economic goals (eg, trafficking of human beings, drugs, weapons, money laundering) or political goals (eg, terrorism). As a result, it may come as no surprise that national jurisdictions have also extended the criminalisation of preparatory acts to atrocity crimes, which, in addition to constituting the most egregious attacks on the core societal values of the international community, are of a 'unique magnitude', have a 'collective nature' and take place in an 'organisational context'.

[66] See the different approaches taken by Cassese and Fletcher on this point in relation to conspiracy to commit genocide: A Cassese, 'Jurisdiction *ratione materiae* – Genocide' in Cassese, Gaeta and Jones (eds), *The Rome Statute of the International Criminal Court* (above n 5) at 347; GP Fletcher, 'Amicus Curiae Brief of Specialists in Conspiracy and International Law in Support of Petitioner' 2006 West Law 53979, filed in *Hamdan v. Rumsfeld*, 548 U.S. 557 (2006) 12. Moreover, according to Schabas the exclusion of conspiracy to commit genocide from the Rome Statute was due to 'an oversight of exhausted drafters' (Schabas, *Genocide in International Law* (above n 54) at 264).

Although the existing provisions on attempt and incitement provide a sufficient basis for the ICC's timely intervention, extending liability for 'planning' and 'preparation' to all atrocity crimes will significantly strengthen the ICC's preventative role.[67]

Moreover, as senior leaders are usually directly involved in the planning and preparation of atrocity crimes,[68] focusing on this early stage of the *iter criminis* will reduce the controversy over some forms of criminal liability underscored by Kai Ambos,[69] George Fletcher,[70] Göran Sluiter,[71] Herman van der Wilt,[72] Elise van Sliedregt,[73] Tomas Weigend[74] or Gerard Werle.[75]

Furthermore, this will be in line with the ICC's gravity threshold, and Luis Moreno-Ocampo's policy of focusing on the 'most responsible persons'.[76]

As long as an individual communication[77] or a referral letter[78] contains tangible indicia of attempt or incitement to commit atrocity crimes, the ICC Prosecutor

[67] In particular, the exclusion of the notion of conspiracy from the realm of art 25(3) ICC Statute (including in relation to the crime of genocide) appears to be unjustified, particularly in light of its broad acceptance in national legal systems for lesser crimes. The *rationale* for the criminalisation of the notion of conspiracy is that the design of a common plan to commit a serious offence by two or more individuals seriously increases the risk of harming the societal value which is affected when the relevant offence is committed. This risk is further increased when those who have designed the plan to commit the offence begin taking the first steps towards preparing to implement their criminal plan. Logically, the higher the hierarchical position of those involved in the planning of the crime, the higher the level of risk will be. Likewise, the more egregious an attack on a core societal value is, the more legitimate an intervention at an earlier stage of the *iter criminis* in order to prevent the commission of the crime will be. As a result, it appears that the notion of conspiracy is particularly well suited to prevent the actual completion of atrocity crimes (the most serious crimes of international concern) by senior political and military leaders. In light of these circumstances, and considering the inclusion of conspiracy in the Genocide Convention, in the statutes of the *Ad hoc* Tribunals and in national jurisdictions, its exclusion from the ICC appears to be unjustified. This is more so if we consider that the definition of the crime of aggression, approved in June 2010 at the first ICC Review Conference, includes the criminalisation of conspiracy-like preparatory acts, such as 'planning'.

[68] This situation is normally accompanied by the conscious acquiescence of another sector of the leadership, which refrains from active involvement but does not take the measures within their power to stop such plans and/or preparations.

[69] K Ambos, 'Joint Criminal Enterprise and Command Responsibility' (2007) 5 *Journal of International Criminal Justice* 159, 167–76.

[70] GP Fletcher and JD Ohlin, 'Reclaiming Fundamental Principles of Criminal Law in the Darfur Case' (2005) 3 *Journal of International Criminal Justice* 539.

[71] A Zahar and G Sluiter, *International Criminal Law: A Critical Introduction* (Oxford, Oxford University Press, 2007) 221–57.

[72] H van der Wilt, 'Joint Criminal Enterprise Possibilities and Limitations' (2007) 5 *Journal of International Criminal Justice* 91.

[73] E van Sliedregt, 'Joint Criminal Enterprise as a Pathway to Convicting Individuals for Genocide' (2007) 5 *Journal of International Criminal Justice* 184.

[74] T Weigend, 'Intent, Mistake of Law and Co-Perpetration in the *Lubanga* Decision on Confirmation of Charges' (2008) 6 *Journal of International Criminal Justice* 471.

[75] G Werle, 'Individual Criminal Responsibility in Article 25 ICC Statute' (2007) 5 *Journal of International Criminal Justice* 953.

[76] See ICC Office of the Prosecutor, 'Paper on Some Policy Issues before the Office of the Prosecutor' (September 2003): www.icc-cpi.int/NR/rdonlyres/1FA7C4C6-DE5F-42B7-8B25-60AA962ED8B6/143594/030905 _Policy_Paper.pdf.

[77] See arts 13(c), 15(1) ICC Statute.

[78] See arts 13(a) and (b), 14, 53(1) ICC Statute.

must initiate a preliminary examination.[79] This examination aims to distinguish between (i) those situations that require a formal investigation, and (ii) those other situations better dealt with by other means.[80] To make such a determination, it is not sufficient to gather and analyse information concerning the allegations of attempt or incitement. It is also necessary to review the available information regarding, inter alia: (i) the admissibility of the relevant situation, due to the inaction, unwillingness or inability of national authorities and the gravity of the violence; and (ii) the possible existence of substantial reasons to believe that the investigation would not serve the interests of justice.[81]

As a result, as Antonio Cassese[82] and David Scheffer[83] have pointed out, the Prosecutor can respond appropriately on grounds of admissibility or interest of justice where national authorities take meaningful steps to actually prevent atrocity crimes. Moreover, according to article 25 of the ICC Statute those who start the execution of atrocity crimes by means of a substantial step shall not be liable if they abandon their efforts to commit such crimes or otherwise prevent their completion.[84] Hence, the Prosecutor can close a preliminary examination into allegations of attempt or incitement if his timely intervention has contributed to successfully defusing the threat of atrocity crimes occurring.

Although the Prosecutor cannot rely at this stage on measures of a coercive nature,[85]

[79] All natural and legal persons have not only been granted the right to access the ICC by way of individual communications and, in the case of States Parties and the Security Council, referral letters, but they have also been granted the right to be informed of the reasons why the ICC Prosecutor does not intend to proceed with an investigation. See arts 15(6), 53(3) ICC Statute and Rules 104 and 105 of the Rules of Procedure and Evidence. See also H Oasolo, *The Triggering Procedure of the International Criminal Court* (Leiden, Martinus Nijhoff Publishers, 2005) 65–70.

[80] Olasolo, *Triggering Procedure*, ibid at 39–47. See also ICC Office of the Prosecutor, 'Regulations of the Office of the Prosecutor' ICC-BD/05-01-09 (23 April 2009) regs 25–29.

[81] According to arts 15(3) and (4), 53(1) ICC Statute, and Rule 48 of the Rules of Procedure and Evidence, these are the different elements of the standard '*reasonable basis* to initiate an investigation', which must be met for the ICC to initiate a formal investigation into a situation. This was underscored in the recent decision of Pre-Trial Chamber II in the relation to the Kenya situation. *Situation in the Republic of Kenya* (Decision Pursuant to Article15 of the Rome Statute on the Authorization of an Investigation into the Situation in the Republic of Kenya) ICC-01/09-19 (31 March 2010) paras 26–35.

[82] A Cassese, *International Criminal Law* 2nd edn (Oxford, Oxford University Press, 2008) 395–409.

[83] D Scheffer and A Cox, 'The Constitutionality of the Rome Statute of the International Criminal Court' (2008) 98 *Journal of Criminal Law and Criminology* 983–1068.

[84] According to art 25(3)(f) ICC Statute: 'Attempts to commit such a crime by taking action that commences its execution by means of a substantial step, but the crime does not occur because of circumstances independent of the person's intentions. However, a person who abandons the effort to commit the crime or otherwise prevents the completion of the crime shall not be liable for punishment under this Statute for the attempt to commit that crime if that person completely and voluntarily gave up the criminal purpose'. See Ambos, 'Individual Criminal Responsibility' (above n 53) at 764. See also Ohlin, 'Attempt to Commit Genocide' (above n 53) at 175–77.

[85] On the initiation of an investigation, the Prosecutor can also rely on measures of a coercive nature, as well as on all forms of State Party cooperation provided for in art 93 of the ICC Statute. See arts 54, 57, 93 ICC Statute. Disguising an art 54 ICC Statute investigation as an art 15(2) ICC Statute preliminary examination would be contrary to the limited scope of the latter. See Olasolo, *Triggering Procedure* (above n 79) at 59. A different opinion is held by M Bergsmo and J Pejic, 'Article 15' in O Triffterer (ed), *Commentary on the Rome Statute of the International Criminal Court* 2nd edn (Oxford, Munich, Hart Publishing and Verlag CH Beck, 2008) 366.

and not all forms of States Party cooperation are available,[86] the potential of preliminary examinations to incentivise national authorities should not be underestimated. As shown by several preliminary examinations, including Georgia,[87] Guinea[88] and Palestine,[89] the Prosecutor, in addition to receiving testimony and seeking information from reliable sources,[90] may: (i) send missions to the relevant states; (ii) receive in The Hague national delegations of members of governments, representatives of high-courts, opposition leaders and NGOs; (iii) provide advice on those measures that should be taken at the national level to defuse the threat of atrocity crimes; (iv) discuss a prevention strategy with the United Nations and other stakeholders; (v) exchange information with national and international actors; and (vi) address in the media the evolution of events and the degree of cooperation by national authorities.[91]

Using diplomatic and media channels to bring the world's attention to the plans of senior leaders to engage in atrocity crimes, along with highlighting the possibility of them escaping ICC prosecution should they abandon their plans and take the necessary preventative measures, can be a powerful tool. Moreover, from the perspective of ensuring a timely reaction to tangible threats of atrocity crimes, the ICC Statute appears to offer unprecedented opportunities. While

[86] Those forms of State Party cooperation provided for in art 93 Rome Statute in which the Prosecution can rely on at this stage are: (i) the identification and location of persons or items; (ii) the voluntary questioning of victims and witnesses in the territory of the States Parties; (iii) the service of documents, including judicial documents; (iv) the provision of records and documents, including official records and documents; (v) the examination of places or sites; and (vi) any other type of assistance not of a coercive nature which is not prohibited by the law of the requested Statute. See Olasolo, *Triggering Procedure* (above n 79) at 60.

[87] In relation to the preliminary examination of the situation in Georgia, since the Prosecutor made public its preliminary examination public on 14 August 2008, the Georgian Minister of Justice visited the Prosecutor in the Hague; Russia, a State not Party to the Statute, sent to the Prosecutor 3817 communications, the Prosecutor requested information from the Governments of Russia and Georgia on 27 August 2008, and both of them responded; and two on-site visits have been conducted in Georgia in November 2008 and June 2010, and one in Russia in March 2010. See ICC Office of the Prosecutor, 'Georgia': www.icc-cpi.int/Menus/ICC/Structure+of+the+Court/Office+of+the+Prosecutor/Comm+And+Ref/Georgia/.

[88] In relation to the preliminary examination of the situation in Guinea, since the Prosecutor made public its preliminary examination on 14 October 2009, consultations were held in January 2010 with President Compaore of Burkina Faso (mediator for the contact group on Guinea) and President Wade of Senegal to ensure that they are informed of Prosecutor's work; two on-sites visits to Guinea have taken place in February and May 2010 to meet, inter alia, the Guinean Minister of Justice, Colonel Lohalamou, and the Guinean judges took place on 19–21 May 2010. See ICC Office of the Prosecutor, 'Guinea': www.icc-cpi.int/Menus/ICC/Structure+of+the+Court/Office+of+the+Prosecutor/Comm+and +Ref/Guinea/.

[89] With regard to the preliminary examination of the Palestine situation, a delegation from the Palestinian National Authority, and Representatives of the Arab League visited the Prosecutor on 15 and 16 October 2009, and on 11 January 2010. See ICC Office of the Prosecutor, 'Palestine': www.icc-cpi.int/Menus/ICC/Structure+of+the+Court/Office+of+the+Prosecutor/Comm+and+Ref/Palestine/.

[90] Art 15(2) ICC Statute; Rules 104, 105 of the Rules of Procedure and Evidence.

[91] See in this regard, W Burke-White, 'Implementing a Policy of Positive Complementarity in the Rome System of Justice' (2008) 19 *Criminal Law Forum* 59, 61; CK Hall, 'Developing and Implementing an Effective Positive Complementarity Prosecution Strategy' in C Stahn and G Sluiter, *The Emerging Practice of the International Criminal Court* (Leiden, Brill, 2009) 220.

other organs of the international community, such as the UN Security Council or the UN General Assembly, usually require long negotiations before deciding to intervene in a situation, the ICC Prosecutor need not consult with interested stakeholders prior to opening a preliminary examination.

Despite the absence of conclusive evidence at this stage, it appears that the preliminary examination in Afghanistan, contributed to NATO (and in particular the United States) subsequently tightening its airstrike policy.[92] The United States also appears to have reaffirmed its commitment to its internal mechanisms of investigation and prosecution,[93] which may have led to the opening in April 2010 of a high profile military inquiry into civilian deaths allegedly caused by US Special Forces.[94]

In turn, the preliminary examination in Iraq, which started on the receipt of numerous individual communications since 2003, was closed in light of the proceedings initiated in the United Kingdom with regard to each instance of war crimes allegedly involving British nationals.[95]

Moreover, the preliminary examination in Kenya appears to have strengthened the message sent by former UN Secretary-General Kofi Annan to caution Kenyan authorities that there will be no impunity for those engaging in atrocity crimes.[96]

Whenever a preliminary examination is unsuccessful in incentivising national authorities, the investigation stage,[97] in which the Prosecutor can rely on coercive measures[98] and all forms of State Party cooperation, may prove to be a useful mechanism to fulfil the ICC's preventative mandate. Article 53 of the ICC Statute

[92] D Schwammenthal, 'Prosecuting American 'War Crimes' *The Wall Street Journal* (The Hague, 26 November 2009) Opinion Europe. See also D Filkins, 'US Tightens Airstrike Policy in Afghanistan' *The New York Times* (21 June 2009) Asia Pacific.

[93] See E Barbour and MC Weed, 'The International Criminal Court (ICC): Jurisdiction, Extradition, and US Policy' (Congressional Research Service 16 March 2010): assets.opencrs.com/rpts/R41116_20100316.pdf, 15.

[94] See L King, 'Inquiry puts Spotlight on US Special Forces in Afghanistan' *The Los Angeles Times* (9 April 2010) referring to the high profile inquiry into alleged civilian deaths caused by special forces who, until then, had been largely shielded from the public spotlight which was opened by the US military in April 2010.

[95] ICC Office of the Prosecutor, 'OTP Response to communications received concerning Iraq' (9 February 2010): www.icc-cpi.int/NR/rdonlyres/04D143C8-19FB-466C-AB77-4CDB2FDEBEF7/143682/OTP_letter_to_senders_re_Iraq_9_February_2006.pdf, 9.

[96] See the research paper by C Bjork and J Goebertus, from Harvard Law School, 'Parallel Paths and Unintended Consequences: The Role of Civil Society and the ICC in Rule of Law Strengthening in Kenya' (forthcoming): works.bepress.com/christine_bjork/1/. See also Kofi Annan Foundation, 'Remarks by Kofi Annan on Conclusion of the Visit to Kenya, 2–8 December 2009' (Press Release December 2009): kofiannanfoundation.org/newsroom/press/2009/12/remarks-he-kofi-annan-conclusion-visit-to-kenya-au-panel-eminent-african. Nevertheless, far more empirical research is necessary to have more certainty about the impact of the Preliminary Examination of the ICC.

[97] In this cases, a qualitative approach to the gravity threshold may still justify the start of an investigation into a situation where atrocity crimes have not been yet committed, or are starting being committed. For a definition of a qualitative approach to the gravity threshold see *Prosecutor v Abu Garda* (Decision on the Confirmation of Charges) ICC-02/05-02/09-243-Red (8 February 2010) paras 31–33; *Situation in the Republic of Kenya* (Decision Pursuant to Article 15 of the Rome Statute on the Authorization of an Investigation into the Situation in the Republic of Kenya) ICC-01/09 (31 March 2010) para 62.

[98] See arts 54–57 ICC Statute.

empowers the Prosecutor to close an investigation when 'there is no sufficient basis for a prosecution'. This standard is comprised of similar criteria to those applicable during the preliminary examination.[99] As a result, the Prosecutor can close an investigation if it has served to prompt reluctant national authorities to take meaningful steps to actually prevent the commission of atrocity crimes.[100]

IV The ICC's Timely Intervention when Atrocity Crimes are already Taking Place

The ICC's timely intervention can also take place in situations in which atrocity crimes are already occurring. The focus in these situations will be on stopping ongoing atrocity crimes.

Moreover, abandonment of future crimes will not exclude liability for those already committed. Therefore, preliminary examinations and investigations could only be brought to an end by the Prosecutor on admissibility or interest of justice grounds.

In this context, prompting national authorities to stop ongoing atrocity crimes goes hand in hand with:[101] (i) encouraging and assisting them to comply with their duties to investigate and prosecute those crimes already occurred ('positive complementarity');[102] and (ii) dividing with the ICC, particularly in cases of substantial capacity deficits, the burden of adjudicating the crimes ('cooperative complementarity').[103] As a consequence, supporting receptive states to strengthen their judicial systems and carry out national proceedings is a core component of the ICC's timely intervention.

[99] Compare art 53(2) ICC Statute with art 53(1) ICC Statute and r 48 of the ICC Rules of Procedure and Evidence.

[100] Moreover, under art 19(11) ICC Statute, the Prosecutor may decide to suspend his investigation and monitor the development of events at the national level prior to formally close it.

[101] Both positive complementarity and cooperative complementarity appear to have been implicitly upheld, to an important extent, by the 22 June 2009 decision of the ICC Appeals Chamber in the *Katanga and Ngudjolo* case. See *Prosecutor v Mr Germain Katanga and Mathieu Ngudjolo Chui* (Decision of the Presiding Judge of the Appeals Chamber in the appeal of Germain Katanga against the Decision of Trial Chamber I of 12 June 2009 on the admissibility of the case) ICC-01/04-01/07-1286 (10 July 2009).

[102] See Burke-White, 'Implementing a Policy' (above n 91) at 61; Hall, 'Developing and Implementing' (above n 91) at 220. See also ME Cross and S Williams, 'Recent Developments at the ICC: Prosecutor v Germain Katanga and Mathieu Ngudjolo Chui: A Boost for Co-operative Complementarity?' (2010) 10 *Human Rights Law Review* 336, 339.

[103] A Cassese, 'The Rome Statute: A Tentative Assessment' in Cassese, Gaeta and Jones (eds), *The Rome Statute of the International Criminal Court* (above n 5) at 1906; C Kress, '"Self-Referrals" and "Waivers of Complementarity": Some Considerations in Law and Policy' (2004) 2 *Journal of International Criminal Justice* 944, 947–48; F Gioia, 'State Sovereignty, Jurisdiction, and "Modern" International Law: The Principle of Complementarity in the International Criminal Court' (2006) 19 *Leiden Journal of International Law* 1095, 1115.

As stated by William Burke-White[104] and Christopher Hall,[105] the Prosecutor, in order to fulfil this mandate during his preliminary examinations and investigations, may rely on those measures referred to in the previous section. In particular, the Prosecutor may train national actors in the adjudication of atrocity crimes, and may assist them in the establishment of protection programmes for victims and witnesses and effective systems of information management. He can also monitor and provide feedback regarding the development of national proceedings, and work in coordination with other ICC organs to increase the efficacy of overall preventative efforts.

It must be stressed that, despite the international cooperation of other stakeholders, the national authorities of receptive states appear to have a strong preference to receive advice and guidance directly from ICC officials. As national authorities are aware that their efforts to adjudicate atrocity crimes will be reviewed by the ICC, the ICC's advice and guidance is considered of the utmost importance to ensure the success of such efforts. As a result, the potential of the ICC to strengthen through timely intervention the rule of law and improve good governance in receptive states is major.[106] The preliminary examination in Colombia provides some indicia of this potential.

Investigations of those paramilitary members demobilised in Colombia since 2003[107] did not start until May 2006, when the Constitutional Court upheld the centrepiece of the demobilisation process: the Peace and Justice Law.[108] Soon afterwards, the ICC Prosecutor made public his preliminary examination,[109] and in October 2007 and August 2008 he personally conducted two on-site visits to Colombia.[110]

[104] Burke-White, 'Implementing a Policy' (above n 91) at 61.

[105] Hall, 'Developing and Implementing' (above n 91) at 220.

[106] See also in this regard, W Burke-White, 'Complementarity in Practice: The International Criminal Court as Part of a System of Multi-level Global Governance in the Democratic Republic of Congo' (2005) 18 *Leiden Journal of International Law* 557, 589–90. See also in this respect the document issued by the prosecution itself which was published just after this inaugural address was delivered: ICC Office of the Prosecutor, 'Draft Policy Paper on Preliminary Examinations' (4 October 2010): www.icc-cpi.int/NR/rdonlyres/9FF1EAA1-41C4-4A30-A202-174B18DA923C/282515/OTP_Draftpolicypaperonpreliminaryexaminations04101.pdf. At the June 2010 ICC Review Conference, a proposal was made by the stocktaking bureau on the complementarity principle to task the Secretariat of the Assembly of States Parties 'facilitating the exchange of information between the Court, States Parties, signatory States, international organizations, civil society and other stakeholders, aimed at strengthening domestic jurisdictions'. (ICC Assembly of States Parties, Bureau on Stocktaking: Complementarity, 'Taking Stock of the Principle of Complementarity: Bridging the Impunity Gap' (18 March 2010) ICC-ASP/8/51, para 54(e)). Although this initiative may constitute an initial first step in the right direction, it is insufficient in light of the potential in strengthening rule of law and improving good governance in receptive states through timely intervention.

[107] The demobilisation process is the result of the Santa Fé de Ralito Accord signed on 15 July 2003. That agreement was between the Colombian national government and the so-called *Autodefensas Unidas de Colombian* (AUC).

[108] See Corte Constitucional de Colombia, sentencia C-370/ 2006 (18 May 2006). See also JE Arvelo, 'International Law and Conflict Resolution in Colombia: Balancing Peace and Justice in the Paramilitary Demobilization Process' (Winter 2006) 77 *Georgetown Journal of International Law* 411.

[109] See ICC Office of the Prosecutor, 'Colombia': www.icc-cpi.int/Menus/ICC/Structure+of+the+Court/Office+of+the+Prosecutor/Comm+and+Ref/Colombia.

[110] See ibid.

Since then, the Supreme Court of Colombia has underscored the importance of focusing investigations under the Peace and Justice Law on (i) the pattern of atrocity crimes committed against the civilian population, and (ii) the structure, membership and external support of those paramilitary organisations through which the crimes were committed.[111] This has been fully reflected in the 16-page *Protocol for the Presentation of Evidence* issued on 23 August 2010 by the Bogotá Peace and Justice Trial Chamber.

Furthermore, since the end of 2007, the Colombian Supreme Court has also been conducting investigations and prosecutions for alleged links with paramilitary groups against a third of the members of the Colombian Parliament,[112] as well as against around 20 governors.[113] These proceedings, which are based on confessions made by demobilised paramilitary leaders, have led so far to more than ten convictions, most of them against members of political parties that supported the Colombian Government in 2007. Such confessions have also led to the investigation in lower courts of several hundred civil servants, local politicians and members of the armed forces and the police.[114]

It is indisputable that only a handful of high ranking military and police officers are currently facing investigation, and that the application of the Peace and Justice Law is facing significant challenges, such as (i) the lack of publicity of the criteria to select those demobilised paramilitary members investigated under such a Law; (ii) the few convictions entered so far; (iii) the extradition to the United States on drug-trafficking charges of 14 key high-level paramilitary leaders; (iv) the lack of demobilisation of guerrilla members; and (v) the new increase in the level of violence, spurred partly by armed groups comprised of former paramilitary members.[115]

Nevertheless, in assessing whether the ongoing Colombian proceedings for atrocity crimes are contributing to strengthening the rule of law and improving good governance, one must take into consideration the long decades of mass violence in which paramilitary groups and their aides enjoyed full impunity in Colombia.

[111] See, inter alia, the appeal decisions of the Penal Chamber of the Colombian Supreme Court, in the cases of (i) Wilson Salazar Carrascal (aka *el loro*) Case No 31539 (31 July 2009); and (ii) Gian Carlos Gutierrez Suarez (aka *el tuerto*) Case No 32022 (21 September 2009).

[112] See Verdad Abierta's information collected up to July 2010 which refers to data provided by the New Rainbow Foundation available at: www.verdadabierta.com/reconstruyendo/1856-estadisticas.

[113] ibid.

[114] ibid.

[115] For a general analysis of the justice and peace process, see K Ambos, *Procedimiento de La Ley de Justicia y Paz (Ley de 2005) y Derecho Penal Internacional* (Bogotá, GTZ, Universidad de Göttingen, 2010); G Gallón Giraldo, M Reed Hurtado and C Lleras Cruz (eds), *Anotaciones sobre la Ley de Justicia y Paz: Una Mirada desde los Derechos de las Víctimas* (Bogotá, Comisión Colombiana de Juristas, 2007). See also the recent publication by Professor Kai Ambos extended within the framework of the roundtable with non-government organisations on the situation in Colombia in The Hague organised by the Office of the ICC on 19 and 20 October 2010: K Ambos and F Huber, 'The Colombian Peace Process and the Principle of Complementarity of the International Criminal Court: Is there sufficient willingness and ability on the part of the Colombian authorities or should the Prosecutor open an investigation now?' (5 January 2011): www.icc-cpi.int/NR/rdonlyres/ 2770C2C8-309A-408E-A41B-0E69F098F421/282850 /civil1.pdf.

As shown by the visits of the Colombian Attorney General and an ample delegation from the Colombian Supreme Court to the ICC in 2010, the Prosecutor's preliminary examination appears to be a contributing factor to the new situation in Colombia. Nevertheless, it is difficult to measure its impact on the Colombian national authorities as there appear to be several other contributing factors, such as the conditions imposed by the US Congress to approve US military aid and favourable trade conditions for Colombia[116] and the judgments of the Inter-American Court of Human Rights against Colombia for paramilitary violence.[117]

In this context, further coordination between the ICC's timely intervention and those other contributing factors will increase the effectiveness in Colombia of the measures taken by the international community pursuant to the notion of responsibility to protect. In this regard, it must be noted that the need for further coordination between the United Nations and the ICC is especially acute,[118] particularly in light of their mutual recognition and commitment to cooperation,[119]

[116] The final certification by the US State Department in connection with the performance by the Colombian armed forces of the conditions relating to compliance with the conditions of respect for human rights imposed by the United States Congress took place on 9 September 2010. See in this regard, United States Embassy in Bogotá, 'Resolución y Certificación del Gobierno Colombiano y de las Fuerzas Armadas con respect a los Condicionamientos en Derechos Humanos' (15 Sep 2010): spanish.bogota.usembassy.gov/pr_117_15092010.html. It can also be found on the website of the Colombian Commission of Jurists report by the US State Department which analyses in detail whether or not the Colombian armed forces in 2009 complied with the requirements of respect for human rights imposed by the United States Congress. (US Department of State, 'Memorandum of Justification concerning Human Rights Conditions with respect to Assistance for the Colombian Armed Forces' (Sep 2010): www.coljuristas.org/LinkClick.aspx?fileticket=ksYH5X9Cvy0%3d&tabid=160&language=es-CO).

[117] See the judgments of the Inter-American Court of Human Rights in *Case of the 19 Comerciantes v Colombia*, Series C, No 93 (5 July 2004); *Case of the Mapiripán Massacre v Colombia*, Series C, no 122 (15 September 2005); *Case of the Pueblo Bello Massacre v Colombia*, Series C, No 140 (31 January 2006); *Case of the Ituango Massacre*, Series C, No 148 (1 July 2006); *Case of Manuel Cepeda Vargas v Colombia*, Series C, No 213 (26 May 2010).

[118] A Cassese, 'Is the ICC Still Having Teething Problems' (2006) 4 *Journal of International Criminal Justice* 434, 436. See also N Jain, 'A Separate Law for Peacekeepers: The Clash between the Security Council and the International Criminal Court' (2005) 16 *European Journal of International Law* 239.

[119] Paras 7 and 9 of the Preamble of the ICC Statute reaffirms the Purposes and Principles of the UN Charter and emphasises the will of the States Parties to have the ICC established in relationship with UN system. Moreover, art 87(7) of the Statute permits the ICC to send a finding of lack of state cooperation to the UN Security Council for its consideration. Other provisions, such as art 87(6) of the ICC Statute, provide that the ICC may ask any intergovernmental organisation, including the United Nations, to provide information or documents, as well as other forms of cooperation agreed upon by the relevant organisation. Furthermore, art 115 of the ICC Statute establishes that the expenses of the Court and the Assembly of States Parties may be provided for by the '[f]unds provided by the United Nations, subject to the approval of the General Assembly, in particular in relation to the expenses incurred due to referrals by the Security Council. In turn, the Negotiated Relationship Agreement between the ICC and the United Nations (elaborated pursuant to article 2 of the ICC Statute) is based on mutual recognition between the UN and the ICC and a commitment to cooperation. Its preamble highlights 'the important role assigned to the International Criminal Court in dealing with the most serious crimes of concern to the international community as a whole [. . .] and which threaten the peace, security and well-being of the world'. On the basis of a general obligation of mutual cooperation, coordination and consultation enshrined in art 3, the Negotiated Relationship Agreement elaborates on the modalities of cooperation between both organisations in a number of areas, including UN Security Council referrals (art 17(1) of the Negotiated Relationship Agreement); UN Security Council requests for suspension of ICC investigations and prosecutions (art 17(2) of the Negotiated Relationship Agreement); UN Security Council cooperation under the condition of confidentiality (art 18(3) of the

as well as the existing safeguards against ICC interference with the role of the Security Council.[120]

V Conclusion

The ICC's preventative mandate is an important means to fulfil the responsibility of the international community under the notion of responsibility to protect. So far, the focus has been on the ICC's efforts on general prevention by ending impunity for past atrocities. Nevertheless, the ICC's contribution to the prevention of future atrocity crimes through timely intervention is potentially even greater.

Realising this potential requires acknowledgment of the ICC's preventative role through timely intervention by the different organs of the institution. It also requires States Parties to recognise this role so as to provide the necessary resources, and extend to all atrocity crimes criminal liability for 'planning' and 'preparation'. Based on this premise, increased coordination between the ICC, the United Nations and other stakeholders will increase the preventive effect of their timely intervention.

In the end, what is at stake is whether the ICC remains one among several mechanisms for accountability with a limited general prevention mandate; or whether, instead, it fully develops its potential to prevent atrocity crimes, strengthen the rule of law and improve good governance through timely intervention.

Negotiated Relationship Agreement); and UN Security Council cooperation with the ICC Prosecutor in the context of a preliminary examination (art 18(2) ICC Statute of the Negotiated Relationship Agreement).

[120] Arts 12, 13 and 16 of the ICC Statute empower the UN Security Council to refer any post-1 July 2002 situation to the ICC without any jurisdictional limitation, and to request the ICC to suspend an investigation or a prosecution for renewable periods of 12 months. Moreover, the Assembly of States Parties has recently approved by consensus at the First Review Conference that the ICC will only exercise its jurisdiction over the crime of aggression after ascertaining whether the UN Security Council has made a determination of an act of aggression committed by the relevant state. In the absence of such a declaration, the ICC could only proceed if it is acting on the basis of a State Party referral or an individual communication and if the plenary of the Pre-Trial Division gives its authorisation to do so (see Assembly of States Parties, 'Amendments to the Rome Statute of the International Criminal Court on the Crime of Aggression' Annex I to Resolution RC/Res.6 (11 June 2010) art 15, para 6).

2

The Admissibility of 'Situations'*

I Introduction

As of March 2009, the International Criminal Court (ICC) is conducting (i) preliminary examinations of a number of 'situations', including those of Colombia, Afghanistan, Chad, Kenya, Ivory Coast and Georgia;[1] (ii) investigations into the 'situations' in the Democratic Republic of Congo (DRC), Northern Uganda, Darfur (Sudan) and the Central African Republic (CAR); and (iii) pre-trial or trial proceedings in three 'cases' (*Lubanga* case, *Katanga and Ngudjolo* case and *Bemba* case). Moreover, trial proceedings in four additional 'cases' are on hold pending the suspects' arrest or voluntary appearance (*Kony et al* case, *Ntaganda* case, *Harun and Kushayb* case and *Al Bashir* case).

The distinction between 'situations and 'cases' is found in the Statute of the International Criminal Court (ICC Statute). Articles 13(a) and (b), 14(1) and 19(3) of the ICC Statute establish that the object of a referral by the UN Security Council or a State Party is to be a 'situation'.[2] Moreover, article 18(1) makes clear that the preliminary examinations and investigations initiated by the Prosecution

* Drafted with E Carnero Rojo (Ph.D Candidate at Utrecht University; Law Degree Deusto University; LLM Leiden University; Associate Legal Adviser at ICC OTP from 2004 to 2009) in September 2009. At the time of submission of the final manuscript of the present work, it was awaiting publication as part of the book: C Stahn and MM El Zeidy (eds), *The International Criminal Court and Complementarity: From Theory to Practice* (Cambridge, Cambridge University Press, 2011). The authors thank Cambridge University Press for authorising the reprint of the present work. The views expressed herein are those of the authors alone and do not necessarily reflect the views of the ICC, the ICTY, the United Nations in general or the Spanish Government.

[1] ICC Office of the Prosecutor, 'ICC Prosecutor confirms situation in Georgia under analysis' (press release) ICC-OTP-20080820-PR346 (20 August 2008).

[2] United Nations General Assembly (UNGA), 'Rome Statute of the International Criminal Court' (17 July 1998) UN Doc A/Conf.183/9 [hereinafter ICC Statute]. With regard to the distinction between 'situations' and 'cases' see H Olasolo, 'The Lack of Attention to the Distinction between Situations and Cases in National Laws on Cooperation with the ICC: Special Attention to the Spanish Case' (2007) 20 *Leiden Journal of International Law* 193. See also L Yee, 'The International Criminal Court and the Security Council' in R Lee (ed), *The International Criminal Court: The Making of the Rome Statute – Issues, Negotiations, Results* (The Hague, Kluwer Law International, 1999) 147; SA Fernández de Gurmendi, 'The Role of the International Prosecutor' in Lee, ibid, 180–82 E Wilmhurst, 'Jurisdiction of the Court' in Lee, ibid, 131; H Olasolo, *The Triggering Procedure of the International Criminal Court* (Leiden, Martinus Nijhoff, 2005) 44.

as a result of such referrals must also refer to 'situations'.[3] Similarly, articles 15(5) and (6) and 18(1) highlight that 'situations' are also the object of the preliminary examinations and investigations resulting from communications made by natural or legal persons other than States Parties and the UN Security Council.[4] Once the investigation into a 'situation' is initiated, the Prosecution may request the issuance of a warrant of arrest or summons to appear pursuant to article 58 against one or more identified individuals, if it considers that there are 'reasonable grounds' to believe that these individuals, are criminally liable for one or more crimes within the jurisdiction of the Court allegedly committed in one or several specific incidents. The issuance by the Pre-Trial Chamber of the requested warrant or summons marks the commencement of a 'case'.[5]

Some authors have expressed the view that 'the complementarity test under article 17 of the ICC Statute applies where the investigation into a given country or conflict *situation* has yielded a *case* (ie, "specific incidents during which one or more crimes within the jurisdiction of the Court seem to have been committed by one or more identified suspects").'[6] Nevertheless, article 53(1)(b) of the ICC Statute and rule 48 of the Rules of Procedure and Evidence of the Court (RPE) appear to request the application of the complementarity test at a much earlier stage of the proceedings. Pursuant to these provisions, the Prosecution must carry out an admissibility assessment before deciding whether to initiate – or, when acting on the receipt of a communication (eg, situations in Colombia and Georgia), to request the Pre-Trial Chamber's authorisation to initiate – an investigation into the relevant situation.

Hence, the question arises as to what is the object of such an admissibility assessment, considering the early stage of the proceedings at which it must be carried out, as well as the fact that a case only arises at a significantly subsequent stage of the proceedings – for instance, the first DRC case (the *Lubanga* case) was initiated a year and a half after the initiation of the investigation into the DRC situation, and the first Darfur case (the *Harun and Kushayb* case) was opened about two years after the initiation of the investigation into the Darfur situation.

[3] HT Holmes, 'The Principle of Complementarity' in R Lee (ed), *The International Criminal Court: The Making of the Rome Statute – Issues, Negotiations, Results* (The Hague, Kluwer Law International, 1999) 71, fn 40; MM El Zeidy, 'The Ugandan Government Triggers the First Tests of the Complementarity Principle: An Assessment of the First State's Party Referral to the ICC' (2005) 5 *International Criminal Law Review* 83, 106.

[4] Olasolo, *Triggering Procedure* (above n 2) at 44. The term 'case' in art 15(4) should not be read in isolation but, rather, in the context of the rest of art 15. Thus, when read together with the references to the notion of situation in art 15(5) and (6) and in view of the drafters' intention to introduce adequate safeguards against the initiation of politically motivated investigations – in particular when the *notitia criminis* is communicated by individuals or legal persons other than States Parties or the UN Security Council – one cannot but conclude that, in spite of the literal reference to the term 'case' in art 15(4), the object of article 15 proceedings are 'situations'.

[5] R Rastan, 'What is a "Case" for the Purpose of the Rome Statute?' (2008) 19 *Criminal Law Forum* 435, 442–43.

[6] C Kress and L Grover, 'International Criminal Law Restraints in Peace Talks to End Armed Conflicts of a Non-International Character' in M Bergsmo and P Kalmanovitz (eds), *Law in Peace Negotiations* (Oslo, Forum for International Criminal and Humanitarian Law Publications, 2009) 29, 45.

This chapter intends to shed some light on this issue. In order to do so, it will first analyse how the ICC Pre-Trial, Trial and Appeals Chambers have interpreted the distinction between the notions of 'situation' and 'case' provided for in the ICC Statute so far. It will then turn its attention to the notion of 'admissibility of situations' (as opposed to 'admissibility of cases'). It will analyse its content, relevance and, most importantly, whether there is any room for such a notion under the current statutory scheme, as interpreted in the ICC case law so far. Finally, the last section of the chapter will advance some guiding criteria for the performance of admissibility assessments of situations.

II The Distinction between 'Situations' and 'Cases'

The distinction between 'situations' and 'cases' was first embraced by the Prosecution, when, in June 2004, the Prosecution announced the opening of an investigation into the DRC 'situation'.[7] Subsequently it announced the opening of investigations into the Northern Uganda 'situation' in July 2004,[8] the Darfur 'situation' in June 2005[9] and the CAR 'situation' in May 2007.[10]

Likewise, all Chambers of the Court have embraced the distinction between 'situations' and 'cases'. The content of both notions, as well as the features that distinguish them, have been particularly elaborated upon in the context of victims' participation in the proceedings. Pre-Trial Chamber I, when issuing the Court's first decision on victim participation in January 2006, explained that

> [s]ituations, which are generally defined in terms of temporal, territorial and in some cases personal parameters, such as the situation in the territory of the Democratic Republic of Congo since 1 July 2002, entail the proceedings envisaged in the Statute to determine whether a particular situation should give rise to a criminal investigation as well as the investigation as such.[11]

In the same decision, the Chamber defined a 'case' by referring to 'specific incidents during which one or more crimes within the jurisdiction of the Court seem to have been committed by one or more identified suspects'.[12] Since then, Pre-Trial Chamber I has recognised 128 applicants as victims allowed to participate in

[7] ICC Office of the Prosecutor, 'The Office of the Prosecutor of the International Criminal Court opens its first investigation' (press release) ICC-OTP-20040623-59 (23 June 2004).

[8] ICC Office of the Prosecutor, 'Prosecutor of the International Criminal Court opens an investigation into Northern Uganda' (press release) ICC-OTP-20040729-65 (29 July 2004).

[9] ICC Office of the Prosecutor, 'The Prosecutor of the ICC opens investigation in Darfur' (press release) ICC-OTP-0606-104 (6 June 2005).

[10] ICC Office of the Prosecutor, 'Prosecutor opens investigation in the Central African Republic' (press release) ICC-OTP-20070522-220 (22 May 2007).

[11] *Situation in the Democratic Republic of Congo* (Decision on the Applications for Participation in the Proceedings of VPRS 1, VPRS 2, VPRS 3, VPRS 4, VPRS 5 and VPRS 6) ICC-01/04-101-tEN-Corr (17 January 2006) para 65.

[12] ibid.

the proceedings at the stage of investigation into the DRC situation.[13] And after the issuance of warrants of arrest against Thomas Lubanga Dyilo, Germain Katanga and Mathieu Ngudjolo Chui, Pre-Trial Chamber I[14] has respectively recognised four and 57 applicants as victims in relation to those two cases.

Pre-Trial Chamber II has also noted the distinction between 'situations' and 'cases' when reaching a conclusion on applications by victims to participate in the proceedings. In fact, Pre-Trial Chamber II has relied on the distinction between those two notions established by Pre-Trial Chamber I in order to specify the rights enjoyed by victims at the 'situation stage'.[15] More recently, the Chamber has noted that for the application of article 19(1),

> the proceedings must have reached the stage of a case (including 'specific incidents during which one or more crimes within the jurisdiction of the Court seem to have been committed by one or more identified suspects'), as opposed to the preceding stage of the situation following the Prosecutor's decision to commence an investigation pursuant to article 53 of the Statute.[16]

[13] ibid at paras 124, 135, 153, 167, 176, 186; *Prosecutor v Thomas Lubanga Dyilo* (Decision on the Applications for Participation in the Proceedings of a/0001/06, a/0002/06 and a/0003/06 in the case of the Prosecutor v Thomas Lubanga Dyilo and of the investigation in the Democratic Republic of the Congo) ICC-01/04-01/06-228-tEN (28 July 2006) para 16; *Situation in the Republic Democratic of the Congo* (Corrigendum to the 'Decision on the Applications for Participation Filed in Connection with the Investigation in the Democratic Republic of the Congo by a/0004/06 to a/0009/06, a/0016/06 to a/0063/06, a/0071/06 to a/0080/06 and a/0105/06 to a/0110/06, a/0188/06, a/0128/06 to a/0162/06, a/0199/06, a/0203/06, a/0209/06, a/0214/06, a/0220/06 to a/0222/06, a/0224/06, a/0227/06 to a/0230/06, a/0234/06 to a/0236/06, a/0240/06, a/0225/06, a/0226/06, a/0231/06 to a/0233/06, a/0237/06 to a/0239/06 and a/0241/06 to a/0250/06') ICC-01/04-423-Corr-tENG) (31 January 2008) paras 137–38, 142–43; *Prosecutor v Germain Katanga and Mathieu Ngudjolo Chui* (Decision on the Applications for Participation in the Proceedings of Applicants a/0327/07 to a/0337/07 and a/0001/08) ICC-01/04-01/07-357 (2 April 2008) para 13; *Prosecutor v Germain Katanga and Mathieu Ngudjolo Chui* (Public Redacted Version of the 'Decision on the 97 Applications for Participation at the Pre-Trial Stage of the Case') ICC-01/04-01/07-579 (10 June 2008) paras 51–52; *Prosecutor v Germain Katanga and Mathieu Ngudjolo Chui* (Decision on the Application for Participation of Witness 166) ICC-01/04-01/07-632 (23 June 2008) para 14.

[14] *Prosecutor v Thomas Lubanga Dyilo* (Decision on the Applications for Participation in the Proceedings Submitted by VPRS 1 to VPRS 6 in the Case the Prosecutor v Thomas Lubanga Dyilo) ICC-01/04-01/06-172-tEN (29 June 2006) paras 8–9; *Prosecutor v Thomas Lubanga Dyilo* (Decision on the Applications for Participation in the Proceedings of a/0001/06, a/0002/06 and a/0003/06 in the case of the Prosecutor v Thomas Lubanga Dyilo and of the investigation in the Democratic Republic of the Congo) ICC-01/04-01/06-228-tEN (28 July 2006) para 16; *Prosecutor v Thomas Lubanga Dyilo* (Decision on the Applications for Participation in the Proceedings a/0004/06 to a/0009/06, a/0016/06, a/0063/06, a/0071/06 to a/0080/06 and a/0105/06 in the case of The Prosecutor v Thomas Lubanga Dyilo) ICC-01/04-01/06-601-tEN (20 October 2006) para 13; *Prosecutor v Germain Katanga and Mathieu Ngudjolo Chui* (Decision on the Applications for Participation in the Proceedings of Applicants a/0327/07 to a/0337/07 and a/0001/08) ICC-01/04-01/07-357 (2 April 2008) para 13; *Prosecutor v Germain Katanga and Mathieu Ngudjolo Chui* (Public Redacted Version of the 'Decision on the 97 Applications for Participation at the Pre-Trial Stage of the Case') ICC-01/04-01/07-579 (10 June 2008) paras 51–52; *Prosecutor v Germain Katanga and Mathieu Ngudjolo Chui* (Decision on the Application for Participation of Witness 166) ICC-01/04-01/07-632 (23 June 2008) para 14.

[15] Situation in Uganda (Decision on victims' applications for participation a/0010/06, a/0064/06 to a/0070/06, a/0081/06 to a/0104/06 and a/0111/06 to a/0127/06) ICC-02/04-101 (10 August 2007) paras 88, 96; *Prosecutor v Joseph Kony et al* (Decision on victims' applications for participation a/0010/06, a/0064/06 to a/0070/06, a/0081/06 to a/0104/06 and a/0111/06 to a/0127/06) ICC-02/04-01/05-252 (10 August 2007) paras 88, 96.

[16] *Prosecutor v Joseph Kony et al* (Decision on the admissibility of the case under article 19(1) of the Statute) ICC-02/04-01/05-377 (10 March 2009) para 14.

All in all, Pre-Trial Chamber II has recognised 21 applicants as 'victims of the situation'[17] and 41 applicants as 'victims of the case' against *Kony et al.*[18]

In turn, in the absence of applications to participate in relation to the CAR situation,[19] Pre-Trial Chamber III has found 54 applicants to be victims in relation to the *Bemba* case.[20]

Trial Chamber I[21] has also acknowledged the existence of 'victims of the Situation in the Democratic Republic of Congo' when deciding that 93 victims were allowed to participate in the trial of Thomas Lubanga.[22] Similarly, Trial Chamber II has recognised 57 applicants as victims of the case against Germain Katanga and Mathieu Ngudjolo.[23]

The Appeals Chamber has also left unchanged this methodological distinction between 'victims of the situation' and 'victims of the case'.[24] In particular, on

[17] Situation in Uganda (Decision on victims' applications for participation a/0010/06, a/0064/06 to a/0070/06, a/0081/06 to a/0104/06 and a/0111/06 to a/0127/06) ICC-02/04-101 (10 August 2007) para 61; Situation in Uganda (Decision on victims' applications for participation a/0010/06, a/0064/06 to a/0070/06, a/0081/06, a/0082/06, a/0084/06 to a/0089/06, a/0091/06 to a/0097/06, a/0099/06, a/0100/06, a/0102/06 to a/0104/06, a/0111/06, a/0113/06 to a/0117/06, a/0120/06, a/0121/06 and a/0123/06 to a/0127/06) ICC-02/04-125 (14 March 2008) para 70; *Situation in Uganda* (Decision on victims' applications for participation a/0066/06, a/0067/06, a/0069/06, a/0070/06, a/0083/06, a/0088/06, a/0091/06, a/0092/06, a/0102/06, a/0114/06, a/0115/06, a/0125/06 and a/0126/06) ICC-02/04-170 (17 November 2008) para 19; *Situation in Uganda* (Decision on victims' applications for participation a/0014/07 to a/0020/07 and a/0076/07 to a/0125/07) ICC-02/04-172 (21 November 2008) para 67.

[18] *Prosecutor v Joseph Kony, et al* (Decision on victims' applications for participation a/0010/06, a/0064/06 to a/0070/06, a/0081/06 to a/0104/06 and a/0111/06 to a/0127/06) ICC-02/04-01/05-252 (10 August 2007) para 61; *Prosecutor v Joseph Kony, et al* (Decision on victims' applications for participation a/0010/06, a/0064/06 to a/0070/06, a/0081/06, a/0082/06, a/0084/06 to a/0089/06, a/0091/06 to a/0097/06, a/0099/06, a/0100/06, a/0102/06 to a/0104/06, a/0111/06, a/0113/06 to a/0117/06, a/0120/06, a/0121/06 and a/0123/06 to a/0127/06) ICC-02/04-01/05-282 (14 March 2008) para 70; *Prosecutor v Joseph Kony, et al* (Decision on victims' applications for participation a/0014/07 to a/0020/07 and a/0076/07 to a/0125/07) ICC-02/04-01/05-356 (21 November 2008) paras 66–67.

[19] *Prosecutor v Jean-Pierre Bemba Gombo* (Second decision on the question of victims' participation requesting observations from the parties) ICC-01/05-01/08-184 (23 October 2008) para 3; *Prosecutor v Jean-Pierre Bemba Gombo* (Third Decision on the question of victims' participation requesting observations from the parties) ICC-01/05-01/08-253 (17 November 2008) para 3.

[20] *Prosecutor v Jean-Pierre Bemba Gombo* (Fourth Decision on Victims' Participation) ICC-01/05-01/08-320 (12 December 2008) paras 36–37. Pre-Trial Chamber III found that a 'case' at the pre-trial stage of the proceedings, in the absence of a decision confirming the charges, is 'delineated by means of the document containing the charges pursuant to article 61(3)(a) of the Statute', ibid, para 63.

[21] *Prosecutor v Thomas Lubanga Dyilo* (Decision on victims' participation) ICC-01/04-01/06-1119 (18 January 2008) para 95; see also ibid at Separate and Dissenting Opinion of Judge René Blattmann, para 6 ('[v]ictims are not abstract entities but rather concrete persons or groups of individuals who have suffered harm as a result of conduct attributed or specified in a particular case or situation').

[22] *Prosecutor v Thomas Lubanga Dyilo* (Decision on the applications by victims to participate in the proceedings) ICC-01/04-01/06-1556-Corr-Anx1 (15 December 2008) para 137; Prosecutor v Thomas Lubanga Dyilo (Decision on the applications by 3 victims to participate in the proceedings) ICC-01/04-01/06-1562 (18 December 2008) paras 13–14.

[23] *Prosecutor v Germain Katanga and Mathieu Ngudjolo Chui* (Décision relative au traitement des demandes de participation) ICC-01/04-01/07-933 (26 February 2009) para 13.

[24] *Prosecutor v Thomas Lubanga Dyilo* (Judgment on the appeal of Mr Thomas Lubanga Dyilo against the decision of Pre-Trial Chamber I entitled 'Décision sur la demande de mise en liberté provisoire de Thomas Lubanga Dyilo') ICC-01/04-01/06-824 (13 February 2007); *Prosecutor v Thomas Lubanga Dyilo* (Decision of the Appeals Chamber on the Joint Application of Victims a/0001/06 to a/0003/06 and a/0105/06 concerning the 'Directions and Decision of the Appeals Chamber' of 2 February 2007) ICC-01/04-01/06-925 (13 June 2007). See also *Prosecutor v Thomas Lubanga Dyilo*

18 December 2008 and 2 February 2009, the Appeals Chamber has found that 'victims are not precluded from seeking participation in any judicial proceedings, including proceedings affecting investigations [of the situation], provided their personal interests are affected by the issues arising for resolution', and therefore even though 'the Appeals Chamber is not in a position to advise the Pre-Trial Chamber as to how applications for participation in judicial proceedings at the investigation stage of a situation should generally be dealt with in the future, in the absence of specific facts', '[i]t is for the Pre-Trial Chamber to determine how best to rule upon applications for participation, in compliance with the relevant provisions of the Court's texts'.[25]

As a result, while 'victims of a situation' may participate in specific 'judicial proceedings' conducted in the framework of the investigation of the said 'situation',[26] 'victims of the case' may participate in the proceedings relating to the confirmation hearings of the relevant 'cases'[27] and in the subsequent trials.[28]

This distinction between 'situations' and 'cases' has been embraced by the Chambers of the Court in contexts other than that of victims' participation in the proceedings.[29] In particular, it must be highlighted that filings and decisions in

(Decision on victims' participation) ICC-01/04-01/06-1119 (18 January 2008) Separate and Dissenting Opinion of Judge René Blattmann, para 9.

[25] *Situation in the Democratic Republic of the Congo* (Judgment on victim participation in the investigation stage of the proceedings in the appeal of the OPCD against the decision of Pre-Trial Chamber I of 7 December 2007 and in the appeals of the OPCD and the Prosecutor against the decision of Pre-Trial Chamber 1 of 24 December 2007) ICC-01/04-556 (19 December 2008) paras 56–57; *Situation in Darfur (Sudan)* (Judgment on victim participation in the investigation stage of the proceedings in the appeal of the OPCD against the decision of Pre-Trial Chamber I of 3 December 2007 and in the appeals of the OPCD and the Prosecutor against the decision of Pre-Trial Chamber I of 6 December 2007) ICC-02/05-177 (2 February 2009) para 7; *Situation in Uganda* (Judgment on the appeals of the Defence against the decisions entitled 'Decision on victims' applications for participation a/0010/06, a/0064/06 to a/0070/06, a/0081/06, a/0082/06, a/0084/06 to a/0089/06, a/0091/06 to a/0097/06, a/0099/06, a/0100/06, a/0102/06 to a/0104/06, a/0111/06, a/0113/06 to a/0117/06, a/0120/06, a/0121/06 and a/0123/06 to a/0127/06' of Pre-Trial Chamber II) ICC-02/04-179 (23 February 2009) para 33.

[26] *Situation in the Democratic Republic of the Congo* (Judgment on victim participation in the investigation stage of the proceedings in the appeal of the OPCD against the decision of Pre-Trial Chamber I of 7 December 2007 and in the appeals of the OPCD and the Prosecutor against the decision of Pre-Trial Chamber 1 of 24 December 2007) ICC-01/04-556 (19 December 2008) paras 45, 55–56, where the Appeals Chamber ruled that victims cannot be acknowledged general participatory rights in the investigation of crimes committed in a situation referred to the Court, but only in respect of 'judicial proceedings' during such investigation.

[27] *Prosecutor v Thomas Lubanga Dyilo* (Decision on the Arrangements for Participation of Victims a/0001/06, a/0002/06 and a/0003/06 at the Confirmation Hearing) ICC-01/04-01/06-462-tEN (22 September 2006) paras 7–8; *Prosecutor v Germain Katanga and Mathieu Ngudjolo Chui* (Decision on the Set of Procedural Rights Attached to Procedural Status of Victim at the Pre-Trial Stage of the Case) ICC-01/04-01/07-474 (13 May 2008) paras 124–45; *Prosecutor v Jean-Pierre Bemba Gombo* (Fourth Decision on Victims' Participation) ICC-01/05-01/08-320 (12 December 2008) paras 101–10.

[28] *Prosecutor v Thomas Lubanga Dyilo* (Decision on victims' participation) ICC-01/04-01/06-1119 (18 January 2008) paras 105, 107, 108–10, 112, 117, 138; *Prosecutor v Thomas Lubanga Dyilo* (Judgment on the appeals of The Prosecutor and The Defence against Trial Chamber I's Decision on Victims' Participation of 18 January 2008) ICC-01/04-01/06-1432 (11 July 2008) para 109.

[29] See, eg, *Situation in the Democratic Republic of Congo* (Decision following the Consultation held on 11 October 2005 and the Prosecution's Submission on Jurisdiction and Admissibility filed on 31 October 2005) ICC-01/04-93 (9 November 2005) 4 ('[t]hat at this stage of the proceedings [investigation of the situation] no warrant of arrest or summons to appear has been issued and thus no case has

each 'situation' and each 'case' are kept by the Registrar within a separate record.[30] Furthermore, on the commencement of a 'case', the Pre-Trial Chamber orders the completion of the 'case' record with copies of the relevant documents from the 'situation' record.[31] As a consequence, it can be stated that the distinction between 'situations' and 'cases' has become a matter of procedural importance in the daily practice of the Court.

III The Notion of Admissibility of 'Situations'

The difference between 'situations' and 'cases' explained above seems to have a firm basis in the legal instruments and the established practice of the Court. 'Situations' are the object of preliminary examinations and investigations.[32] 'Cases' are subsequently initiated by the issuance of a warrant of arrest or a summons to appear by the competent Pre-Trial Chamber at the request of the Prosecution.[33] Articles 15, 18 and 53 suggest that the Prosecution cannot investigate a 'case' without previously opening an investigation of the relevant 'situation' in the context of which that case has taken place. In fact, before the Prosecution has opened an investigation of the situation, it does not know with any certainty what evidence it will gather, against which persons and for what conduct.[34]

arisen'), in the context of article 56 proceedings ('unique investigative opportunity'); *Situation in Darfur, Sudan* (Décision relative aux conclusions aux fins d'exception d'incompétence et d'irrecevabilité) ICC-02/05-34 (22 November 2006) 3–4 (' [à] ce stade de la procédure [investigation of the situation], aucun mandat d'arrêt ni citation à comparaître n'ont été délivrés' and therefore no case has arisen), in the context of rule 103 proceedings ('amicus curiae and other forms of submission').

[30] ICC Registry, 'Regulations of the Registry', ICC-BD/03-01-06-Rev.1 (25 September 2006) regs 20 ('Opening of a situation or case record') and 21 ('Content of a situation or case record').

[31] See, eg, *Prosecutor v Thomas Lubanga Dyilo* (Decision concerning Pre-Trial Chamber I's Decision of 10 February 2006 and the Incorporation of Documents into the Record of the Case against Mr Thomas Lubanga Dyilo) ICC-01/04-01/06-8-Corr (24 February 2006) 4–5; *Prosecutor v Thomas Lubanga Dyilo* (Order Concerning the Incorporation of Certain Documents into the Record of the Case against Mr Thomas Lubanga Dyilo) ICC-01/04-01/06-35 (16 March 2006) 3; *Prosecutor v Germain Katanga* (Decision on the Incorporation of Documents in the Record of the Case and Convening a Hearing) ICC-01/04-01/07-27 (18 October 2007) 3; *Prosecutor v Germain Katanga* (Decision on the Incorporation of Documents in the Record of the Case and Convening a Hearing) ICC-01/04-01/07-59 (5 November 2007) 3; *Prosecutor v Germain Katanga and Mathieu Ngudjolo Chui* (Decision on the Set of Procedural Rights Attached to Procedural Status of Victim at the Pre-Trial Stage of the Case) ICC-01/04-01/07-474 (13 May 2008) para 133; *Prosecutor v Jean-Pierre Bemba Gombo* (Decision on unsealing and re-classification of certain documents and decisions) ICC-01/05-01/08-20 (20 June 2008) 6.

[32] *Situation in the Democratic Republic of the Congo* (Decision on the Applications for Participation in the Proceedings of VPRS 1, VPRS 2, VPRS 3, VPRS 4, VPRS 5, and VPRS 6) ICC-01/04-101-tEN-Corr (17 January 2006) para 65.

[33] *Situation in the Democratic Republic of the Congo* (Decision following the Consultation held on 11 October 2005 and the Prosecution's Submission on Jurisdiction and Admissibility filed on 31 October 2005) ICC-01/04-93 (9 November 2005) 4; *Situation in the Democratic Republic of the Congo* (Decision on the Applications for Participation in the Proceedings of VPRS-1, VPRS-2, VPRS-3, VPRS-4, VPRS-5, VPRS-6) ICC-01/04-101-tEN-Corr (17 January 2006) para 65.

[34] Rastan, 'What is a "Case"?' (above n 5) at 441.

As seen in the previous section, the distinction between 'situations' and 'cases' is a matter of procedural importance, which has brought about the distinctions between 'situation record' and 'case record', and between 'victims of the situation' and 'victims of the case'. The question arises as to whether the dichotomy between 'situations' and 'cases' also has an impact on the object of the admissibility assessment: can there be an admissibility analysis of the situations?; and as a result of it, can there be 'admissible' and 'inadmissible' situations?

The express wording of article 17 of the ICC Statute ('issues of admissibility') only refers to the admissibility assessment of 'cases' and not of 'situations'. Similarly, article 53(1)(b) of the ICC Statute and rule 48 of the RPE, which require the undertaking of an admissibility analysis prior to the initiation of an investigation, also refer only to the admissibility assessment of 'cases' pursuant to article 17 of the ICC Statute.

Based on a literal interpretation of these provisions, some authors have stated that the admissibility analysis only applies 'where the investigation into a given country or conflict *situation* concerned has yielded a *case*'.[35] Prior to this stage, the complementarity test provided for in article 17 of the ICC Statute, and therefore, the admissibility analysis required by article 53(1)(b) of the ICC Statute and rule 48 of the RPE would not be applicable.[36]

Nevertheless, if, as shown above, the initiation of an investigation into a 'situation' precedes the subsequent opening of one or more 'cases' relating to such a situation, this interpretation would deprive article 53(1)(b) and rule 48 of any meaning. Indeed, no admissibility assessment could be conducted at a time when there is no 'case', and when the analysis focuses on whether an investigation into a 'situation' must be initiated.

Interpretative criteria aim at defining the precise content of a provision, not at depriving the relevant provision of any meaning. Being that the nature of the ICC Statute is that of an international treaty, the interpretative criteria contained in articles 31 and 32 of the Vienna Convention on the Law of Treaties are applicable.[37] In this regard, the interpretation of the above-mentioned provisions in 'good faith in accordance with the ordinary meaning to be given to the terms of the treaty in their context and in the light of its object and purpose', as well as its drafting history, supports the conclusion that there may be admissible and inadmissible situations.

First, the fact that the word 'situation' is absent from articles 17 and 53(1)(b) of the ICC Statute and rule 48 of the RPE is not due to the inapplicability of the admissibility test to situations. Quite the contrary, the problem lies in the fact that

[35] Kress and Grover, 'International Criminal Law Restraints' (above n 6) at 29, 45.

[36] ibid.

[37] *Situation in the Democratic Republic of the Congo* (Judgment on the Prosecutor's Application for Extraordinary Review of Pre-Trial Chamber I's 31 March 2006 Decision Denying Leave to Appeal) ICC-01/04-168 (13 July 2006) para 33; *Prosecutor v Germain Katanga and Mathieu Ngudjolo Chui* (Judgment on the Appeal against the Decision on Joinder rendered on 10 March 2008 by the Pre-Trial Chamber in the Germain Katanga and Mathieu Ngudjolo Chui Cases) ICC-01/04-01/07-573 (9 June 2008) para 5.

articles 17 and 53(1)(b) were drafted before the distinction between 'situations' and 'cases' was fully introduced, and before articles 15 and 18, which refer to 'situations', were either proposed or discussed in depth.[38] Indeed, by the end of the fourth session of the preparatory committee in August 1997, the core of current articles 17 and 53(1)(b) of the ICC Statute had already been agreed upon.[39] However, the current article 15 comes from proposals made by the Argentinian and Swiss delegations during the same session[40] and article 18 was first proposed by the US delegation at the last session of the preparatory committee immediately before the Rome Conference.[41] In fact, the main elements of articles 15 and 18 were only agreed upon hours before the end of the Rome Conference and there was no time subsequently to adjust the definition of the notion of admissibility in articles 17 and 53(1)(b) to the notion of 'situation' in the former articles.[42]

Concerning the absence of the word 'situation' in rule 48 of the RPE, this is explained by the fact that the sole aim of this provision is to clarify that those criteria provided for in article 53(1)(a), (b) and (c) of the ICC Statute must be applied to decide whether to open an investigation, regardless of whether the Court acts on the receipt of a referral by a State Party or the UN Security Council, or on a communication by any other natural or legal person.[43] As a consequence, rule 48 limits itself to literally reproduce the wording of article 53(1)(a), (b) and (c).

Secondly, article 18, dealing with 'preliminary rulings regarding admissibility', refers to 'situations', and is therefore a positive indication that an article 17 admissibility analysis must be carried out when an investigation is initiated with regard to 'situations'. This view is supported by the informal expert paper on the principle of complementarity in practice prepared in 2003, where it is indicated that 'at such points [when the Prosecutor decides whether to proceed with an investigation upon the referral of a situation or when determining whether to seek authorisation for an investigation in accordance with article 15], admissibility is not an issue for litigation and judicial determination, but rather a matter for the OTP to consider and assess in reaching decisions' and that 'the object of the early pro-

[38] Olasolo, *Triggering Procedure* (above n 2) at 44, fn 67 and 148, fn 158.

[39] Holmes, 'The Principle' (above n 3) at 45–47, 51. Regarding art 53(1)(b), see Preparatory Committee on the Establishment of an International Criminal Court, 'Decisions taken by the Preparatory Committee at its session held from 4 to 15 August 1997' (14 August 1997) UN Doc A/AC.249/1997/L.8/Rev.1 Annex II, art 26(1bis)(b)(ii); Preparatory Committee on the Establishment of an International Criminal Court, 'Report of the inter-sessional meeting from 19 to 30 January 1998 in Zutphen, The Netherlands' (4 February 1998) UN Doc A/AC.249/1998/L.13 art 47[26](1bis)(b)(ii); Preparatory Committee on the Establishment of an International Criminal Court, 'Report of the Preparatory Committee on the Establishment of an International Criminal Court' (14 April 1998) UN Doc A/CONF.183/2/ADD.1, Part One, Draft Statute of the International Criminal Court, art 54(2)(b)(ii).

[40] Fernández de Gurmendi, 'The Role' (above n 2) at 179.

[41] DD Ntanda Nsereko, 'Article 18: Preliminary Rulings Regarding Admissibility' in O Triffterer (ed), *Commentary on the Rome Statute of the International Criminal Court* 2nd edn (Oxford and Munich, Hart Publishing and Verlag CH Beck, 2008) 628.

[42] Fernández de Gurmendi, 'The Role' (above n 2) at 187; Holmes, 'The Principle' (above n 3) at 69.

[43] E Haslam, 'Victim Participation at the International Criminal Court: A Triumph of Hope over Experience?' in R Lee (ed), *The International Criminal Court: Elements of Crimes and Rules of Procedure and Evidence* (New York, Transnational Publishers, 2001) 315, 330–31.

ceedings [under articles 15, 18 and 53] should be referred to as a "situation" [instead of "case" '].[44] El Zeidy,[45] Rastan[46] and Guariglia[47] also support the application of the admissibility test to situations on the basis of articles 17 and 18.

Thirdly, article 53(1)(b) of the ICC Statute and rule 48 of the RPE require admissibility assessments to be conducted during the preliminary examination, prior to the initiation of an investigation. Considering that, at this stage, the Prosecution does not know with certainty what evidence it will gather, against which persons and for what conduct – and that, as shown by the DRC and Darfur investigations, 'cases' only arise at a much later stage of the proceedings (1.5 to 2 years after the start of the investigation) – the object of article 53(1)(b) and rule 48 admissibility assessments can only be 'situations'.

Finally, the aim of the admissibility assessments is to preserve the complementary nature of the ICC – as well as to provide states with an incentive to take action with regard to crimes provided in the ICC Statute – by making sure that the Court does not intervene when national jurisdictions (which are capable and willing to conduct their national proceedings with regard to crimes provided for in the ICC Statute) are 'genuinely' investigating and prosecuting.[48] In order to effectively preserve the ICC's complementary nature, the admissibility assessment cannot be postponed until a case arises; it must be conducted during the preliminary examination of a situation, prior to the commencement of its investigation. Otherwise, the ICC and national jurisdictions may conduct parallel investigations over the same crimes for years, with great uncertainty as to the efficacy of such parallel investigative efforts.

This is particularly relevant in those scenarios in which national investigations and/or prosecutions are conducted in the framework of alternative legislative measures to full investigation and prosecution in a transitional justice context,[49] including conditional amnesty laws (such as in South Africa), alternative reduced sentences (such as in Colombia) or traditional forms of justice (such as in Rwanda).

[44] X Aguirre, A Cassese, RE Fife, H Friman, CK Hall, JT Holmes, J Kleffner, H Olasolo, NH Rashid, D Robinson, E Wilmshurst and A Zimmermann, 'Informal Experts Paper: The Principle of Complementarity in Practice' (2003) www.icc-cpi.int/library/organs/otp/complementarity.pdf, paras 24–26, fn 10.

[45] MM El Zeidy, *The Principle of Complementarity in International Criminal Law: Origin, Development and Practice* (Leiden, Boston, Martinus Nijhoff, 2008) 159, 161, 174, 182–83, 192–93, 197, 202, 209, 214, 256–57, 265, 275–76, 279.

[46] Rastan, 'What is a "Case"?' (above n 5) at 441.

[47] F Guariglia, 'The Selection of Cases by the Office of the Prosecutor of the International Criminal Court' in C Stahn and G Sluiter (eds), *The Emerging Practice of the International Criminal Court* (The Hague, Martinus Nijhoff, 2009) 213, fn 17.

[48] S Williams, 'Article 17: Issues of Admissibility' in O Triffterer (ed), *Commentary on the Rome Statute of the International Criminal Court: Observers' Notes, Article by Article* (Baden Baden, Nomos, 1999) 606–07; Ntanda Nsereko, 'Article 18' in Triffterer, ibid (above n 41) at 628, para 2, 632, para 15; JT Holmes, 'Complementarity: National Courts versus the ICC' in A Cassese, P Gaeta and JRWD Jones (eds), *The Rome Statute of the International Criminal Court: A Commentary* (Oxford, Oxford University Press, 2002) 672–74.

[49] For an overview of the several alternative measures to prosecution that have been resorted to in the context of transitional justice, see C Stahn, 'The Geometry of Transitional Justice: Choices of Institutional Design' (2005) 18 *Leiden Journal of International Law* 425.

In this regard, it is important to keep in mind the ongoing debate among legal scholars as to whether certain types of amnesty laws could pass the complementarity test provided for in the ICC Statute[50] – especially those laws closely following the South African model,[51] according to which a Truth and Reconciliation Commission (TRC), invested with investigative powers, has the power to grant amnesty (exemption from criminal responsibility) in exchange for full cooperation in the disclosure of the truth, the identification of victims and their whereabouts and the provision of reparations to victims.

For some authors, the activities conducted by TRCs under a conditional amnesty law framework would pass the ICC complementarity test insofar as they would amount to national investigations within the sense of article 17 of the ICC Statute, at the end of which a decision not to prosecute within the meaning of article 17(1)(c) of the ICC Statute would be taken if the conditions for granting amnesty had been met. These decisions would not be due to the concerned state's unwillingness or inability to prosecute insofar as: (i) they are due neither to bias (lack of independence or impartiality) or delay on the part of national authorities (article 17(2)(b) and (c)), nor to a total or substantial collapse of the concerned state (article 17(3)); and (ii) their ultimate purpose is to establish the conditions for peace and stability in the concerned state, as opposed to shielding the perpetrators from their alleged criminal liability (article 17(2)(a)).[52]

For other authors, the activities conducted by TRCs under the above-mentioned legal framework would not pass the ICC complementarity test, as the 'justice component' of such a framework is too fragile. For these authors, the investigative activities of TRCs do not amount to national investigations within the sense of article 17 of the ICC of the Statute because they do not have a judicial nature. Moreover, the decisions not to prosecute taken on the completion of the investigation (if the conditions for granting amnesty have been met) either amount to the concerned state's *a posteriori* inaction, or show the state's unwillingness to prosecute, as the purpose of such decisions is to shield the perpetrators from their

[50] For a recent overview of the main aspects of the debate, see Kress and Grover, 'International Criminal Law Restraints' (above n 6) at 29, 45.

[51] A Boraine, *A Country Unmasked: Inside South Africa's Truth and Reconciliation Commission* (Oxford, Oxford University Press, 2001); J Dugard, 'Dealing with Crimes of a Past Regime. Is Amnesty an Option?' (1999) 12 *Leiden Journal of International Law* 1001; C Jenkins, 'A Truth Commission for East Timor: Lessons from South Africa?' (2002) 7 *Journal of Conflict and Security Law* 233; V Nerlich, 'Lessons for the International Criminal Court: The Impact of Criminal Proceedings on the South African Amnesty Process' in G Werle (ed), *Justice in Transition: Prosecution and Amnesty in Germany and South Africa* (Berlin, Berliner Wissenschaftsverlag, 2006) 55; J Sarkin, *Carrots and Sticks: TRC and the South African Amnesty Process* (Oxford/Antwerp, Intersentia, 2004); P Van Zyl, 'Unfinished Business: The Truth and Reconciliation Commission's Contribution to Justice in Post-Apartheid South Africa' in MC Bassiouni (ed), *Post-Conflict Justice* (Ardsley, Transnational Publishers 2002) 745.

[52] See, inter alia, C Cárdenas, 'The Admissibility Test before the ICC under Special Considerations of Amnesties and Truth Commissions' in JK Kleffner and G Kor (eds), *Complementary Views on Complementarity* (The Hague, TMC Asser Press, 2006) 115, 135–36; D Robinson, 'Comments on Chapter 4 of Claudia Cárdenas Aravena' in JK Kleffner and G Kor (eds), *Complementary Views on Complementarity* (The Hague, TMC Asser Press, 2006) 141, 146; G Werle, *Principles of International Criminal Law* (The Hague, TMC Asser Institute, 2005) 66; K Ambos, *El Marco Jurídico de la Justicia de Transición. Especial Referencia al Caso Colombiano* (Bogotá, Temis, 2008) 146–47.

criminal responsibility (regardless of whether such decision may also ultimately aim at establishing the conditions for peace and stability).[53]

A similar debate exists with regard to other alternative measures, such as alternative reduced sentences or traditional forms of justice, which prima facie appear to have a stronger 'justice component' than conditional amnesty laws.[54] For instance, in Colombia, the 2005 Justice and Peace Act provides for the imposition of alternative reduced sentences of a minimum of five years and a maximum of eight years of imprisonment if the following three conditions are met: (i) demobilisation and surrender of the weapons; (ii) full acknowledgement of criminal responsibility before the Prosecution during the investigation stage (*versión libre*) and entering of a guilty plea before a trial chamber (*aceptación de cargos*); and (iii) transfer of personal property to provide for reparations to victims.[55] Under this legal framework, and subject to its effective implementation, there seems to be less controversy as to whether the investigations conducted by the Justice and Peace Prosecution Unit and the prosecutions held before the Justice and Peace magistrates may amount to genuine investigations and prosecutions within the meaning of article 17(1)(a) and (b) of the ICC Statute. Nevertheless, the question arises as to whether the provision of the alternative reduced sentence could constitute evidence of the unwillingness of the concerned state, insofar as it may aim at partially shielding perpetrators from their alleged criminal responsibility.

Likewise, it is not yet clear whether the use of traditional forms of justice to deal with crimes provided for in the ICC Statute – such as the *Gacaca* courts in Rwanda – would pass the ICC complementarity test. In particular, concerns have been raised in relation to the level of compliance with the 'principles of due process recognized by international law' and the types of traditional sentences available.[56]

Regardless of whether all, some, or none of the above-mentioned alternative measures to full investigation and prosecution in a transitional justice context are deemed to meet the ICC complementarity test, the goals of preserving the ICC complementary nature and providing a solid incentive to the concerned states can

[53] See, inter alia, C Stahn, 'Complementarity, Amnesties and Alternative Forms of Justice: Some Interpretative Guidelines for the International Criminal Court' (2005) 3 *Journal of International Criminal Justice* 695, 715; H Olasolo, 'The Triggering Procedure of the International Criminal Court, Procedural Treatment of Complementarity and the Role of the Office of the Prosecutor' (2005) 5 *International Criminal Law Review* 121.

[54] H Olasolo, 'Admisibilidad de Situaciones y Casos Objeto de Procesos de Justicia de Transición ante la Corte Penal Internacional' in H Olasolo (ed), *Ensayos sobre la Corte Penal Internacional* (Universidad Javeriana/Dyke, Bogotá, 2009) 107–13.

[55] P Burbridge, 'Justice and Peace? – The Role of Law in Resolving Colombia's Civil Conflict' (2008) 8 *International Criminal Law Review* 557; P Kalmanovitz, 'Introduction: Law and Politics in the Colombian Negotiations with Paramilitary Groups' in M Bergsmo and P Kalmanovitz (eds), *Law in Peace Negotiations* (Oslo, Forum for International Criminal and Humanitarian Law Publications, 2009) 7; R Petersen and S Zukerman, 'Revenge or Reconciliation: Theory and Method of Emotions in the Context of Colombia's Peace Process' in Bergsmo and Kalmanovitz, ibid, 151.

[56] LD Tully, 'Human Rights Compliance and the Gacaca Jurisdictions in Rwanda' (2003) 26 *Boston College International and Comparative Law Review* 385, 402–13; J Fierens, '*Gacaca* Courts: Between Fantasy and Reality' (2005) 3 *Journal of International Criminal Justice* 896, 910–12; W Schabas, 'Genocide Trials and *Gacaca* Courts' (2005) 3 *Journal of International Criminal Justice* 879, 895.

only be effectively achieved if all actors involved have an early and clear understanding of whether the relevant legal framework meets the ICC complementarity test.

Only if, after an initial admissibility assessment is made, the legal framework providing for a conditional amnesty, an alternative reduced sentence or a traditional form of justice is deemed to meet the ICC complementarity test, one should continue to monitor, for the purpose of subsequent admissibility assessments, the manner in which such legal framework is implemented in practice by the concerned state. If, on the contrary, the relevant legal framework is deemed not to meet the relevant complementarity test, the concerned states must soon be told the consequences: unless the necessary amendments to meet the test are made, the analysis of whether an investigation into the relevant situation should be initiated will move from the complementarity analysis level to the 'interests of justice' level (the last level provided for in article 53(1)(c) of the ICC Statute and rule 48 of the ICC RPE).

Postponing any admissibility analysis until such a late stage of the proceedings as when a case arises has the following pernicious consequences: (i) lesser efficacy in preserving the ICC complementary nature and in avoiding duplication of investigative efforts by the ICC and national authorities; (ii) lesser efficacy in providing concerned states with an incentive to investigate and prosecute crimes within ICC jurisdiction in a manner consistent with the complementarity test (article 17 criteria); and (iii) a higher degree of uncertainty as to the effectiveness of those investigative activities conducted during years by the ICC and the concerned states.

Moreover, if properly conducted, the admissibility analysis of situations does not involve any determination on the compliance of the judicial system of the concerned states with internationally recognised human rights standards (particularly those relating to the principles of due process). Indeed, this risk can be avoided by limiting such analysis first to (i) those specific measures adopted at the national level in relation to the investigation and prosecution of crimes within ICC jurisdiction; and subsequently to (ii) those national proceedings that are related to the type of cases that, according to pre-established guiding criteria for the selection of cases, may be initiated before the ICC.

As a result, it can be stated that the interpretation of articles 17 and 53(1)(b) of the ICC Statute and rule 48 of the ICC RPE in accordance with the criteria provided for in articles 31 and 32 of the Vienna Convention on the Law of Treaties supports the conclusion that (i) there can be an admissibility analysis of the situations, and thus (ii) there may be admissible and inadmissible situations. This conclusion is further reinforced by the fact that the Prosecution's activities and the ICC case law to date seem to support admissibility considerations regarding 'situations' and not only 'cases'.

In this regard, it must be noted that, when starting the investigation into the situation in the DRC in July 2004, the Prosecutor informed the President of the Court that

> [a]s required under article 53 of the Statute and Rule 104, my Office has conducted analysis and sought additional information in order *to support a determination under*

> *article 53 on the DRC situation.* Having considered *all of the criteria,* I have determined that there is a reasonable basis to initiate an investigation.[57]

In turn, when explaining its decision not to open an investigation into the situation in Iraq, the Prosecution indicated that it 'must select situations in accordance with the article 53 criteria',[58] which suggests that the Prosecution understands admissibility as applicable also to situations.[59] The Prosecution's subsequent paper on the 'interests of justice' (article 53(1) and (2)(c) of the ICC Statute) also refers to a determination of whether 'the situation is of sufficient gravity' to justify further action by the Court pursuant to article 17(1)(d).[60] Likewise, the recently adopted Regulations of the ICC Office of the Prosecutor prescribe that

> [i]n acting under article 15, paragraph 3, or article 53, paragraph 1, the Office shall produce an internal report analysing the seriousness of the information and considering the factors set out in article 53, paragraph 1 (a) to (c), namely issues of jurisdiction, admissibility (including gravity), as well as the interests of justice, pursuant to rules 48 and 104.[61]

In turn, in April 2005, Pre-Trial Chamber I, when dealing with the first 'unique investigative opportunity' within the investigation into the DRC situation, referred to the Prosecution's analysis under article 53(1) of the ICC Statute and to the fact that the Prosecution had received no information from any state pursuant to article 18(2) of the ICC Statute.[62] Later on, in February 2006, when issuing a warrant of arrest against Thomas Lubanga Dyilo, the same Pre-Trial Chamber indicated that the decision '[wa]s limited to the determination of the content of the gravity threshold [. . .] when it must be applied to a *case* arising from the investigation of a situation',[63] but clarified that

> according to a contextual interpretation, [. . .] the gravity threshold provided for in article 17(1)(d) of the Statute must be applied at two different stages: (i) at the stage of initiation of the investigation of a situation, the relevant situation must meet such gravity threshold and (ii) once a case arises from the investigation of a situation, it must also meet the gravity threshold.[64]

[57] *Prosecutor v Thomas Lubanga Dyilo* (Decision Assigning the Situation in the Democratic Republic of Congo to Pre-Trial Chamber I) ICC-01/04-01/06-10 (5 July 2004) Annex I.

[58] L Moreno-Ocampo, 'Communication Concerning the Situation in Iraq' (9 February 2006): www.icc-cpi.int/Menus/ICC/Structure+of+the+Court/Office+of+the+Prosecutor/Comm+and+Ref/Iraq/, 8.

[59] KJ Heller, 'Situational Gravity under the Rome Statute' in C Stahn and L van den Herik (eds), *Future Directions in International Criminal Justice* (The Hague, TMC Asser/CUP, 2009) 4.

[60] ICC Office of the Prosecutor, 'Policy Paper on the Interests of Justice' Ref-ICC-OTP-InterestsofJustice (September 2007) 5.

[61] ICC Office of the Prosecutor, 'Regulations of the Office of the Prosecutor' ICC-BD/05-01-09 (23 April 2009), reg 29(1) ('Initiation of an investigation or prosecution').

[62] *Situation in the Democratic Republic of Congo* (Decision to hold Consultation under Rule 114) ICC-01/04-19 (21 April 2005) 2–5.

[63] *Prosecutor v Thomas Lubanga Dyilo* (Decision concerning Pre-Trial Chamber's I Decision of 10 February 2006 and the Incorporation of Documents into the Record of the Case against Mr Thomas Lubanga Dyilo) ICC-01/04-01/06-8-Corr (24 February 2006) Annex I, para 44.

[64] ibid.

IV Assessing the Admissibility of 'Situations'

There exist several procedural mechanisms whereby the admissibility of a situation is determined. First, article 53(1)(b) of the ICC Statute and rule 48 of the RPE call for an admissibility assessment to be conducted during the preliminary examination of a situation, prior to the initiation of an investigation.[65] Secondly, pursuant to article 18 of the ICC Statute, within 30 days of the Prosecution's notification of the initiation of an investigation into a situation, a state may allege the inadmissibility of the relevant situation as a result of its national proceedings, and obtain a deferral of the Prosecution's investigation unless the Pre-Trial Chamber, upon a request by the Prosecution, decides to authorise such an investigation.[66] In this event, the Pre-Trial Chamber (and eventually the Appeals Chamber pursuant to article 82(1)(a)) will be called to decide on the admissibility of the situation.[67] Finally, pursuant to article 19(11) of the ICC Statute, the Prosecution may, at any time while it is conducting the investigation into a situation, refer such an investigation to the relevant state(s). In light of the development of national proceedings, and having regard to the matters referred to in article 17 of the ICC Statute, the Prosecution may also decide thereafter to proceed with an investigation of the deferred situation and notify, pursuant to article 19(11), the state to which deferral of the proceedings has taken place.[68]

The question arises, however, as to the content of the admissibility assessment of situations and the determination of guiding criteria to conduct it. As the notion of 'situation admissibility assessments' is a novelty, little attention has been paid to this issue by legal scholars so far.[69]

In the view of the authors, one has to distinguish two main areas in the admissibility assessment of situations. The first area refers to the analysis of national legal frameworks providing for conditional amnesties, reduced sentences or traditional forms of justice as alternative measures to full investigation and prosecution in a transitional justice context. The second area refers to the review of those national criminal proceedings that are being conducted, or have been conducted, in relation to crimes within the ICC jurisdiction allegedly committed in the situation under scrutiny.

With regard to the first area of the admissibility analysis of situations, the dilemmas posed by conditional amnesties, reduced sentences or traditional forms of justice from a complementarity perspective have already been described in the

[65] Regardless of whether the Prosecution conducts its preliminary examination upon the receipt of a referral by a State Party or the UN Security Council, or upon the receipt of a communication by any other natural or legal person.

[66] Pursuant to its literal wording, art 18 of the ICC Statute does not appear to be applicable when the Prosecution opens an investigation as a result of a referral by the UN Security Council.

[67] Olasolo, *Triggering Procedure* (above n 2) at 157.

[68] ibid.

[69] See, for instance, the guiding criteria for conducting situation admissibility analyses provided for by ibid at 164–72.

previous section. The academic debate on the matter has been particularly rich in recent years. Nevertheless, the ICC has not yet entertained in a clear manner the following two tasks: (i) the distinction between the 'complementarity' and the 'interests of justice' levels of analysis of the national legal frameworks providing for the said alternative measures; and (ii) the elaboration on the basis of the criteria provided for in article 17 of the Statute of a set of unambiguous conditions, if any, under which conditional amnesties, alternative reduced sentences and traditional forms of justice could meet the ICC complementarity test.

Undoubtedly, the impact of the ICC on the concerned states would be significantly increased if, in addition to the above-mentioned two tasks, clear guiding criteria in the application of the notion of 'interests of justice' were developed with regard to situations in which the said alternative measures have been adopted. Nevertheless, the lack of this last set of guiding criteria would not prevent the ICC from conducting an appropriate admissibility analysis of the relevant situations: one must always keep in mind the distinction between the 'complementarity' and the 'interests of justice' levels of analysis.

Regarding the second area of the admissibility analysis of situations – namely the review of national criminal proceedings – it is unfeasible, except for cases of inaction of the states concerned, to review all investigations and prosecutions carried out at the national level within the relevant situation in relation to crimes within the jurisdiction of the ICC. As a result, the main difficulty is the determination of guiding criteria pursuant to which national proceedings are selected for review for the purpose of conducting an admissibility assessment of the relevant situation.

According to Rastan, the analysis should not focus on the situation 'as a whole', but on 'the type of cases that would be investigated in the situation'.[70] Guariglia also deems it necessary to consider 'the likely set of cases that would arise from investigation of the situation'.[71] This approach is similar to the one adopted by Olasolo:

> [T]he content of the admissibility test cannot be the same when it is carried out against the backdrop of situations as when it is carried out against the backdrop of cases. On the one hand, in order to ascertain the admissibility of a situation, one has to look at the investigations, prosecutions, decisions not to prosecute and final judgements of the States concerned in relation to those types of crimes that, committed in a widespread or systemic manner, are at the core of the criminal activities which occurred in the situation at hand. Besides, if broad political discretion granted to the OTP, the PTC and the AC is used de facto to limit the personal scope of the Court's dormant jurisdiction to those who bear the greatest responsibility, such as the leaders of States, groups or organisations allegedly responsible for the systematic or widespread criminality that has taken place in the situation at hand, the admissibility analysis will focus on the national proceedings of the States concerned against the group of persons that fall within the category of persons ultimately responsible. On the other hand, in order to ascertain the

[70] Rastan, 'What is a "Case"?'(above n 5) at 441.
[71] Guariglia, 'The Selection of Cases' (above n 47) at 213, fn 17.

> admissibility of a case, one has to look at the investigations, prosecutions, decisions not to prosecute and final judgements in relation to a given individual and a limited set of incidents. As a result, though the standard of review does not necessarily have to vary when the admissibility of situations and cases is assessed, the level of scrutiny of national proceedings needs to be lower when ascertaining the admissibility of a situation than when ascertaining the admissibility of a case. This phenomenon is recognized under the heading of art 18 RS that refers to the PTC's and AC's 'preliminary' rulings on admissibility. Logically, the different scope of the admissibility analysis of situations and cases and the different level of scrutiny of national proceedings prevent PTC and AC decisions on the admissibility of situations from having the effect of res judicata regarding the admissibility of cases.[72]

As a result, conducting an admissibility assessment of a situation for the purpose of deciding whether to initiate an investigation into the relevant situation requires the prior formulation of clear and precise criteria according to which cases are to be selected for examination. In defining these criteria there is always a tension between the need for securing a certain degree of flexibility to prevent them from becoming inapplicable as a result of the evidence gathered during the future investigation, and moving away from very broad criteria that provide for excessive leeway in their application. In finding the appropriate balance, it is important to keep in mind that the broader the chosen criteria are, the higher the number of national proceedings that must be taken into consideration for conducting admissibility assessments of situations. Needless to say, the broader the scope of investigations, prosecutions, decisions not to prosecute and final judgements of the states concerned that must be taken into consideration, the more complex the admissibility analysis of situations becomes.

A good example of the complexity of this matter is provided by the interpretation of the criterion 'those who bear the greatest responsibility', which, endorsed by the ICC Office of the Prosecutor,[73] could be a criterion to establish a distinction between those national proceedings that must be reviewed in conducting the admissibility assessment of a situation, and those which fall outside the scope of that analysis.

According to Seils, former head of the Situation Analysis Section of the ICC Office of the Prosecutor:

> The concept of those bearing the greatest degree of responsibility is not only evidence dependent, but can embrace a relatively large number of people depending on the crimes in question. This is seen for example in the case of Ali Kushayb in the first case brought in relation to the Darfur situation. If one were to have applied the logic of the Pre-trial Chamber it is extremely doubtful that one would ever have reached a local commander of the Janjaweed, but a proper understanding of the concept – relying on

[72] Olasolo, *Triggering Procedure* (above n 2) at 165–66.

[73] ICC Office of the Prosecutor, 'Paper on some policy issues before the Office of the Prosecutor' (September 2003): www.icc-cpi.int/NR/rdonlyres/1FA7C4C6-DE5F-42B7-8B25-60AA962ED8B6/143594/030905_Policy_Paper.pdf, para 2.1; ICC Office of the Prosecutor, 'Report on Prosecutorial Strategy' (14 September 2006): www.icc-cpi.int/NR/rdonlyres/D673DD8C-D427-4547-BC69-2D363E07274B/143708/ ProsecutorialStrategy20060914 _English.pdf, para 2(b).

evidence concerning the specific crimes, not the position of the person in general – renders the selection of Kushayb eminently justified as being one of the most responsible *for those particular crimes.*[74]

As a result, in the view of Seils, this criterion would pay, inter alia, attention to the following four factors: (i) the scale of the crime in question, including the numbers of victims and possible consideration of temporal and geographic intensity; (ii) the nature of the crime itself; (iii) the manner of the crime (taking into account especially aggravating factors such as particular cruelty, targeting of especially vulnerable victims, the abuse of authority); and (iv) the impact of the crime.[75]

Nevertheless, if one follows this interpretation, the clarity and precision for the purpose of conducting situation admissibility assessments of the criterion 'those who bear the greatest responsibility' is, to an important extent, lost. Under this interpretation, the standard becomes very broad and leaves too much leeway for its subsequent application as the investigation progresses. As a result, it does not provide much guidance to decide at the stage of initiating an investigation (and thus prior to the gathering of the evidence) which national proceedings must be reviewed in conducting a situation admissibility analysis, and those which fall outside the scope of the said analysis.

In interpreting the article 17(1)(d) gravity threshold, Pre-Trial Chamber I put forward the criterion 'most senior leaders suspected of being most responsible'. According to Pre-Trial Chamber I, the content of this criterion was as follows:

> The Chamber holds that the following two features must be considered. First, the conduct which is the subject of a case must be either systematic (pattern of incidents) or large-scale [. . .] Second, in assessing the gravity of the relevant conduct, due consideration must be given to the social alarm such conduct may have caused in the international community [. . .] According to a teleological interpretation, the Chamber observes that the activities of the Court must seek 'to put an end to impunity for the perpetrators of these crimes'. The Chamber also notes that the preamble and article 1 of the Statute make clear that the Court can by no means replace national criminal jurisdictions, but it is complementary to them, and that the drafters of the Statute emphasised 'the duty of every State to exercise its criminal jurisdiction over those responsible for international crimes' and affirmed the need to ensure their effective prosecution 'by taking measures at the national level and by enhancing international cooperation' [. . .] In the Chamber's view, the analysis of the additional gravity threshold provided for in article 17(1)(d) of the Statute against the backdrop of the preamble of the Statute leads to the conclusion that such an additional gravity threshold is a key tool provided by the drafters to maximise the Court's deterrent effect. As a result, the Chamber must conclude that any retributory effect of the activities of the Court must be subordinate to the higher purpose of prevention [. . .] In this regard, the Chamber considers that the additional gravity threshold provided for in article 17(1)(d) of the Statute is intended to

[74] P Seils, 'The Selection and Prioritization of Cases by the Office of the Prosecutor of the International Criminal Court' in M Bergsmo (ed), *Criteria for Prioritizing and Selecting Core International Crimes Cases* (Oslo, Forum for International Criminal and Humanitarian Law Publications, 2009) 56 (emphasis added).

[75] ibid at 57.

> ensure that the Court initiates cases only against the most senior leaders suspected of being the most responsible for crimes within the jurisdiction of the Court allegedly committed in any given situation under investigation.[76]

Although this criterion would allow distinguishing with clarity between those national proceedings that must be reviewed in conducting the situation admissibility analysis, and those which fall outside the scope of that analysis, it presents, according to several writers, insurmountable problems. In this regard, Seils has pointed out that the 'most senior leaders suspected of being most responsible' criterion used by Pre-Trial Chamber I constituted 'a rigid, formulaic fashion, running a serious risk of entering the treacherous waters of strict liability, but also in an excessively narrow sense, guaranteeing impunity to all but the very top level'.[77] In a similar way, for Guariglia, this type of criterion could become 'a permanent legal barrier providing permanent *ex ante* impunity to entire classes of perpetrators, and enabling perpetrators to bring legal challenges demanding evidence showing that they are not only guilty but the most guilty'.[78]

Most importantly, the Appeals Chamber has expressly rejected the 'most senior leaders suspected of being most responsible' criterion as the controlling standard for the interpretation of the article 17(1)(d) gravity threshold.[79] In so doing, however, the Appeals Chamber did not find it necessary to provide for any alternative controlling criterion for the purpose of the article 17(1)(d) gravity threshold.[80]

As a result, in order to properly conduct situation admissibility assessments, it will be necessary in the coming years for the content of the case selection criteria used by the Prosecution to be further elaborated, and the content of the gravity

[76] *Prosecutor v Thomas Lubanga Dyilo* (Decision concerning Pre-Trial Chamber I's Decision of 10 February 2006 and the Incorporation of Documents into the Record of the Case against Mr Thomas Lubanga Dyilo) ICC-01/04-01/06-8-Corr (24 February 2006) Annex I, paras 47–49, 51 (footnotes omitted, emphasis added). In this regard see X Aguirre, 'Gravity of Crimes and Responsibility of Suspect' in M Bergsmo (ed), *Criteria for Prioritizing and Selecting Core International Crimes Cases* (Oslo, Forum for International Criminal and Humanitarian Law Publications, 2009) 147, 156–62, when analysing the case selection criteria applied by international and mixed tribunals since 1945, explains that art 1(1) of the Statute of the Special Court of Sierra Leone embraces the standard of 'persons who bear the greatest responsibility', in application of which 92 per cent of the indicted persons are high level military or political leaders; and that the Statute of the Extraordinary Chambers of the Courts of Cambodia limit their jurisdiction to 'senior leaders of Democratic Kampuchea and those who were most responsible', in application of which the four highest members of the 1977–79 Government of the Republic of Kampuchea, who are still alive, are being investigated, along with the commander of the S-21 detention centre (the most notorious detention centre at the time). To these references, it could be added that the UN Security Council, in light of the fact that more than half of those indicted prior to 2004 by the ICTY and the ICTR were material executioners or low level superiors, provided for in Resolutions 1503 (UN Security Council, 'Resolution 1503' (28 August 2003) UN Doc S/RES/1503 (2003)), and 1534 (UN Security Council 'Resolution 1534' (26 March 2004) UN Doc S/RES/1534 (2004)) that further indictments could only be brought against the 'most senior leaders suspected of being most responsible'.

[77] Seils, 'The Selection' (above n 74) at 55–56.

[78] Guariglia, 'The Selection of Cases' (above n 47) at 215.

[79] *Situation in the Democratic Republic of Congo* (Judgment on the Prosecutor's appeal against the decision of Pre-Trial Chamber I entitled 'Decision on the Prosecutor's Application for Warrants of Arrest, Article 58') ICC-01/04-169 (13 July 2006) paras 70–73, 78–82.

[80] ibid at para 89.

threshold provided for in article 17(1)(d) of the Statute to be interpreted in further detail.

V Conclusion

The distinction between 'situations' and 'cases' has already been endorsed by ICC Chambers and constitutes today a matter of procedural importance in the daily practice of the Court, bringing about, inter alia, the distinction between 'situation record' and 'case record', and between 'victims of the situation' and 'victims of the case'. This dichotomy between 'situations' and 'cases' also has an impact on the object of the admissibility assessment. As a result, there can be an admissibility analysis of situations – as opposed to the admissibility analysis of cases – and situations can thus be admissible or inadmissible.

Situation admissibility assessments include the analysis of national legal frameworks providing for conditional amnesties, reduced sentences or traditional forms of justice as alternative measures to full investigation and prosecution in a transitional justice context. Such assessments also include the review of those national criminal proceedings that are being conducted, or have been conducted, in relation to crimes within the ICC jurisdiction allegedly committed in the situation under scrutiny.

Given the novelty of the notion of 'situation admissibility assessments', little attention has been paid so far by scholars in the determination of guiding criteria to conduct such assessments. Likewise, the ICC has not yet entertained in a clear manner: (i) the distinction between the 'complementarity' and the 'interests of justice' levels of analysis of the national legal frameworks providing for the said alternative measures; (ii) the elaboration, on the basis of the criteria provided for in article 17 of the ICC Statute, of a set of unambiguous conditions, if any, under which conditional amnesties, alternative reduced sentences and traditional forms of justice can meet the ICC complementarity test; and (iii) the formulation of clear and precise criteria according to which national proceedings are to be selected for review for the purpose of conducting situation admissibility assessments.

As a result, and considering the important role of situation admissibility assessments in the initiation and development of ICC investigations, the Court, in the coming years, is bound to strive to find clear guiding criteria under which situation admissibility assessments are to be conducted. In so doing, a balance must be struck between the need for securing a certain degree of flexibility to prevent such criteria from becoming inapplicable as a result of the evidence gathered during the eventual investigation, and moving away from very broad criteria that provide for excessive leeway in their application. In this regard, it is important to keep in mind that the 'most senior leaders suspected of being most responsible' criterion has been criticised for its alleged lack of flexibility and has been rejected by the

Appeals Chamber. In turn, the interpretation of the criterion 'those who bear the greatest responsibility' as a purely 'evidence dependent' standard does not permit achievement of the above-mentioned balance, as it is far too broad and, thus, provides little guidance in selecting which national proceedings must be reviewed in conducting a situation admissibility analysis.

3

The Admissibility Analysis of the 'Situation' in the Republic of Kenya Before the International Criminal Court*

I Introduction

On 31 March 2010 Pre-Trial Chamber II of the International Criminal Court (ICC) authorised the Prosecutor of the Court to start a *proprio motu* investigation into the 'situation' in the Republic of Kenya in relation to crimes against humanity within the jurisdiction of the Court allegedly committed on the territory of the Republic of Kenya between 1 June 2005 and 26 November 2009.[1] Pursuant to article 15(1) of the Statute of the International Criminal Court (ICC Statute), the Pre-Trial Chamber concluded that there was a 'reasonable basis to proceed with an investigation' after finding that: (i) the crimes alleged by the Prosecutor fell within the jurisdiction of the Court; (ii) the 'situation' was admissible; and (iii) opening an investigation on these crimes would not be against the interests of justice. This was the first (and at the time of writing these lines, the only) decision of the Court authorising the Prosecutor to start an investigation.

The 31 March 2010 Pre-Trial Chamber II decision is a remarkable decision in many aspects. Nevertheless, this chapter will focus only on one specific aspect: its findings concerning the notion of admissibility of 'situations'. In this regard, it must be noted that until the 31 March 2010 Pre-Trial Chamber II decision, the Court had issued several decisions touching on the admissibility of 'cases'. However, it had not discussed in detail the possibility of undertaking admissibility analysis of 'situations' in order to declare them admissible or inadmissible. The absence of judicial decisions on the admissibility of 'situations' was due to the fact that all previous investigations had been opened upon referrals by States Parties to the ICC Statute (Uganda, Democratic Republic of the Congo, Central African

* Drafted with Enrique Carnero-Rojo in March 2011, PhD candidate at the Willem Pompe Institute for Criminal Law and Criminology of the University of Utrecht; Associate Legal Adviser at ICC OTP (2004–09); LLM Leiden University; law degree Deusto University. The views expressed herein are those of the authors in their personal capacity and do not necessarily represent the views of the ICC.

1 *Situation in the Republic of Kenya* (Decision Pursuant to Article 15 of the Rome Statute on the Authorization of an Investigation into the Situation in the Republic of Kenya) ICC-01/09-19 (31 March 2010).

Republic) or by the United Nations (UN) Security Council (Darfur). Pursuant to the ICC Statute, the opening of investigations on the basis of such 'referrals' does not require prior judicial authorisation but only the Prosecutor's prior assessment.[2]

II The Notions of 'Situation' and 'Case'

The ICC Statute makes a clear distinction between 'situations' and 'cases'. Articles 13(a) and (b), 14(1) and 19(3) of the ICC Statute establish that the object of a 'referral' by a State Party to the Statute or by the UN Security Council is to be a 'situation'.[3] Moreover, article 18(1) states that the 'preliminary examinations' and investigations initiated by the Prosecution as a result of the said referrals must also refer to 'situations'.[4] Similarly, articles 18(1) and 15(5) and (6) highlight that 'situations' are also the object of the 'preliminary examinations' and investigations resulting from 'communications' sent by natural or legal persons other than States Parties and the UN Security Council.[5]

Concerning the 'cases', it is only after the start of an investigation into a 'situation' that the Prosecutor may request the issuance of a warrant of arrest or a summons to appear pursuant to article 58 against one or more identified individuals if he considers that there are 'reasonable grounds' to believe that these individuals

[2] United Nations General Assembly (UNGA), 'Rome Statute of the International Criminal Court' (17 July 1998) UN Doc A/Conf.183/9 [hereinafter, ICC Statute] art 15 in relation to art 13(a). See also Office of the Prosecutor of the ICC (ICC-OTP), 'The Office of the Prosecutor of the International Criminal Court opens its first investigation' ICC-OTP-20040623-59 (23 June 2004); ICC-OTP, 'Prosecutor of the International Criminal Court opens an investigation into No[r]thern Uganda' ICC-OTP-20040729-65 (29 July 2004); ICC-OTP, 'The Prosecutor of the ICC opens investigation in Darfur' ICC-OTP-0606-104 (6 June 2005); ICC-OTP, 'Prosecutor opens investigation in the Central African Republic' ICC-OTP-20070522-220 (22 May 2007).

[3] H Olasolo, 'The Lack of Attention to the Distinction between Situations and Cases in National Laws on Cooperation with the ICC: Special Attention to the Spanish Case' (2007) 20 *Leiden Journal of International Law* 193; H Olasolo and E Carnero-Rojo, 'The Application of the Principle of Complementarity to Decide where to Open an Investigation: The Admissibility of *Situations*' in C Stahn and MM El Zeidy (eds), *The International Criminal Court and Complementarity: From Theory to Practice* (Cambridge, Cambridge University Press, 2011). See also L Yee, 'The International Criminal Court and the Security Council' in R Lee (ed), *The International Criminal Court: The Making of the Rome Statute – Issues, Negotiations, Results* (The Hague, Kluwer Law International, 1999) 147; SA Fernández de Gurmendi, 'The Role of the International Prosecutor' in Lee, ibid, 180–82; E Wilmshurst, 'Jurisdiction of the Court' in Lee, ibid, 131; H Olasolo, *The Triggering Procedure of the International Criminal Court* (Leiden, Martinus Nijhoff, 2005) 44.

[4] JT Holmes, 'The Principle of Complementarity' in R Lee (ed), *The International Criminal Court: The Making of the Rome Statute – Issues, Negotiations, Results* (The Hague, Kluwer Law International, 1999) 71, fn 40; MM El Zeidy, 'The Ugandan Government Triggers the First Test of the Complementarity Principle: An Assessment of the First State's Party Referral to the ICC' (2005) 5 *International Criminal Law Review* 83, 106.

[5] Olasolo, *Triggering Procedure* (above n 3) at 44. The term 'case' in art 15(4), read together with the references to the notion of situation in art 15(5) and (6) and in view of the drafters' intention to introduce adequate safeguards against the initiation of politically motivated investigations, cannot literally refer to 'cases' but to 'situations', in accordance with the object of art 15.

are criminally liable for one or more crimes within the jurisdiction of the Court. The commencement of a 'case' is marked by an issuance of the requested warrant or summons by a Pre-Trial Chamber.[6]

Despite this distinct reference to 'situations' and 'cases' in the legal texts of the ICC, neither the Statute nor the Rules of Procedure and Evidence of the ICC provide a definition of 'situation' and 'case'. Both notions, as well as the features that distinguish them, have been elaborated upon by the Court itself in different scenarios.

The clearest judicial elaboration of the notions of 'situations' and 'cases' so far has taken place in the context of the participation of victims in the proceedings. Pre-Trial Chamber I, when issuing the Court's first decision on victims' participation in January 2006, clarified that

> situations, which are generally defined in terms of temporal, territorial and in some cases personal parameters, such as the situation in the territory of the Democratic Republic of Congo since 1 July 2002, entail the proceedings envisaged in the Statute to determine whether a particular situation should give rise to a criminal investigation as well as the investigation as such.[7]

In the same decision, the Chamber defined a 'case' by referring to 'specific incidents during which one or more crimes within the jurisdiction of the Court seem to have been committed by one or more identified suspects'.[8]

On the basis of this distinction between 'situations' and 'cases', the ICC Pre-Trial, Trial and Appeals Chambers have subsequently ruled that victims of a 'situation' may participate only in specific 'judicial proceedings' conducted in the framework of the investigation of their respective 'situation',[9] whereas victims of a

[6] *Situation in the Republic of Kenya* (Decision Pursuant to Article 15 of the Rome Statute on the Authorization of an Investigation into the Situation in the Republic of Kenya) ICC-01/09-19 (31 March 2010) para 44. See also R Rastan, 'What is a "Case" for the Purpose of the Rome Statute?' (2008) 19 *Criminal Law Forum* 435, 442–43; K Ambos, *Procedimiento de La Ley de Justicia y Paz (Ley de 2005) y Derecho Penal Internacional* (Bogota, GTZ, Göttingen University, 2010) paras 331–34.

[7] *Situation in the Democratic Republic of the Congo* (Decision on the Applications for Participation in the Proceedings of VPRS 1, VPRS 2, VPRS 3, VPRS 4, VPRS 5, VPRS 6) ICC-01/04-101-tEN-Corr (17 January 2006) para 65.

[8] ibid. See also *Prosecutor v Thomas Lubanga Dyilo* (Decision concerning Pre-Trial Chamber's I Decision of 10 February 2006 and the Incorporation of Documents into the Record of the Case against Mr Thomas Lubanga Dyilo) ICC-01/04-01/06-8-Corr (24 February 2006) Annex I, para 31.

[9] *Situation in the Democratic Republic of the Congo* (Judgment on victim participation in the investigation stage of the proceedings in the appeal of the OPCD against the decision of Pre-Trial Chamber I of 7 December 2007 and in the appeals of the OPCD and the Prosecutor against the decision of Pre-Trial Chamber 1 of 24 December 2007) ICC-01/04-556 (19 December 2008) paras 45, 55–57; *Situation in Darfur (Sudan)* (Judgment on victim participation in the investigation stage of the proceedings in the appeal of the OPCD against the decision of Pre-Trial Chamber I of 3 December 2007 and in the appeals of the OPCD and the Prosecutor against the decision of Pre-Trial Chamber I of 6 December 2007) ICC-02/05-177 (2 February 2009) para 7; *Prosecutor v Joseph Kony et al* (Judgment on the appeals of the Defence against the decisions entitled 'Decision on victims' applications for participation' a/0010/06, a/0064/06 to a/0070/06, a/0081/06, a/0082/06, a/0084/06 to a/0089/06, a/0091/06 to a/0097/06, a/0099/06, a/0100/06, a/0102/06 to a/0104/06, a/0111/06, a/0113/06 to a/0117/06, a/0120/06, a/0121/06 and a/0123/06 to a/0127/06' of Pre-Trial Chamber II) ICC-02/04-01/05-371 (23 February 2009) para 33.

'case' may participate also in the proceedings related to the confirmation hearing of the 'case' concerning the crimes they have allegedly suffered[10] and in the subsequent trial.[11]

These notions of 'situation' and 'case' have also been relied on by the Chambers of the Court when dealing with other substantive legal issues, such as jurisdictional matters,[12] 'unique investigative opportunities'[13] and the possibility for *amici curiae* to participate in the proceedings.[14] Furthermore, the concepts of 'situation' and 'case' have also become a matter of procedural importance in the daily practice of the Court since filings and decisions are kept by the Registrar within separate records for each 'situation' and each 'case'.[15] On the commencement of a 'case', the Pre-Trial Chamber orders the completion of the 'case' record with copies of the relevant documents from the 'situation' record.[16]

In conclusion, 'situations' and 'cases' are different notions pursuant to the legal instruments and the established practice of the Court. 'Situations' are the object

[10] *Prosecutor v Thomas Lubanga Dyilo* (Decision on the Arrangements for Participation of Victims a/0001/06, a/0002/06 and a/0003/06 at the Confirmation Hearing) ICC-01/04-01/06-462-tEN (22 September 2006) 7–8; *Prosecutor v Germain Katanga and Mathieu Ngudjolo Chui* (Decision on the Set of Procedural Rights Attached to Procedural Status of Victim at the Pre-Trial Stage of the Case) ICC-01/04-01/07-474 (13 May 2008) paras 124–45; *Prosecutor v Jean-Pierre Bemba Gombo* (Fourth Decision on Victims' Participation) ICC-01/05-01/08-320 (12 December 2008) paras 101–10.

[11] *Prosecutor v Thomas Lubanga Dyilo* (Judgment on the appeals of the Prosecutor and the Defence against Trial Chamber I's Decision on Victims' Participation of 18 January 2008) ICC-01/04-01/06-1432 (11 July 2008) para 109.

[12] *Prosecutor v Joseph Kony et al* (Decision on the admissibility of the case under article 19(1) of the Statute) ICC-02/04-01/05-377 (10 March 2009) para 14 (to decide whether an admissibility determination should be made pursuant to art 19(1) of the ICC Statute, 'the proceedings must have reached the stage of a case (including "specific incidents during which one or more crimes within the jurisdiction of the Court seem to have been committed by one or more identified suspects"), as opposed to the preceding stage of the situation following the Prosecutor's decision to commence an investigation pursuant to article 53 of the Statute').

[13] *Situation in the Democratic Republic of the Congo* (Decision following the Consultation held on 11 October 2005 and the Prosecution's Submission on Jurisdiction and admissibility filed on 31 October 2005) ICC-01/04-93 (9 November 2005) 4 ('that at this stage of the proceedings [investigation of the situation] no warrant of arrest or summons to appear has been issued and thus no case has arisen').

[14] *Situation in Darfur (Sudan)* (Décision relative aux conclusions aux fins d'exception d'incompétence et d'irrecevabilité) ICC-02/05-34 (22 November 2006) 3–4 ('qu'à ce stade de la procédure [investigation of the situation], aucun mandat d'arrêt ni citation à comparaître n'ont été délivrés' [and therefore no case has arisen]).

[15] ICC, 'Regulations of the Registry' ICC-BD/03-01-06-Rev.1 (25 September 2006) regs 20 ('Opening of a situation or case record') and 21 ('Content of a situation or case record').

[16] See, eg, *Prosecutor v Thomas Lubanga Dyilo* (Decision concerning Pre-Trial Chamber I's Decision of 10 February 2006 and the Incorporation of Documents into the Record of the Case against Mr Thomas Lubanga Dyilo) ICC-01/04-01/06-8-Corr (24 February 2006) 4–5; *Prosecutor v Thomas Lubanga Dyilo* (Order Concerning the Incorporation of Certain Documents into the Record of the Case against Mr Thomas Lubanga Dyilo) ICC-01/04-01/06-35 (16 March 2006) 3; *Prosecutor v Germain Katanga* (Decision on the Incorporation of Documents in the Record of the Case and Convening a Hearing) ICC-01/04-01/07-27 (18 October 2007) 3; *Prosecutor v Germain Katanga* (Decision on the Incorporation of Documents in the Record of the Case and Convening a Hearing) ICC-01/04-01/07-59 (5 November 2007) 3; *Prosecutor v Germain Katanga and Mathieu Ngudjolo Chui* (Decision on the Set of Procedural Rights Attached to Procedural Status of Victim at the Pre-Trial Stage of the Case) ICC-01/04-01/07-474 (13 May 2008) para 133; *Prosecutor v Jean-Pierre Bemba Gombo* (Decision on unsealing and re-classification of certain documents and decisions) ICC-01/05-01/08-20 (20 June 2008) 6.

of preliminary examinations and investigations.[17] 'Cases' within a 'situation' are subsequently initiated by the issuance of a warrant of arrest or a summons to appear by the competent Pre-Trial Chamber at the request of the Prosecutor.[18]

III The Notion of 'Admissibility' and its Application to 'Situations' and 'Cases'

Article 17 of the ICC Statute, entitled 'issues of admissibility', literally refers to the admissibility and inadmissibility of 'cases'. Its provisions set up a test of admissibility comprised of two parts, namely 'complementarity' and 'gravity'.[19]

The first part of the test relates to national investigations, prosecutions and trials concerning the 'case'. Article 17(1)(a)–(c) provides that a 'case' is inadmissible where: (i) it is being genuinely investigated or prosecuted by a state which has jurisdiction over it; (ii) it has been genuinely investigated by a state which has jurisdiction over it and the state has decided not to prosecute the person concerned; or (iii) the person concerned has already been genuinely tried for conduct which is the subject of the complaint and a trial by the Court would therefore constitute *bis in idem*. Accordingly, a 'case' will be admissible only if those states with jurisdiction over it remain inactive in relation to that 'case', or if they are 'unwilling' or 'unable' to investigate and prosecute it within the meaning of article 17(2) and (3).[20]

The second part of the admissibility test refers to the 'gravity' of the case. Article 17(1)(d) provides that a 'case' is inadmissible where it is not of sufficient gravity to justify further action by the Court.

Accordingly, pursuant to article 17 of the ICC Statute, a 'case' is admissible only if national authorities are inactive, unwilling or unable and the case is grave enough.[21] The Court can investigate and prosecute such 'cases' as appropriate.

The ICC Pre-Trial, Trial and Appeals Chambers have already applied article 17 of the ICC Statute to several 'cases'. Although a finding of admissibility is not

[17] *Situation in the Democratic Republic of the Congo* (Decision on the Applications for Participation in the Proceedings of VPRS 1, VPRS 2, VPRS 3, VPRS 4, VPRS 5 and VPRS 6) ICC-01/04-101-tEN-Corr (17 January 2006) para 65.

[18] *Situation in the Democratic Republic of the Congo* (Decision following the Consultation held on 11 October 2005 and the Prosecution's Submission on Jurisdiction and Admissibility filed on 31 October 2005) ICC-01/04-93 (9 November 2005) para 4; *Situation in the Democratic Republic of the Congo* (Decision on the Applications for Participation in the Proceedings of VPRS 1, VPRS 2, VPRS 3, VPRS 4, VPRS 5 and VPRS 6) ICC-01/04-101-tEN-Corr (17 January 2006) para 65.

[19] *Situation in the Republic of Kenya* (Pre-Trial Chamber II, Decision Pursuant to Article 15 of the Rome Statute on the Authorization of an Investigation into the Situation in the Republic of Kenya) ICC-01/09-19 (31 March 2010) para 52.

[20] Interpretation *a contrario* of art 17(1)(a)–(c) of the ICC Statute.

[21] See, eg, *Prosecutor v Thomas Lubanga Dyilo* (Decision concerning Pre-Trial Chamber's I Decision of 10 February 2006 and the Incorporation of Documents into the Record of the Case against Mr Thomas Lubanga Dyilo) ICC-01/04-01/06-8-Corr (24 February 2006) Annex I, para 29.

required for the issuance of a warrant of arrest or a summons to appear,[22] several Pre-Trial Chambers have passed rulings on admissibility on finding reasonable grounds to believe that a person has committed a crime within the jurisdiction of the Court pursuant to article 58 of the ICC Statute. Furthermore, two persons have challenged the admissibility of their 'cases' after appearing before the Court. Moreover, in one instance the Court has felt the need to rule on the admissibility of a 'case' concerning persons still a large. As a consequence, up to the time of writing, no case has been found to be inadmissible, and seven cases haven been found to be admissible on the basis of article 17 of the ICC Statute, namely the *Ntaganda* case, the *Lubanga* case, the *Kony et al* case, the *Katanga and Ngudjolo* case, the *Harun and Kushayb* case, the *Abu Garda* case and the *Bemba* case.

Regarding the *Ntaganda* case, in 2006 the Appeals Chamber quashed the decision of Pre-Trial Chamber I not to grant the Prosecutor's application for an arrest warrant against the suspect on the basis that the 'case' was inadmissible for lack of sufficient gravity (article 17(1)(d) of the ICC Statute).[23] The Appeals Chamber stated that, contrary to the Pre-Trial Chamber's findings, the 'gravity' component of the admissibility analysis does not necessarily require the 'case' to involve 'systematic or large-scale' conduct, to cause 'social alarm' to the international community and to refer to 'the most senior leaders suspected of being the most responsible'.[24] Therefore, the Appeals Chamber reversed the Pre-Trial Chamber's finding of inadmissibility and remanded the matter back to the Pre-Trial Chamber, which subsequently issued an arrest warrant against *Bosco Ntaganda*.[25]

By contrast, Pre-Trial Chamber I issued an arrest warrant against *Thomas Lubanga* in 2006, after declaring admissible the 'case' against him. The Pre-Trial Chamber found that there was inaction by the Democratic Republic of the Congo (DRC) and any other state with regard to the *Lubanga* 'case'. It also found that such 'case', which was comprised of the alleged enlistment, conscription and use to participate actively in hostilities of children under the age of 15, was grave enough (article 17(1)(d) of the ICC Statute).[26] This finding on the admissibility of the 'case' was left untouched by Pre-Trial Chamber I in its decision confirming the charges against *Thomas Lubanga* in 2007.[27]

[22] *Situation in the Democratic Republic of the Congo* (Judgment on the Prosecutor's appeal against the decision of Pre-Trial Chamber I entitled 'Decision on the Prosecutor's Application for Warrants of Arrest, Article 58') ICC-01/04-169 (13 July 2006) para 42.

[23] *Prosecutor v Bosco Ntaganda* (Decision on Prosecutor's Application for Warrants of Arrest, Article 58) ICC-01/04-02/06-20-Anx2 (10 February 2006) para 89.

[24] *Situation in the Democratic Republic of the Congo* (Judgment on the Prosecutor's appeal against the decision of Pre-Trial Chamber I entitled 'Decision on the Prosecutor's Application for Warrants of Arrest, Article 58') ICC-01/04-169 (13 July 2006) para 82.

[25] Prosecutor v *Bosco Ntaganda* (Warrant of arrest) ICC-01/04-02/06-2-Anx-tENG (22 August 2006).

[26] *Prosecutor v Bosco Ntaganda* (Decision on Prosecutor's Application for Warrants of Arrest, Article 58) ICC-01/04-02/06-20-Anx2 (10 February 2006) paras 40, 74–75.

[27] *Prosecutor v Thomas Lubanga Dyilo* (Decision on the Confirmation of Charges) ICC-01/04-01/06-803-tEN (29 January 2007) paras 165–66. The Appeals Chamber later dismissed Mr Lubanga Dyilo's appeal against this decision. See *Prosecutor v Thomas Lubanga Dyilo* (Decision on the admissibility of the appeal of Mr Thomas Lubanga Dyilo against the decision of Pre-Trial Chamber I entitled 'Décision sur la confirmation des charges' of 29 January 2007) ICC-01/04-01/06-926 (13 June 2007).

Similarly, on the basis of the acknowledged inability and lack of will of the Government of Uganda, Pre-Trial Chamber II found admissible the 'case' against *Joseph Kony, Vincent Otti, Okot Odhiambo* and *Dominic Ongwen* (all commanders of the Lord's Resistance Army) when it issued an arrest warrant against them in 2005 for crimes against humanity and war crimes.[28] In 2009 this finding was *proprio motu* confirmed by Pre-Trial Chamber II in proceedings held in the absence of the accused persons but in the presence of the Prosecutor, victims, representatives of the government of Uganda and a counsel appointed to represent the interests of the Defence. The Chamber concluded that the Agreement on Accountability and Reconciliation between the Republic of Uganda and the Lord's Resistance Army and its Annexes, which had been drafted after the warrants of arrest were issued, did not change the scenario of state inaction concerning the investigation and prosecution of this case.[29] The Appeals Chamber found no error in this finding.[30]

Regarding *Germain Katanga* and *Mathieu Ngudjolo*, Pre-Trial Chamber I found the 'cases' against them to be admissible when issuing arrest warrants in 2007, on the ground of state inaction concerning the crimes against humanity and war crimes alleged by the Prosecutor.[31] In 2009, Trial Chamber II dismissed *Germain Katanga*'s challenge to the admissibility of his 'case' on the grounds, inter alia, that the decision of the DRC Government not to investigate and prosecute his case and to let the Court do it instead did not fall within any of the causes of inadmissibility listed in article 17(1)(a)–(c) of the ICC Statute and was in fact consistent with the principle of 'complementarity' on which the Court was founded.[32] This understanding of the admissibility of a 'case' was later supported and further clarified by the Appeals Chamber when dismissing the defendant's appeal against the Trial Chamber's decision finding his 'case' admissible.[33]

Pre-Trial Chamber I also found the 'case' against *Ahmed Harun* and *Ali Kushayb* to be admissible when issuing warrants of arrest against them in 2007 on the ground of state inaction.[34] By contrast, the Chamber did not find it necessary

[28] *Prosecutor v Joseph Kony et al* (Warrant of Arrest for Joseph Kony issued on 8 July 2005 as amended on 27 September 2005) ICC-02/04-01/05-53 (27 September 2005) paras 36–38.

[29] *Prosecutor v Joseph Kony et al* (Decision on the admissibility of the case under article 19(1) of the Statute) ICC-02/04-01/05-377 (10 March 2009).

[30] *Prosecutor v Joseph Kony et al* (Judgment on the appeal of the Defence against the 'Decision on the admissibility of the case under article 19(1) of the Statute' of 10 March 2009) ICC-02/04-01/05-408 (16 September 2009).

[31] *Prosecutor v Germain Katanga* (Decision on the evidence and information provided by the Prosecution for the issuance of a warrant of arrest for Germain Katanga) ICC-01/04-01/07-4 (6 July 2007) paras 17–21; *Prosecutor v Mathieu Ngudjolo Chui* (Decision on the evidence and information provided by the Prosecution for the issuance of a warrant of arrest for Mathieu Ngudjolo Chui) ICC-01/04-02/07-3 (6 July 2007) paras 17–22.

[32] *Prosecutor v Germain Katanga and Mathieu Ngudjolo Chui* (Reasons for the Oral Decision on the Motion Challenging the Admissibility of the Case (Article 19 of the Statute)) ICC-01/04-01/07-1213-tENG (16 June 2009) paras 77–79.

[33] *Prosecutor v Germain Katanga and Mathieu Ngudjolo Chui* (Judgment on the Appeal of Mr Germain Katanga against the Oral Decision of Trial Chamber II of 12 June 2009 on the Admissibility of the Case) ICC-01/04-01/07-1497 (25 September 2009) paras 85–86.

[34] *Prosecutor v Ahmad Harun and Ali Kushayb* (Decision on the Prosecutor's Application under Article 58(7) of the Statute) ICC-02/05-01/07-1-Corr (27 April 2007) paras 18–25.

to address the admissibility of the 'cases' against *Omar Al Bashir*, *Abu Garda*, and *Banda and Jerbo* at that stage, considering that: (i) these persons could not have access to the Prosecutor's applications at that time; (ii) the Prosecutor had indicated that there were no national proceedings in relation to these cases; and (iii) there was no ostensible cause or self-evident factor impelling the Chamber to exercise its discretion to rule on the admissibility of the 'case'.[35] Nonetheless, once *Abu Garda* appeared before the Court, Pre-Trial Chamber I confirmed the admissibility of his 'case', on the grounds of state inaction and sufficient gravity.[36]

Concerning Jean-Pierre Bemba, Pre-Trial Chamber III found the 'case' against him for crimes against humanity and war crimes to be admissible when it issued a warrant of arrest in 2007. The Chamber concluded that Jean-Pierre Bemba was not being prosecuted at the national level for the crimes alleged by the Prosecutor and that the judicial authorities of the Central African Republic (CAR) had abandoned any attempt to prosecute him because he enjoyed immunity by virtue of his status as Vice President of the DRC.[37] This finding on the admissibility of the 'case' was left untouched by Pre-Trial Chamber II in its decision confirming the charges against Jean-Pierre Bemba in 2009.[38] In 2010, Trial Chamber III also declared admissible the 'case' against Jean-Pierre Bemba when dismissing an admissibility challenge filed by the accused. The Trial Chamber found, inter alia, that the CAR had not taken a decision 'not to prosecute' the 'case' against Jean-Pierre Bemba in the sense of article 17(1)(b) of the ICC Statute, but had instead sought the prosecution of the 'case' by the ICC.[39] The Chamber also found that the national judicial system of the CAR was 'unable' to conduct the trial because it did not have the capacity to handle the complexity and extent of the 'case' against the accused and was therefore 'unavailable' (article 17(3) of the ICC Statute).[40] Moreover, the Trial Chamber relied on the Pre-Trial Chamber's finding regarding the gravity of the 'case'.[41] This understanding of the admissibility of the 'case' against Jean-Pierre Bemba was later supported by the Appeals

[35] *Prosecutor v Omar Al Bashir* (Decision on the Prosecution's Application for a Warrant of Arrest against Omar Hassan Ahmad Al Bashir) ICC-02/05-01/09-3 (4 March 2009) paras 47–51; *Prosecutor v Bahr Idriss Abu Garda* (Decision on the Prosecutor's Application under Article 58) ICC-02/05-02/09-1 (7 May 2009) para 4; *Prosecutor v Abdallah Banda Abakaer Nourain and Saleh Mohammed Jerbo Jamus* (Second Decision on the Prosecutor's Application under Article 58) ICC-02/05-03/09-1 (27 August 2009) para 4.

[36] *Prosecutor v Bahar Idriss Abu Garda* (Decision on the Confirmation of Charges) ICC-02/05-02/09-243-Red (8 February 2010) paras 29–34.

[37] *Prosecutor v Jean-Pierre Bemba Gombo* (Decision on the Prosecutor's Application for a Warrant of Arrest against Jean-Pierre Bemba Gombo) ICC-01/05-01/08-14-tENG (10 June 2008) para 21.

[38] *Prosecutor v Jean-Pierre Bemba Gombo* (Decision Pursuant to Article 61(7)(a) and (b) of the Rome Statute on the Charges of the Prosecutor against Jean-Pierre Bemba Gombo) ICC-01/05-01/08-424 (15 June 2009) paras 25–26.

[39] *Prosecutor v Jean-Pierre Bemba Gombo* (Decision on the Admissibility and Abuse of Process Challenges) ICC-01/05-01/08-802 (24 Jun 2010) paras 241–44.

[40] ibid at paras 245–46.

[41] ibid at para 249.

Chamber when dismissing the defendant's appeal against the Trial Chamber's decision.[42]

By contrast with the above-mentioned judicial decisions on the admissibility of 'cases', until the 31 March 2010 Pre-Trial Chamber II decision authorising the Prosecutor to start an investigation into the 'situation' in the Republic of Kenya, the Chambers of the Court had not paid much attention to the applicability of article 17 of the ICC Statute to 'situations'.

In April 2005, when dealing with the first 'unique investigative opportunity' within the investigation into the situation in the DRC, Pre-Trial Chamber I made references to the Prosecutor's preliminary examination prior to opening his investigation into the said situation and to the fact that the Prosecutor had received no information from any state pursuant to article 18(2) of the ICC Statute.[43] More clearly, in February 2006, when issuing a warrant of arrest against *Thomas Lubanga*, the same Pre-Trial Chamber indicated that such decision was 'limited to the determination of the content of the gravity threshold . . . when it must be applied to a *case* arising from the investigation of a situation',[44] but clarified that

> according to a contextual interpretation, . . . the gravity threshold provided for in article 17(1)(d) of the Statute must be applied at two different stages: (i) at the stage of initiation of the investigation of a situation, the relevant situation must meet such gravity threshold and (ii) once a case arises from the investigation of a situation, it must also meet the gravity threshold.[45]

Moreover, in November 2006, Pre-Trial Chamber I dismissed the request of an '*ad hoc*' counsel for the Defence to analyse the admissibility of the 'situation' in Darfur (Sudan) in the following terms:

> ATTENDU d'une part qu'aucune disposition du Statut et du Règlement ne mentionne que la Chambre doit sursoir à statuer suite à une contestation de la recevabilité et de la compétence de la Cour déposée par le conseil ad hoc pour la Défense dans le cadre de l'enquête sur une situation.[46]

However, by the time of these judicial decisions, the Prosecutor of the Court had already made reference to his admissibility assessment of 'situations'. For instance, when starting the investigation into the situation in the DRC in July 2004, the Prosecutor informed the President of the Court that

[42] *Prosecutor v Jean-Pierre Bemba Gombo* (Judgment on the appeal of Mr Jean-Pierre Bemba Gombo against the decision of Trial Chamber III of 24 June 2010 entitled 'Decision on the Admissibility and Abuse of Process Challenges') ICC-01/05-01/08-962 (19 October 2010) paras 74, 107–09.

[43] *Situation in the Democratic Republic of the Congo* (Decision to hold Consultation under Rule 114) ICC-01/04-19 (21 April 2005) 2–5.

[44] *Prosecutor v Thomas Lubanga Dyilo* (Decision concerning Pre-Trial Chamber's I Decision of 10 February 2006 and the Incorporation of Documents into the Record of the Case against Mr Thomas Lubanga Dyilo) ICC-01/04-01/06-8-Corr (24 February 2006) Annex I, para 44.

[45] ibid. See also Olasolo and Carnero-Rojo, 'The Admissibility of *Situations*' (above n 3).

[46] *Situation in Darfur (Sudan)* (Décision relative aux 'Conclusions aux fins d'in limine litis sursis à statuer' déposées par le conseil ad hoc de la Défense) ICC-02/05-25 (2 November 2006) 4.

> as required under Article 53 of the Statute and Rule 104, my Office has conducted analysis and sought additional information in order *to support a determination under Article 53 on the DRC situation.* Having considered *all of the criteria,* I have determined that there is a reasonable basis to initiate an investigation.[47]

In turn, when explaining his decision not to open an investigation into the situation in Iraq in 2006, the Prosecutor indicated that he 'must select situations in accordance with the Article 53 criteria',[48] which suggested that the Prosecutor understood admissibility at that time as applicable also to 'situations'.[49] The Prosecutor's subsequent paper on the 'interests of justice' (article 53(1) and (2)(c) of the Statute), released in 2007, also referred to a determination of whether 'the situation is of sufficient gravity' to justify further action by the Court pursuant to article 17(1)(d).[50] Likewise, the Regulations of the ICC Office of the Prosecutor adopted in 2009 prescribed that

> in acting under article 15, paragraph 3, or article 53, paragraph 1, the Office shall produce an internal report analysing the seriousness of the information and considering the factors set out in article 53, paragraph 1 (a) to (c), namely issues of jurisdiction, admissibility (including gravity), as well as the interests of justice, pursuant to rules 48 and 104.[51]

Finally, in October 2010 the Prosecutor issued a draft policy paper on 'preliminary examinations'.[52] This document confirms that the Prosecutor analyses the admissibility of 'situations' before starting an investigation thereof: 'In order to distinguish those situations that warrant investigation from those that do not, the Office has established a filtering process comprising four phases: . . . (c) Phase 3 focuses on an analysis of admissibility'.[53] Moreover, the draft policy paper examines how each of the admissibility factors set out in article 17 of the ICC Statute are applied by the Prosecutor in order to determine whether there is a 'reasonable basis' to proceed with an investigation of a 'situation', be it *proprio motu* or upon referral by States Parties to the ICC Statute or by the UN Security Council.[54]

[47] *Prosecutor v Thomas Lubanga Dyilo* (Decision Assigning the Situation in the Democratic Republic of Congo to Pre-Trial Chamber I) ICC-01/04-01/06-10 (5 July 2004) Annex I.

[48] ICC-OTP, 'OTP Response to communications received concerning Iraq' (9 February 2010): www.icc-cpi.int/NR/rdonlyres/04D143C8-19FB-466C-AB77-4CDB2FDEBEF7/143682/OTP_letter_to_senders_re_Iraq_9_February_2006.pdf, 8.

[49] KJ Heller, 'Situational Gravity under the Rome Statute' in C Stahn and L van den Herik (eds), *Future Directions in International Criminal Justice* (The Hague, TMC Asser/Cambridge University Press, 2009) 4.

[50] ICC-OTP, 'Policy Paper on the Interests of Justice' (September 2007): www.icc-cpi.int/Menus/Go?id=772c95c9-f54d-4321-bf09-73422bb23528&lan=en-GB, 5.

[51] ICC Office of the Prosecutor, 'Regulations of the Office of the Prosecutor' ICC-BD/05-01-09 (23 April 2009) Regulation 29(1) ('Initiation of an investigation or prosecution').

[52] ICC-OTP, 'Draft Policy Paper on Preliminary Examinations' (4 October 2010): www.icc-cpi.int/Menus/Go?id=e278f5a2-a4f9-43d7-83d2-6a2c9cf5d7d7&lan=en-GB.

[53] ibid at para 86.

[54] ibid at paras 51–72. In 2011, the Prosecutor announced the opening of an investigation on the basis of the referral by the UN Security of the 'situation' in Libya since 15 February 2011 after concluding that 'following a preliminary examination of available information . . . an investigation is warranted'. See ICC-OTP, 'ICC Prosecutor to open an investigation in Libya' (2 March 2011): www.icc-cpi.int/Menus/Go?id=3eee2e2a-2618-4d66-8ecb-c95beccc300c &lan= En-GB.

Therefore, the practice of the Court so far appears to disprove scholarly claims that the complementarity test under article 17 of the ICC Statute only applies where the investigation into a given country or conflict 'situation' has yielded a 'case'.[55] By contrast, such analysis must be carried out before the investigation of a 'situation' starts, as confirmed by Pre-Trial Chamber II in its decision authorising the Prosecutor to start an investigation into the 'situation' in the Republic of Kenya.

IV The Admissibility of the 'Situation' in the Republic of Kenya

In February 2008, the Prosecutor of the Court issued a statement in relation to the post-election violence that started in six of the eight provinces of the Republic of Kenya in December 2007. The Prosecutor informed that he was conducting a 'preliminary examination' of this 'situation':

> Kenya is a State Party to the Rome Statute. The OTP considers carefully all information relating to alleged crimes within its jurisdiction committed on the territory of States Parties or by nationals of States Parties, regardless of the individuals or group alleged to have committed the crime.[56]

One year later, the Prosecutor reaffirmed that the 'situation' in Kenya was being monitored by his office. He explained, in particular, that 'the OTP continues to follow-up whether national proceedings into the post-election violence in Kenya in early 2008 are being conducted'.[57] The Prosecutor also indicated that since January 2008, he had received 'communications' under article 15 of the ICC Statute by individuals and non-governmental organisations (NGOs) related to the post-election violence in Kenya.[58]

[55] C Kress and L Grover, 'International Criminal Law Restraints in Peace Talks to End Armed Conflicts of a Non-International Character' in M Bergsmo and P Kalmanovitz (eds), *Law in Peace Negotiations* (Oslo, Forum for International Criminal and Humanitarian Law Publications, 2009) 45. See, however, the guiding criteria for conducting situation admissibility analyses provided in Olasolo, *Triggering Procedure* (above n 3) at 164–72; H Olasolo, 'The Role of the International Criminal Court in Preventing Atrocity Crimes through Timely Intervention', above ch 1, this volume at 6; Olasolo and Carnero Rojo, 'The Admissibility of *Situations*' (above n 3); Ambos, *Procedimiento de La Ley* (above n 6) paras 329, 334, 336–37; K Ambos, 'The Colombian Peace Process and the Principle of Complementarity of the International Criminal Court: Is there sufficient willingness and ability on the part of the Colombian authorities or should the Prosecutor open an investigation now?' (Göttingen University, 5 January 2011): www.icc-cpi.int/NR/rdonlyres/ 2770C2C8-309A-408E-A41B-0E69F098F421/282850/civil1.pdf, para 3(a).

[56] ICC-OTP, 'Statement in relation to the events in Kenya' (5 February 2008): www.icc-cpi.int/Menus/Go?id=4ad85aa7-0272-4721-8d73-f527a55ecd54&lan=en-GB.

[57] ICC-OTP, 'Prosecutor reaffirms that the situation in Kenya is monitored by his office' (11 February 2009): www.icc-cpi.int/Menus/Go?id=06455318-783e-403b-8c9f-8e2056720c15&lan= en-GB.

[58] ibid.

In July 2009, the Prosecutor met at the seat of the Court with a delegation of the Kenyan Government. The latter agreed to provide the Prosecutor with a report of the investigations and prosecutions arising in Kenya out of the post-election violence and informed the Prosecutor that a special tribunal or other judicial mechanism should be adopted by the Kenyan Parliament to investigate and prosecute those responsible for the 2008 violence. Ultimately both parties agreed that the Kenyan Government would refer the 'situation' to the Prosecutor in accordance with article 14 of the ICC Statute if no parliamentary agreement to achieve the 'end of impunity of the most responsible of the most serious crimes' was reached over the next 12 months.[59]

As a consequence of the agreement with the Kenyan Government, the Prosecutor subsequently received a report from the Kenyan Attorney-General on crimes committed during the post-election violence.[60] Moreover, the Commission of Inquiry into the Post-Election Violence in Kenya (the Waki Commission) also transmitted to the Prosecutor the materials it had collected, together with a sealed envelope containing a list of persons who could be implicated in such violence.[61] On receipt of these materials, the Prosecutor stated that

> We will consider in particular the existence of national proceedings. The Kenyan authorities are discussing options to establish a national court to prosecute these cases. In accordance with the Rome Statute, the primary responsibility for investigating and prosecuting these crimes rests with Kenya . . . The findings of the Waki Commission are important but they do not bind the Office; I should reach an impartial conclusion.[62]

After holding more consultations with the Kenyan Government, in September 2009 the Prosecutor suggested a three pronged-approach to address the post-election violence of early 2008 in Kenya: (i) the ICC would be prosecuting 'those most responsible'; (ii) national proceedings set up by the Kenyan parliament would deal with 'other perpetrators'; and (iii) a 'Justice, Truth and Reconciliation Commission' would be established in Kenya to shed light on the full history of past events and to suggest mechanisms to prevent similar crimes in the future.[63]

In November 2009, however, the Kenyan Parliament lacked enough quorum to discuss a Bill for the establishment of a domestic special tribunal for the post-election violence and the Kenyan Government did not refer the 'situation' in Kenya to the Prosecutor. As a consequence, the Prosecutor, after informing the

[59] ICC-OTP, 'Agreed Minutes of the meeting between Prosecutor Moreno-Ocampo and the delegation of the Kenyan Government' (3 July 2009): www.icc-cpi.int/NR/rdonlyres/6D00562 5-2248-477A-9485-FC52B4F1F5AD/280560/20090703AgreedMinutesofMeetingProsecutor KenyanDele.pdf.

[60] ICC-OTP, 'ICC Prosecutor receives materials on post-election violence in Kenya', ICC-OTP-20090716-PR438 (16 July 2009).

[61] ICC-OTP, 'Waki Commission list of names in the hands of ICC Prosecutor', ICC-OTP-20090716-PR439 (16 July 2009).

[62] ICC-OTP, 'ICC Prosecutor receives materials on post-election violence in Kenya', ICC-OTP-20090716-PR438 (16 July 2009).

[63] ICC-OTP, 'ICC Prosecutor Supports Three-Pronged Approach to Justice in Kenya', ICC-OTP-20090930-PR456 (30 September 2009).

Kenyan authorities,[64] notified the President of the ICC that he intended to request authorisation to proceed with an investigation into the 'situation' in Kenya pursuant to article 15(3) of the ICC Statute. The Prosecutor also issued a public notice informing victims of the possibility of sending their comments to the Pre-Trial Chamber on whether an investigation in respect of crimes allegedly committed in Kenya during the post-election violence of 2007–08 should be opened.[65]

Once the 'situation' in Kenya was assigned to Pre-Trial Chamber II,[66] on 26 November 2009 the Prosecutor filed before this Chamber a request to get an authorisation to commence an investigation into the Kenyan post-election violence of 2007–08.[67] Based on public reports by Kenyan authorities, the United Nations and several NGOs, the Prosecutor alleged in his request that acts committed on the territory of Kenya at the end of 2007 and early 2008 amounted to crimes within the jurisdiction of the Court – namely crimes against humanity of murder, rape and other forms of sexual violence, deportation or forcible transfer of population and other inhumane acts allegedly committed on a State Party after its ratification of the ICC Statute.[68]

More interestingly, the Prosecutor's application also addressed the admissibility of the 'situation', taking into account the 'potential cases' that would likely arise from an investigation of the 'situation'.[69] The Prosecutor submitted that the 'cases' that would arise from his investigation of the 'situation' would be admissible at that time because no national investigations or proceedings were pending against 'those bearing the greatest responsibility for the crimes against humanity allegedly committed'. The Prosecutor asserted that according to the reports of Kenyan authorities only a limited number of proceedings for less serious offences had been started in Kenya in connection with the crimes allegedly committed during the post-election violence. Furthermore, the Prosecutor submitted that the information available at that time did not indicate the existence of national proceedings in other states with jurisdiction in relation to the post-election violence (article 17(1)(a)–(c) of the ICC Statute).[70] Moreover, the Prosecutor asserted that the crimes allegedly committed in the situation were grave enough, considering their number

[64] ICC-OTP, 'Kenyan authorities committed to cooperate as ICC Prosecutor informs them that in December he will request ICC judges to open an investigation into post-election violence', ICC-01/09-3-Anx20 (5 November 2009).

[65] *Situation in the Republic of Kenya* (Decision Assigning the Situation in the Republic of Kenya to Pre-Trial Chamber II) ICC-01/09-1 (6 November 2009) Annex I; ICC-OTP, 'Victims of post-election violence in Kenya have 30 days to make representations to ICC in the Hague' (23 November 2009): www.icc-cpi.int/Menus/Go?id=7a34b336-9611-430f-a668-ca5d209471ca&lan=en –GB.

[66] *Situation in the Republic of Kenya* (Decision Assigning the Situation in the Republic of Kenya to Pre-Trial Chamber II) ICC-01/09-1 (6 November 2009).

[67] *Situation in the Republic of Kenya* (Request for authorisation of an investigation pursuant to Article 15) ICC-01/09-3 (26 November 2009).

[68] ibid at paras 48, 61–101.

[69] ibid at para 51.

[70] ibid at para 55.

of victims, their organisation and planning, and their impact on the local communities (article 17(1)(d) of the ICC Statute).[71]

Prior to making a decision on the Prosecutor's request, Pre-Trial Chamber II also showed its intention to analyse the admissibility of the 'situation'. In February 2010, the Chamber requested from the Prosecutor additional information on the 'admissibility within the context of the situation in the Republic of Kenya'. In particular the Chamber requested information on: (i) the incidents that were likely to be the focus of the Prosecutor's investigation; (ii) the groups of persons involved that were likely to be the target of the investigation; and (iii) the existing domestic investigations, if any, with respect to the 'potential cases' as constituted by the previous two elements.[72]

On the basis of the information submitted by the Prosecutor and the comments received from alleged victims,[73] on 31 March 2010 the Pre-Trial Chamber authorised the opening of an investigation into the 'situation' in Kenya.[74] The Majority of the Chamber found that the crimes alleged by the Prosecutor fell within the jurisdiction of the Court,[75] the 'situation' was admissible and the opening of an investigation on these crimes would not be against the interests of justice.

Regarding admissibility, the Majority of the Pre-Trial Chamber found that the requirement that 'the case is or would be admissible under Article 17' (article 53(1)(b) of the ICC Statute) called on the Chamber to review the Prosecutor's finding on admissibility 'exceptionally' prior to the start of a *proprio motu* investigation of the 'situation' because otherwise such review could only take place pursuant to a Prosecutor's application under article 18. After underlining that the ICC Statute is drafted in a manner which tends to solve questions related to admissibility at different stages of the proceedings before trial, the Majority of the Pre-Trial Chamber concluded that at this stage of the proceedings the Prosecutor and the Pre-Trial Chamber operated within the parameters of a 'situation' rather than in relation to a specific 'case'. Accordingly, relying on a literal and contextual

[71] ibid at paras 56–59.

[72] *Situation in the Republic of Kenya* (Decision Requesting Clarification and Additional Information) ICC-01/09-15 (18 February 2010) paras 11, 14.

[73] *Situation in the Republic of Kenya* (Public Redacted Version of Corrigendum to the Report on Victims' Representations) ICC-01/09-17-Corr-Red (29 March 2010).

[74] *Situation in the Republic of Kenya* (Decision Pursuant to Article 15 of the Rome Statute on the Authorization of an Investigation into the Situation in the Republic of Kenya) ICC-01/09-19 (31 March 2010).

[75] Judge Kaul could not see an attack directed against the civilian population in Nairobi, North Rift Valley, Central Rift Valley, South Rift Valley, Nyanza Province, Western Province, Coast Province and Central Province pursuant to or in furtherance of the policy of an organisation or a state, because of the lack of a common purpose, hierarchical structure and membership of the organisations over a prolonged period of time, and the lack of adoption or endorsement of a policy at a high level of the state. His overall assessment of the information led him to conclude that several centres of violence in several provinces existed and each did not rise to the level of crimes against humanity. See *Situation in the Republic of Kenya* (Decision Pursuant to Article 15 of the Rome Statute on the Authorization of an Investigation into the Situation in the Republic of Kenya) ICC-01/09-19 (31 March 2010) Dissenting Opinion of Judge Hans-Peter Kaul, paras 82–83, 93–94, 102–03, 112–13, 119–20, 127–28, 137–38, 146–47 and 150.

interpretation of articles 13(a) and (b), 14(1), 15(5) and (6), 18(1) and 53(1)(b) of the ICC Statute, the Majority of the Pre-Trial Chamber found that the admissibility assessment necessary for the authorisation of an investigation should be related to a 'situation' and used the expression 'admissibility of a situation'.[76]

After reviewing the drafting history of the Statute, the Majority of the Chamber concluded that the drafters advertently retained the terminology of a 'case' in all relevant provisions addressing admissibility, including article 17 of the Statute, thereby leaving it for the Court to harmonise the meaning according to the different stages of the proceedings. Accordingly, the Majority of the Chamber concluded that since it is not possible to have a concrete 'case' involving an identified suspect for the purpose of prosecution prior to the commencement of the investigation of a 'situation', the admissibility assessment at this stage actually refers to the admissibility of one or more 'potential cases' within the context of the 'situation'.[77] This approach is similar to the one advanced by authors like Rastan, Guariglia and Ambos.[78] Moreover, the Majority clarified that the determination of the admissibility of a 'situation' in order to authorise its investigation was not binding on it for future admissibility challenges based on complementarity arguments regarding the actual 'cases' subsequently brought to the Court.[79]

As a result, the Majority found that the admissibility of the 'situation' should be assessed against 'potential cases' within such a 'situation', defined with criteria such as the groups of persons and the alleged crimes within the jurisdiction of the Court that are likely to be the focus of an investigation for the purpose of shaping the future case(s).[80]

[76] *Situation in the Republic of Kenya* (Decision Pursuant to Article 15 of the Rome Statute on the Authorization of an Investigation into the Situation in the Republic of Kenya) ICC-01/09-19 (31 March 2010) paras 41–45. Judge Kaul did not address the admissibility issue in his dissenting opinion. See also in this regard, Olasolo, *Triggering Procedure* (above n 3) at 40–45; Olasolo and Carnero-Rojo, 'The Admisibility of *Situations*' (above n 3); H Olasolo, 'Admisibilidad de situaciones y casos objeto de procesos de justicia de transición ante la Corte Penal Internacional' in J Almqvist and C Espósito (eds), *El papel de los tribunales en contextos de justicia transicional: oportunidades y desafíos actuales en la región Iberoamericana* (Madrid, Centro de Estudios Constitucionales y Políticos, AECID, 2009).

[77] *Situation in the Republic of Kenya* (Decision Pursuant to Article 15 of the Rome Statute on the Authorization of an Investigation into the Situation in the Republic of Kenya) ICC-01/09-19 (31 March 2010) paras 47–48.

[78] According to these authors, the complementarity analysis of the Court at the 'situation' stage should be limited to 'the type of cases that would be investigated in the situation', 'the likely set of cases that would arise from investigation of the situation' or 'the group of probable cases that would come out from the investigation of a situation'. See respectively Rastan, 'What is a "Case"?' (above n 6) at 441; F Guariglia, 'The Selection of Cases by the Office of the Prosecutor of the International Criminal Court' in C Stahn and G Sluiter (eds), *The Emerging Practice of the International Criminal Court* (The Hague, Martinus Nijhoff, 2009) 213, fn 17; Ambos, *Procedimiento de La Ley* (above n 6) para 334.

[79] *Situation in the Republic of Kenya* (Decision Pursuant to Article 15 of the Rome Statute on the Authorization of an Investigation into the Situation in the Republic of Kenya) ICC-01/09-19 (31 March 2010) para 50.

[80] ibid at paras 49–50. Nonetheless, the Chamber clarified that the Prosecutor's selection of the incidents or groups of persons that were likely to shape his future case(s) was preliminary in nature and not binding for future admissibility assessments. This meant that the Prosecutor's selection of 'potential cases' for this particular phase may change at a later stage, depending on the development of the investigation.

As mentioned above, any admissibility assessment requires a complementarity analysis and a gravity analysis. This is also applicable to the admissibility assessments of 'situations'. The Majority of Pre-Trial Chamber II, relying on the above-mentioned interpretation, considered that a complementarity analysis with regard to a 'situation' requires an examination as to whether the relevant state(s) are conducting or have conducted national proceedings in relation to the groups of persons and the crimes allegedly committed during the incidents which together will likely form the object of the Prosecutor's investigations (article 17(1)(a)–(c) of the ICC Statute).

In this regard, relying on the 25 September 2009 judgment of the Appeals Chamber in the *Katanga and Ngudjolo* case,[81] the Majority concluded that there was no need to examine questions of unwillingness and inability since there was a scenario of state inactivity with respect to the elements that were likely to shape the 'potential cases' of the 'situation' in the Republic of Kenya.[82] The Majority of the Chamber found that although there were references to a number of domestic investigations and prosecutions concerning the post-election period in relation to minor offences, there was a lack of national proceedings in Kenya or in any third state with respect to the 'main elements which could shape the "potential case(s)" of the Court', namely the 'senior business and political leaders' related to or associated with the Party of National Unity and the Orange Democratic Movement, and the 'crimes against humanity allegedly committed in the context of the most serious criminal incidents' referred to by the Prosecutor upon request from the Chamber.[83]

Regarding the gravity assessment (article 17(1)(d) of the ICC Statute), the Majority concluded that the gravity of the 'situation' should also be examined against the backdrop of the likely set of 'potential case(s)' that would arise from investigating the 'situation'.[84] In particular, the Majority found that such assessment involved a general assessment of whether the group of persons that was likely to form the object of investigation captured 'those who may bear the greatest responsibility for the alleged crimes committed', and an assessment of the gravity of the crimes committed within the incidents which were likely to be the focus of an investigation, taking into account their scale, nature, manner of commission, impact on victims and the existence of aggravating circumstances.[85]

Applying this theory to the overall 'situation' in the Republic of Kenya through the study of the 'potential cases' put forward by the Prosecutor at the request of

[81] See above (n 33).

[82] *Situation in the Republic of Kenya* (Decision Pursuant to Article 15 of the Rome Statute on the Authorization of an Investigation into the Situation in the Republic of Kenya) ICC-01/09-19 (31 March 2010) paras 53–54, 182.

[83] ibid at paras 185–87. The Prosecutor had filed *ex parte* a list of the most serious criminal incidents and a list of 20 leaders who appeared to bear the greatest responsibility for the most serious crimes. See *Situation in the Republic of Kenya* (Prosecution's Response to Decision Requesting Clarification and Additional Information) ICC-01/09-16 (3 March 2010).

[84] ibid at para 58.

[85] ibid at paras 60–62, 188.

the Chamber, the Majority of Pre-Trial Chamber II found that the Kenyan situation met the requisite gravity threshold. The Chamber´s conclusion was based on the following two arguments: (i) the target group of persons likely to be the focus of the Prosecutor's future investigations concerned the high-ranking positions that allegedly played a role in the violence; and (ii) some of the specific crimes committed in the context of the potential incidents suggested by the Prosecutor satisfied the elements of scale and/or brutality[86] and had a devastating impact on the victims.[87]

Despite the important efforts of Pre-Trial Chamber II, one can observe some limitations in its gravity analysis of the situation in the Republic of Kenya. In particular, the Chamber did not provide concrete guidance on how the 'potential cases' approach should be applied. It simply enumerated some general factors, such as 'high-ranking positions', 'scale', 'brutality' and 'impact on victims', and applied them to the facts of the 'situation'. As these factors had already been adopted by the Prosecutor for the purpose of conducting gravity assessments of specific 'cases',[88] the question arises as to controlling criteria to distinguish between gravity analysis of 'situation' and 'cases'.

One can only regret that Pre-Trial Chamber II missed the opportunity to provide further clarity on the content of article 17(1)(d) gravity threshold. This is more so considering that the Appeals Chamber, after declining to embrace the criterion of 'the most senior leaders suspected of being the most responsible' to declare 'cases' inadmissible,[89] has not provided for any alternative controlling criterion for the purpose of the article 17(1)(d) gravity threshold.[90]

[86] ibid at paras 198–99.

[87] ibid at paras 191, 193, 195–96.

[88] These general factors had already been adopted by the ICC Office of the Prosecutor for the purpose of assessing the gravity of specific 'cases'. See ICC-OTP, 'Paper on some policy issues before the Office of the Prosecutor' (September 2003): www.icc-cpi.int/Menus/Go?id=1fa7c4c6-de5f-42b7-8b25-60aa962ed8b6&lan=en-GB, para 2.1; ICC-OTP, 'Report on Prosecutorial Strategy' (14 September 2006): www.icc-cpi.int/Menus/Go?id=d673dd8c-d427-4547-bc69-2d363e07274b&lan=en-GB, para 2.b.

[89] See above (n 24). In this regard, Seils has supported such decision by pointing out that the 'most senior leaders suspected of being most responsible' criterion constitutes 'a rigid, formulaic fashion, running a serious risk of entering the treacherous waters of strict liability, but also in an excessively narrow sense, guaranteeing impunity to all but the very top level' and has argued that such standard should be purely 'evidence dependent' with reference to each 'case' (P Seils, 'The Selection and Prioritization of Cases by the Office of the Prosecutor of the International Criminal Court' in M Bergsmo (ed) *Criteria for Prioritizing and Selecting Core International Crimes Cases* (Oslo, Forum for International Criminal and Humanitarian Law Publications, 2009) 56). In a similar way, for Guariglia this type of criterion could become 'a permanent legal barrier providing permanent *ex ante* impunity to entire classes of perpetrators, and enabling perpetrators to bring legal challenges demanding evidence showing that they are not only guilty but the most guilty' (Guariglia, 'The Selection of Cases' (above n 78) at 215).

[90] *Situation in the Democratic Republic of the Congo* (Judgment on the Prosecutor's appeal against the decision of Pre-Trial Chamber I entitled 'Decision on the Prosecutor's Application for Warrants of Arrest, Article 58') ICC-01/04-169 (13 July 2006) para 89. In his separate and partly dissenting opinion, Judge Pikis elaborated on the criterion under art 17(1)(d), stating that 'a crime is insignificant itself if, notwithstanding the fact that it satisfies the formalities of the law . . ., the acts constituting the crime are wholly peripheral to the objects of the law in criminalizing the conduct. Both, the inception and consequences of the crime must be negligible. In those circumstances the Court need not concern itself with the crime nor will it assume jurisdiction for the trial of such an offence, when national courts fail

As a result – in order to properly conduct gravity analysis and admissibility assessments of any future 'situations' – it will be necessary in the coming years for the content of the gravity threshold provided for in article 17(1)(d) of the ICC Statute to be interpreted in further detail.[91]

V Conclusion

The law and practice of the ICC endorses a clear distinction between 'situations' and 'cases'. 'Situations' are generally defined in terms of temporal, territorial and in some cases personal parameters, whereas 'cases' entail specific incidents during which one or more crimes within the jurisdiction of the Court seem to have been committed by one or more identified suspects. As practical examples of this distinction, the ICC refers to 'victims of the situation' and to 'victims of the case' and keeps separate records of the proceedings within each 'situation' and each 'case'.

Although the letter of the ICC Statute appears to limit the admissibility analysis to 'cases', 'situations' must also undergo an admissibility analysis pursuant to a literal and contextual reading of the ICC Statute. However, until the 31 March 2010 Pre-Trial Chamber II decision authorising the commencement of an investigation into the 'situation' in the Republic of Kenya, the Chambers of the Court had only tangentially referred to the admissibility of 'situations' and had instead focused their attention on the admissibility of 'cases'. For this reason, the 31 March 2010 Pre-Trial Chamber II decision is of a fundamental value.

Admissibility assessments of 'situations' require a complementarity analysis and a gravity analysis. Pre-Trial Chamber II found that the complementarity analysis of a 'situation' (article 17(1)(a)–(c) of the ICC Statute) must be directed to 'potential cases' within the relevant 'situation', defined with criteria such as the groups of persons and the alleged crimes within the jurisdiction of the Court that are likely to be the focus of an investigation for the purpose of shaping the future case(s).

to do so . . . The subject-matter must be minimal, so much that it can be ignored by the Court'. See ibid at 'Separate and Partly Dissenting Opinion of Judge Georghios M Pikis', para 40. For a similar criticism and suggestions on the interpretation of gravity, see Ambos, *Procedimiento de La Ley* (above n 6) paras 339–43.

[91] In spite of being outside the scope of this chapter, it is important to highlight that the dilemmas posed by amnesties, pardons, alternative reduced sentences or traditional forms of justice from a complementarity perspective were also left unaddressed by Pre-Trial Chamber II in its 31 March 2010 decision. As a consequence, this approach still does not provide much direction to address the main problem posed by such dilemmas: deciding at the stage of initiating an investigation (and thus prior to the gathering of the evidence) which national proceedings must be reviewed in conducting a 'situation' admissibility analysis and which proceedings fall outside the scope of that analysis. The authors have addressed these dilemmas elsewhere. See in particular, Olasolo and Carnero-Rojo, 'The Admissibility of *Situations*' (above n 3); and Olasolo, 'La Admisibilidad de Situaciones y Casos' (above n 76). In these works, the authors argue that a key element for the proper conduct of future complementarity assessments of situations is that in the coming years the content of the selection criteria used by the Prosecutor to target 'cases' for investigation and prosecution be further elaborated in the context of art 17(1)(a)–(c) of the ICC Statute.

Pre-Trial Chamber II also found that the gravity analysis of a 'situation' (article 17(1)(d) of the ICC Statute) must be directed to assess whether the group of persons that is likely to form the object of investigation captures both 'those who may bear the greatest responsibility for the alleged crimes committed', and the crimes committed within the incidents which are likely to be the focus of an investigation, considering their scale, nature, manner of commission, impact on victims and the existence of aggravating circumstances.

Conducting admissibility assessments of 'situations' is a very complex task, particularly when it is done for the first time; hence, the merit of Pre-Trial Chamber II in carrying out the admissibility assessment of the 'situation' in the Republic of the Kenya must be acknowledged.

Nevertheless, this should not prevent us from underlining the shortcomings observed in the Chamber's analysis. In particular, it is worth noting the opportunity missed by Pre-Trial Chamber II to provide further clarity on the content of the gravity threshold provided for in article 17(1)(d) of the ICC Statute, when applied to 'situations' as part of the admissibility assessment.[92] As a result, the question arises as to controlling criteria to distinguish between the gravity analysis of 'situation' and 'cases'.

As a consequence, and considering the vital role of the admissibility assessment of 'situations' for the initiation and development of ICC investigations, the Court is bound to continue to clarify in the coming years the guiding criteria under which the admissibility assessment of 'situations' in general, and their gravity analysis in particular, are to be conducted.

[92] ibid.

4

The Distinction Between Situations and Cases in National Laws of Cooperation with the ICC*

I Introduction

In its decision of 17 January 2006, Pre-Trial Chamber I (PTC I) of the International Criminal Court (ICC or the Court) clarified the distinction between situations and cases under the ICC Statute. The Chamber made it clear that situations and cases form the object of the different proceedings before the Court. The Chamber explained this differentiation in the following terms:

> The Chamber considers that the Statute, the Rules of Procedure and Evidence and the Regulations of the Court draw a distinction between situations and cases in terms of the different kinds of proceedings, initiated by any organ of the Court, that they entail. Situations, which are generally defined in terms of temporal, territorial and in some cases personal parameters, such as the situation in the territory of the Democratic Republic of the Congo since 1 July 2002, entail the proceedings envisaged in the Statute to determine whether a particular situation should give rise to a criminal investigation as well as the investigation as such. Cases, which comprise specific incidents during which one or more crimes within the jurisdiction of the Court seem to have been committed by one or more identified suspects, entail proceedings that take place after the issuance of a warrant of arrest or a summons to appear.[1]

PTC I also established that the issuance of a warrant of arrest or a summons to appear marks the demarcation line between proceedings concerning the situation and proceedings concerning the case. As PTC I put it concerning VPRS-1–PRS-6's application for participation at all stages of the proceedings:

> With regard to the applications currently under consideration, the Chamber notes that, for the time being, no case has been initiated through the issuance of a warrant of arrest

* Published in (2007) 20 *Leiden Journal of International Law* 193. The author thanks the *Leiden Journal of International Law* for authorising the reprint of the present work. The views expressed herein are those of the author alone and do not necessarily reflect the views of the ICC, the ICTY, the United Nations in general or the Spanish Government.

[1] *Situation in the Democratic Republic of the Congo* (Decision on the Applications for Participation in the Proceedings of VPRS 1, VPRS 2, VPRS 3, VPRS 4, VPRS 5 and VPRS 6) ICC-01/04-101-tEN-Corr (17 January 2006) para 65.

> or a summons to appear by the Chamber under article 58 of the Statute in the light of the investigation of the situation in the territory of the DRC under way since 1 July 2002. At this stage, therefore, the Chamber can accord the status of victim only in connection with the situation in the DRC. As the applicants have applied to be accorded the status of victim 'at the investigation, trial or sentencing stage', once a case ensues from the investigation of the DRC situation, the Chamber will automatically address the question of whether the applicants seem to meet the definition of victims set out in rule 85 of the Rules in connection with such a case.[2]

The distinction between situations (eg, the armed conflict in the territory of the former Yugoslavia between 1991 and 1995 or the crisis situation in the territory of Rwanda after 6 April 1994) and cases (eg, the criminal responsibility of Dario Kordic for crimes committed during the attack to the village of Ahmici on the morning of 16 April 1993, or the criminal responsibility of General Krstic for the massacre following the fall of Srebrenica on 11 July 1995) is a core feature of the procedural regime of the Statute which has multiple implications for the proceedings of the Court.

In its decision of 17 January 2006, PTC I highlighted the consequences of the situation/case distinction for the procedural status of victims.[3] The Chamber distinguished the procedural status of victims of the situation and victims of the case. The Chamber pointed out:

> In the light of this distinction, the Chamber considers that, during the stage of investigation of a situation, the status of victim will be accorded to applicants who seem to meet the definition of victims set out in rule 85 of the Rules of Procedure and Evidence in relation to the situation in question. At the case stage, the status of victim will be accorded only to applicants who seem to meet the definition of victims set out in rule 85 in relation to the relevant case.
>
> The Chamber notes that, according to regulation 86 (2) (g) of the Regulations of the Court, when a natural or legal person makes an application to be accorded the status of victim, the applicant is required to provide, to the extent possible, '[i]nformation on the stage of the proceedings in which the victim wishes to participate'. It follows that where any natural or legal person applying for the status of victim in respect of a situation also requests to be accorded the status of victim in any case ensuing from the investigation of such a situation, the Chamber automatically takes this second request into account as soon as such a case exists, so that it is unnecessary to file a second application.[4]

Moreover, in a subsequent decision dated 10 February 2006, the Chamber found that the distinction between situations and cases has implications for the admissibility analysis under the Statute. PTC I noted:

[2] ibid at para 68.

[3] For a general discussion of victims'participation at the pre-trial stage, see C Stahn, H Olasolo and K Gibson,'Participation of Victims in Pre-Trial Proceedings of the ICC' (2006) 4 *Journal of International Criminal Justice* 219.

[4] *Situation in the Democratic Republic of the Congo* (Decision on the Applications for Participation in the Proceedings of VPRS 1, VPRS 2, VPRS 3, VPRS 4, VPRS 5 and VPRS 6) ICC-01/04-101-tEN-Corr (17 January 2006) paras 66–67.

> According to a contextual interpretation, the Chamber observes that the gravity threshold provided for in article 17 (1) (d) of the Statute must be applied at two different stages: (i) at the stage of initiation of the investigation of a situation, the relevant situation must meet such a gravity threshold, and (ii) once a case arises from the investigation of a situation, it must also meet the gravity threshold provided for in that provision. In this regard, the Chamber would emphasize that the scope of the present decision is limited to the determination of the content of the gravity threshold under article 17 (1) (d) of the Statute when it must be applied to a case arising from the investigation of a situation.[5]

National legislatures have not always paid sufficient attention to the distinction between situations and cases when drafting national laws on cooperation with the ICC. This distinction is, in particular, often disregarded in relation to a referral of a situation to the ICC Office of the Prosecutor pursuant to articles 13(a) and 14 of the ICC Statute, a request to the Prosecutor to defer an investigation under article 18(2), or a challenge to the admissibility of a case under article 19(2).

As a result, the application of domestic law is likely to raise a number of problems that might hamper the functioning of the Court. The lack of attention to the distinction between situations and cases, may, in particular, lead to a loss of valuable evidence or an ineffective application of the complementarity principle due to simultaneous investigations and prosecutions by the Court and national jurisdictions.

The chapter focuses on the Spanish Organic Law 18/2003 of 10 December 2003 on Cooperation with the International Criminal Court (OLCICC) as a paradigmatic example of the lack of attention to the distinction between situations and cases. It treats problems that are likely to arise in three different areas: (i) the communication of the *notitia criminis* to the Court; (ii) admissibility issues in proceedings under articles 18 and 19 of the ICC Statute; and (iii) the efficacy of admissibility rulings by the Court at the national level.

It should be noted that these problems are not particular to Spanish legislation. Similar deficits can be identified in a number of national laws or draft national laws on cooperation with the ICC, such as for instance the Colombian and the Argentinian draft Bills on Cooperation with the ICC. Furthermore, other national laws, such as the 2001 International Criminal Court Act of the United Kingdom or 2002 Australian International Criminal Court Act, present similar problems.[6] The deficiencies identified here are therefore of broader relevance to ICC implementing legislation.

[5] *Prosecutor v Thomas Lubanga Dyilo* (Decision concerning Pre-Trial Chamber I's Decision of 10 February 2006 and the Incorporation of Documents into the Record of the Case against Mr Thomas Lubanga Dyilo) ICC-01/04-01/06-8-Corr (24 February 2006) Annex I, para 44.

[6] The lack of specific provisions dealing with the three areas which are the focus of this chapter in the cooperation laws of Australia and the United Kingdom has been highlighted by H Brady, 'Australia' in C Kress, B Broomhall, F Lattanzi and V Santori (eds), *The Rome Statute and Domestic Legal Orders Vol II: Constitutional Issues, Cooperation and Enforcement* (Baden-Baden, Nomos/Il Sirente, 2005) 11–12; P Lewis, 'The United Kingdom' in Kress, Broomhall, Lattanzi and Santori (eds), ibid, 460.

II Communication of the *Notitia Criminis* to the Court according to the OLCICC

A Referral of a Situation by a State Party

The Preamble of the OLCICC states that one of the goals of the law is to regulate the procedure for referrals of situations of crisis to the Court by Spain with particular care. Article 7(1) of the law vests the government with the competence to make a referral of a situation, since it is the organ responsible for foreign policy under the Spanish Constitution and thus able to make a decision that could affect such policy. The referral of a situation under articles 13(a) and 14 of the ICC Statute has to be agreed on by the Council of Ministers on the basis of a joint proposal of the Ministers of Justice and Foreign Affairs. The same procedure must be followed to request the PTC under article 53(3)(a) of the ICC Statute to review the decision of the ICC Office of the Prosecutor not to investigate or not to prosecute in accordance with article 53(1) or (2) of the ICC Statute.[7] This approach is also reflected in article 7 of the Colombian draft Bill on Cooperation with the ICC and article 24 of the Argentinian draft Bill on Cooperation with the ICC.

Although some scholars have voiced concern with respect to this rule,[8] this author shares the view that there are a number of reasons that support the legislature's choice to leave the decision whether or not to refer a situation under articles 13(a) and 14 of the ICC Statute in the hands of the government. Articles 13(a) and 14 of the ICC Statute direct states to refer armed conflicts or situations of crisis that are defined by territorial and temporal (and sometimes also personal) criteria to the Court. The referral of a situation automatically initiates the triggering procedure to determine whether the Court will activate its dormant jurisdiction regarding the armed conflict or crisis situation in question and, thus, whether the Court will initiate an investigation into the crimes allegedly committed in the situation.[9] Moreover, by referring a situation under articles 13(a) and 14 of the ICC Statute, Spain becomes a party to the triggering procedure before the Court, and the states concerned by the conflict or situation referred by Spain will likely become opposing parties under article 18(2) of the ICC Statute. The referral of a situation under articles 13(a) and 14 of the ICC Statute may therefore have far greater implications for Spanish foreign policy than the transmission of a simple criminal complaint against a particular individual which is tied to a limited set of acts.

[7] Art7(1) OLCICC.

[8] See, inter alia, L Bujosa Vadell, *La Cooperación Procesal de los Estados con la Corte Penal Internacional* (Barcelona, Atelier, 2006) section 4.3.

[9] H Olasolo, *Corte Penal Internacional: Dónde Investigar? Especial Referencia a la Fiscalía en el Proceso de Activación* (Valencia, Tirant lo Blanch, 2003) 107, 391–403.

B Transmission of Communications under Article 15 of the ICC Statute

Article 7(2) of the OLCICC directs Spanish judicial organs, public prosecutors and ministerial departments to abstain from taking any action when the *notitia criminis* is communicated to them or when they receive a criminal complaint or request concerning crimes within the jurisdiction of the Court allegedly committed by non-nationals outside Spain. In such circumstances, Spanish authorities shall solely inform the persons or entities filing the criminal complaint or request of their right to communicate the matter to the ICC Office of the Prosecutor. Judicial organs and public prosecutors are also barred from acting ex officio regarding such crimes. The only exception to this rule is included in the Third Additional Disposition of the OLCICC, which allows such action with respect to the jurisdiction of judicial organs of the Spanish military over actions or omissions carried out by Spanish troops outside Spain or the exercise of jurisdictional functions by the judicial military organs accompanying Spanish military troops outside Spain.[10]

At the same time, article 7(2) of the OLCICC contains an important safeguard that allows competent judicial organs and public prosecutors to adopt urgent preliminary measures aimed, inter alia, at avoiding the loss of evidence. Furthermore, article 7(3) of the OLCICC provides an option to bring criminal complaints or

[10] During the parliamentary debate, some pointed out that this provision restricted the scope of the principle of universal jurisdiction as enshrined in art 23.4 of the Organic Law 6/1985 of 1 July 1985 on the Judicial Power (OLJP) in such a way as to make it no longer applicable by the Spanish judicial organs regarding crimes within the jurisdiction of the Court. As a result, the creation of the ICC would entail a decline of the principle of universal jurisdiction in Spain (see Proposed amendment 1 to the draft OLCICC, presented in the Congress of Deputies by B Lasagabáster, of the Mixed Parliamentarian Group). Others affirmed that this proposal was not in line with the object and purpose behind the creation of a permanent International Criminal Court which operates on the basis of the principle of complementarity. In their view, the Court is not supposed to substitute any of the mechanisms in place at the national or international level to fight against impunity in relation to the most serious crimes of concern to the international community. On the contrary, the Court constitutes an additional mechanism aimed at providing states with the necessary incentives to make the existing mechanisms more effective; and it only takes direct action when national jurisdictions have shown themselves unwilling or unable to properly fight against impunity. Therefore, the creation of the Court could not be interpreted as supporting the restriction of some of the mechanisms available under Spanish law to investigate and prosecute the crimes within the jurisdiction of the Court. Quite the opposite, the creation of the Court should promote their more effective exercise. This position was supported by important voices in doctrine, including Bujosa Vadell, *La Cooperación* (above n 8) at 97–102, section 2.5; MP Pozo Serrano, 'Medidas Nacionales adoptadas para la ratificación y la aplicación del Estatuto de la Corte Penal Internacional: Un balance provisional' (2003) 18 *Anuario de Derecho Internacional* 299, 345; J Pueyo Losa, 'Un nuevo modelo de cooperación internacional en materia penal: entre la justicia universal y la jurisdicción internacional' in S Álvarez González and JR Remacha y Tejada (eds), *Cooperación jurídica internacional* (Madrid, Colección Escuela Diplomática, 2001) 141–203, 145. However, the great majority of Spanish parliamentarians favoured an understanding of the formal primacy of Spanish jurisdiction in accordance with the principle of complementarity as limited to those crimes committed in Spanish territory or by Spaniards abroad. This position has also been supported by some scholars, including A Sánchez Legido, *Jurisdicción Universal Penal y Derecho Internacional* (Valencia, Tirant lo Blanch, 2004) 394; F Lattanzi, 'Compétence de la Cour pénale internationale et consentement des états' (1999) *Revue Générale de Droit International Public* 425, 430–31.

requests before competent Spanish judicial organs, public prosecutors or ministerial departments if the Court declines to act because no investigation is initiated by the ICC Office of the Prosecutor or there is a declaration of inadmissibility. This system was introduced in order to ensure that the principle of universal jurisdiction can be exercised with regard to the crimes within the jurisdiction of the Court, but only in those circumstances where the Court fails to act.

One problem of the Spanish approach (which is also reflected in article 7 of the Colombian draft Bill on Cooperation with the ICC)[11] is that the second and third paragraphs of article 7 of the OLCICC have inverted the meaning of the relationship of complementarity between the Court and Spanish jurisdiction. The duty to stop proceedings and inform complainants of the possibility of communicating the matter to the ICC Office of the Prosecutor is based on the idea that the Court serves as a substitute for Spanish judicial organs. Even if the Spanish legislature intended to base its choice on the recent jurisprudence of the Spanish Supreme Court's Penal Chamber, by establishing the necessity of the intervention of Spanish jurisdiction as a pre-requisite for the application of universal jurisdiction, the legislature did not lend enough weight to the difference between the *ultima ratio* jurisdiction of the ICC and the primary responsibility of national jurisdictions to investigate and prosecute crimes committed on their territory.

Moreover, article 7(2) of the OLCICC has been drafted on the premise that the Court can directly open an investigation against a particular individual for a well-defined set of acts under the ICC Statute. This assumption is misguided. It conflicts with the general distinction between situations and cases under the ICC Statute and the fact that situations (as opposed to cases) form the object of the triggering procedure of the Court and the object of separate investigations. As a consequence, a scenario may occur under which:

1. An initial criminal complaint or administrative request is filed with a Spanish judicial organ, public prosecutor or ministerial department.
2. The organ with which the criminal complaint or administrative request is filed informs the complainant of his or her right to transmit the *notitia criminis* to the ICC Office of the Prosecutor.
3. The complainant sends a communication to the ICC Office of the Prosecutor pursuant to article 15(1) of the ICC Statute.
4. The ICC Office of the Prosecutor, pursuant to article 15(2) of the ICC Statute, carries out a preliminary examination of the situation in the context of which the acts object of the said communication have allegedly taken place.
5. After the preliminary examination of the overall situation, the ICC Office of the Prosecutor, unless the gravity of the systematic and/or widespread crimes allegedly committed in the said situation otherwise requires, decides not to request authorisation from PTC to initiate the investigation of the situation under preliminary examination.

[11] Similar provisions are lacking, however, in the Argentinian draft Bill on Cooperation with the ICC.

6. The ICC Office of the Prosecutor, according to article 15(6) of the ICC Statute, informs the complainant of its decision not to request the authorisation to initiate the investigation of the said situation.
7. The complainant, at this point, can only file a new criminal complaint or administrative request with the Spanish judicial organ, public prosecutor or ministerial department with which it filed – years before – his or her first criminal complaint or administrative request.
8. According to article 7(3) of the OLCICC, only now can the relevant acts be investigated by the competent Spanish authorities.

As a consequence, the very same Spanish judicial or prosecutorial organs which must abstain from acting after receiving the first criminal complaint, may be forced years afterwards to investigate the relevant acts pursuant to the principle of universal jurisdiction embraced by article 23(4) of the Spanish Organic Law 6/1985 of the Judicial Power (OLJP). It is evident that this sequence of events (caused by the inversion of the meaning of the relationship of complementarity between the Court and Spanish jurisdiction and the disregard for the distinction between situations and cases when drafting the OLCICC) compromises the efficiency of proceedings since investigations can only be started years after the first criminal complaint is filed.

The danger is even greater in those cases in which Spanish judicial or prosecutorial organs acquire *notitia criminis* in relation to the alleged commission of crimes by non-Spaniards outside the territory of Spain when acting *propio motu*. In such cases, Spanish authorities are even prevented from taking the necessary investigative steps pursuant to the principle of universal jurisdiction under article 7(2) of the OLCICC. Furthermore, insofar as the OLCICC does not grant Spanish judicial and prosecutorial organs the power to transmit the *notitia criminis* to the ICC Office of the Prosecutor, they will have to remain inactive; and this despite the fact that criminal investigations are guided by the principle of legality (as opposed to the principle of political discretion) under articles 105 and 299 of the Spanish Code of Criminal Procedure (*Ley de Enjuiciamiento Criminal).*

III Admissibility Issues in the OLCICC

A Deferral Requests under Article 18(2) of the ICC Statute

The Preamble of the OLCICC highlights that it is an important rationale of the law to regulate potential jurisdictional conflicts between the Court and Spanish jurisdiction. Several articles address this matter. Article 8 of the OLCICC establishes the procedure to decide whether or not to request, pursuant to article 18(2) of the ICC

Statute, the deferral of the investigation of a situation[12] provisionally initiated by the Court in accordance with articles 15(4) or 53(1) of the ICC Statute.

Article 8(1) OLCICC establishes that on reception of the notification provided for in article 18(1) of the ICC Statute, the Ministry of Justice must request information on any investigation or prosecution conducted by Spanish judicial or prosecutorial organs from the Attorney General (*Fiscal General del Estado*). Similarly, the Ministry of Justice must request information from the Attorney General on the jurisdictional basis claimed by Spanish judicial organs to be seized with the crimes allegedly committed in the situation under investigation by the Court.

If the information provided by the Attorney-General indicates that Spain has exercised its jurisdiction, is exercising its jurisdiction, or has started an investigation as a result of the notification provided for in article 18(1) of the ICC Statute, the Ministry of Justice in conjunction with the Ministry of Foreign Affairs must send the proposal to request the deferral of the Court's investigation to the Council of Ministers, no later than 20 days after reception of the Court's notification.[13] Though article 8(3) of the OLCICC is not completely clear on this point, its Preamble makes clear that the Council of Ministers has the duty to request the deferral of the Court's investigation, and thus to uphold the Spanish jurisdiction. After obtaining clearance from the Council of Ministers, the Ministry of Justice will be responsible for making the deferral request urgently under article 18(2) of the ICC Statute and rule 53 of the Rules of Procedure and Evidence (RPE).

It is noteworthy that this procedure is not applicable in relation to crimes allegedly committed by non-Spaniards outside the territory of Spain. Hence, the mandate to uphold the formal primacy of the Spanish jurisdiction vis-à-vis the Court contained in the Preamble of the OLCICC is limited to those situations in which Spanish tribunals act pursuant to the principles of territoriality or nationality of the suspect or accused person.[14]

One should not overlook that, according to article 23 OLJP, the extent of Spanish jurisdiction goes beyond these two principles. Indeed, as provided for in

[12] Proceedings under art 18 of the ICC Statute concern situations as opposed to cases. This is, inter alia, reflected in the 'preliminary' character of the admissibility rulings under United Nations General Assembly (UNGA), 'Rome Statute of the International Criminal Court' (17 July 1998) UN Doc A/Conf.183/9, arts 1, 4 [hereinafter ICC Statute] art 18(2) and (4), Art) ve n 12), rocedurecle 9 19 which are not meant to be final decisions with the respect to the admissibility of the case (ie, the more limited set of acts occurring within the broader context of those situations). Moreover, this conception makes sense in practical terms since the degree of scrutiny exercised with respect to national proceedings concerning a situation cannot be as detailed as the admissibility analysis focused on a single case. For a more detailed explanation of the role of art 18 of the ICC Statute proceedings as the second part of the *triggering procedure*, see H Olasolo, *The Triggering Procedure of the International Criminal Court* (Leiden, Martinus Nijhoff Publishers, 2005) 72–89.

[13] Art 8 (2) OLCICC.

[14] A similar regulation can be found in art 8 of the Colombian draft Bill on Cooperation with the ICC and in art 25 of the Argentinian draft Bill on Cooperation with the ICC. However, it must be highlighted that, according to art 8 of the Colombian draft Bill, the aforementioned procedure is not applicable with regard to crimes allegedly committed by non-Colombians outside the territory of Colombia, whereas art 25 of the Argentinian draft Bill does not contain such a restriction.

article 23 OLJP, Spanish tribunals can act pursuant other jurisdictional bases, such as nationality of the victim, the protective principle or the principle of universal jurisdiction.

As a result, Spanish legislators have distinguished between jurisdictional bases of first and second class insofar as only the proceedings carried out pursuant to the principles of territoriality and nationality of the suspect or accused person merit to be upheld before the Court through a deferral request under article 18 of the ICC Statute.

Moreover, article 8 of the OLCICC is not consistent with the aim of the deferral mechanism provided for in article 18 (2) of the ICC Statute. This mechanism is aimed at avoiding an investigation by the Court when national jurisdictions have already investigated, or are investigating, the crimes within the jurisdiction of the Court allegedly committed in the situation under scrutiny. It is, hence, a procedural tool to guarantee the effective application of the complementarity principle so as to ensure that the Court only investigates a given situation when those national jurisdictions concerned are inactive, unwilling or unable (thus, avoiding simultaneous investigations by the Court and national tribunals).

However if, as in the Spanish case, article 23 OLJP permits Spanish tribunals to investigate crimes within the jurisdiction of the Court pursuant to the jurisdictional basis of the nationality of the victim, the protective principle and the principle of universal jurisdiction, and article 8 of the OLCICC ignores this reality, it is likely that the same crimes be simultaneously investigated for months or years by the Court and national tribunals. In fact, such a situation may not be resolved until it is revealed by way of a possible refusal by Spanish authorities to comply with Court's cooperation request on the basis of the ongoing investigation by Spanish tribunals;[15] or an admissibility challenge by the person against whom a warrant of arrest or a summons to appear has been issued on the ground of an ongoing investigation by Spanish tribunals.[16]

B Admissibility Challenges under Article 19(2) of the ICC Statute

Article 9(1) of the OLCICC entrusts the Spanish Council of Ministers, on the basis of a joint proposal of the Ministries of Justice and Foreign Affairs, with the decision to make a challenge on jurisdiction or admissibility pursuant to article 19 of the ICC Statute. However, unlike in cases of deferral requests under article 18(2) of the ICC Statute, the Council of Ministers is not obliged to make an admissibility challenge even if Spanish tribunals are conducting, or have conducted, proceedings with regard to the relevant case. This distinction is grounded, according to the Preamble of the OLCICC, on the recent jurisprudence of the Second and Third Chambers of the Spanish Supreme Court on the duty/right to resort to external judicial organs.

[15] Art 93(3) of the ICC Statute.
[16] Art 19(2)(a) of the ICC Statute.

As a result, at the stage of article 18(2) of the ICC Statute proceedings, when no admissibility ruling has been issued yet by the Court, the Council of Ministers is obliged to uphold the Spanish jurisdiction. However, once an admissibility ruling has been issued, the Council of Ministers' duty to uphold the Spanish jurisdiction through article 19 of the ICC Statute admissibility challenge turns into a discretional power.

On the other hand, due to the Council of Ministers' duty to make a deferral request under article 8 of the OLCICC, Spanish legislators have assumed that, after article 18 of the ICC Statute proceedings, an admissibility ruling will automatically exist. As a result, article 9 (1) of the OLCICC leaves the decision to make a challenge on jurisdiction or admissibility pursuant to article 19 of the ICC Statute at the discretion of the Spanish Council of Ministers.

In the author's view, Spanish legislators have not paid due attention to the fact that article 18 proceedings concern situations, whereas article 19 proceedings are related to cases.[17] The object of the Court's analysis of admissibility under articles 18(2) and 19 varies accordingly. At the time when a case arises pursuant to article 58 of the ICC Statute, the Court may have declared, at best, the admissibility of the situation in the context of which the case takes place. However, no admissibility ruling concerning any newly-arisen case will exist at that time.

A different matter is the practice set out by PTC I and PTC II after the approval of the OLCICC, according to which the issuance of an arrest warrant or of a summons to appear may be subject to a previous finding of admissibility of the case brought forward by the ICC Office of the Prosecutor.[18]

The question arises as to whether the prima facie determination of the admissibility of a case required by PTC II would suffice, according to article 9 of the OLCICC, to turn the Spanish Government's duty to uphold the Spanish jurisdiction through an article 19 of the ICC Statute admissibility challenge into

[17] This position has also been defended by MC Bassiouni, *Introduction to International Criminal Law* (Ardsley, Transnational Publishers, 2003) 518–19; WA Schabas, *An Introduction to the International Criminal Court* (Cambridge, Cambridge University Press, 2004) 125–26; CK Hall, 'Article 19: Challenges to the Jurisdiction of the Court and the Admissibility of the Case' in O Triffterer, *Commentary on the Rome Statute of the International Criminal Court: Observers' Notes, Article by Article* (Baden Baden, Nomos, 1999) 405–17, 407; MM El Zeidy, 'The Ugandan Government Triggers the First Tests of the Complementarity Principle: An Assessment of the First State's Party Referral to the ICC' (2005) 5 *International Criminal Law Review* 83, 110.

[18] The public version of PTC I's decision of 10 February 2006 can be found in *Prosecutor v Thomas Lubanga Dyilo* (Decision concerning Pre-Trial Chamber's I Decision of 10 February 2006 and the Incorporation of Documents into the Record of the Case against Mr Thomas Lubanga Dyilo) ICC-01/04-01/06-8-Corr (24 February 2006) Annex I (see in particular para 20). See also *Prosecutor v Joseph Kony et al* (Warrant of Arrest for Joseph Kony issued on 8 July 2005 as amended on 27 September 2005) ICC-02/04-01/05-53 (27 September 2005) para 38; *Prosecutor v Joseph Kony et al* (Warrant of Arrest for Vincent Otti) ICC-02/04-01/05-54 (8 July 2005) para 38; *Prosecutor v Joseph Kony et al* (Warrant of Arrest for Raska Lukwiya) ICC-02/04-01/05-55 (8 July 2005) para 26; *Prosecutor v Joseph Kony et al* (Warrant of Arrest for Okot Odhiambo) ICC-02/04-01/05-56 (8 July 2005) para 28; *Prosecutor v Joseph Kony et al* (Warrant of Arrest for Dominic Ongwen) ICC-02/04-01/05-57 (8 July 2005) para 26. For a discussion, see MM El Zeidy, 'Some Remarks on the Question of the Admissibility of a Case during Arrest Warrant Proceedings before the International Criminal Court' (2006) 19 *Leiden Journal of International Law* 741–51.

a discretionary power. The same question arises when, according to PTC I's practice, an admissibility ruling is made on the basis of the limited information provided for by the ICC Office of the Prosecutor in the context of an application for an arrest warrant or a summons to appear (particularly if such information does not include the proceedings of the Spanish tribunals in relation to the case at hand).

Article 9(1) of the OLCICC appears to be based on the assumption that an admissibility ruling by the Court (prior to any plausible admissibility challenge by Spain under article 19(2) of the ICC Statute) will have taken into consideration the proceedings of the Spanish tribunals with regard to the relevant case. However, the practice of PTC I and PTC II shows that it is possible for the Court to declare the admissibility of a case without having analysed the proceedings of Spanish tribunals in relation to the same case.

Hence, the author considers that no admissibility ruling should be able to turn the Spanish Government's duty to uphold the formal primacy of the Spanish jurisdiction vis-à-vis the Court into a discretional power. On the contrary, article 9(1) of the OLCICC should be interpreted in a manner in which such a transformation only takes place when the Court's admissibility ruling has taken into consideration the proceedings of Spanish tribunals with regard to the case at hand. Otherwise, the ultimate aim of the OLCICC – which is to promote the formal primacy of the Spanish jurisdiction vis-à-vis the Court in application of the complementarity principle – will not be achieved.

A similar interpretation should be adopted under articles 8 and 9 of the draft Colombian Bill on Cooperation with the ICC, which contain provisions similar to those under articles 8 and 9 of the OLCICC.[19]

IV The OLCICC and the Efficacy of Admissibility Rulings at the National Level

One of the most difficult issues of any law on cooperation is to determine the impact of an admissibility decision by the ICC on the national system that has been under scrutiny of the Court.

In such circumstances, it may be necessary to determine the status of national investigations and prosecutions that do not meet the standards provided for in article 17 of the ICC Statute and hence justify an inadmissibility ruling. Moreover, there may be a need to define the status of final decisions by national tribunals that according to the Court justify an inadmissibility ruling.

[19] Note that art 26(1) of the draft Argentinian Bill on Cooperation with the ICC constitutes a remarkable example of the lack of attention to the distinction between situations and cases insofar as it jointly deals with deferral requests under art 18(2) of the ICC Statute and admissibility challenges under art 19(2) of the ICC Statute as if both had cases as their object.

Article 10 of the OLCICC addresses the first question. According to this provision, Spanish tribunals must stay their proceedings if the Court declares the admissibility of the relevant situation or case despite a deferral request or an admissibility challenge by Spain under articles 18(2) of the ICC Statute or 19(2) of the ICC Statute, and must transfer the record of such proceedings to the Court, if the Court so requires. Article 10 of the Colombian draft Bill on Cooperation with the ICC and article 27 of the Argentinian draft Bill on Cooperation with the ICC have embraced the same approach.

This approach acknowledges the material primacy of the Court vis-à-vis the Spanish jurisdiction. However, it presents a number of problems as a result of disregarding the distinction between situations and cases. For instance, it is not reasonable to require that a ruling on the admissibility of a situation would prevent Spanish tribunals from investigating or prosecuting any of the crimes allegedly committed in the relevant situation.

In the view of the author, the stay of national proceedings and the transmission to the Court of the record of such proceedings is a necessary measure to avoid the paralysis of the Court as a result of the dynamic nature of the complementarity principle. Otherwise, there is a risk that, after an admissibility ruling, the states concerned resurrect their national proceedings in order to subsequently uphold the formal primacy of their national jurisdictions vis-à-vis the Court.

However, one should not forget that the ultimate aim of the complementarity principle (and of the procedural right to challenge the admissibility of a case pursuant to article 19(2) and (4) of the ICC Statute until just before the commencement of the trial) is to provide an incentive for national investigations and prosecutions of crimes within the jurisdiction of the Court.

Hence, a strict application of article 10 of the OLCICC would impede the fulfilment of this aim because an admissibility ruling at such an early stage of the Court's proceedings as that of article 18 of the ICC Statute proceedings would prevent Spanish tribunals from investigating and prosecuting any of the crimes allegedly committed in the situation which is the object of that admissibility ruling.

As a consequence, this author considers that the scope of application of article 10 of the OLCICC should have been expressly limited to those admissibility rulings taken by the Court at the case stage pursuant to article 19 of the ICC Statute. It is precisely in the framework of the criminal procedure before the Court (whose object is a case as opposed to a situation) where the stay of national proceedings and the transmission to the Court of the record of such proceedings as a result of the Court's declaration of the admissibility of a case are fully consistent with the ultimate aim of the complementarity principle.

However, in dealing with this issue it is important to pay attention to the practice of PTC I and PTC II, which shows that proceedings of Spanish tribunals may not always be analysed prior to the issuance of an admissibility ruling by the Court.

In this scenario, the stay of national proceedings and the transmission of the record of such proceedings to the Court pursuant to article 10 of the OLCICC would be contrary to the principle of formal primacy of the Spanish jurisdiction vis-à-vis the Court and to the ultimate aim of the complementarity principle, which aims to promote national investigations and prosecutions of the crimes within the jurisdiction of the Court.

Indeed, if article 10 of the OLCICC is applied in this scenario, Spanish tribunals would be bound to stay their proceedings and to transfer the record of such proceedings to the Court without having been declared by the Court as unwilling or unable in relation to the case at hand.

Therefore, according to the author, article 10 of the OLCICC should only be applied after the Court´s issuance of a decision under article 19 of the ICC Statute which declares the admissibility of a case and shows that due attention has been paid to those proceedings of Spanish tribunals in relation to the case at hand. In the absence of the second prerequisite, the Spanish Government, acting pursuant to article 9(1) of the OLCICC (as interpreted in light of the Preamble of the OCCICC), should make a challenge to the admissibility of the case as soon as practicable.

Only if, as a result of such a challenge, the Court reaffirms the admissibility of the case due to the unwillingness or inability of the Spanish jurisdiction, Spanish tribunals should stay their proceedings and transmit the record of such proceedings to the Court as provided for in article 10 of the OLCICC.

On the other hand, the OLCICC (like many other laws on cooperation with the Court passed to date)[20] is silent on the question of the efficacy of those final national judicial resolutions which are affected by a Court's admissibility ruling.

The problems arising in this context have already been underscored in the following terms:

> From a purely national perspective, the proceedings of the ICC concerning acts and individuals which have been the object of national final judgments would constitute a violation of the *ne bis in idem* principle as defined in many national systems. In order to avoid this problem it is submitted that the States Parties should incorporate into their national legislation mechanisms depriving of any effect those national final judgments and decisions not to prosecute that for the purpose of the RS are declared ineffective by the ICC's competent organ. Otherwise, it is likely that the violation from a national perspective of the *ne bis in idem* principle will prevent the States Parties concerned, and particularly those in which the *ne bis in idem* principle has constitutional rank, from complying with their obligations to cooperate with the ICC.[21]

In the view of the author, this legislative gap is the result of the resistance of national legislators to acknowledge the far-reaching effects of the material primacy of the Court vis-à-vis national jurisdictions.

In order to solve this problem, it is useful to take into account, once again, the distinction between situations and cases. Indeed, the nullity of final national

[20] Art 10 of the Colombian draft Bill on Cooperation with the ICC, art 27 of the Argentinian draft Bill on Cooperation with the Court and the 2001 and 2002 International Criminal Court Acts of the United Kingdom and Australia are also silent on this matter.

[21] Olasolo, *Triggering Procedure* (above n 12) at 154.

judicial resolutions must be subject to a decision by the Court under article 19 of the ICC Statute which declares the admissibility of a case and shows that the national decision concerned has been examined by the Court.

On the basis of this premise, and having regard to the particular characteristics of the Spanish legal system, the author considers it necessary to amend article 238 OLJP in order to introduce a fifth ground of nullity of final judicial resolutions along the lines set out above.

V Final Remarks

This short chapter has shown that Spanish legislators have not paid enough attention to the core distinction between situations and cases when drafting the OLCICC. This shortcoming may be explained by the fact that this distinction was not yet developed in the Court's jurisprudence at the time of the drafting of the OLCICC. However, this deficit needs to be addressed in due course, otherwise Spanish authorities and other jurisdictions are likely to face a number of problems in areas such as the communication of the *notitia criminis* to the Court, admissibility issues in proceedings under articles 18 and 19 of the ICC Statute and the efficacy of the Court's admissibility rulings at the national level.

The Court has clarified some of the parameters governing the distinction between situations and cases under the ICC Statute in its first practice. The case law has, in particular, identified some of the implications of this distinction in the fields of victims' participation and admissibility analysis. It is therefore necessary and timely to rethink domestic implementation of legislation from this perspective.

5

Complementarity Analysis of National Sentencing*

I Introduction

As seen recently in the context of the criminal proceedings held by Rwandan national courts and the International Criminal Tribunal for Rwanda (ICTR), those political and military leaders who are ultimately responsible for the bloodshed may end up being tried by an international tribunal where the death penalty is not an option, whereas lower level perpetrators will be tried by national courts and subject to the death penalty. Due to the material limitations of the International Criminal Court (ICC), this phenomenon may also take place in the context of the ICC.

However, being tried by national courts does not necessarily mean exposure to higher penalties. Indeed, one can envisage the opposite scenario, particularly concerning cases of superior responsibility that are considered by the relevant national criminal justice system as crimes of pure omission and are punished with relatively short penalties depending on the negligent or intentional nature of the superior's breach of duties. Therefore, whether the persons tried by national courts may also be exposed to lower penalties or to higher ones will largely depend on the general principles inspiring the relevant national criminal justice system.

The close link in any given national criminal justice system between the principles that lie at its roots and sentencing, and the fact that the ICC's complementarity analysis is not only limited to national proceedings, but extends to national sentencing, may prompt the ICC to play a role in shaping the foundations of national criminal justice systems in order to put an end to either the inhuman and disproportionate character or the leniency of national penalties. However, a number of reasons which are analysed throughout this chapter call for a more cautious approach based on respect, to the extent possible, to the general principles inspiring national criminal justice systems.

* Published in R Haveman and O Olusanya (eds), *Sentencing and Sanctioning in Supranational Criminal Law* (Antwerp/Oxford, Intersentia, 2006) 37. The author thanks Intersentia for authorising reprint of the present work. The views expressed herein are those of the author alone and do not necessarily reflect the views of the ICC, the ICTY, the United Nations in general or the Spanish Government.

II The Relevance of National Sentencing in a Complementarity Analysis

The ICC, unlike the other international criminal tribunals, is a permanent institution. Its relationship with national jurisdictions is based on the principle of complementarity provided for in articles 1, 17, 18, 19 and 20 of the ICC Statute,[1] as opposed to the principle of primacy that govern the relationship between the other international criminal tribunals and national jurisdictions. According to the principle of complementarity, the ICC constitutes an *ultima ratio* jurisdiction that can only act as a result of the inaction, unwillingness or inability of national jurisdictions.

The ICC Statute embraces the principle of formal primacy of national jurisdictions over the ICC[2] and, at the same time, grants the Court the power to decide on the inaction, unwillingness or inability of national jurisdictions. This constitutes the most important transfer of sovereignty by the States Parties through the ICC Statute and places the ICC in a position of material primacy over national jurisdictions.[3] As a result, one can say that the principle of complementarity is composed of two main elements: the formal primacy of national jurisdictions and the ICC's material primacy.[4]

Each of the above-mentioned two elements is linked to one of the two main goals of the principle of complementarity. On the one hand, through the principle of formal primacy of national jurisdictions, the complementarity principle intends to promote the investigation and prosecution by national jurisdictions of 'the most serious crimes of international concern'[5] with full respect to the principles of justice contained in the ICC Statute.[6] On the other hand, the principle of

[1] JT Holmes, 'The Principle of Complementarity' in RS Lee (ed), *The International Criminal Court: The Making of the Rome Statute – Issues, Negotiations, Results* (The Hague, Kluwer Law International, 1999) 73; SA Williams, 'Article 17: Issues of Admissibility' in O Triffterer (ed), *Commentary on the Rome Statute of the International Criminal Court: Observers' Notes, Article by Article* (Baden Baden, Nomos, 1999) 383, 384.

[2] C Escobar Hernandez, 'La Progresiva Institucionalización de la Jurisdicción Penal Internacional' in M Garcia Aran and D Lopez Garrido (eds), *Crimen Internacional y Jurisdicción Universal (el Caso Pinochet)* (Valencia, Tirant lo Blanch, 2000) 225, 258. See also Williams, 'Article 17' (above n 1) at 384.

[3] Escobar Hernandez, 'La Progresiva' (above n 2) at 260.

[4] The same view is held by ibid at 260; J Alcaide Fernandez, 'La Complementariedad de la Corte Penal Internacional y de los Tribunales Nacionales: ¿Tiempos de "Ingeniería Jurisdiccional"?' in JA Carrillo Salcedo (ed), *La Criminalización de la Barbarie: La Corte Penal Internacional* (Madrid, Consejo General del Poder Judicial, 2000) 383, 416–17; JL Rodriguez-Villasante y Prieto, 'Análisis del Estatuto del Tribunal Penal Internacional' in Miño and Dávila (eds), *Jornadas 'Fuerrzas Armadas y Derechos Humanos: EsPosible Alcanzar el Equilibrio? (1999: Sevilla, Spain)* (Madrid, Miño and Dávila, 2000) 1–14; F Jimenez Garcia, 'Hacia una Jurisdicción Internacional Obligatoria en el Siglo XXI: El Estatuto del Tribunal Penal Internacional Adoptado en Roma el 17 de Julio de 1998' (1999) 3 *Studia Carande* 103, 120–22.

[5] United Nations General Assembly (UNGA), 'Rome Statute of the International Criminal Court' (17 July 1998) UN Doc A/Conf.183/9, art 1 [hereinafter ICC Statute].

[6] The same view is held by B Broomhall, 'The International Criminal Court: A Checklist for National Implementation' in MC Bassiouni (ed), *ICC Ratification and National Implementing Legislation, Nouvelles Études Pénales* vol 13 (Érès, Nouvelles Études Pénales, 1999) 113, 159. See also Escobar Hernandez, 'La Progressiva' (above n 2) at 261.

material primacy of the Court aims to extirpate, through the ultimate action of the ICC, the virus of the impunity for the perpetrators of such crimes which is preventing national jurisdictions from investigating and prosecuting.[7]

As the principle of formal primacy of national jurisdictions prevents the action of the Court as a result of the investigations and prosecutions undertaken by national jurisdictions, the first hypothesis of admissibility is the inaction of the latter with regard to the crimes provided for in the ICC Statute allegedly committed in the situation or case at hand. Here one can distinguish between *a priori* inaction, which takes place when the states concerned have not taken any action whatsoever with regard to the relevant crimes, and *a posteriori* inaction, which occurs when national proceedings are *de facto* or *de jure* stopped for reasons other than those technical reasons provided for in the laws of criminal procedure of the states concerned.[8] However, this first hypothesis of admissibility is not relevant from the perspective of a complementarity analysis focused on national sentencing because in scenarios of *a priori* or *a posteriori* inaction national proceedings will not have reached the stage of sentencing.

Even when the states concerned are taking, or have taken, action regarding the crimes allegedly committed in the situation or case at hand, the ICC could act if the states concerned are 'unwilling or unable genuinely' to carry on their national proceedings. Thus, the unwillingness or inability of the states concerned constitutes the second hypotheses of admissibility.

Article 17(3) of the ICC Statute defines the 'inability' scenario as the inability of the states concerned to obtain the accused or to gather the necessary evidence or to carry out their own national proceedings as a result of 'total or substantial collapse or unavailability of their national judicial system'.[9] As several authors have put it, this notion of 'inability' covers only very exceptional scenarios, such as those where there is no central government[10] or where exceptional circumstances such as civil wars or natural disasters lead to the total or substantial collapse of the administration of justice.[11] As a result, one can affirm that the 'inability' scenario is not relevant for a complementarity analysis focused on national sentencing because in such a scenario national proceedings cannot reach the sentencing stage.

[7] Escobar Hernandez, 'La Progresiva' (above n 2) at 261; Holmes, 'The Principle' (above n 1) at 73–74.

[8] For instance, as a result of the passing of a sweeping amnesty law or the coming into power of a new government which opposes any investigation or prosecution at the national level. A brief discussion of the notion of *a posteriori* inaction can be found in X Aguirre, A Cassese and RE Fife et al, 'Informal Experts Paper: The Principle of Complementarity in Practice' (2003): www.icc-cpi.int/icc-docs/doc/doc654724.PDF, 20, n 26.

[9] Art 15(2) of the draft statute of the preparatory committee referred to 'total or partial collapse'. However, a number of delegations insisted during the Rome Conference that the expression 'partial collapse' was too low of a threshold. As a result, the adjective 'partial' was replaced by the adjective 'substantial'. See Holmes, 'The Principle' (above n 1) at 54–55.

[10] For instance, the case of Somalia in the 1990s.

[11] Williams, 'Article 17' (above n 1) at 394; Holmes, 'The Principle' (above n 1) at 54–55.

Thus, one is left with unwillingness as the only possible scenario where national sentencing may be a relevant factor for the purpose of a complementarity analysis. In this regard, the joint interpretation of articles 17(1)(c) *in fine* and 20(3) of the ICC Statute, makes clear that final judgments delivered by national courts are important components of the notion of unwillingness from a double perspective: (i) the delivery of a final judgment does not cure the unwillingness of the acting states, as evidenced by the way in which their national proceedings were conducted; and (ii) the acting states will also be considered unwilling if, despite the propriety of their national proceedings, any of the two alternative criteria included in article 20(3) of the ICC Statute,[12] which mirror those contained in article 17(2)(a) and (c) of the ICC Statute, is met in connection with the national judgment at hand.

From this last perspective, it can be stated that national sentencing is a relevant factor for a complementarity analysis. In fact, according to articles 17(1)(c) and (2) and 20(3) of the ICC Statute, final judgments delivered by national courts will not have the effect of *res judicata* vis-à-vis the ICC, and thus the *ne bis in idem* principle will not apply, if – regarding the norms of due process recognised by international law – one of the following criteria is met:

1. The sentence imposed responds to the 'purpose of shielding the person concerned from criminal responsibility for crimes within the jurisdiction of the Court';[13] or
2. The sentence was not imposed in an independent or impartial manner, nor was it consistent with the intention to bring the person concerned to justice.[14]

However, at the same time that it can be stated that national sentencing is a relevant factor for a complementarity analysis, one cannot obviate the fact that its role in such analysis is not a primary one insofar as it seems to be limited, for the most part, to those scenarios in which the sentence imposed on the convicted

[12] It is important to highlight that there is a translation error in the Spanish version of art 20(3)(b) ICC Statute because it uses the conjunction 'o' ('or') as opposed to 'y' ('and'). However, the two requirements contained in art 20(3)(b) ICC Statute are cumulative and not alternative. See I Tallgreen, 'Article 20. Ne Bis in Idem' in O Triffterer (ed), *Commentary on the Rome Statute of the International Criminal Court: Observers' Notes, Article by Article* (Baden Baden, Nomos, 1999) 419, 432.

[13] This subjective criteria, solely based on the specific intent of the acting state, aims at guaranteeing the ICC's action when the acting state intends to protect the alleged perpetrators of 'the most serious crimes of international concern to the international community as a whole'. The same view is held by L Arbour and M Bergsmo, 'Conspicuous Absence of Jurisdictional Overreach' in H Von Hebel, JG Lammers and J Schukking (eds), *Reflections on the International Criminal Court. Essays in Honour of Adriaan Bos* (The Hague, TMC Asser Press, 1999) 131; Broomhall, 'The International Criminal Court' (above n 6) at 145; Williams, 'Article 17' (above n 1) at 393; Holmes, 'The Principle' (above n 1) at 50.

[14] Due to the lack of guidance in arts 17(2)(c) and 20(3)(b) ICC Statute, some authors have stated that the reference to lack of independence or impartiality, insofar as it was first proposed as a hypothesis of inability, has a very limited scope. For these authors, it would only cover the scenario in which the acting state does not have the specific intention of shielding the persons concerned from criminal responsibility, but certain individuals manipulate the national proceedings for the purpose of violating the fundamental rights of the persons concerned and, by doing so, cause their acquittal or their release without charge. See Holmes, 'The Principle' (above n 1) at 50; Williams, 'Article 17' (above n 1) at 394.

person is manifestly insufficient in light of the gravity of the crimes and the form of participation of the accused in their commission.[15]

III National Sentencing as the Object of a Complementarity Analysis

As seen in the previous section, a complementarity analysis of national sentencing has quite limited scope. In this regard, it is important to distinguish between a complementarity analysis of national sentencing and a complementarity analysis of other potentially relevant factors which, despite having an impact on the final sentence, fall outside the scope of the former analysis. Among these other factors, the following can be mentioned:

(a) The fact that the overall investigative steps are manifestly insufficient in light of the investigative steps that are shown to have been available to the acting state.
(b) The fact that the charges and modes of liability provided for in the indictment against the person concerned are manifestly inadequate in light of the evidence gathered by the acting state during its investigation, including:

    i. Charging offences that are punished with far lower penalties under the applicable national law.
    ii. Charging ordinary crimes, as opposed to the so-called 'international crimes', when the latter are provided for in the applicable national law.[16]
    iii. Charging negligent, as opposed to intentional, modes of liability.
    iv. Charging modes of liability, such as aiding and abetting, that only give rise to accessory liability as opposed to modes of principal liability such as perpetration by means or co-perpetration.
    v. Charging attempt as opposed to the actual commission of the crime.

(c) The fact that the evidence put forward at trial against the person concerned is manifestly insufficient in light of the evidence gathered against him or her by the acting state during the investigation.
(d) The fact that the evidence put forward at trial is assessed in a manifestly inadequate manner, and as a result:

    i. A judgment of acquittal is rendered either because the underlying facts of the charges are not proven or a manifestly implausible defence is upheld.

[15] Broomhall, 'The International Criminal Court' (above n 6) at 153. See also United Nations General Assembly (UNGA), 'Report of the Preparatory Committee on the Establishment of an International Criminal Court' (1996) UN Doc A/51/22, suppl no 22, vol I, para 173.

[16] The analysis of the limitations to the role played by this factor in a complementarity analysis as a result of the principle *ne bis in idem* falls outside the scope of the present study.

ii. A conviction for a lesser offence or for an ordinary crime is entered.
iii. A conviction for a negligent mode of liability is entered.
iv. A conviction for an accessory mode of liability is entered.
v. A conviction for the attempted commission of the crimes is entered.

Hence, it can be affirmed that the object of a complementarity analysis of national sentencing, whether such analysis is carried out at the situation stage or at the case stage,[17] must be always confined to the examination of the national process of determining the appropriate penalty (*individualización de la pena*). This process starts with the a priori determination by the national legislature of the applicable penalty range for any given crime and concludes once the stage of enforcement of sentence is over. It is comprised of three main stages:

1. Legislative determination of penalties

   At this initial stage the national legislature establishes in the applicable national criminal law both the kind of penalty and the penalty range[18] (particularly in cases of imprisonment and fines) that can be imposed for any given crime. Besides, the national legislature may also establish mandatory guidelines to be applied by the judicial organs in order to decide which specific amount of penalty should be imposed within the mandatory range. It must be highlighted that national laws greatly differ on the breadth of the applicable penalty ranges and the content of mandatory guidelines for the judicial determination of the penalties.

2. Judicial determination of penalties

   At this stage, the national competent judicial organ determines the appropriate penalty within the mandatory range provided for in the applicable national criminal law. One can distinguish between a qualitative judicial determination of penalties in a scenario in which the competent judicial organ may choose among several kinds of penalties, and a quantitative determination of the time of imprisonment to be served or the amount of money to be paid within the statutory penalty ranges.

3. Executive determination of penalties

   During the stage of enforcement of sentence, the penalty may be de facto amended as a result of the application by the national custodial authorities of some provisions that allow for, inter alia, the reduction of the time to be served, the granting of daylight release, or even the granting of parole. As seen below in further detail, the relevance of the executive determination of penalties for the purpose of a complementarity analysis depends on the applicability of the principle of complementarity during the stage of enforcement of sentences.

[17] See below, section VII.

[18] The determination of the applicable penalty ranges is made through the establishment of mandatory minimum and maximum levels of penalty for each offence.

IV The Complementarity Analysis of the Legislative Determination of Penalties

A A Priori Determination of the Penalties Applicable to a Given Crime

Penal norms may be seen as determinative norms, evaluative norms or a combination thereof. The first approach is taken by those who consider that penal norms are mandates or prohibitions that aim at influencing citizens to carry out, or not to carry out, certain conduct.[19] According to this approach, the function of penal norms is to protect the highest values of the society through the prevention of those acts that most seriously undermine them.[20] In order to achieve this goal, three different sets of functions are assigned to punishment:

1. The function of general deterrence, which is understood as the likelihood of influencing other potential criminals to not commit the same crime as a result of punishing a given offender.
2. The function of special deterrence, which is understood as the likelihood that the convicted persons will be deterred from future offences after their release.
3. The function of rehabilitation, which is understood as the likelihood that the convicted persons, as a result of their treatment during incarceration, will be cured of their impulses to commit any kind of criminal activity.[21] As a result, according to a determinative conception of penal norms, retribution plays – at the very best – a secondary role.

An evaluative conception of penal norms considers that such norms are purely negative evaluations of conduct, which are grave enough to justify the imposition of a penalty. However, according to this conception, penal norms do not contain any mandate or prohibition aimed at influencing citizens to undertake, or refrain from undertaking, some acts. According to an evaluative conception of penal norms, the main function of these norms is retribution insofar as the penalty is understood as an expression of the negative evaluation of a given conduct.[22] In other words, 'what makes punishment just, regardless of the social good that might follow, is that it is a fitting social response to the commission of the crime'.[23]

The conception of the penal norms and the functions of punishment embraced by any given national system of criminal justice have a direct impact on the definition of the available penalties and, to a lesser extent, on the determination of the statutory penalty range provided for any given conduct. For instance, the death

[19] DM Luzón Peña, *Curso de Derecho Penal. Parte General* (Madrid, Editorial Universitas SA, 1999) 64.
[20] ibid at 68.
[21] GP Fletcher, *Rethinking Criminal Law* (New York, Oxford University Press, 2000) 414.
[22] Luzón Peña, *Curso* (above n 19) at 68.
[23] Fletcher, *Rethinking Criminal Law* (above n 21) at 415.

penalty is incompatible with the making of the rehabilitation of convicted persons one of the functions of punishment. Likewise, the more emphasis a national criminal justice system puts on the retribution aim of punishment, the higher the mandatory penalty range provided for a given crime tends to be.

The determination of the penalties provided for crimes against humanity, war crimes and genocide in a given national criminal justice system is not alien to this phenomenon and, therefore, is inextricably linked to the core principles of that system. Among these principles, one can highlight the principle of *minimal intervention of the penal law*. According to this principle, penal norms are an instrument of last resort that should always be used in a limited manner and should always be subject to the rule of law, for the protection of the highest values of a society against those conduct that most severely undermine them.[24] The most important manifestations of this principle are the following: (i) the principle of retroactivity *pro reo* of the penal norms; and (ii) the principles of humanity and proportionality in the determination of penalties.

The idea behind this approach to criminal law is that, insofar as the restoration of the legal order is guaranteed, the lesser penalty should be preferred over the graver. In this context, the principle of humanity requires the acknowledgement that the convicted person, no matter which crime he has committed, is a human being and thus has the right to be treated humanely and, given the social dimension of all human beings, to be reintegrated into the community with the same rights as any other member.[25] Likewise, the principle of proportionality requires that, for the purpose of determining which penalty is proportional to the gravity of the crime, such gravity must be exclusively assessed in light of the importance of the values of the community that have been undermined and the manner in which such values have been attacked by the criminal conduct.[26] Those national criminal justice systems that are founded on this so-called minimalist approach to criminal law are particularly zealous in safeguarding the idea of proportionality and in avoiding any increase in the hardship of penalties as a result of an increase in criminality.

A complementarity analysis of the national legislative determination of the penalties provided for crimes against humanity, war crimes and genocide will have to be carried out against the backdrop of the conception of the penal norms, the principles of criminal law that develop such conception and the functions of punishment embraced by the relevant national system of criminal justice. But, at the same time, such analysis will have to be carried out on the basis of a second set of considerations that result from the careful selection of the crimes included in the ICC Statute, which has left out a number of 'treaty-crimes' such as mercenarism, drug-trafficking and terrorism.[27] In this regard, it must be highlighted

[24] F Muñoz Conde and M Garcia Aran, *Derecho Penal. Parte General* (Valencia, Tirant lo Blanch, 1998) 78.

[25] ibid at 92.

[26] ibid at 93.

[27] A Zimmermann, 'Article 5. Crimes within the Jurisdiction of the Court' in O Triffterer (ed), *Commentary on the Rome Statute of the International Criminal Court: Observers' Notes, Article by Article* (Baden Baden, Nomos, 1999) 98–100.

that the ICC Statute only contains those gravest attacks against the highest values of the international community[28] that, according to many, are criminalised by norms of *ius cogens*.[29] Moreover, a similar a priori selection process on the basis of gravity took place with regard to any specific crime included within the general categories of genocide, crimes against humanity and war crimes.[30] As a result, there is some conduct, such as the unjustifiable delay in the repatriation of prisoners of war and civilians,[31] which despite giving rise to individual criminal responsibility according to the international law of armed conflict, has been left out from the ICC Statute.[32]

Besides, any given crime contained in the ICC Statute has been defined in a manner so as to include contextual elements relating to the necessary level of gravity.[33] For instance, the crime of genocide requires that the criminal conduct takes place 'in the context of a manifest pattern of similar conduct directed against that group' or be of such magnitude that it can cause in and of itself the destruction in whole or in part of the targeted group.[34] Likewise, any crime against humanity requires that the criminal conduct be committed 'as part of a widespread or systematic attack directed against any civilian population'.[35] Finally, concerning war crimes, article 8(1) of the ICC Statute provides that 'the Court shall have jurisdiction in respect of war crimes in particular when committed as part of a plan or policy or as part of a large-scale commission of such crimes'.[36] As

[28] Preamble to the ICC Statute, paras 3 and 4; arts 1 and 5(1) ICC Statute.

[29] MC Bassiouni, 'International Crimes: Ius Cogens and Obligatio Erga Omnes' (1996) 59 *Law and Contemporary Problems* 63; M Morris, 'High Crimes and Misconceptions: The ICC and Non-Party States' (2000) 64 *Law and Contemporary Problems* 13, 57; K Henrad, 'The Viability of National Amnesties in View of the Increasing Recognition of Individual Criminal Responsibility at International Law' (1999) 8 *Michigan State University-DCL Journal of International Law* 595, 645.

[30] H Von Hebel and D Robinson, 'Crimes within the Jurisdiction of the Court' in R Lee (ed), *The International Criminal Court: The Making of the Rome Statute – Issues, Negotiations, Results* (The Hague, Kluwer Law International, 1999) 79, 104.

[31] Included as a grave breach in art 85(4)(b) of the Additional Protocol I to the Geneva Conventions.

[32] Only those violations of the international law of armed conflict that met the following three criteria were included in the Rome Statute: (i) that the norm violated had the status of customary international law and, thus, was binding on all States members of the international community; (ii) that the violation gave rise to individual criminal responsibility under customary international law; and (iii) that the violation was serious enough to merit inclusion in the Rome Statute. See Von Hebel and Robinson, 'Crimes within the Jurisdiction of the Court' (above n 30) at 104.

[33] H Olasolo, 'Apuntes Prácticos sobre el Tratamiento de los Crímenes de Guerra en el Estatuto de Roma de la Corte Penal Internacional' (2005) 86 *Revista Española de Derecho Militar* 107, section 2.

[34] See elements of the crime of genocide (art 6(a)–(e) ICC Statute) in the 'Elements of the Crimes'.

[35] Art 7(1) ICC Statute.

[36] As shown below in section VII, the contextual elements relating to the level of gravity must first be applied in the context of situations. Only subsequently will those contextual elements be applied with regard to those specific incidents that will be the basis of an arrest warrant or a summons to appear against one or several identified individuals. The question arises as to whether at this second stage it will be necessary to prove that those war crimes allegedly committed in such specific incidents were part of a plan or policy or large-scale commission of war crimes. Despite the fact that this would constitute the best way of proving the sufficient gravity of such crimes, arts 8(1) and 17(1)(d) ICC Statute do not seem *stricto sensu* to contain such evidentiary requirement. The same conclusion is reached by F Pignatelly y Meca, *La Sanción de los Crímenes de Guerra en el Derecho Español* (Madrid, Ministerio de Defensa, 2002) 74–75.

a result, it can be stated that isolated criminal activity, that is criminal activity that does not take place in a systematic ('pattern of similar conduct', 'plan' or 'policy') or widespread ('large-scale') manner, have been excluded from the ICC Statute.[37]

However, this does not mean that the wrongdoing derived from the commission of the different crimes contained in the ICC Statute is the same. This would not hold true even if one were to accept that any of these crimes severely undermines the existence of the international community.[38] Indeed, not much analysis is necessary to realise that the gravity of the crime of looting property of enemy civilians, even if carried out as part of a policy to compensate one's own combatants, falls far short of the gravity of the imposition of measures intended to prevent births within a given ethnic group with a view to drastically reducing its membership in a generation. As a result, it would come at no surprise if the penalties imposed on the perpetrators of these crimes differ substantially.

In this scenario, it is of the utmost importance to be aware of the fact that by using the power to declare the inadmissibility of a situation or a case on the basis of the inappropriateness of the penalties provided for crimes against humanity, war crimes and genocide in the relevant national criminal law, the ICC may indirectly cause the state concerned to revise the conception of the penal norms, the principles of criminal law and the functions of punishment embraced by its national criminal justice system. This holds equally true in connection with those systems based on an evaluative conception of the penal norms and a retribution function of punishment (such as those providing for the death penalty) as with regard to those others that are founded on the principle of *minimal intervention of the penal law*. Moreover, the risk is even higher for customary systems of criminal law that are based on tradition and, thus, lack a sophisticated written articulation.

The question that then arises is whether or not the ICC must play a role in indirectly shaping the foundations of national criminal justice systems or whether it must be respectful, to the greatest possible extent, with those general principles inspiring such systems, no matter whether the penalties provided for crimes against humanity, war crimes and genocide are considered to be inhuman and disproportionate from the perspective of the principle of *minimal intervention of the penal law* (that is because they resort to the death penalty) or far too lenient from a purely retribution perspective of punishment in connection with the 'most serious crimes of concern for the international community as a whole'.

The first relevant factor to answer this question can be found in the Preamble to the ICC Statute. Its initial paragraph refers to the delicate mosaic of all peoples' cultures that are pieced together in a shared heritage. Moreover, its third paragraph makes clear that the ICC Statute is confined to those crimes that threaten

[37] H Olasolo, *The Triggering Procedure of the International Criminal Court* (Leiden, Martinus Nijhoff, 2005) 183.

[38] Even in those national criminal justice systems, as the Spanish one, in which genocide, crimes against humanity and war crimes are all included in a specific section on crimes against the international community because they are considered to undermine the highest values of the international community (Pignatelly y Meca, *La Sanción* (above n 36) at 41, there are important differences in the penalty ranges provided for any such crimes. See arts 407–16 of the Spanish Criminal Code.

the peace, security and wellbeing of the world, and thus may shatter the mentioned delicate mosaic of all peoples' cultures. As a result, it can be stated that the ICC Statute is founded on the acknowledgement of the cultural differences among the peoples of the world, including something so linked to the core values of any given society as the principles that are at the root of their national criminal justice systems. On this basis, the ICC Statute is shaped as a tool for the protection of values that are common to all people's cultures from those acts which due to their exceptional gravity may seriously undermine them.

From this perspective, it can be stated that the object and purposes of the ICC Statute, as defined in its Preamble, call for being respectful, to the greatest possible extent, of the general principles inspiring national systems of criminal justice. Only in the exceptional scenario in which such general principles appear manifestly inconsistent with those highest values of the international community that the ICC Statute intends to protect, the ICC may play a role in indirectly shaping the foundations of national criminal justice systems as a result of its admissibility decisions following a complementarity analysis of national sentencing. This could be the case, for instance, if a national criminal justice system considers that, absent any kind of duress or mistake of law, the mere fact of having the intention to implement a state policy through the commission of the crimes automatically diminishes the level of wrongdoing and, thus, justifies the provision of a significantly lower penalty range.

This approach is reaffirmed by the indetermination of the ICC Statute sentencing system. In this regard, it must be highlighted that the ICC Statute sentencing system is confined to the general definition of the three kinds of penalties provided for in the ICC Statute:[39]

i. Imprisonment up to 30 years unless the extreme gravity of the crimes and the individual circumstances of the convicted person justify life imprisonment.
ii. A fine to be determined according to the criteria established in the Rules of Procedure and Evidence (RPE).
iii. A forfeiture of proceeds, property and assets derived directly or indirectly from the relevant crimes.

Moreover, rule 145 RPE establishes open-ended lists of aggravating and mitigating circumstances[40] and of additional factors for the determination of the penalty according to the personal circumstances of the convicted person.[41] However, neither the ICC Statute nor the RPE provide for any particular penalty range for any of the crimes contained in the ICC Statute, nor do they include rules on the legal weight of aggravating and mitigating circumstances. As a result, given the level of discretionary powers conferred on the ICC and the absence of close links between the general principles of criminal law contained in the ICC Statute and

[39] I Lirola Delgado and M Martín Martínez, *La Corte Penal Internacional. Justicia versus Impunidad* (Barcelona, Ariel Derecho, 2001) 236–38.

[40] R 145(2) and (3) RPE.

[41] R 145 (1)(c) RPE.

its sentencing system, it can be stated that the ample deference towards the general principles inspiring national criminal justice systems called for by the Preamble to the ICC Statute is reaffirmed.

Article 80 of the ICC Statute is a corollary to the above approach insofar as it expressly provides that nothing in the ICC Statute sentencing system 'affects the application by States of penalties prescribed by their national law, nor the law of States which do not provide for penalties prescribed in this Part'. This provision makes clear that states may continue applying penalties, such as the death penalty, loss of rights, disqualification or disfranchisement, which are not provided for in the ICC Statute, and that they do not have any obligation whatsoever to introduce in their internal legal orders those penalties, such as life imprisonment, provided for in the ICC Statute.[42] Hence, it can be stated that article 80 of the ICC Statute is the best proof of the adoption by the ICC Statute of an approach that grants ample deference to the principles informing national criminal justice systems as reflected in their respective sentencing schemes.

Therefore, it can be concluded that any complementarity assessment of the penalties provided for in national legislations for crimes against humanity, war crimes and genocide should be based on an intra-systemic analysis so as to compare the penalties provided for these crimes and the penalties provided for crimes of similar gravity. Besides, any comparison with other national or international criminal justice systems should be based on the broadest possible deference to the general principles informing the national system at hand.

B Variation in Penalty Ranges on the Basis of the Subjective Element

Though the categories used to define the subjective element of the crimes present their own specificities in every national criminal justice system, one can observe that a number of national systems contain rules providing for different penalty ranges for the same crime depending on the *mens rea* (intent/*dolus* or negligence)[43] with which the *actus reus* is carried out. The question arises as to whether these rules are relevant for the purpose of a complementarity analysis of national sentencing.

The answer to the above-mentioned question is closely linked to the definition in article 30 of the ICC Statute of the subjective element of the crimes and modes of liability provided for in the ICC Statute. In the author's view, this provision includes *dolus directus* of the first degree, which consists of the intent to cause the forbidden result through one's action or omission. It also includes *dolus directus*

[42] RE Fife, 'Article 80. Non-Prejudice to National Application of Penalties and National Laws' in O Triffterer (ed), *Commentary on the Rome Statute of the International Criminal Court: Observers' Notes, Article by Article* (Baden Baden, Nomos, 1999) 1009, 1014.

[43] Athough common law systems also use an intermediate category which is referred to as recklessness. See Fletcher, *Rethinking Criminal Law* (above n 21) at 443 *et seq*.

of the second degree, which consists of the awareness that the forbidden result will be a necessary consequence of one's action or omission.[44] Besides, it can also be argued that the general subjective element provided for in article 30 of the ICC Statute includes the civil law notion of *dolus eventualis*,[45] which, apart from the specificities of every national legal system, it can be said to be comprised of the awareness of the risk that the forbidden result may take place as a result of one's action or omission, and the acceptance of such result by making peace or reconciling oneself with the idea that it will occur.[46]

It is important to highlight that in those civil law systems that have embraced the notion of *dolus eventualis*, the acceptance of the forbidden result constitutes the lowest possible threshold of the notion of intent. In these systems, anything short of this falls within the category of negligence, including those cases in which one is aware of the possibility – or even likelihood – that the forbidden result will occur as a result of one's action or omission and, despite that, one takes the risk in the belief that one's expertise will suffice to avoid the forbidden result.[47]

In general terms, it can be stated that this last scenario corresponds to the common law category of subjective recklessness. In this regard, it must be highlighted that subjective recklessness presupposes the awareness of the risk that in the ordinary course of events the forbidden result would occur as a result of one's action or omission.[48] The required level of risk varies among national systems from mere possibility[49] to likelihood.[50] Moreover, subjective recklessness also requires the acceptance of the risk, which is normally considered to be inherent to the carrying out of a risky action or omission in the awareness of the existence of such risk.[51] It

[44] A Eser, 'Mental Elements – Mistakes of Fact and Law' in A Cassese, P Gaeta and JRWD Jones (eds), *The Rome Statute of the International Criminal Court: A Commentary* (Oxford, Oxford University Press, 2002) 898–99.

[45] JL Rodriguez-Villasante y Prieto, 'Los Principios Generales del Derecho Penal en el Estatuto de Roma' (2000) 75 *Revista Española de Derecho Militar* 381, 417; DK Piragoff, 'Article 30. Mental Element' in O Triffterer (ed), *Commentary on the Rome Statute of the International Criminal Court: Observers' Notes, Article by Article* (Baden Baden, Nomos, 1999) 527–36, 534.

[46] In defining the notion of *dolus eventualis*, the *Prosecutor v Milomir Stakić* (Judgment) IT-97-24-T (31 July 2003) para 587, stated 'The technical definition of *dolus eventualis* is the following: if the actor engages in life-endangering behaviour, his killing becomes intentional if he "reconciles himself" or "makes peace" with the likelihood of death'.

[47] For instance, the truck driver who, despite being aware of the risk of driving at a very high speed on a local road, believes that nothing will happen as a result of the expertise accumulated by his many years on the road.

[48] As Fletcher, *Rethinking Criminal Law* (above n 21) has pointed out (at 443): 'Recklessness is a form of culpa – equivalent to what German scholars call 'conscious negligence'. 'The problem of distinguishing "intention" and "recklessness" arises because in both cases the actor is aware that his conduct might generate a specific result'.

[49] Regarding the crime of homicide, the 'possibility' standard is sufficient in South Africa. See CR Snyman, *Criminal Law* (Oxford, Butterworths, 1995) 169.

[50] Regarding the crime of homocide, the 'probability' standard is required in Australia (*The Queen v Crabbe* (1985) 156 CLR 464; see also B Fisse, *Howard's Criminal Law* 5th edn (Sydney, Law Book Company, 1990) 59); Bahamas (ss 311 and 11(2) of the Criminal Code of 1987); Kenya (ss 203 and 206 (b) of the Criminal Code of 1985); Malawi (ss 209 and 212(b) of the Criminal Code); Sierra Leone (B Thompson, *The Criminal Law of Sierra Leone* (Lanham, University Press of America, 1999) 61); and Zambia (ss 200 and 204(b) of the Criminal Code).

[51] KW Simons, 'Rethinking Mental States' (1992) 72 *Boston University Law Review* 463, 486.

does not require, however, the acceptance of the forbidden result in the sense of making peace or reconciling oneself with it, and it is here where the main difference with the civil law category of *dolus eventualis* lies.

Some could make the argument that article 30(2) and (3) of the ICC Statute define the notions of 'intent' and 'knowledge' in a way that would include subjective recklessness because both definitions refer to the awareness of the fact that the forbidden result will occur in the ordinary course of events. However, in the author's view, the absence of the acceptance of the forbidden result in the sense of making peace or reconciling oneself with it makes it difficult to conceptualise the production of such forbidden result as truly intentional. Besides, several authors have pointed out,[52] that the cumulative requirements of 'intent' and 'knowledge' provided for in article 30(1) ICC of the Statute militates in favour of the interpretation that excludes the subjective recklessness standard from the system of the ICC Statute. This interpretation is also reinforced by the manifestation of the principle *nullum crime sine lege* provided for in article 22(2) of the ICC Statute, which requires that the definition of the crimes provided for in the ICC Statute be construed strictly and not be extended by analogy.

Ad magiorem, the notion of objective recklessness would also be excluded insofar as it merely refers to the adoption of a socially unacceptable high level of risk, whether or not the person concerned is aware of such risk.[53]

As a result, it can be stated that those national rules which provide for different penalty ranges depending on the *mens rea* with which the *actus reus* is committed, do not have any relevance for the purpose of a complementarity analysis. The reason is that – except for cases of superior responsibility – the ICC Statute only punishes intentional conduct. Hence, for the purpose of a complementarity analysis, the provision of a lesser penalty as a result, for instance, of a conviction for the negligent commission of any of the war crimes provided for in the ICC Statute, should not be analysed from the perspective of the penalty imposed on the convicted person, but from the perspective of his acquittal of the intentional commission of the relevant war crime.

The main exception to the general requirement of 'intent' and 'knowledge' under article 30(1) of the ICC Statute is the 'should have known' standard adopted in article 28(a)(i) of the ICC Statute in connection with the superior responsibility of military commanders. This provision requires that the relevant military commander 'knew or, owing to the circumstances at the time, should have known that the forces were committing or about to commit such crimes'. Thus, it can be stated that criminal liability arises from the commander's failure to act with the diligence required of an average commander in the relevant circumstances in order to gather information about the activities of his subordinates for the purpose of being in a position to comply with his duties to prevent and punish.

[52] See, among others, Piragoff (above n 45) at 535; Eser, 'Mental Elements' (above n 44) at 898–99.

[53] In England and Wales, the judgment of the House of Lords in the *Cadwell* case highlighted the distinction between the *inadvertent, objective or Cadwell recklessness* and the *advertent, subjective or Cunningham recklessness* (*R v Caldwell* [1982] AC 341).

Hence, the 'should have known' standard is not only far lower than the 'intent and knowledge' required under article 30(1) of the ICC Statute, it is also lower than the 'had reason to know' standard provided for in article 7(3) of the statute of the ICTY and article 6(3) of the statute of the ICTR. In this regard, it is important to highlight that the Appeals Chamber of the *Ad hoc* Tribunals has distinguished between both standards by stating that the 'had reason to know standard', as opposed to the 'should have known standard', does not punish the commander's failure to obtain information and, at the very minimum, requires that the military commander had at his disposal information that should have put him on notice of the need for a further investigation of the matter.[54]

In the particular context of the superior responsibility of military commanders,[55] those national rules providing for different penalty ranges depending on the intentional or negligent commission of the crime, or participation therein, are relevant for the purpose of a complementarity analysis. Indeed, the analysis of these rules will be at the core of any complementarity analysis of the penalties imposed by national courts on military commanders for their failure to fulfil their duties to prevent the commission of crimes by their subordinates and to punish the latter.

The departing point will be to determine whether the penalty imposed on the relevant military commander is the result of a conviction for an intentional or a negligent breach of the above-mentioned duties. If the application of a lower penalty range is the result of a conviction for a negligent breach of duties, one should then answer the question as to whether the application of a lower penalty range could be reasonably justified by the lesser level of the wrongdoing of a negligent, as opposed to an intentional action or omission. If the answer is in the affirmative, the following step would consist of analysing whether the provision of a lower penalty range for negligent conduct is a general rule in the relevant national criminal justice system, and thus is a manifestation of the conception of the penal norms, the general principles of criminal law and the functions of punishment at the roots of such system. Or, on the other hand, whether it is a unique phenomenon within that system which happens to be only applicable to the crimes contained in the ICC Statute that are committed by military commanders. It is submitted that only in this last scenario a finding of admissibility can be justified. Otherwise, one risks having the ICC censoring the ultimate principles on which the relevant national system of criminal justice is based.

[54] *Prosecutor v Zejnil Delalic et al* (Judgment) IT-96-21-A (20 February 2001) para 241; *Prosecutor v Bagilishema* (Judgment) ICTR-95-1A-A (3 July 2002) para 42; *Prosecutor v Milorad Krnojelac* (Judgment) IT-97-25-A (17 September 2003) para 151; *Prosecutor v Tihomir Blaskic* (Judgment) IT-95-14-A (29 July 2004) para 62. See also K Ambos, 'Superior Responsibility' in A Cassese, P Gaeta and JRWD Jones (eds), *The Rome Statute of the International Criminal Court: A Commentary* (Oxford, Oxford University Press, 2002) 823, 867.

[55] According to art 28(b)(ii) ICC Statute, non-military superiors are only responsible if they 'either knew, or consciously disregarded information which clearly indicated, that the subordinates were committing or about to commit such crimes'. Thus, one can see how art 28(b)(ii) ICC Statute brings the subjective element of the non-military superiors' responsibility close to the boundaries of the general subjective element provided for in art 30 ICC Statute.

Due to the fact that mistakes of fact are often treated in the Roman-Germanic systems as cases of negligent commission of crimes, a number of the above-mentioned comments are applicable to them. First, it is important to highlight that the analysis of the definition of mistake of fact, as any other defence allowed in the relevant national system of criminal justice falls outside the scope of this study. What concerns this study is the mitigating weight given to mistakes of facts for sentencing purposes.

Broadly speaking,[56] a mistake of fact takes place when the actor is mistaken about any of the elements of the *actus reus* of the crime. For instance, a hunter shoots at and kills a farmer in the belief that he is shooting at a wild boar. In systems such as the German or Spanish, this kind of mistake is considered to exclude the *dolus* or intent to kill the farmer. As a result, if the hunter's mistake was due to the lack of due diligence in ascertaining the nature of the target, the hunter could at best be held liable for the negligent homicide. However, if the hunter's mistake was due to no fault of his own, the hunter will not be criminally liable for the death of the farmer.[57] This treatment of mistake of fact is based on one of the cornerstones of this group of national criminal justice systems according to which every element of the *actus reus* must be carried out with the required subjective element. As a result – as far as this treatment of mistakes of fact is not shaped in a way that only applies with regard to crimes contained in the ICC Statute – the Court should be respectful of it. Hence, as the ICC Statute only punishes intentional conduct, the imposition of a lower penalty as a result of a conviction for the negligent commission of the relevant crime due to the convicted person's mistake of fact should not be analysed, for the purpose of complementarity, from a sentencing perspective. On the contrary, the focus of the analysis should be on the evidentiary basis that brought about the determination of the existence of a mistake of law, which according to the relevant national legislation automatically resulted in an acquittal for the intentional commission of the relevant crime.[58]

[56] As Fletcher, *Rethinking Criminal Law* (above n 21) has pointed out (at 684), the classification of mistakes in the categories of mistakes of fact and mistakes of law 'is insensitive to the wide variety of mistakes that can arise in criminal cases'.

[57] Muñoz Conde and Garcia Aran, *Derecho Penal* (above n 24) at 308.

[58] Slightly different is the problem posed by mistakes of law. These are cases where the perpetrator is not aware that her conduct is contrary to criminal law as a result of a lack of awareness about the existence of the relevant penal norm or a belief that her conduct is justified in the particular circumstances of the case. For common law systems, mistakes of law are for the most part irrelevant. Concerning this approach to mistakes of law some authors have pointed out that '[t]he maxim that mistakes of law do not excuse specifies a category of irrelevant mistakes even though a mistake about the legality of one's conduct bears on whether one can be fairly blamed for violating the law. Mistakes are sometimes genuinely irrelevant to a just determination of liability and sometimes, as in many cases of mistake of law, they are deemed irrelevant for practical or utilitarian reasons. We shall refer to the latter cases, where mistakes are ignored even though they bear on culpability as instances of strict liability'. (Fletcher, *Rethinking Criminal Law* (above n 21) at 691). In the Roman-Germanic system, mistakes of law are often given mitigating weight if they are due to a lack of due diligence. They can also exclude criminal liability if they are due to no fault of the perpetrator of the crime. In any case, apart from some minority doctrinal approaches, mistakes of law are not considered as cases of negligent behaviour, but are given a mitigating weight (Muñoz Conde and Garcia Aran, *Derecho Penal* (above n 24) at 428–32); one can apply to them the comments below on the complementarity analysis of aggravating and mitigating circumstances.

C Variation in Penalty Ranges on the Basis of the Modes of Liability

Some national systems of criminal justice contain rules providing for a higher penalty range for the perpetrators of crimes (also known as principals to the crimes) who are considered to be directly liable for the violation of penal norms, and a lower penalty range for the accessories to the crimes (such as instigators or aidors and abettors) seen as derivatively liable for the offences committed by others.

Challenging the *rationale* behind these rules, some authors have posed the following question: 'Why should it matter whether one is a perpetrator or an accomplice and, even more discriminatingly, whether one is a perpetrator, instigator, accessory or perpetrator by means?'[59] Indeed, a number of national criminal justice systems – such as the French and the Anglo-American ones – have embraced the principle that accessories and perpetrators should be punished alike. These systems are based on the premise that 'aiding another person to commit a crime renders one an accomplice, and being an accomplice is simply one way of "being guilty of an offence" '.[60]

However, many other national systems of the Roman-Germanic tradition, such as the German[61] and Spanish,[62] are based on the principle that principals and accessories to the crime should be punished differently. These national criminal justice systems base this distinction of the level of punishment on the premise that 'punishment should be inflicted in proportion both to wrongdoing and culpability'.[63] These two rationales can be defined as: (i) each participant in the crime should be punished according to his individual culpability; and (ii) although the wrongdoing of the perpetrator sets the maximum level of permissible punishment, the wrongdoing of the accessory is less than that of the perpetrator and therefore should be subject to a lesser level of punishment. As a result, in this group of national systems, those rules adjusting the applicable penalty ranges to the way in which the convicted persons participated in the commission of the crimes have a direct impact on the final determination of the penalty and, as such, are relevant to a complementarity analysis of national sentencing. One has, however, to distinguish between this set of rules and those other national rules that define the applicable theories of perpetration by means and co-perpetration in order to distinguish principals and accessories to those crimes in which a plurality of persons participated in the preparation and execution of their *actus reus*. This second set of rules, despite its relevance in the context of the crimes provi-

[59] Fletcher, *Rethinking Criminal Law* (above n 21) at 649.
[60] ibid at 650.
[61] See s 27(2) of the German Criminal Code.
[62] See art 63 of the Spanish Criminal Code.
[63] Fletcher, *Rethinking Criminal Law* (above n 21) at 651.

ded for in the ICC Statute,[64] falls outside a complementarity analysis of national sentencing.

Irrespective of the conceptual merits of the distinction between principals and accessories to the crime for sentencing purposes, and regardless of whether the ICC's case law will also embrace it, a complementarity analysis of national sentencing should primarily consist of an intra-systemic analysis aimed at determining whether the mentioned distinction is consistently applied throughout the relevant national criminal justice system; or whether, on the contrary, it is a special phenomenon that is only applicable to those crimes provided for in the ICC Statute. Moreover, the Court should also be careful to avoid treating as a sentencing problem any charging or evidentiary issue that – as a result of the normal application of national sentencing rules – may result in a low penalty which manifestly does not reflect the gravity of the convicted person's involvement in the commission of the crimes.

Likewise, in cases of seemingly low sentences for superiors who fail to punish those subordinates who committed crimes contained in the ICC Statute, the Court should pay due attention to whether this is the result of having conceptualised the superior's failure to punish as a crime of pure omission that excludes any superiors' criminal responsibility for those crimes committed by their subordinates. This conceptual approach to the superior's failure to punish, which can be

[64] One can get an idea of the importance of these rules and the different theories embraced by them by taking a look at art 25(3) of the ICC Statute. This provision seems to contain a sort of scale of gravity concerning the modes of liability. It starts by defining forms of perpetration, co-perpetration and perpetration by means (art 25(3)(a) of the ICC Statute). Then, it describes different modes of accomplice liability (particularly in art 25(3)(c) of the ICC Statute). And finally, it deals with less important forms of contribution to the execution of a common criminal plan (art 25(3)(d) of the ICC Statute contains a mode of liability according to which those less important contributions that would normally not give rise to individual criminal liability are considered criminal on account of their being carried out with: (i) the purpose of implementing a common criminal plan; or (ii) the knowledge to assist in the implementation of a common criminal plan). As a result, one can state that art 25(3)(d) of the ICC Statute constitutes a sort of residual provision of accomplice liability which is only applicable when the contribution to the commission of the crime does not objectively reach a substantial level. By contrast, the case law of the ICTY has made clear that any participant in the implementation of a common criminal plan is a co-perpetrator (principal to the crime) no matter what the objective level of his contribution is (common purpose or joint criminal enterprise doctrine). See H Olasolo and A Pérez Cepeda, 'The Notion of Control of the Crime and its Application by the ICTY in the *Stakić* Case' (2004) 4 *International Criminal Law Review* 475, 476–78. See also *Prosecutor v Dusko Tadic* (Judgment) IT-94-1-A (15 July 1999) paras 227–28; *Prosecutor v Anto Furundzija* (Judgment) IT-95-17/1-A (21 July 2000) para 118; *Prosecutor v Zejnil Delalic et al* (Judgment) IT-96-21-A (20 February 2001) paras 365–66; *Prosecutor v Milorad Krnojelac* (Judgment) IT-97-25-A (17 September 2003) para 29; *Prosecutor v Miroslav Kvocka et al* (Judgment) IT-98-30/1-A (28 February 2005) paras 81–86, 91, 97; *Prosecutor v Zoran Kupreskic et al* (Judgment) IT-95-16-T (14 January 2000) para 772; *Prosecutor v Dario Kordic and Mario Cerkez* (Judgment) IT-95-14/2-T (26 February 2001) para 397; *Prosecutor v Radislav Krstic* (Judgment) IT-98-33-T (2 August 2001) para 601; *Prosecutor v Miroslav Kvocka et al* (Judgment) IT-98-30/1-T (2 November 2001) para 265; *Prosecutor v Milorad Krnojelac* (Judgment) IT-97-25-T (15 March 2002) para 81; *Prosecutor v Mitar Vasiljevic* (Judgment) IT-98-32-T (29 November 2002) para 65; *Prosecutor v Milomir Stakić* (Judgment) IT-97-24-T (31 July 2003) para 431; *Prosecutor v Blagoje Simic, Miroslav Tadić and Simo Zaric* (Judgment) IT-95-9-T (17 October 2003) para 149. See also *Prosecutor v Milan Milutinovic et al* (Decision on Dragoljub Ojdanić's Motion Challenging Jurisdiction – Joint Criminal Enterprise) IT-99-37-AR72 (21 May 2002) para 20 *et seq.*

found for instance in section 14 of the German Code of Crimes against International Law,[65] causes the legislative determination of lower penalty ranges, and is just the opposite of the approach adopted by the *Ad hoc* Tribunals, where superiors are punished for their alleged responsibility for the crimes committed by their subordinates.[66]

In this regard, one has to keep in mind that there can be no causal link between the superior's failure to punish and the actual commission of the crimes.[67] An *a posteriori* punishment can in no way prevent subordinates from executing the *actus reus* of the crimes. As a result, one cannot see in the superior's failure to punish a case of commission by omission of the subordinates' crimes. Hence, the only possible way to hold superiors liable for crimes committed by their subordinates is by understanding the superior's failure to punish as a *tertium genus* under international law, which is distinct from the traditional notions of criminal law of commission by omission and pure omission. This *tertium genus* would allow holding superiors criminally liable for subordinates' crimes that are not linked in any way to the superiors' own conduct.[68] Otherwise, superiors' failure to punish will have to be considered as a crime of pure omission, and thus superiors will only be criminally liable for the breach of their duties to punish and not for the principal crimes committed by their subordinates. This last approach will be the one preferred by the principle of culpability that requires the careful determination of the specific wrongdoing of any given individual and the necessary adjustment of punishment in light of it.

Regardless of the approach finally adopted by the ICC's case law, it is important to highlight that the Court should be sensitive to the core principles on which

[65] According to s 14(1) of the German Code of Crimes against International Law: 'A military commander or a civilian superior who omits immediately to draw the attention of the agency responsible for the investigation or prosecution of any offence pursuant to this Act, to such an offence committed by a subordinate, shall be punished with imprisonment for not more than five years'. Even the breach of the superiors' duty to prevent the commission of crimes by their subordinates is considered by s 13(a) and (b) of the German Code of Crimes against International Law as a crime of pure omission. As a result, according to s 13(d): 'Intentional violation of the duty of supervision shall be punished with imprisonment for not more than five years, and negligent violation of the duty of supervision shall be punished with imprisonment for not more than three years'.

[66] This approach is closely related to the fact that the *Ad hoc* Tribunals do not require any causal link between the superiors' breach of duties and the commission of crimes by their subordinates in order for the former to be criminally liable for the crimes committed by the latter. See *Prosecutor v Tihomir Blaskic* (Judgment) IT-95-14-A (29 July 2004) para 77.

[67] This causal link would hypothetically consist of the likelihood that the execution of the *actus reus* would have been avoided had the commander adopted the measures within his power to punish those subordinates that committed the crimes.

[68] As the Appeals Chamber has recently put it in the *Blaskic* case with regard to the superiors' failure to prevent: 'The Appeals Chamber is therefore not persuaded by the Appellant's submission that the existence of causality between a commander's failure to prevent subordinates' crimes and the occurrence of these crimes, is an element of command responsibility that requires proof by the Prosecution in all circumstances of a case. Once again, it is more a question of fact to be established on a case by case basis, than a question of law in general'. (*Prosecutor v Tihomir Blaskic* (Judgment) IT-95-14-A (29 July 2004) para 77). Following the *rationale* of the Appeals Chamber, this argument is *ad magiorem* applicable in cases of superiors' failure to punish insofar as the superiors' omission always takes place after the commission of the crimes by the subordinates.

national criminal justice systems are based, particularly if they play such a key role as the principle of culpability plays in the Roman-Germanic tradition. Therefore, it is only if the relevant national system solely resorts to the category of crimes of pure omission in the context of superiors' failure to punish subordinates for the commission of crimes contained in the ICC Statute, that a finding of admissibility might be justified.

D Variation in Penalty Ranges on the Basis of the Lack of Completion of the Actus Reus

In some national systems of criminal justice, the punishment of attempt is justified on the basis of subjective theories that do not see any reason to provide for lower penalty ranges in cases of attempt than in cases of completion of the crime. According to these subjective theories the *rationale* behind punishment is the fact that the perpetrator has shown through her conduct a criminal purpose. As a result, the wrongdoing is the same whether the *actus reus* of the relevant crime is completed, and thus the penalty must be also the same.[69] This approach has been adopted not only in those national systems that have embraced an evaluative conception of the penal norms, but in some national systems that have opted for a determinative conception. The reason is that if penal norms are mandates or prohibitions addressed to the citizens' conscience, their violation – and consequently the wrongdoing – is the same no matter whether the *actus reus* of the crime is completed or not.[70]

However, a number of national criminal justice systems provide for lower penalty ranges if the *actus reus* of the crime is not completed.[71] For most of these systems, although the wrongdoing of the convicted person's action or omission may be the same, it is evident that the damage caused is far lower when the forbidden result is not achieved. Thus, the overall wrongdoing derived from the criminal action or omission is less in cases of attempt, and thus the punishment must also be less grave. Other national systems justify the provision of lower penalty ranges in cases of attempt from a purely objective perspective. For these systems, the punishment of attempt is justified by the fact that it puts objectively at risk those highest values of the community protected by the infringed penal norms. However, the risk occasioned by an attempt will always be lower than that occasioned by the effective undermining of such values as a result of the completion of the *actus reus* of the crime.[72]

Regardless of the approach finally adopted by the ICC's case law, it is important to highlight once again the need for the Court to be deferential, to the greatest

[69] M Quintero Olivares, *Manual de Derecho Penal. Parte General* (Cizur Menor (Navarra), Aranzadi, 2002) 591.
[70] ibid at 592.
[71] See, for instance, s 30(1) of the German Criminal Code and art 62 of the Spanish Criminal Code.
[72] Quintero Olivares, *Manual de Derecho Penal* (above n 69) at 592.

extent possible, to the principles that are at the root of national criminal justice systems no matter whether they might result in the imposition at the national level of lower sentences in cases of attempt. Therefore, a complementarity analysis of sentencing should take the form of an intra-systemic analysis aimed at the determination of whether the penalty ranges provided for the attempted commission of any of the crimes included in the ICC Statute follow the general approach adopted by the relevant national system concerning the punishment of attempt.

E Concursus Delictorum

The problem of the legislative determination of penalties is particularly complex in scenarios in which one action has caused more than one crime or when one person has committed several crimes.[73] For numerous national legal systems, if the person who undermines one of the values of the community protected by criminal law is punished with a penalty, the person who undermines more than one of such values should be punished with two or more penalties. Moreover, as in the case of imprisonment, two or more penalties cannot be served simultaneously; the convicted person should first serve the gravest one and subsequently the others. On the other hand, for some national legal systems, it is neither reasonable nor useful to maintain an individual in prison forever. As a result, they acknowledge the need to provide for certain limitations in the accumulation of penalties.

Concursus delictorum is in the final analysis just a way of solving a problem of legislative determination of penalties. Traditionally, it has distinguished between the scenario in which one action causes a plurality of crimes, and the other scenario in which the same person carries out a plurality of actions that causes a plurality of crimes. An additional variant of *concursus delictorum* can be found in the notion of continuous crimes, which is a legal fiction originally created to benefit those convicted persons as a result of treating all their offences as one crime as opposed to several different crimes whose penalties would have been added. The notion of continuous crimes is based on three basic requirements: (i) the existence of a previous plan or the fact that the convicted person took advantage of similar circumstances to commit the different crimes; (ii) a plurality of actions or omissions; and (iii) the infringement of the same penal norm or different penal norms which protect similar values.[74]

The rules on *concursus delictorum* – apart from dealing with a problem of legislative determination of penalties – are closely related to the general principles of criminal law which are at the root of national criminal justice systems. Indeed, the need to provide for certain limitations in the accumulation of penalties is closely related to the rehabilitation function of punishment, which sees the unending

[73] Muñoz Conde and Garcia Aran, *Derecho Penal* (above n 24) at 511–12; Quintero Olivares, *Manual de Derecho Penal* (above n 69) at 747–48.

[74] Muñoz Conde and Garcia Aran, *Derecho Penal* (above n 24) at 519–20.

maintenance of individuals in prison as unreasonable and useless. As a result, any complementarity analysis focused on the rules on *concursus delictorum* should be deferential, to the greatest extent possible, to the general principles which inform such rules, and should take the form of an intra-systemic analysis of the definition and application of such rules.

V The Complementarity Analysis of the Judicial Determination of Penalties

At the stage of judicial determination of penalties, the competent judicial organ determines the appropriate penalty within the mandatory range provided for in the applicable national law. It is at this stage that its discretionary powers come into play. No matter what the level of discretion entrusted with the competent judicial organ by the relevant national legislation is, the judicial determination of the penalty is a necessary stage which has important political implications. Indeed, though the case law tends to be somewhat irrational, one cannot obviate the fact that, to an important extent, it is influenced by the conception of the penal norms and the functions of punishment embraced by the relevant national system. Indeed, any decision advancing the retribution, prevention or rehabilitation functions of punishment has clear ideological implications.

Resorting to judicial discretion in the determination of the penalty is inevitable and constitutes a common feature of the different national criminal justice systems. However, apart from the level of discretion conferred on the competent judicial organs, what varies greatly among national systems is the set of principles that guides the exercise of judicial discretion and which is closely related to the core policy choices that lie at the root of any given national system. For instance, in a good number of national criminal justice systems, judicial discretion is subject to the principle of proportionality, which operates not only in the legislative determination of the penalty ranges, but in the judicial determination of the penalty within the mandatory range.[75]

On the other hand, a number of national criminal justice systems have embraced the prohibition against the aggravation of punishment for reasons related to general or special prevention. As a result, the personal conditions of the convicted person, his criminal record or any other personal characteristic that may reveal a certain degree of danger above average, may preclude the mitigation of the penalty or the resort to an alternative penalty, but cannot serve as a basis for an increase in the penalty assigned.[76]

Among the set of principles which guides the exercise of judicial discretion, one can highlight a feature common of many national systems, which consists of the

[75] Quintero Olivares, *Manual de Derecho Penal* (above n 69) at 715.
[76] ibid at 714–15.

predetermination of aggravating and mitigating circumstances. These circumstances consist – to an important extent – of situations that surround the carrying out of the *actus reus* of the crime, or that shows a particular condition concerning the convicted person. Though not necessarily clear prima facie, the essence of the aggravating and mitigating circumstances is closely linked to the general principles which inform a given national criminal justice system insofar as they refer to circumstances that, without altering the existence of the crimes, increase their gravity or the culpability of the convicted persons. As a result, in a number of national systems, their definition and legal weight is closely related to the principle of proportionality, which is not only applicable at the stage of legislative determination of the mandatory penalty ranges, but is also applicable at the stage of judicial determination of the penalty within those ranges. Moreover, the definition and legal weight of the aggravating circumstances are also directly linked to the different approaches adopted by national criminal justice systems, as to whether or not punishment may be aggravated for reasons of general and special prevention.

As a result of the establishment of guiding principles for the exercise of judicial discretion, the role to be played by the judges' personal motivations in the determination of the penalty is, to an important extent, limited. However, by no means is such a role left aside. On the contrary, in any national system the judges' personal motivations play a role – no matter whether such a role is broader or narrower. Besides, every national system has its own mechanisms to minimise the risks derived from the role granted to the judges' personal motivations in the judicial determination of the penalty. These mechanisms may range from carefully drafted procedures for the review of the penalties imposed on the convicted persons, to the strict limitation of judicial discretion through the establishment of narrower mandatory penalty ranges and more precise binding criteria for the exercise of judicial discretion.

A complementarity analysis of the judicial determination of the penalty should be particularly deferential, with those binding criteria for the exercise of judicial discretion that are closely connected to the core policy choices of the relevant national criminal justice system. However, a different approach can be undertaken with regard to the exercise by the judges of the role given to their personal motivations in the judicial determination of penalties. It is in this ambit where a complementarity analysis of national sentencing acquires a more prominent role, and where the level of deference to national judgments can, to a certain extent, be diminished. As a result, it can be stated that those judgments in which – after an inter-systemic analysis – the judges' personal motivations appear to have played an unusually prominent role, are undoubtedly the main candidates to be the objects of admissibility rulings. Indeed, it is the *rationale* behind these judgments that can be best analysed against the backdrop of the two criteria provided for in articles 17(1)(c) and (2) and 20(3) of the ICC Statute: (i) that the sentence imposed responds to the 'purpose of shielding the person concerned from criminal responsibility for crimes within the jurisdiction of the Court'; or (ii) that the sentence was not imposed in an independent or impartial manner, nor was it consistent with the intention to bring the person concerned to justice.

VI The Irrelevance of the Executive Determination of Penalties for the Purpose of a Complementarity Analysis

As stated above, during the stage of enforcement of sentence, the penalties provided for in national judgments may be *de facto* amended by the national custodial authorities (executive determination of penalties). This takes place through the application of a series of legal provisions that allow in certain instances for the reduction of the time to be served, the granting of daylight release, or even the granting of parole. Needless to say, the most stringent of these measures is the concession of administrative pardons.

The question arises as to the relevance of the executive determination of penalties for the purpose of a complementarity analysis. The answer to this question depends on whether the application of the complementarity principle extends as well to the stage of enforcement of sentence.

From a temporal perspective, the drafters of the ICC Statute had to choose between a static and a dynamic configuration of the principle of complementarity. According to the static configuration, the principle of complementarity would operate only until the moment at which either national jurisdictions or the ICC initiated proceedings regarding a given situation. In contrast – according to the dynamic configuration – the temporal scope of application of the principle of complementarity could be extended, while the national jurisdictions or the ICC exercised their respective functions of investigation, prosecution, declaration of individual criminal responsibility and enforcement of sentences.

The solution finally adopted by the drafters in articles 15(3) and (4), 17, 18, 19, 20(3) and 53(1)(b) and (2)(b) of the ICC Statute, consists of a dynamic configuration of the principle of complementarity.[77] According to it, the principle of complementarity is applicable when national jurisdictions and the ICC exercise their respective functions of investigation, prosecution and declaration of the individual criminal responsibility derived from the commission of the crimes provided for in the ICC Statute. At the same time, the dynamic configuration of the principle of complementarity excludes from its temporal scope of application: the stage of enforcement of sentences.[78] Therefore, once a final judgment has been pronounced by the ICC in any given case, the latter assumes exclusive jurisdiction

[77] H Olasolo, 'The Triggering Procedure of the International Criminal Court, Procedural Treatment of the Principle of Complementarity, and the Role of the Office of the Prosecutor' (2005) 5 *International Criminal Law Review* 121, 138.

[78] The same view is held by Broomhall, 'The International Criminal Court' (above n 6) at 144; Holmes, 'The Principle' (above n 1) at 59.

in relation to its execution.[79] Likewise, if a final judgment is delivered by a national court, the latter acquires exclusive jurisdiction over its execution, as long as the ICC does not declare that any of the criteria provided for in article 20(3) of the ICC Statute has been met by the national judgment.[80]

Hence, as the principle of complementarity does not extend to the stage of enforcement of sentences,[81] the executive determination of penalties during the stage of enforcement of sentences is irrelevant for the purpose of any complementarity analysis.

VII The Complementarity Analysis of National Sentencing against the Backdrop of Situations and Cases

The object of the complementarity analysis of national sentencing depends on the object of the ICC proceedings in connection with which such analysis is undertaken. When such analysis takes place during the triggering procedure pursuant

[79] In addition, under art 20(2) of the ICC Statute, the states concerned will be precluded from trying the accused for the same crimes for which that person has already been convicted or acquitted by the Court.

[80] H Olasolo, 'Reflexiones sobre el Principio de Complementariedad en el Estatuto de Roma' (2003) 82 *Revista Española de Derecho Militar* 47, 62. Concerning the problems occasioned by the non-extension of the temporal scope of application of the principle of complementarity to the stage of enforcement of sentences, see Holmes, 'The Principle' (above n 1) at 76–77.

[81] There are several reasons as to why the temporal scope of the principle of complementarity was not extended to the enforcement stage in order to foreclose any impunity gap that could be caused by the granting of administrative pardons. Among them, two must be highlighted. First, such extension would inevitably have led to problems of *ne bis in idem*. Indeed, unless such an extension had implied the automatic acknowledgement of final judgments delivered by national courts for the purpose of their enforcement by the ICC, the Court would have had to conduct new prosecutions of the very same crimes which were the object of national judgments that do not meet any of the criteria provided for in art 20(3) of the ICC Statute before being able to enforce its own final judgments. As a result, the same crimes would have been prosecuted twice, which would have violated the *ne bis in idem* principle as provided for in art 20(3) of the ICC Statute and could have given rise to two different final judgments. In this sense, it is important to underline that the *ne bis in idem* principle contained in art 14(7) International Covenant of Civil and Political Rights (ICCPR) has traditionally been interpreted as being limited to criminal proceedings conducted in a particular jurisdiction. However, one cannot forget that the level of protection offered by the *ne bis in idem* principle in art 10 of the statute of the ICTY, art 9 of the statute of the ICTR and art 20 of the ICC Statute is greater than that which is traditionally offered by art 14(7) ICCPR. See JRWD Jones, *The Practice of the International Criminal Tribunals for the Former Yugoslavia and Rwanda* (Irvington-on-Hudson, Transnational Publishers, 2000) 151–54, 504–05. Secondly, the extension of the temporal scope of the principle of complementarity to the stage of enforcement of sentences would have caused the provisional suspension of the enforcement of the ICC's final judgments as a result of the initiation of national investigations and prosecutions of those very same crimes which were the objects of the ICC's final judgments. In this regard, one cannot forget that the principle of complementarity acts in a twofold manner insofar as it affects not only the proceedings of national courts, but those of the ICC. See Olasolo, *Triggering Procedure* (above n 37) at 162–63.

to articles 15(3) and (4), 18(2), 53(1) or 82(1)(a) of the ICC Statute,[82] or during the investigation of a situation under articles 19(11) and 53(2)(b) ICC Statute,[83] its object will be situations defined by personal, temporal and territorial parameters.[84] However, when such analysis, pursuant to article 19(1), (2) and (3) of the ICC Statute, takes place in the context of the criminal procedure initiated through the issue of an arrest warrant or a summons to appear, its object will be cases consisting of a set of specific incidents in which crimes contained in the ICC Statute were allegedly committed by one or more identified individuals.[85]

On the other hand, although articles 17 and 20(3) of the ICC Statute provide for the same set of criteria, the application of those criteria and the level of scrutiny of national judgments cannot be the same when the complementarity analysis of national sentencing is carried out against the backdrop of situations than when it is carried out against the backdrop of cases. Indeed, although the standard of review does not necessarily have to vary,[86] the level of scrutiny of national judgments will be lower when situations, as opposed to cases, are the object of the complementarity analysis of national sentencing. This phenomenon is recognised under the heading of article 18 of the ICC Statute that refers to the PTC's and AC's 'preliminary' rulings on admissibility.[87]

In this regard, it is important to highlight that, for the purpose of a complementarity analysis of national sentencing with regard to a situation, one will have to look at the national judgments of the acting states in relation to those types of crimes that – committed in a widespread or systematic manner – are at the core of the criminal activities which occurred in the situation at hand. Moreover, if the broad political discretion granted to the Office of the Prosecutor, the Pre-Trial Chamber and the Appeals Chamber is used to limit de facto investigations and prosecutions to those who are the ultimately responsible persons or bear the greatest responsibility, such as the leaders of states, groups or organisations allegedly

[82] MC Bassiouni, *Introduction to International Criminal Law* (Ardsley, Transnational Publishers, 2003) 518–19; WA Schabas, *An Introduction to the International Criminal Court* (Cambridge, Cambridge University Press, 2004) 125–26; CK Hall, 'Article 19. Challenges to the Jurisdiction of the Court or the Admissibility of a Case' in O Triffterer (ed), *Commentary on the Rome Statute of the International Criminal Court: Observers' Notes, Article by Article* (Baden Baden, Nomos, 1999) 405, 407; MM El Zeidy, 'The Ugandan Government Triggers the First Test of the Complementarity Principle: An Assessment of the First State's Party Referral to the ICC' (2005) 5 *International Criminal Law Review* 83, 110.

[83] As Hall, 'Article 19' (above n 82) has pointed out (at 418): 'Paragraph 11 appears to address a voluntary deferral by the Prosecutor of an investigation based on article 18 paragraph 2 or a suspension of an investigation pursuant to paragraph 7 after an admissibility challenge'.

[84] Olasolo, 'Reflexiones' (above n 80) at 125–26.

[85] H Olasolo, *Corte Penal Internacional:¿Dónde Investigar? Especial Referencia a la Fiscalía en el Proceso de Activación* (Valencia, Tirant lo Blanch/Cruz Roja Española, 2003) 112–13.

[86] Aguirre et al, 'Informal Experts Paper' (above n 8) at 16. No provision in the Rome Statute, including art 19 of the ICC Statute, specifies the applicable standard of review for the admissibility of situations and cases. Thus, the Pre-Trial Chamber (PTC) and the Appeals Chamber (AC) will have to give some guidance as to whether they embrace a balance of probabilities standard, an 'intimate conviction' standard or any other conceivable standard.

[87] The different scope of the admissibility analysis of situations and cases and the different level of scrutiny of national proceedings prevent the PTC's and AC's decisions on the admissibility of situations from having the effect of *res judicata* regarding the admissibility of cases. For a broader discussion of this matter, see Olasolo, *Triggering Procedure* (above n 37) at 44–45.

responsible for the systematic or widespread criminality that has taken place in the situation at hand,[88] the complementarity analysis of national sentencing will focus only on those national judgments issued against that limited group of persons which may fall within that category.[89] On the other hand, for the purpose of a complementarity analysis of national sentencing with regard to a case, one will have to look at the national judgment(s) issued against the person concerned for those incidents in which the crimes charged against her in the proceedings before the Court were allegedly committed.

VIII Conclusion

As a result of the material limitations of the ICC, the architects of the crimes provided for in the ICC Statute, such as those political and military leaders who are ultimately responsible for the bloodshed, may end up being tried by the ICC where the death penalty is not an option; whereas lower level perpetrators will be tried by national courts and subject to the death penalty. A situation of this kind has already arisen in the context of the criminal proceedings held by Rwandan national courts[90]

[88] ICC Office of the Prosecutor, 'Paper on some policy issues before the Office of the Prosecutor' (September 2003): www.icc-cpi.int/NR/rdonlyres/1FA7C4C6-DE5F-42B7-8B25-60AA962ED8B6/143594/030905 _Policy_Paper.pdf.

[89] It is only then that due regard should be given to the length of the sentences contained in such national judgments in light of the gravity of crimes, the modes of liability and the rest of circumstances analysed throughout this study.

[90] The Rwandese Organic Law No 08/96 of 30 August 1996 on the Organization of the Prosecution of Offences Constituting the Crime of Genocide or Crimes Against Humanity, *Official Gazette of the Republic of Rwanda* (1 September 1996) [hereinafter The Genocide Law], established four categories of offenders subject to prosecution: (i) Organisers or leaders of genocide, notorious killers, and persons who committed acts of sexual torture (category I); (ii) murderers or accomplices to murder or serious attacks (category III); (iii) persons who committed serious attacks without the intent to cause death (category III); and (iv) those responsible for property damage (category IV). Art 14(1) of The Genocide Law reads as follows: 'The penalties imposed for the offences set out in Article I shall be those provided under the Penal Code, except: (a) that persons whose acts place them in Category 1 are liable to the death penalty; (b) that for persons whose acts place them in Category 2, the death penalty is replaced by life imprisonment; (c) where a confession and guilty plea have been accepted, in which case articles 15 and 16 of this organic law apply; (d) that the acts committed by persons placed in Category 4 shall only give rise to civil damages determined by amicable agreement between the parties with the assistance of the community, failing which the rules pertaining to criminal proceedings and civil actions shall apply. If the accused is sentenced to a term of imprisonment, the sentence is suspended'. The Rwandese Organic Law No 40/2000 of 26/01/2001 Setting Up 'Gacaca Jurisdictions' and Organizing Prosecutions for Offences Constituting the Crime of Genocide or Crimes Against Humanity Committed between October 1, 1990 and December 31, 1994 [2001 Gacaca Law], *Official Gazette of the Republic of Rwanda*, 15 March 2001 (hereinafter the 2001 Gacaca Law), amended the 1996 genocide law. Art 51 of the 2001 Gacaca Law expanded category I, the most serious category of crimes, to include the crime of rape. Besides, the 2001 Gacaca Law made persons accused of genocide or related crimes in categories II, III and IV eligible for reduction of their sentences through plea-bargaining in accordance with the provisions of the Gacaca Law. This was not, however, the case for persons accused of genocide or related crimes, including rape, in category I. More recently, the Rwandese Organic Law No 16/2004 of 19/6/2004 Establishing the Organisation, Competence and Functioning of Gacaca Courts Charged with Prosecuting and Trying the Perpetrators of the Crime of Genocide and Other Crimes Against

and the ICTR[91] concerning crimes under the subject matter jurisdiction of the latter.

However, one can also envisage the opposite scenario in which those tried by national courts are exposed to lower penalties than those tried by the ICC. This will particularly be the case if the relevant national criminal justice system is founded in a determinative conception of the penal norms and has embraced general and special prevention and rehabilitation as the main functions of punishment. In this regard, one can foresee that this scenario is likely to happen regarding cases of superior responsibility that are considered by the relevant national criminal justice system as crimes of pure omission and are punished with a maximum penalty of three to five years of imprisonment depending on the negligent or intentional nature of the superiors' breach of duties.[92]

Considering the relevance of national sentencing for the purpose of a complementarity analysis, and in light of the Court's power to indirectly cause the state concerned to revise the foundations of its criminal justice system as a result of admissibility decisions based on the inappropriateness of the penalties imposed at the national level, the Court could be tempted to play a role in shaping the foundations of national criminal justice systems for a variety of reasons, such as the inhuman and disproportionate character of national penalties or the leniency of such penalties.

However, a variety of reasons which have been analysed throughout this chapter call for a cautious approach that – save for those exceptional scenarios in which such general principles appear manifestly inconsistent with those highest values of the international community that the ICC Statute intend to protect – is respectful, to the greatest possible extent, of the general principles inspiring national criminal justice systems. As a result, a complementarity analysis of national sentencing should primarily have an intra-systemic nature and be particularly focused in the judges' exercise of the role given to their personal motivations in the judicial determination of penalties.

Humanity, Committed Between 1 October 1990 and 31 December 1994, *Official Gazette of the Republic of Rwanda*, 19 June 2004 (hereinafter 'the 2004 Gacaca Law'), reshaped partially the system by, inter alia, merging categories I, II and III into only two categories (as a result, category IV become category III). Besides, according to arts 55 and 72 of the 2004 Gacaca Law, for the first time, persons accused of genocide or related crimes in category I who confess are eligible for reduction of their sentences.

[91] According to art 23(1) of the statute of the ICTR, '[t]he penalty imposed by the Trial Chamber shall be limited to imprisonment'. Besides, art 23(3) adds that '[i]n addition to imprisonment, the Trial Chambers may order the return of any property and proceeds acquired by criminal conduct, including by means of duress, to their rightful owners'.

[92] See, for instance, ss 13(d) and 14(1) of the German Code of Crimes against International Law.

6

The Application of Indirect Perpetration through Organised Structures of Power at the International Level*

I Introduction

On 4 March 2009, Pre-Trial Chamber I of the International Criminal Court (ICC Pre-Trial Chamber I) issued a landmark decision justifying, for the first time ever, the issuance of a warrant of arrest against a sitting head of state (Sudanese President Omar Al Bashir). At the core of this decision was the application of the notion of indirect perpetration through organised structures of power,[1] insofar as, according to ICC Pre-Trial Chamber I,[2] Al Bashir, either by himself, or acting in a coordinated manner with other high-ranking Sudanese political and military leaders, directed the different branches of the Sudanese 'state-apparatus' to carry out crimes against humanity and war crimes during a five-year counter-insurgency campaign (2003–08).[3]

According to ICC Pre-Trial Chamber I, the notion of indirect perpetration through organised structures of power is based on the consideration that an organised structure of power has a life of its own, irrespective of the identity of its replaceable members.[4] Therefore, the superior who controls it: (i) can, in general, be certain that his wishes will be carried out by his subordinates, and does not need to bother with who will carry them out; (ii) does not need to resort to coercion or deception of the physical perpetrators because he knows that should a member of his organisation refuse to carry out his instructions, someone else would replace him and carry them out; and (iii) keeps control over the crime

* Drafted in September 2010. The views expressed herein are those of the author alone and do not necessarily reflect the views of the ICC, the ICTY, the United Nations in general or the Spanish Government.

[1] *Prosecutor v Omar Hassan Ahmad Al Bashir* (Decision on the Prosecution's Application for a Warrant of Arrest against Omar Hassan Ahmad Al Bashir) ICC-02/05-01/09-3 (4 March 2009) para 223.

[2] ibid at paras 214, 215.

[3] ibid.

[4] *Prosecutor v Germain Katanga and Mathieu Ngudjolo Chui* (Decision on the Confirmation of the Charges) ICC-01/04-01/07-717 (30 September 2008) paras 515, 516. See also H Olasolo, *The Criminal Responsibility of Senior Political and Military Leaders as Principals to International Crimes* (Oxford, Hart Publishing, 2009) 116–25, 318–27.

because its commission cannot be stopped by the opposition or resistance of his subordinates.[5] As a result, as highlighted by ICC Pre-Trial Chamber I, from the perspective of those senior political leaders and high military commanders who control organised structures of power, they appear as the main perpetrators because they do not leave the decision on whether to commit the crimes up to those subordinates who physically execute them. Such subordinates are not perceived as free responsible individuals, but they are actually perceived as anonymous and replaceable members of the organisations.[6]

For ICC Pre-Trial Chamber I, the hierarchical structure of an organisation and the replaceable character of the physical perpetrators are the key factors which sustain the superior's control of the will of their subordinates, in the sense that the superior's dominant will has ultimate control of the crime. Therefore, the justification of the notion of indirect perpetration through organised structures of power is not the specific psychological activities of the superior who issued the order, but rather the way in which the relevant organised structures of power are organised which ensure automatic compliance with the superior's orders. This has been underscored by ICC Pre-Trial Chamber I in the following way:

> In addition, particular characteristics of the organized and hierarchical apparatus enable the leader to actually secure the commission of crimes. In essence, the leader's control over the apparatus allows him to utilise his subordinates as 'a mere gear in a giant machine' in order to produce the criminal result 'automatically' [. . .] Above all, this 'mechanisation' seeks to ensure that the successful execution of the plan will not be compromised by any particular subordinate's failure to comply with an order. Any one subordinate who does not comply may simply be replaced by another who will; the actual executor of the order is merely a fungible individual. As such, the organization also must be large enough to provide a sufficient supply of subordinates. The main attribute of this kind of organization is a mechanism that enables its highest authorities to ensure automatic compliance with their orders. Thus, '[s]uch Organization develops namely a life that is independent of the changing composition of its members. It functions, without depending on the individual identity of the executant, as if it were automatic.' An authority who issues an order within such an organization therefore assumes a different kind of responsibility than ordinary cases of criminal ordering. In the latter cases, article 25(3)(b) of the Statute provides that a leader or commander who orders the commission of a crime may be regarded as an accessory.[7]

The *Bashir* case before the ICC follows a number of cases at the national and international levels which have applied the notion of indirect perpetration through organised structures of power after the *Argentinian Juntas* trial, including, inter alia, the *German Border* case in Germany, several Argentinian cases relating to crimes committed during the 1976–83 military regime, the case against general Manuel Contreras in Chile, the case against former national senator Alvaro Alfonso García Romero in Colombia, the cases against former Shining

[5] ibid.
[6] ibid.
[7] ibid.

Path leader Abimael Guzmán and former president Alberto Fujimori in Peru,[8] as well as the cases against Milomir Stakić, Radoslav Brđanin, Momcilo Krajišnik, Milan Martić and Fatmir Limaj et al at the International Criminal Tribunal for the former Yugoslavia (ICTY), the case against Protais Zigiranyirazo at the International Criminal Tribunal for Rwanda (ICTR) and the cases against Jean-Pierre Bemba, Germain Katanga and Mathieu Ngudjolo Chui, Omar Al Bashir and Abu Garda at the International Criminal Court (ICC).

Given the growing application of the notion of indirect perpetration through organised structures of power, this chapter analyses how the ICTY, the ICTR and the ICC at the international level have resorted to this notion to justify the convictions of senior political leaders and high military commanders as principals to the crimes committed by subordinate members of their organisations.[9]

II Initial Reluctance and Subsequent Development of the Notion of Indirect Perpetration through Organised Structures of Power

In 1963, Claus Roxin developed in his book entitled *Täterschaft und Tatherrschaft* the notion of indirect perpetration through organised structures of power.[10] The same year he wrote an article,[11] partially contained in his previous work, in which

[8] See K Ambos, 'The *Fujimori* Judgment: A President's Responsibility for Crimes Against Humanity as Indirect Perpetrator by Virtue of an Organised Power Apparatus' (2011) 9 *Journal of International Criminal Justice* 137; F Muñoz Conde and H Olasolo, 'The Application of the Notion of Indirect Perpetration through Organised Structures of Power in Latin America and Spain' (2011) 9 *Journal of International Criminal Justice* 113.

[9] For a comprehensive analysis of the origins and application of this notion in international criminal law see Olasolo, *Criminal Responsibility* (above n 4) at chs 3, 5.

[10] C Roxin, *Täterschaft und Tatherrschaft* 1st edn (Berlin, De Gruyter, 1963) 242 *et seq*. The first edition of this book is the one taken as a reference in the present chapter. The seventh edition of this work has already been published in 2004. In all seven editions, Roxin maintains his original explanation concerning the notion of indirect perpetration through organised structures of power. He has added, nevertheless, several appendices providing information on the impact that such notion has had on criminal law theory, as well as on the case law of Germany and other countries.

[11] C Roxin, 'Straftaten im Rahmen organisatorischer Machtapparate' (1963) *Goldtdammers'Archiv für Strafrecht* 193–207 (an English version of this article is contained in the same volume). Subsequently, Roxin has published several articles in which he updates and partially adjusts the contours of the notion of indirect perpetration through organised structures of power supported in his first article. See, for instance, C Roxin, 'Probleme von Täterschaft und Teilnahme bei der organisierten Kriminalität' in E Samson, F Dencker, P Frisch, H Frister and W Reiss (eds), *Festschrift für Grünwald* (Baden Baden, Nomos, 1999) 549 *et seq*. The Spanish translation of this article can be found in J Ferré Olivé and E Anarte Borrallo (eds), *Problemas de autoría y participación en la criminalidad organizada* (Huelva, Universidad de Huelva, 1999) 91 *et seq*. There is an additional article by C Roxin, 'El dominio de la organización como forma independiente de autoría mediata' (2006) 7 *Revista de Estudios de la Justicia* 11. Some of the translations into Spanish of Roxin's work have also been published in legal journals in Latin American. For a summary of Roxin's approach to the notion of indirect perpetration through organised structures of power, and the main critics made to this notion, see Strafrecht, Allgemeiner Teil, vol. II, 2003, at 17 *et seq*.

he applied the said notion to the *Eichmann* case. This case concerned Adolf Eichmann, a member of the Nazi SS, who was unlawfully kidnapped by the Israeli Secret Service in Buenos Aires and subsequently accused before a district court in Jerusalem of being one of the main responsible persons of the Holocaust. The starting point of Roxin's new approach to the notion of indirect perpetration was the difficulty that the traditional approach presented for the consideration of senior political leaders and high military commanders who were at the top of organised structures of power as principals to the crimes committed by the subordinate members of their organisations. According to Roxin:

> One must acknowledge that war crimes, State crimes and organizational crimes, as the ones hereby analyzed, cannot be properly understood with the criteria used to analyze ordinary crimes [. . .] Hence, the notions of principal liability, instigation and complicity, which have been shaped in light of ordinary crime, cannot be adjusted to analyze a collective phenomena as the one in which the above-mentioned crimes takes place [. . .] Nevertheless, this does not release us from our duty to individually analyze the conduct of each person participating in the commission of the crime.[12]

In order to resolve these difficulties, Roxin developed a notion, according to which, when the organisations through which the crimes are committed have certain distinctive features that ensures automatic compliance with the superior's orders, those superiors behind the scene are those persons who dominate the commission of the crimes, in the sense that they decide whether the crimes will be committed and how they will be carried out.[13] As a result, they can be considered as indirect perpetrators, even in cases in which the physical perpetrators are fully liable for the crimes. As Roxin explained, the justification for this notion is not the specific psychological activities of the superiors who issue the orders, but rather the way in which the relevant organised structures of power are organised.[14]

The notion of indirect perpetration through organised structures of power strongly put into question those attempts to portray the criminal liability of senior Nazi political and military leaders, as well as mid-level superiors of the Nazi organisation, as mere accessories to the crimes committed in execution of the Final Solution. Nevertheless, such notion was met initially with reluctance at the national and international level because of three main reasons. The first is the absence of any specific reference to such a notion in national or international legislation. Secondly, the belief that the scope of application of the notion of indirect perpetration was limited to situations in which superiors use innocent agents who are not fully criminally liable to have the crimes committed.[15] Thirdly,

[12] Roxin, *Täterschaft* (above n 10) at 243. Authors' translation.

[13] For a more detailed analysis and critique of such a notion, see A Pérez Cepeda, *La responsabilidad de los administradores de sociedades: criterios de atribución* (Barcelona, Cedecs Editorial, 1997) 369.

[14] Roxin, *Täterschaft* (above n 10) at 244.

[15] This is, for example, the case when the direct perpetrators are mistaken about the factual circumstances on which an element of the *actus reus* of the crime is based, or about a cause of justification as a result of having been mislead by their superiors (eg, a military commander directs his subordinates to shell an undefended village by misleading them about the location of the enemy's artillery in that

the application of the notion of indirect perpetration did not necessarily have an impact on the penalty to be imposed on superiors, even in national jurisdictions belonging to the Romano-Germanic tradition, such the Spanish or the Latin American ones, where the principle of mitigation for accessorial liability constitutes an important reason for the distinction between principals and accessories to the crime.[16]

Only over time have national and international courts increasingly found that their traditional approach did not adequately reflect the nature of the superiors' contribution to the crimes (planning and controlling the means through which the criminal activity is carried out) because it relegates them to a secondary role which does not correspond to their actual relevance. As a result, they have progressively resorted to the notion of indirect perpetration through organised structures of powers to better encapsulate the criminal liability of senior political and military superiors. This took place for the first time at the national level in the 9 December 1985 landmark judgment of the Cámara Federal Nacional de Apelaciones en lo Criminal y Correccional de la Capital Buenos Aires (the 'Buenos Aires Federal Court of Appeals'), which convicted the military commanders of the three consecutive Argentinian Military Juntas that run the authoritarian military regime that governed Argentina from 1976 to 1983.[17] In turn, the 31 July 2003 judgment of ICTY Trial Chamber II in the case against Milomir Stakić (former mayor of the town of Prijedor in Bosnia and Herzegovina), constitutes the first application of the notion of indirect perpetration through organised structures of power at the international level.[18]

Since then, the notion of indirect perpetration through organised structures of power has been applied in a number of cases at the international level. Nevertheless,

area). It is also the case when the direct perpetrators' actions are justified by necessity because the harm that they avoid by carrying out the illegal orders given by their superiors is higher than the harm inflicted as a result of carrying them out (eg, a camp warden directs members of the police providing security to the camp to deport a number of camp prisoners, and the police officers know that should they reject doing so). See the numerous instances of the application of the notion of indirect perpetration in this type of situation referred to by H Olasolo and A Pérez Cepeda, 'The Notion of Control of the Crime and its Application by the ICTY in the *Stakić* Case' (2004) 4 *International Criminal Law Review* 475, 485. However, when the person who physically carried out the *actus reus* of the crime acted subject to *a vis absoluta* (eg, someone is pushed by his superior against the special envoy of the enemy who is standing next to a railway when the train is approaching. As a result, the special envoy of the enemy falls on the railway and it is mortally wounded by the train), it is not necessary to resort to the notion of indirect perpetration because the superior is considered a direct perpetrator who used his subordinate as he could have used any other non-human tool, such a hammer or a pistol.

[16] For instance, in most Latin American Penal Codes (such as in Argentina, Chile, Peru, Colombia or Uruguay) as well as in the Spanish Penal Code, the same penalty is attached to the modes of liability of instigation and necessary contribution (material assistance without which the crime would not have taken place) than to perpetration. See Muñoz Conde and Olasolo, 'The Application' (above n 8).

[17] Judgments Supreme Court, vol 29, I–II at 36–1657. The text of this judgment and the judgment of the Argentine Supreme Court referred to in the next footnote can be found at: www.derechos.org/nizkor/arg/causa13. For a complete report and translation of the judgment, see American Society of International Law (1987) 26 *International Legal Materials* 2. The Introductory Note and English translation were prepared for International Legal Materials by E Dahl, Visiting Professor of Law, Southern Methodist University School of Law, and AM Garro, Lecturer in Law, Columbia University.

[18] See *Prosecutor v Milomir Stakic* (Judgment) ICTY-97-24-T (31 July 2003) paras 808–16.

save for the *Bashir* case before the ICC, in most of these cases the notion of indirect perpetration through organised structures of power has been applied in combination with the notion of co-perpetration based on joint control over the crime.[19] According to this last notion, when a plurality of persons participate in the commission of a crime pursuant to a division of tasks in the execution of a common plan, those persons who share the control over its implementation as a result of the essential tasks assigned to them (without performing them, the plan would be ruined) are to be considered co-perpetrators (principals to the crime).[20] The joint application of the notions of indirect perpetration through organised structures of power and co-perpetration based on joint control over the crime is usually referred to as indirect co-perpetration. Indirect co-perpetration is applicable to two types of scenarios: (i) when several senior superiors who have joint control over one organised structure of power jointly use it to secure the commission of the crimes;[21] and (ii) when several senior superiors, who are each in control of one organised structure of power (or a part thereof), direct their different organisations to implement a common criminal plan in a coordinated manner[22] – the latter is the factual scenario in the *Stakić, Brđanin, Krajišnik* and *Martić* cases before the ICTY, as well as in the *Bemba, Katanga and Ngudjolo* and *Abu Garda* cases before the ICC.[23]

Moreover, as shown by the cases against Milomir Stakić and Radoslav Brđanin before the ICTY, and Germain Katanga and Mathieu Ngudjolo Chui before the ICC, the notion of indirect perpetrators through organised structures of power

[19] For a comprehensive study on the application of the notions of indirect perpetration through organised structures of power, co-perpetration based on joint control and indirect co-perpetration (joint application of the first two) see Olasolo, *Criminal Responsibility* (above n 4) at chs 3 and 5. See also in relation to the *Katanga and Ngudjolo* case, H Olasolo, 'El Desarrollo de la Coautoria Mediata en Derecho Penal Internacional' (2009) 7 *Iter Criminis* 121 and in relation to the *Stakić* case, Olasolo and Pérez Cepeda, 'The Notion' (above n 15).

[20] *Prosecutor v Thomas Lubanga Dyilo* (Decision on the Confirmation of Charges) ICC-01/04-01/06-803-tEN (29 January 2007) paras 342, 347; *Prosecutor v Germain Katanga and Mathieu Ngudjolo Chui* (Decision on the Confirmation of Charges) ICC-01/04-01/07-717 (30 September 2008) paras 515–25. See also Olasolo, *Criminal Responsibility* (above n 4) at 265–67, 273–96, 318–29.

[21] This is the factual situation in the German Border case, where the National Defence Council, which was the organ responsible for defence and security in East Germany, was comprised of several members who acted jointly. As a result, one should have considered them as indirect co-perpetrators because they jointly controlled the decisions of the Council. However, the German Federal Supreme Court did not treat the link among the different defendants and found them guilty of homicide as indirect perpetrators. See *Entscheidungen des Bundesgerichtshofs in Strafsachen* 40, at 218.

[22] One could envisage a third scenario where not all co-perpetrators control one organised structure of power. In this scenario, those co-perpetrators who do not control any organised structure of power would co-ordinate the implementation of the common criminal plan by those other co-perpetrators who use their organised structures of power to have the crimes committed.

[23] In the *Argentinian Military Juntas* case, where each military junta was comprised of the commanders-in-chief of the Argentinian army, navy and air forces, there were three different organised structures of power (the army, the navy and the air forces). However, unlike in the *Stakić* case, the Buenos Aires Federal Court of Appeals considered that such organisations did not act in a coordinated manner in the commission of the crimes. As a result, their respective commanders-in-chief were only convicted as indirect perpetrators for the crimes committed by their own subordinates. See Judgment of the Federal Appeals Court (9 December 1985) at 29, 804. See also the analysis by MA Sancinetti, *Derechos Humanos en la Argentina Postdictatorial* (Buenos Aires, Lerner, 1988).

has been used at the international level to prosecute individuals who were not *stricto sensu* at the top of their organisations. This is consistent with Roxin's view that those at the intermediate echelons of the organised structures of power who can give 'orders' to their subordinates are also principals to the crime due to their control of the will, in case they use their power for the execution of criminal activities.[24] Indeed, when Roxin defined the notion of indirect perpetration through organised structures of power for the first time in 1963, he had in mind the Holocaust and the network of Nazi organisation and the concentration and extermination camps. Although Adolf Hitler and Heinrich Himmler were at the top of the Nazi organisation, the effective functioning of the Nazi organisation required coordinated action of thousands of additional members who, according to a strict chain of command, operated at the different levels of the Nazi organisation. As a result, the notion was never confined to the highest echelons of the Nazi political and military leadership. Quite the contrary, it was defined in light of the case against Adolf Eichmann, who despite not being part of the highest echelons of the Nazi political and military leadership, played from his office (he was never present at the scene of the crimes) a key role for the effective execution of the so-called Final Solution of the Jewish Question.

As Ambos has also pointed out, crimes are committed through an organised structure of power because its members, at different levels, direct the part of the organisation that is under their control at securing the commission of the crimes.[25] From the perspective of the senior political and military leaders, members of the organised structure of power at the intermediate level are replaceable links within the organisation. Nevertheless, from the perspective of such intermediate superiors, they retain ultimate control of the criminal actions of their subordinates because they have full knowledge of the underlying factual circumstances of the objective elements of the crime; they act under no coercion when deciding whether to direct the part of the organised structure of power under their control at securing the commission of the crimes; and they perceive the members of the part of the organisation under their control as anonymous and replaceable, and, thus, do not leave up to the autonomous decision of the physical perpetrators whether the objective elements of the crimes will be performed.[26]

[24] Roxin, *Täterschaft* (above n 10) at 248.

[25] See K Ambos and C Grammer, 'Dominio del Hecho por Organizacion. La Responsabilidad de la Conduccion Militar Argentina por la Muerte de Elisabeth Kasemann' (2003) 12 *Revista Penal* 28, 31. These authors have pointed out that the traditional formula to distinguish between perpetrators (principals) and other participants (accessories) in the crime has been replaced by three levels. The first level – the highest – is comprised of the indirect perpetrators who plan and organise the crimes, that is, those who control and put in motion the organisation. The second level is comprised of the intermediate superiors who control a part of the organisation and direct it towards the implementation of the plan. They can, thus, also be considered indirect perpetrators. The third level – the lowest – is comprised of the physical perpetrators who play only an auxiliary role in the global criminal event.

[26] Roxin, *Täterschaft* (above n 10) at 245.

III The Application of the Notion of Indirect Perpetration through Organised Structures of Power at the ICTY and the ICTR

A The ICTY

i The Stakic *Case*

The notion of indirect perpetration through organised structures of power was for the first time applied by the ICTY in the 31 July 2003 judgment of ICTY Trial Chamber II in the case against Milomir Stakic, former mayor of the town of Prijedor (Bosnia and Herzegovina), which was located a few kilometers away from the infamous Omarska detention camp.[27] The case referred to the campaign of persecution against the non-Serb population of the Bosnian Municipality of Prijedor, which included mass murders, torture, physical violence, rapes and sexual assaults, constant humiliation and degradation, destruction and looting of residential and commercial properties, destruction of religious and cultural buildings, mass deportations and denial of fundamental rights.[28]

According to the ICTY Trial Chamber II, this campaign of persecution was the core crime committed in the Municipality of Prijedor. Such campaign took place, to an important extent, inside camps and detention centres, and during military operations against the civilian population, and could only be carried out through the joint action of all three organised structures of power existing in Prijedor in 1992:[29] (i) the civil administration of Prijedor, which was under the direction of the Prijedor Municipal Assembly/Crisis Staff/War Presidency headed by the defendant Milomir Stakic, who was also the mayor of Prijedor; (ii) the civil police of Prijedor; and (iii) the military units posted in Prijedor (mainly the JNA/VRS Garrison and the Territorial Defence of Prijedor).[30] Furthermore, the political and military leaders at the top of each structure were in control over them and knew that their orders would be implemented by their subordinates, and that they had the power to stop the commission of crimes by their subordinates at any time.[31]

[27] For a comprehensive analysis of this case, see Olasolo and Pérez Cepeda, 'The Notion' (above n 15) at 500–24.

[28] *Prosecutor v Milomir Stakic* (Judgment) ICTY-97-24-T (31 July 2003) paras 808–16.

[29] ibid at para 490.

[30] The Trial Chamber stated that, in general, the associates of Stakić included the authorities of the Self-proclaimed Assembly of the Serbian People in the Prijedor Municipality, the SDS, the Prijedor Crisis Staff, the Territorial Defence, the police and the military. In particular Stakic acted together with: (a) the chief of Police (Simo Drljaca); (b) the military commanders of the military units posted in Prijedor (Colonel Vladimir Arsic and Major Radmilo Zeljaja); (c) the president of the Executive Committee of the Prijedor Municipality (Dr Milan Kovacevic); and (d) the commander both of the Municipal Territorial Defence Staff and the Trnopolje camp (Slobodan Kurozovic).

[31] *Prosecutor v Milomir Stakic* (Judgment) ICTY-97-24-T (31 July 2003) paras 486-101, 469–488.

As a consequence, ICTY Trial Chamber II found that Milomir Stakic and the heads of the civil police and army divided the essential tasks for the implementation of the campaign of persecution among themselves.

In addition to designing the persecutorial campaign against the non-Serb population of Prijedor, the main contribution of Stakic and the heads of the civil police and the army to the implementation of such a campaign was to instruct their respective subordinates to carry out the tasks respectively assigned to the civil administration, the civil police and the army. Although the members of the civil administration did not physically carry out the objective elements of the crime (the civil administration headed by Stakić was mainly in charge of providing logistics and financial assistance to the civil police and the army),[32] the civil police and the army could not have implemented the campaign of persecution by themselves.[33] Furthermore, Stakić coordinated the cooperation among all three organised structures of power.[34] As a result, ICTY Trial Chamber II decided to convict Milomir Stakić as an indirect co-perpetrator.[35]

Although the 22 March 2006 ICTY Appeals Chamber judgment in the *Stakić* case overturned the joint application of the notions of indirect perpetration through organised structures of power and co-perpetration based on joint control over the crime,[36] the subsequent ICTY case law continued relying on the former notion in combination with the notion of co-perpetration based on joint criminal enterprise.[37]

ii The Brdanin, Krajinik and Limaj et al *Cases*

For instance, in the case against Radoslav Brdanin, former President of the Crisis Staff and War Presidency of the Autonomous Region of Krajina (ARK), for war crimes and crimes against humanity committed in the ARK territory between 1991 and 1995, the ICTY Appeals Chamber expressly stated that physical perpetrators need not be part of the joint criminal enterprise, and that they can be used as tools to have the crimes committed by those senior political leaders and high military commanders who are members of the joint criminal enterprise. As the ICTY Appeals Chamber explained:

[32] ibid at paras 482, 486.
[33] ibid at para 490. The only exception was the crime of deportation, the physical execution of which members of the civil administration participated under the orders of Stakić. See ibid at para 712.
[34] ibid at para 482.
[35] ibid at paras 490–97.
[36] *Prosecutor v Milomir Stakic* (Judgment) ICTY-97-24-A (22 March 2006) para 62. See also H Olasolo, 'Reflections on the Treatment of the Notions of Control of the Crime and Joint Criminal Enterprise in the *Stakić* Appeal Judgment' (2007) 7 *International Criminal Law Review* 143.
[37] See Olasolo, *Criminal Responsibility* (above n 4) at chapter 4, sections V.B and V.D. See also *Prosecutor v Radoslav Brđanin* (Judgment) ICTY-99-36-A (3 April 2007) paras 409–14; *Prosecutor v Milan Martić*(Judgment) ICTY-95-11-A (8 October 2008) para 82; *Prosecutor v Fatmir Limaj, Haradin Bala and Isak Musliu* (Judgment) ICTY-03-66-A (27 September 2007) para 120; *Prosecutor v Momcilo Krajisnik* (Judgment) ICTY-00-39-T (27 September 2006) para 883.

> In light of the above discussion of relevant jurisprudence, persuasive as to the ascertainment of the contours of joint criminal enterprise liability in customary international law, the Appeals Chamber is of the view that what matters in a first category [Joint Criminal Enterprise (JCE)] is not whether the person who carried out the *actus reus* of a particular crime is a member of the JCE, but whether the crime in question forms part of the common purpose. In cases where the principal perpetrator of a particular crime is not a member of the JCE, this essential requirement may be inferred from various circumstances [. . .] As the Prosecution recognizes, for it to be possible to hold an accused responsible for the criminal conduct of another person, there must be a link between the accused and the crime as legal basis for the imputation of criminal liability. According to the Prosecution, this link is to be found in the fact that the members of the joint criminal enterprise use the principal perpetrators as 'tools' to carry out the crime. Considering the discussion of post-World War II cases and of the Tribunal's jurisprudence above, the Appeals Chamber finds that, to hold a member of a JCE responsible for crimes committed by non-members of the enterprise, it has to be shown that the crime can be imputed to one member of the joint criminal enterprise, and that this member – when using a principal perpetrator – acted in accordance with the common plan. The existence of this link is a matter to be assessed on a case-by-case basis [. . .] From a reading of the Prosecution Brief, it appears that the fact that the RPPs [Relevant Physical Perpetrators] were used as mere 'tools' by their superiors was, actually, the most likely explanation for what happened in the territory of the ARK during the indictment period.[38]

Likewise, in the case against Momcilo Krajisnik, former Vice-President and President of the Parliament of the self-proclaimed Serbian Republic of Bosnia (*Republika Srpska*), for crimes against humanity and war crimes committed in the territory of the said Republic between 1991 and 1995, ICTY Trial Chamber I held that the members of the joint criminal enterprise in which the defendant also participated included, first and foremost, a Pale based Bosnian-Serb leadership component comprised of, inter alia, Momcilo Krajisnik, Radovan Karadzic, Biljana Plavsic, Nikola Koljevic, Momcilo Mandic, Velibor Ostojic, Mico Stanisic and, as of 12 May 1992, General Ratko Mladic. Moreover, the rank and file of the members of the joint criminal enterprise consisted of local politicians, military and police commanders, paramilitary leaders, and others, who were based in the regions and municipalities of the *Republika Srpska* and maintained close links with Pale.[39] As a result, the Trial Chamber did not include the physical perpetrators among the participants in the joint criminal enterprise because they were 'tools' or 'instruments' used by the political and military leaders who participated in the enterprise to secure the commission of the crimes.[40]

Subsequent ICTY case law such as, inter alia, the ICTY Appeals Judgments in the cases against former Kosovo Liberation Army members Fatmir Limaj, Haradin Bala and Isak Musliu,[41] and former Minister of Interior, former Minister of Defence and former President of the self-proclaimed 'Serbian Autonomous

[38] *Prosecutor v Radoslav Brđanin* (Judgment) ICTY-99-36-A (3 April 2007) paras 410, 412–13, 448.

[39] *Prosecutor v Momcilo Krajisnik* (Judgment) ICTY-00-39-T (27 September 2006) para 1087.

[40] ibid.

[41] *Prosecutor v Fatmir Limaj, Haradin Bala and Isak Musliu* (Judgment) ICTY-03-66-A (27 September 2007) para 120.

Region of Krajina', Milan Martic,[42] have referred with approval to the above-mentioned legal findings of the *Brdanin* Appeals Judgment concerning the joint application of the notions of indirect perpetration through organised structures of power and co-perpetration based on joint criminal enterprise.[43]

B The ICTR: The Case against Protais Zigiranyirazo

The joint application of the notions of indirect perpetration through organised structures of power and co-perpetration based on joint criminal enterprise has also been recently accepted by the ICTR in the case against Protais Zigiranyirazo (uncle-in-law of the late Rwandan President Habyarimana), who was found guilty of having participated in a joint criminal enterprise with the common purpose of committing genocide and extermination of thousands of Tutsi individuals at Kesho Hill.

Although, given the particular circumstances surrounding the case, ICTR Trial Chamber III found that the physical perpetrators were also members of the joint criminal enterprise to which the accused belonged, it explicitly highlighted in its 18 December 2008 judgment that:

> [t]he principal perpetrators carrying out the *actus reus* of the crimes do not have to be members of the JCE. What matters in such cases is whether the crime in question forms part of the common purpose and whether at least one member of the JCE used the principal perpetrator acting in accordance with the common plan.[44]

IV The Application of the Notion of Indirect Perpetration through Organised Structures of Power at the ICC

A The *Bashir* Case

The *Bashir* case constitutes to date the only case before an international jurisdiction in which the notion of indirect perpetration through organised structures of power has been applied by itself, as opposed to as part of the notion of indirect co-perpetration. According to the *Bashir* Case Arrest Warrant Decision, the facts of the case are as follows. Soon after the attack on El Fasher airport in April 2003,

[42] See *Prosecutor v Milan Martić* (Judgment) ICTY-95-11-T (12 June 2007) para 438. This finding has been quoted with approval by *Prosecutor v Milan Martić* (Judgment) ICTY-95-11-A (8 October 2008) paraa 68.

[43] For the problems arising out of the joint application of these two notions, see the conclusions reached by Olasolo, *Criminal Responsibility* (above n 4) at ch 4, section V.E.

[44] *Prosecutor v Protais Zigiranyirazo* (Judgment) ICTR-01-73-T (18 December 2008) para 384.

the Government of Sudan, in response to the activities of the Sudan Liberation Movement/Army (SLM/A), the Justice and Equality Movement (JEM) and other opposition armed groups in Darfur, issued a general call for the mobilisation of the Janjaweed Militia, and thereafter conducted a counter-insurgency campaign, through the so-called forces of the Government of Sudan that included the Sudanese armed forces and their allied Janjaweed Militia, the Sudanese police forces, the National Intelligence and Security Service (NISS) and the Humanitarian Affairs Commission (HAC).[45] The said counter-insurgency campaign continued for well over five years. One of its core components was the unlawful attack on the part of the civilian population of Darfur – belonging largely to the Fur, Masalit and Zaghawa groups – that were perceived by the Government of Sudan as being close to the SLM/A, the JEM and other opposition armed groups.[46] This unlawful attack was large in scale, as it affected hundreds of thousands of individuals and took place across a large part of the territory of the Darfur region, and systematic because the acts of violence of which it was comprised followed, to a considerable extent, a similar pattern.[47] In furtherance of this unlawful attack, the forces of the Government of Sudan carried out numerous unlawful attacks, followed by systematic acts of pillage, on towns and villages; subjected thousands of civilians to acts of murder and extermination; subjected thousands of civilian women to acts of rape; subjected hundreds of thousands of civilians to acts of forcible transfer; and subjected civilians to acts of torture.[48]

For ICC Pre-Trial Chamber I, Omar Al Bashir and other high-ranking Sudanese political and military leaders directed the branches of the 'apparatus' of the State of Sudan that they led, in a coordinated manner, in order to jointly implement the above-mentioned counter-insurgency campaign.[49] This was, to a very important extent, implemented through local Security Committees comprised of the head of the locality and representatives of the Sudanese armed forces, the Sudanese police forces and the NISS at the local level,[50] and State Security Committees comprised of the state governor and representatives of the Sudanese armed forces, the Sudanese police forces and NISS at the state level.[51] While the local Security Committees worked together with Janjaweed Militia at the local level, State Security Committees worked together with Janjaweed Militia leaders at the regional level.[52] The Deputy Federal Minister of the Interior was entrusted with the tasks of supervising the three Darfurian State Security Committees and acting as a link between the governments of the three Darfurian states and the highest level of the Government of Sudan in Khartoum.[53]

[45] *Prosecutor v Omar Hassan Ahmad Al Bashir* (Decision on the Prosecution's Application for a Warrant of Arrest against Omar Hassan Ahmad Al Bashir) ICC-02/05-01/09-3 (4 March 2009) para 74.
[46] ibid at paras 75, 76.
[47] ibid at paras 84, 85.
[48] ibid at para 192.
[49] ibid at para 216.
[50] ibid at paras 217, 218.
[51] ibid at paras 217, 219.
[52] ibid at paras 218, 219.
[53] ibid at para 220.

In this context, according to ICC Pre-Trial Chamber I, there were reasonable grounds to believe that Omar Al Bashir, as de jure and de facto President of Sudan and Commander-in-Chief of the Sudanese Armed Forces at all relevant times, played, at the very least, an essential role in coordinating the design and implementation of the common plan.[54]

Furthermore, ICC Pre-Trial Chamber I also found that, in the alternative, there also existed reasonable grounds to believe that Omar Al Bashir played a role that went beyond coordinating the implementation of the counter-insurgency campaign, was in full control of all branches of the 'apparatus' of the State of Sudan, including the Sudanese armed forces and their allied Janjaweed Militia, the Sudanese police forces, the NISS and the HAC and used such control to secure the implementation of the common plan.[55]

As a result, ICC Pre-Trial Chamber I issued a warrant of arrest against Omar Al Bashir in light of his alleged criminal liability pursuant to article 25(3)(a) of the ICC Statute as an indirect co-perpetrator, or, in the alternative, as an indirect perpetrator for those war crimes and crimes against humanity committed as part of the counter-insurgency campaign of the Government of Sudan by members of the forces of the Government of Sudan, including the Sudanese armed forces and their allied Janjaweed Militia, the Sudanese police forces, the NISS and the HAC.[56]

B The *Bemba* Case

The *Bemba* Case Warrant of Arrest Decision, issued by ICC Pre-Trial Chamber III on 10 June 2008, applied, for the first time before the ICC, the notion of indirect co-perpetration,[57] in which, as seen above, the notion of indirect perpetration through organised structures of power plays a key role. Although, given the limited evidence presented by the Prosecution on the alleged co-perpetrators' mental state, the subsequent *Bemba* Case Confirmation of the Charges Decision, issued on 15 June 2009, had to resort to the notion of superior responsibility pursuant to article 28 of the ICC Statute to confirm the charges brought by the Prosecution against Jean-Pierre Bemba,[58] the value of the *Bemba* Case Warrant of Arrest Decision as the first ICC decision to ever use the notion of indirect co-perpetration remains unaffected.

The *Bemba* Case Warrant of Arrest Decision highlights that the case concerns war crimes and crimes against humanity (wilful killings, torture, rapes, outrages upon personal dignity and pillage) allegedly committed against the civilian popu-

[54] ibid at para 221.

[55] ibid at para 222.

[56] ibid at para 223.

[57] *Prosecutor v Jean-Pierre Bemba Gombo* (Decision on the Prosecutor's Application for a Warrant of Arrest against Jean-Pierre Bemba Gombo) ICC-01/05-01/08-14-TENG (10 June 2008) paras 69–84.

[58] *Prosecutor v Jean-Pierre Bemba Gombo* (Decision Pursuant to Article 61 (7)(a) and (b) of the Rome Statute on the Charges of the Prosecutor against Jean-Pierre Bemba Gombo) ICC-01/05-01/08-424 (15 June 2009) paras 114–78.

lation of the southern part of the Central African Republic (CAR) between 25 October 2002 and 15 March 2003.[59] According to ICC Pre-Trial Chamber III, the crimes were allegedly the result of the implementation of a common plan between Angel-Félix Patassé, former CAR president, and Jean-Pierre Bemba, the de jure and de facto president and commander-in-chief of the Mouvement pour la Libération du Congo (MLC).[60] The common plan consisted of Jean-Pierre Bemba's deployment of an important part of the MLC in the CAR territory to provide military support to Angel-Félix Patassé in the conflict in which the latter was engaged against the armed *forces* loyal to current CAR President François Bozizé,[61] and Angel-Félix Patassé's strategic and logistical support to Jean-Pierre Bemba against the current Democratic Republic of the Congo (DRC) President Joseph Kabila.

As the *Bemba* Case Warrant of Arrest Decision highlighted, according to the common plan, MLC forces, once in CAR territory, would act jointly and in a coordinated manner with CAR forces still loyal to Angel-Félix Patassé (mainly the Presidential Security Unit) in order to stop the offensive of François Bozizé's forces.[62] For ICC Pre-Trial Chamber III, the common plan was not aimed at the commission of the crimes. Moreover, the commission of crimes was not the necessary result of the implementation of the common plan. The commission of the crimes was thus not an integral part of the common plan.[63]

Nevertheless, as the *Bemba* Case Warrant of Arrest Decision pointed out, the commission of the crimes was a likely outcome of the implementation of the common plan, given the numerous acts of violence against the civilian population (murders, thefts, destruction of property and rapes) that the MLC forces that were about to be deployed in CAR territory had carried out in recent military campaigns in several parts of the DRC.[64] Therefore, the common plan had an 'element of criminality' within the meaning of the *Lubanga* Case Confirmation of Charges Decision.[65]

Furthermore, for ICC Pre-Trial Chamber III, Angel-Félix Patassé and Jean-Pierre Bemba did not implement the common plan with the aim of having the crimes committed or even with the awareness that its implementation would necessarily bring about the commission of the crimes. On the contrary, as ICC Pre-Trial Chamber III highlighted, Angel-Félix Patassé and Jean-Pierre Bemba acted with shared *dolus eventualis* because they were merely aware of the fact that the commission of crimes against the civilian population of southern CAR was a

[59] *Prosecutor v Jean-Pierre Bemba Gombo* (Decision on the Prosecutor's Application for a Warrant of Arrest against Jean-Pierre Bemba Gombo) ICC-01/05-01/08-14-TENG (10 Jun 2008) paras 45, 68.

[60] ibid at paras 69–72.

[61] ibid.

[62] ibid at paras 74-6.

[63] ibid at paras 72–74, 82.

[64] ibid at para 80.

[65] *Prosecutor v Thomas Lubanga Dyilo* (Decision on the Confirmation of Charges) ICC-01/04-01/06-803-tEN (29 January 2007) para 377.

likely outcome of the implementation of the common plan, and had mutually accepted this likely outcome.[66]

The *Bemba* Case Warrant of Arrest Decision also pointed out that Angel-Félix Patassé and Jean-Pierre Bemba did not carry out any of the objective elements of the crimes directly.[67] As a result, unlike in the *Lubanga* case, the notion of co-perpetration based on joint control was not applicable, because neither member of the common plan had made a contribution by way of directly committing the crimes. Instead, they had each made their contribution to the common plan by using their subordinates in the armed groups that they controlled de jure and de facto.

Furthermore, according to ICC Pre-Trial Chamber III, the physical perpetrators were allegedly members of the MLC, of which Jean-Pierre Bemba was the de jure and de facto leader. This could, in principle, have made it possible to consider Jean-Pierre Bemba as an indirect perpetrator, who committed the crimes through his subordinates in the organised structure of power that he controlled (the MLC). However, the *Bemba* Case Warrant of Arrest Decision highlighted that the evidence presented by the Prosecution showed reasonable grounds to believe that the crimes were committed as a result of Jean-Pierre Bemba and Angel-Félix Patassé's *coordinated* efforts to implement their common plan.[68] In the final analysis, the commission of the crimes was possible due to the coordinated action of their respective subordinates in order to stop François Bozizé's attempted coup d'état. As a result, although ICC Pre-Trial Chamber III did not state it expressly, Jean-Pierre Bemba was considered an indirect co-perpetrator of the crimes who – with full awareness of the essential nature of his functions in the implementation of the common plan – carried them out via the organised armed group (the MLC) that he controlled de jure and de facto.[69]

C The *Katanga and Ngudjolo* Case

ICC Pre-Trial Chamber I in the *Katanga and Ngudjolo* Case Confirmation of Charges decision developed the approach to the notion of indirect co-perpetration initially taken by ICC Pre-Trial Chamber III in the *Bemba* case. The *Katanga and Ngudjolo* case refers to events that occurred during the armed conflict that took place in the Ituri District (DRC) in the second half of 2002 and in 2003. The suspects were the two ex commanders-in-chief of the Ngiti (the *Front des Nationalistes et Intégrationnistes* (FNI)) and Lendu (the *Forces de Résistance Patriotique d'Itrui*

[66] *Prosecutor v Jean-Pierre Bemba Gombo* (Decision on the Prosecutor's Application for a Warrant of Arrest against Jean-Pierre Bemba Gombo) ICC-01/05-01/08-14-TENG (10 June 2008) paras 82–83.

[67] ibid at paras 80–82.

[68] ibid at paras 73–74, 81.

[69] ibid at paras 52–55 (on the MLC hierarchical structure); paras 75– 81 (on the essential nature of Jean-Pierre Bemba's contribution to the implementation of the common plan); para 83 (on the Jean-Pierre Bemba's awareness of his leadership position within the MLC, as well as his essential role in the execution of the common plan).

(FRPI)) armed groups, who fought, with the support of the Uganda People's Defence Force (UPDF), against the provisional government of Ituri, which at that time was controlled by the main Hema political movement (*Union des Patriotes Congolais pour la Reconciliation et la Paix* (UPC/RP)) and its military branch (*Forces Patriotiques pour la Libération du Congo* (FPLC)).[70]

According to the *Katanga and Ngudjolo* Case Confirmation of Charges Decision, the only two members of the common plan were Germain Katanga (former FRPI commander-in-chief) and Mathieu Ngudjolo Chui (former FNI commander-in-chief),[71] who had already worked closely together in the past.[72] They both agreed to launch a joint attack on 24 February 2003 against the village of Bogoro, which at that time had an undeniable military value derived from its strategic location at the crossroads between the Bunia-Beni[73] and the Kasenyi-Mongwalu[74] roads.[75]

According to ICC Pre-Trial Chamber I, the common plan had two main objectives: on the one hand, obtaining the control of Bogoro, which was an important military objective given its strategic value[76] and on the other, securing that such control would be subsequently maintained through the destruction of the civilian population of Bogoro, which, to a large extent, belonged to the Hema ethnic group and supported the FPLC forces defending the village.[77] As a result, the *Katanga and Ngudjolo* Case Confirmation of Charges Decision found that the common plan was integrally criminal because it specifically aimed at attacking the civilian population of Bogoro.[78]

For ICC Pre-Trial Chamber I, Germain Katanga and Mathieu Ngudjolo Chui did not directly commit any of the crimes that occurred during the attack on Bogoro. On the contrary, once the launch of the attack was agreed, their role was to ensure: (i) coordination in its implementation by discussing the details of the attack with those commanders in charge of leading the troops in the field; (ii) the supply of the necessary weapons; (iii) the deployment of their respective forces; and (iv) the issuance to the field commanders of the order to launch the attack against Bogoro.[79] As a result, both suspects carried out their contributions *via* the

[70] *Prosecutor v Germain Katanga and Mathieu Ngudjolo Chui* (Decision on the Confirmation of the Charges) ICC-01/04-01/07-717 (30 September 2008) paras 71–75.

[71] ibid at paras 548–53.

[72] ibid at para 552.

[73] Bunia and Beni are respectively the capitals of the Ituri District and North Kivu Province.

[74] Kasenyi is the most important village in the Congolese side of Lake Albert, whereas one of the most important gold mines of the Great Lakes region is located in Mongwalu.

[75] *Prosecutor v Germain Katanga and Mathieu Ngudjolo Chui* (Decision on the Confirmation of the Charges) ICC-01/04-01/07-717 (30 September 2008) paras 275–83, 548.

[76] ibid at paras 273, 275.

[77] ibid at paras 273, 275, 548–49.

[78] This difference has played a fundamental role in the manner in which ICC Pre-Trial Chamber I dealt with the subjective elements in the *Katanga and Ngudjolo* case. See Olasolo, *Criminal Responsibility* (above n 4) at ch 5.

[79] *Prosecutor v Germain Katanga and Mathieu Ngudjolo Chui* (Decision on the Confirmation of the Charges) ICC-01/04-01/07-717 (30 September 2008) paras 555–61.

organised armed groups that they controlled de jure and de facto,[80] and which, in the view of ICC Pre-Trial Chamber I, complied with the requirements of hierarchical organisation and interchangeability of their members as required by the notion of indirect perpetration through organised structures of power.[81]

Moreover, as ICC Pre-Trial Chamber I pointed out, Germain Katanga and Mathieu Ngudjolo Chui belonged to different ethnic groups (Ngiti and Lendu) and had control over organised armed groups with different ethnic compositions.[82] As a consequence: '[t]he distinction between the Ngitis and the Lendus made it unlikely for combatants to comply with the orders of a leader who was not of the same ethnicity'.[83] Hence, the success of the attack was, therefore, dependent on the joint and coordinated action between Germain Katanga and Mathieu Ngudjolo Chui because their respective subordinates would not execute orders given by the other (essential coordinated contributions giving rise to joint control over the crime).[84] Confronted with this situation, ICC Pre-Trial Chamber I decided to apply the notion of indirect co-perpetration.

D The *Abu Garda* Case

The notion of indirect co-perpetration has also been recently applied in the *Abu Garda* Case Summons to Appear[85] issued by ICC Pre-Trial Chamber I on 7 May 2009. This case, which arises out of the investigation into the Darfur situation, refers to the alleged unlawful attack by a group of splinter forces which had broken away from the JEM, and were acting in concert with the forces of a second armed group, on the African Union Mission in Sudan (AMIS) personnel and property stationed at the Military Group Site Haskanita (MGS Haskanita) on 29 September 2007.[86]

The attack on MGS Haskanita took place in the context of an armed conflict not of an international character, which occurred in Darfur from approximately August 2002 to – at least – November 2008, between the Government of Sudan and various armed groups, including the JEM. According to ICC Pre-Trial Chamber I, Abu Garda, who was in command of the said splinter forces of JEM, which were hierarchically organised, had a common plan, which included the commission of war crimes, to attack the MGS Haskanita with the other com-

[80] ibid at paras 540–41.

[81] ibid at paras 543–47.

[82] The FRPI was mainly comprised of members of the Ngiti ethnic group to which Germain Katanga belonged. In turn, the FNI was mainly comprised of members of the Lendu ethnic group to which Mathieu Ngudjolo Chui belonged.

[83] *Prosecutor v Germain Katanga and Mathieu Ngudjolo Chui* (Decision on the Confirmation of the Charges) ICC-01/04-01/07-717 (30 September 2008) para 519.

[84] ibid at para 560.

[85] *Prosecutor v Bahar Idriss Abu Garda* (Decision on the Prosecutor's Application under Article 58) ICC-02/05-02/09-1 (7 May 2009) paras 24–28.

[86] ibid at para 12.

manders whose troops participated in the said attack.[87] Moreover, as commander of the splinter forces of JEM, Abu Garda, along with the other commanders whose troops participated in the said attack, exercised joint control over the commission of the alleged crimes[88] and their respective contributions to the perpetration of the alleged crimes were essential.[89]

Insofar as some evidence pointed to the presence of Abu Garda at the scene of the crime during the attack on MGS Haskanita, Pre-Trial Chamber I found that there were reasonable grounds to believe that Abu Garda was criminally responsible as a co-perpetrator, or, in the alternative, as an indirect co-perpetrator.[90] Nevertheless, it is important to highlight that in the *Abu Garda* Case Confirmation of the Charges,[91] issued on 8 February 2010, Pre-Trial Chamber I decided not to confirm the charges due to insufficient evidence on the alleged criminal liability of Abu Garda.[92] Subsequently, the Prosecutor has stated that he intends again to request the confirmation of the charges on the basis of new evidence.

V Conclusion

Despite the initial reluctance of national and international case law to resort to the notion of indirect perpetration through organised structures of power, the situation has, to a very important extent, changed over time. In the last decade, this notion has been applied in a number of the cases. In particular, the ICC and the ICTY have resorted to it in order to prosecute the highest political and military leaders, as well as other individuals who were not *stricto sensu* at the top of their organisations. Moreover, as explained in the following excerpt of the *Bashir* Case Warrant of Arrest Decision, the notion of indirect perpetration through organised structures of power has often been applied in combination with the notion of co-perpetration based on joint control over the crime:

> At the outset, the Chamber highlights that, in the Lubanga and the Katanga and Ngudjolo cases, the Chamber has held that article 25(3)(a) of the Statute embraces the notion of control of the crime as the determining criterion to distinguish between principal and accessory liability. Furthermore, as the Chamber has held in the said cases, article 25(3)(a) of the Statute also embraces the following four manifestations of the notion of control of the crime: direct perpetration, perpetration through another person or indirect perpetration, co-perpetration based on joint control and indirect co-perpetration.[93]

[87] ibid at paras 12, 26.
[88] ibid at para 27.
[89] ibid.
[90] ibid at para 28.
[91] *Prosecutor v Bahar Idriss Abu Garda* (Decision on the Confirmation of the Charges) ICC-02/05-02/09-243-Red (8 February 2010) paras 158–236.
[92] ibid at paras 158–236.
[93] *Prosecutor v Omar Hassan Ahmad Al Bashir* (Decision on the Prosecution's Application for a Warrant of Arrest against Omar Hassan Ahmad Al Bashir) ICC-02/05-01/09-3 (4 March 2009) para 210.

As a consequence, as Ambos has recently underscored, the notion of indirect perpetration through organised structures of power is today 'a serious option to hold criminal leaders to account'.[94] This is the result of a growing perception that the application of notions of accessorial liability in this type of case – such as instigation or necessary contribution – even if it may have no impact on the penalty, relegates superiors to a secondary role which does not correspond to their actual relevance.

[94] Ambos, 'The *Fujimori* Judgment' (above n 8) at 1.

7

Shedding Some Light on the Nature of the Notion of Joint Criminal Enterprise and its Extended Form*

I Introduction

On 20 May 2010, the Pre-Trial Chamber (PTC) of the Extraordinary Chambers of the Courts of Cambodia (ECCC) issued its Decision on the Appeals against the Co-Investigative Judges Order on Joint Criminal Enterprise (JCE), in which it analysed the customary status of the notion of joint criminal enterprise based on Second World War case law.[1] The ECCC PTC concluded that the London Charter of the International Military Tribunal and the Control Council Law No 10,[2] as well as the *Justice* and *RuSHA* cases,[3] presented a strong support for 'the state of customary international law with respect to the basic form and systemic form of JCE (JCE 1 and JCE 2)'.[4] In the same decision, the ECCC PTC also stated that there were compelling arguments[5] leading to the conclusion that the extended form of joint criminal enterprise was not part of customary international law at the time relevant to ECCC Case 002.[6] Only two months afterwards, on 26 July 2010, the

* Revised and updated version of the work published in (2009) 20(2) *Criminal Law Forum* 263 *et seq*. The author thanks Lachezar Yanev for his research on case law and doctrine. The author thanks Springer for authorising printing of the present revised and updated version of the 2009 work. The views expressed herein are those of the author alone and do not necessarily reflect the views of the ICC, the ICTY, the United Nations in general or the Spanish Government.

[1] *Prosecutor v Ieng Sary, Ieng Thirith and Khieu Samphan* (Decision on the Appeals against the Co-Investigative Judges Order on Joint Criminal Enterprise) 002/19-09-2007-ECCC/OCIJ (PTC38) (20 May 2010). See also K Gustafson, 'ECCC Tackles JCE: An Appraisal of Recent Decisions' (2010) 8 *Journal of International Criminal Justice* 1323–32.

[2] *Prosecutor v Ieng Sary, Ieng Thirith and Khieu Samphan* (Decision on the Appeals against the Co-Investigative Judges Order on Joint Criminal Enterprise) 002/19-09-2007-ECCC/OCIJ (PTC38) (20 May 2010) para 57.

[3] ibid at para 65.

[4] ibid.

[5] ibid at paras 78–83. The Pre-Trial Chamber gave several reasons for its finding. First, it observed that the Nuremberg Charter and Control Council Law No 10 do not offer support for the extended JCE. Following that, the ECCC PTC stated that some of the cases on which the *Tadić* Appeals Chamber relied to support its findings on JCE 3 lacked reasoned judgments, others were of Italian domestic law origin and did not reflect international criminal law. Overall, the ECCC PTC stated that all these cases were insufficient to uphold that the extended form of JCE was part of customary international law.

[6] ibid at para 77.

ECCC Trial Chamber delivered its first judgement in the *Duch* case, also known as ECCC Case 001, in which it refused to make a pronouncement on the customary status of the extended form of joint criminal enterprise.[7] Once again, the recent proceedings before the ECCC have shown that the nature and customary status of the joint criminal enterprise doctrine continues to be an unsettled matter.

This chapter does not intend to make a comprehensive analysis of the numerous issues raised by the notion of joint criminal enterprise,[8] also known as 'common purpose doctrine';[9] quite the contrary, it only aims at shedding some light on the nature and problems posed by the application of the third or extended category of joint criminal enterprise. Nevertheless, in order to fully address this matter, it is necessary to first analyse: (i) the development of the notions of control over the crime; (ii) the development of joint criminal enterprise to address the specific features of international crimes; and (iii) how the overall notion of joint criminal enterprise, which was originally conceived as a notion of partnership in crime or accomplice liability in a common law sense, has been turned into a theory of co-perpetration by the case law of the *Ad hoc* Tribunals after the International Criminal Tribunal for the former Yugoslavia (ICTY) Appeals Chamber Decision on Joint Criminal Enterprise on 21 May 2003.

II The Development of the Notion of Control over the Crime to Address the Specific Features of International Crimes

International crimes have a number of distinctive features. They usually take place in situations of large scale or widespread criminality. They are also generally carried out by 'groups of individuals, military details, paramilitary units or governmental officials acting in unison or in pursuance to a policy'.[10] Furthermore, individuals who plan and set into motion international crimes are often geographically remote from the scene of the crimes when they take place and have no contact with those low level members of their organisations who physically carry out the crimes.[11]

[7] *Prosecutor v Kaing Guek Eav, alias 'Duch'* (Judgment) 001/18-07-2007/ECCC/TC (26 July 2010) para 513.

[8] The author has undertaken such a comprehensive analysis in H Olasolo, *The Criminal Responsibility of Senior Political and Military Leaders as Principals to International Crimes* (Oxford, Hart Publishing, 2009).

[9] *The Prosecutor v Milan Milutinovic et al* (Decision on Dragoljub Ojdanic's Motion Challenging Jurisdiction – Joint Criminal Enterprise) ICTY-99-37-AR72 (21 May 2003) para 36.

[10] A Cassese (*Prosecutor v Kaing Guek Eav, alias 'Duch' Amicus Curiae* Brief of Professor Antonio Cassese and Members of the Journal of International Criminal Justice on Joint Criminal Enterprise Doctrine) 001/18-07-2007-ECCC/OCIJ (PTC 02) - D99-3-24 (27 October 08) para 30.

[11] Those individuals who physically carry out the objective elements of the crimes have been referred to with different expressions such as 'direct perpetrators', 'principal perpetrators', 'material perpetrators',

As a result, according to some authors:

> When such crimes are committed, it is extremely difficult to point out the specific contribution made by each individual participant in the collective criminal enterprise, because (i) not all participants acted in the same manner, but rather each of them may have played a different role in planning, organizing, instigating, coordinating, executing, or otherwise contributing to the criminal conduct, and (ii) the evidence related to each individual's conduct may prove difficult if not impossible to find [. . .] To obscure responsibility in the fog of collective criminality and let the crimes go unpunished would be immoral and contrary to the general purpose of criminal law of protecting the community from deviant behavior that causes serious damage to the general interest. This damage is all the more severe in the context of collective criminality.[12]

Nevertheless, the legality and fair trial principles – which are cornerstones of international criminal law[13] – prohibit the expansion of any theory of criminal liability in order to circumvent the lack of evidence on the specific role played by those individuals somehow involved in the planning, preparation and execution of large scale or widespread campaigns of criminality. As a result, in the view of the author, the main problem posed by the specific features of international crimes resides on the fact that the application of the traditional modes of liability to such crimes in national criminal law leads to the conclusion that senior political and military leaders who plan and set into motion large-scale or systematic campaigns of criminality are mere accessories (as opposed to principals) to the crimes physically committed by their subordinates. This does not reflect the central role that senior political and military leaders usually play in the commission of international crimes, and often results in a punishment which is inappropriately low considering the wrongdoing of their actions and omissions.[14]

As a result, international criminal law has put a particular emphasis on the development of notions,[15] such as 'control over the crime' and 'joint criminal

'physical perpetrators', 'relevant physical perpetrators' or 'perpetrators behind the direct perpetrators/actors'. See *Prosecutor v Radoslav Brđanin* (Judgment) ICTY-99-36-A (3 April 2007) para 362 (*Brđanin* Case Appeals Judgment).

[12] Cassese, *Amicus Curiae* Brief (above n 10) para 30.

[13] R Cryer, H Friman, D Robinson and E Wilmshurst, *An Introduction to International Criminal Law and Procedure* 2nd edn (Cambridge, Cambridge University Press, 2010) 301.

[14] As the ICTY Appeals Chamber has emphasised in *Prosecutor v Dusko Tadić* (Judgment) ICTY-94-1-A (15 July 1999) para 192: 'Under these circumstances, to hold criminally liable as a perpetrator only the person who materially performs the criminal act would disregard the role as co-perpetrators of all those who in some way made it possible for the perpetrator physically to carry out that criminal act. At the same time, depending upon the circumstances, to hold the latter liable only as aiders and abettors might understate the degree of their criminal responsibility'. See also S Manacorda and C Meloni, 'Joint Perpetration *versus* Joint Criminal Enterprise: Concurring Approaches in the Practice of International Criminal Law?' (2011) 9 *Journal of International Criminal Justice* 161.

[15] However, international criminal law has not created these notions, as they have been since long resorted to at the national level in the context of ordinary crimes. For instance, the notion of joint criminal enterprise was originally conceived in common law jurisdictions to deal with 'mob-crimes' as well as other crimes, such as bank robberies, which were committed by a plurality of persons acting in a concerted manner to implement a common criminal purpose. See generally (i) Australia: *R v Johns* [1978] 1 NSWLR 282, 290; *R v McAuliffe* (1995) 69 ALJR 621; Western Australian Criminal Code Act

enterprise', which aim at better reflecting the central role played by senior political and military leaders in campaigns of large scale and systematic criminality.

The notion of control over the crime reflects a material-objective approach to the notion of perpetration, and therefore to the distinction between principal (perpetration) and accessorial or derivative liability (participation).[16] As PTC I of the International Criminal Court (ICC) has held, according to this notion, perpetrators or principals to the crime are those who dominate the commission of the

§ 8(1) (1913); Queensland Criminal Code Act § 8 (1899). (ii) England and Wales: *R v Powell, R v English* [1997] 4 All ER 545; *R v Hyde* [1991] 1 QB 134.; *R v Anderson, R v Morris* [1966] 2 QB 110, and (iii) The United States of America: *Pinkerton v United States*, 328 US 640 (1946); *State of Connecticut v Diaz*, 679 A.2d 902 (1996); Iowa Code § 703.2 (1997); Kansas Statute Annotated § 21-3205 (1997); 17 Maine Criminal Code § 57 (1997); Minnesota Statute § 609.05 (1998); Wisconsin Statute § 939.05 (1995); *State v Walton*, 630 A.2d 990 (1993). Civil law jurisdictions have also resorted to theories of criminal liability somehow akin to the notion of joint criminal enterprise. For instance, the Spanish Supreme Court followed for the most part the 'doctrine of the previous agreement' (*doctrina del acuerdo previo*) until the approval of the new Spanish Criminal Code of 1995. See the Judgments of the Spanish Supreme Court of 22 February 1985, 31 May 1985 and 13 May 1986.

Likewise, the notion of control over the crime was first utilised at the national level to address situations where a person uses an innocent agent, such as a child or a mentally disabled person, to commit a crime. In relation to common law jurisdictions, see generally (i) Australia: P Rush and S Yeah, *Criminal Law Sourcebook* (Sydney, Butterworths, 2000) 662; L Waller and C Williams, *Criminal Law Text and Cases* (Sydney, Butterworths, 2001) 560. (ii) England: *Regina v Cogan and Leak* [1976] QB 217. (iii) South Africa: CR Snyman, *Criminal Law* (Oxford, Butterworths, 1995) 246–47. (iv) United States: Model Penal Code s 2.06(1)–(4); *State v Ward*, 396 A.2d 1041, 1046 (1978). In relation to civil law jurisdictions, see generally (i) Argentina: C Fontán Balestra, *Tratado de Derecho Penal: Parte General* (Albany, Lexis Publishing, 1995) Lexis No 1503/001660. (ii) France: Cour de Cassation, Chambre Criminelle Dalloz (6 Mars 1964) 562. (iii) Germany: Bundesgerichtshof, Entscheidungen des Bundesgerichtshofs in Strafsachen 32, 35, 41, 351. (iv) Spain: J Gonzalez Rus, 'Autoría Única Inmediata, Autoría Mediata y Coautoría' in Consejo General del Poder Judicial (ed), *Cuadernos de Derecho Judicial No XXXIX* (Madrid, 1994) and (v) Switzerland: Entscheidungen des Schweizerischen Bundesgerichts 101 IV 310; Entscheidungen des Schweizerischen Bundesgerichts 85 IV 23.

Subsequently, both notions have been used at the national level in relation to organised crime, such as drug-trafficking, economic crime or even terrorism, where the number of persons involved is higher than in ordinary crimes, but is still limited. See, for instance, *Prosecutor v Milomir Stakic* (Judgment) ICTY-97-24-T (31 July 2003) para 439, fn 942, where ICTY Trial Chamber II refers to the use of the notion of control over the crime in the context of white collar crime and other forms of organised crime.

[16] According to the material-objective approach, perpetration and participation are distinguished on the basis of the level and intensity of the contribution to the execution of the objective elements of the crime. Perpetration requires that the contribution be essential for the completion of the crime in the sense that without it the crime would not have been committed. Those favouring this approach justify it on the higher dangerousness of principals to the crime in comparison with accessories due to the different level and intensity of their respective contributions to the commission of the crime. See for all C Roxin, *Autoria y Dominio del Hecho en Derecho Penal* 6th edn (Madrid, Marcial Pons, 1998) 58; A Gimbernat Ordeig, *Autor y Cómplice en Derecho Penal* (Madrid, Universidad de Madrid, 1966) 115–17; F Muñoz Conde and M García Aran, *Derecho Penal: Parte General* 5th edn (Valencia, Tirant lo Blanch, 2002) 448–49; JM Zugaldia Espinar (ed), *Derecho Penal: Parte General* (Valencia, Tirant lo Blanch, 2002) 734–35. See also H Olasolo, 'Reflections on the Treatment of the Notions of Control of the Crime and Joint Criminal Enterprise in the *Stakic* Appeal Judgment' (2007) 7 *International Criminal Law Review* 143; Manacorda and Meloni, 'Joint Perpetration *versus* JCE' (above n 14) at 168; H van der Wilt, 'The Continuous Quest for Proper Modes of Criminal Responsibility' (2009) 7 *Journal of International Criminal Justice* 311–12; N Farrell, 'Attributing Criminal Liability to Corporate Actors: Some Lessons from the International Tribunals' (2010) 8 *Journal of International Criminal Justice* 880.

crime in the sense that they decide whether the crime will be carried out and how it will be performed.[17]

The notion of control over the crime combines an objective element consisting of the factual circumstances that lead to control over the crime, and a subjective element consisting of the awareness of the factual circumstances that leads to such control.[18] Moreover, it has three main manifestations:

1. Direct perpetration, according to which, those persons, who physically carry out the objective elements of the crime with the subjective elements required by the crime in question, have the control over the crime (also known as 'control of the action').
2. Indirect perpetration, according to which, those persons, who do not physically carry out the objective elements of the crime, can also have the control over the crime if they indirectly commit the crime by using the physical perpetrators as an 'instrument' or a 'tool' who is controlled by their dominant will (also known as 'control of the will').
3. Co-perpetration based on functional control, according to which, when the objective elements of a crime are completed as a result of the sum of individual contributions of several persons on the basis of the principle of divisions of tasks, those persons who can ruin the implementation of the common plan by withholding their essential contributions have also control over the crime.[19]

As ICC PTC I has highlighted, 'indirect co-perpetration' based on a combined application of indirect perpetration and co-perpetration based on joint control, constitutes a fourth manifestation of the notion of control over the crime, which is mainly applicable to two types of scenarios:[20]

[17] As *Prosecutor v Thomas Lubanga Dyilo* (Decision on the Confirmation of Charges) ICC-01/04-01/06-803-tEN (29 January 2007) para 330 has explained: 'The concept of control over the crime constitutes a third approach for distinguishing between principals and accessories which, contrary to the Defence claim, is applied in numerous legal systems. The notion underpinning this third approach is that principals to a crime are not limited to those who physically carry out the objective elements of the offence, but also include those who, in spite of being removed from the scene of the crime, control or mastermind its commission because they decide whether and how the offence will be committed'. See also *Prosecutor v Germain Katanga and Mathieu Ngudjolo Chui* (Decision on the Confirmation of Charges) ICC-01/04-01/07-717 (30 September 2008) para 485.

[18] It is for this reason that, ICC PTC I has recently stated in *Prosecutor v Germain Katanga and Mathieu Ngudjolo Chui* (Decision on the Confirmation of Charges) ICC-01/04-01/07-717 (30 September 2008) para 484, that the notion of control over the crime is: '[O]ne that synthesises both objective and subjective components, since: [...] the doctrine of control over the crime corresponds to an evolution of subjective and objective approaches, such that it effectively represents a synthesis of previously opposed views and doubtless owes its broad acceptance to this reconciliation of contrary positions'.

[19] *Prosecutor v Thomas Lubanga Dyilo* (Decision on the Confirmation of Charges) ICC-01/04-01/06-803-tEN (29 January 2007) para 332; *Prosecutor v Germain Katanga and Mathieu Ngudjolo Chui* (Decision on the Confirmation of Charges) ICC-01/04-01/07-717 (30 September 2008) para 488; *Prosecutor v Jean-Pierre Bemba Gombo* (Decision on the Confirmation of Charges) ICC-01/05-01/08 (15 June 2009) para 348. See also Manacorda and Meloni, 'Joint Perpetration *versus* JCE' (above n 14) at 167.

[20] One could even imagine a third scenario in which this fourth manifestation of the notion of control over the crime could be applicable. This would take place when not all co-perpetrators control one organisation (or a part thereof). In this scenario, those co-perpetrators who do not control any organisation would coordinate the implementation of the common criminal plan by those other co-perpetrators who use their organisations to have the crimes committed.

1. When several political and military leaders who have joint control over one hierarchical organisation (or a part thereof), such as the military, the police, large paramilitary groups or certain organised armed groups, use it to secure the commission of the crimes.[21]
2. When several political and military leaders, who are each of them in control of a different hierarchical organisation (or a part thereof) direct their different organisations to implement in a coordinated manner a common criminal plan.[22]

III The Development of the Notion of Joint Criminal Enterprise to Address the Specific Features of International Crimes

A First Approach to the Notion of Joint Criminal Enterprise

The notion of 'joint criminal enterprise', or the 'common purpose' doctrine, provides that where a crime is committed by a plurality of persons acting together in pursuance of a common criminal purpose, every member of the group who made

[21] This is the factual situation in the *German Border* case, where the East Germany National Defence Council, which was the organ responsible for defence and security matters, was comprised of several members, which jointly issued those decisions, in execution of which crimes were committed at the border between East and West Germany. Nevertheless, the German Federal Supreme Court failed to address the horizontal relationship between the members of the Council, and only applied the notion of indirect perpetration. See *Entscheidungen des Bundesgerichtshofs in Strafsachen* 40 at 218.

[22] This is the factual scenario in the *Katanga and Ngudjolo* and *Bemba* cases before the ICC, and in the *Stakic* case before the ICTY. See *Prosecutor v Germain Katanga and Mathieu Ngudjolo Chui* (Decision on the Confirmation of Charges) ICC-01/04-01/07-717 (30 September 2008) paras 540–82; *Prosecutor v Jean-Pierre Bemba Gombo* (Decision on the Prosecutor's Application for a Warrant of Arrest against Jean-Pierre Bemba Gombo) ICC-01/05-01/08-14-tENG (10 June 2008) paras 69–84. See also *Prosecutor v Milomir Stakic* (Judgment) ICTY-97-24-T (31 July 2003) paras 738–44, 774, 818, 822, 826. In this last case, the ICTY Trial Chamber II used the expression 'co-perpetratorship' to refer to the combined application of the notions of indirect perpetration in its variant of Organised Structure of Power and co-perpetration based on joint control. See the explanation by H Olasolo and A Pérez Cepeda, 'The Notion of Control of the Crime and its Application by the ICTY in the Stakic Case' (2004) 4 *International Criminal Law Review* 475, 512–14. In the *Juntas* Trial (Argentina), one of the most important issues was whether the commanders-in-chief of the three branches of the armed forces were criminally responsible as individuals, or collectively responsible as members of a governing junta. The Prosecution argued that each member of the three juntas was collectively responsible for all acts committed by any of the three organisations (army, navy and air force). That would have made the commander-in-chief of the air force equally responsible for the crimes committed by those who acted under the command of the army and navy. Nevertheless, the Federal Court of Appeals rejected this argument, accepting the Defence's argument that the commanders-in-chief of the separate services remained autonomous, not subject to any general orders of the Junta as a whole. See Judgment of the Federal Appeals Court of Buenos Aires (9 December 1985) at 29, 804. See also the analysis by MA Sancinetti, *Derechos Humanos en la Argentina Postdictatorial* (Buenos Aires, Lerner, 1988).

a significant contribution is criminally liable.[23] In order to become a participant in a joint criminal enterprise, is not sufficient to agree with the common criminal purpose; it is also necessary to make a contribution to its implementation with a view to commit the crimes that are either the ultimate goal of the enterprise or the means through which the goal of the enterprise is to be achieved.[24] The contribution need not be essential or substantial, as it suffices if the contribution is 'significant'.[25] Minor contributions that do not reach the threshold of 'significant' are considered irrelevant, and therefore do not give rise to criminal liability.[26] The intent must be shared by all participants in a joint criminal enterprise, no matter whether they are physical perpetrators or senior political and military leaders.[27]

[23] *Prosecutor v Dusko Tadić*(Judgment) ICTY-94-1-A (15 July 1999) paras 227, 229. At first, the ICTY Appeals Chamber seemed to accept that the accused's contribution to the criminal enterprise did not have to reach any particular threshold, as long as he shared the intent of the other participants in the JCE. See, for instance, *Prosecutor v Mitar Vasiljevic* (Judgment) ICTY-98-32-A (25 February 2004) para 100; *Prosecutor v Kvocka, et al (*Judgment) ICTY-98-30/1-A (28 February 2005) paras 97, 187. Presently, however, there seems to be a consensus that although the contribution to a common criminal plan does not need to be necessary or substantial, it has to be *at least* significant. See, for instance, *Prosecutor v Radoslav Brdanin* (Judgment) IT-99-36-A (3 April 2007) para 430; *Prosecutor v Momcilo Krajišnik* (Judgment) ICTY-00-39-A (17 March 2009) para 215; *Prosecutor v Popovic, et al* (Judgment) ICTY-05-88-T (10 June 2010) para 1027; *Prosecutor v Vlastimir Djordjevic* (Judgment) IT-05-87/1-T (23 February 2011) para 1863; *Prosecutor v Gotovina, et al* (Judgment) IT-06-90-T (15 April 2011) para 1953; *Prosecutor v Kanyarukiga* (Judgment) ICTR-02-78-T (1 November 2010) paras 624, 643; *Prosecutor v Jean-Baptiste Gatete* (Judgment) ICTR-00-61-T (31 March 2011) para 577; *Prosecutor v Sesay, Kallon and Gbao* (Judgment) SCSL-04-15-A (26 October 2009) paras 313, 401, 611 1169; *Decision on the Applicable Law: Terrorism, Conspiracy, Homicide, Perpetration, Cumulative Charging* (Decision) STL-11-01/1 (16 February 2011) para 237. On the importance of the notion of Joint Criminal Enterprise, see N Piacente, 'Importance of the JCE Doctrine for the ICTY Prosecutorial Policy' (2004) 2 *Journal of International Criminal Justice* 446, 448; M Osiel, 'The Banality of the Good: Aligning Incentives against Mass Atrocity' (2005) 105 *Columbia Law Review* 1751, 1783.

[24] *Prosecutor v Dusko Tadić* (Judgment) ICTY-94-1-A (15 July 1999) para 227. See also *Prosecutor v Milorad Krnojelac* (Judgment) ICTY-97-25-A (17 September 2003) para 31; *Prosecutor v Mitar Vasiljevic* (Judgment) ICTY-98-32-A (25 February 2004) para 100; *Prosecutor v Kvocka, et al (*Judgment) ICTY-98-30/1-A (28 February 2005) para 96; *Prosecutor v Milomir Stakić* (Judgment) ICTY-97-24-A (22 March 2006) para 64; *Prosecutor v Momcilo Krajišnik* (Judgment) ICTY-00-39-T (27 September 2006) para 883; *Prosecutor v Radoslav Brđanin* (Judgment) ICTY-99-36-A (3 April 2007) para 364; *Prosecutor v Milan Marti* (Judgment) ICTY-95-11-A (8 October 2008) para 82; *Prosecutor v Momcilo Krajišnik* (Judgment) ICTY-00-39-A (17 March 2009) para 215; *Prosecutor v Vlastimir Djordjevic* (Judgment) IT-05-87/1-T (23 February 2011) para 1863; *Prosecutor v Gotovina, et al* (Judgment) IT-06-90-T (15 April 2011) para 1953; *Prosecutor v Kanyarukiga* (Judgment) ICTR-02-78-T (1 November 2010) para 624; *Prosecutor v Jean-Baptiste Gatete* (Judgment) ICTR-00-61-T (31 March 2011) para 577; *Prosecutor v Sesay, Kallon and Gbao* (Judgment) SCSL-04-15-A (26 October 2009) para 313; *Decision on the Applicable Law: Terrorism, Conspiracy, Homicide, Perpetration, Cumulative Charging* (Decision) STL-11-01/1 (16 February 2011) para 237.

[25] See above (n 23). See also Farrell, 'Attributing Criminal Liability' (above n 16) at 878.

[26] See, for instance, *Prosecutor v Gotovina, et al* (Judgment) IT-06-90-T (15 April 2011) para 2548. There, the Trial Chamber held with respect to Ivan Cermak's criminal liability, that 'his misleading assurances to the international community that action to stop the crimes was being and/or would be taken, and his denial and concealment of the crimes committed . . . did not constitute a significant contribution to the JCE'.

[27] *Prosecutor v Dusko Tadić* (Judgment) ICTY-94-1-A (15 July 1999) para 228; *Prosecutor v Milorad Krnojelac* (Judgment) ICTY-97-25-A (17 September 2003) paras 32–33; *Prosecutor v Mitar Vasiljevic* (Judgment) ICTY-98-32-A (25 February 2004) para 101; *Prosecutor v Kvocka, et al* (Judgment) ICTY-98-30/1-A (28 February 2005) paras 82, 83, 89; *Prosecutor v Milomir Stakic* (Judgment) ICTY-97-24-A (22 March 2006) para 65; *Prosecutor v Radoslav Brđanin* (Judgment) ICTY-99-36-A (3 April 2007)

As a result, it can be stated that, once the contribution becomes relevant because it reaches the threshold of being 'significant', the specific level of contribution (notable, substantial, essential) of those participating in a joint criminal enterprise to the achievement of the common criminal purpose is secondary. What really matters is that they make their contributions with the aim of furthering the common criminal purpose.[28] Hence, non-essential, or even non-substantial contributions – including further planning and preparation of the actual commission of the crimes – may suffice as long as the common criminal purpose is shared.[29] Likewise, substantial, or even essential contributions with knowledge of the common criminal purpose, but without sharing in it, will not suffice for criminal liability to arise under the notion of joint criminal enterprise.[30]

As a result, for the notion of joint criminal enterprise or the common purpose doctrine, the essence of the wrongdoing lies in the shared intent by all the participants in the enterprise to commit the crimes encompassed by the common crim-

para 365; *Prosecutor v Blagoje Simic, et al* (Judgment) ICTY-95-9-T (17 October 2003) para 158; *Prosecutor v Momcilo Krajišnik* (Judgment) ICTY-00-39-T (27 September 2006) paras 879, 883; *Prosecutor v Momcilo Krajišnik* (Judgment) ICTY-00-39-A (17 March 2009) paras 200, 707; *Prosecutor v Vlastimir Djordjevic* (Judgment) IT-05-87/1-T (23 February 2011) paras 1864–65; *Prosecutor v Gotovina, et al* (Judgment) IT-06-90-T (15 April 2011) para 1953; *Prosecutor v Kanyarukiga* (Judgment) ICTR-02-78-T (1 November 2010) para 625; *Prosecutor v Jean-Baptiste Gatete* (Judgment) ICTR-00-61-T (31 March 2011) para 578; *Prosecutor v Sesay, Kallon and Gbao* (Judgment) SCSL-04-15-A (26 October 2009) paras 398-400; *Decision on the Applicable Law: Terrorism, Conspiracy, Homicide, Perpetration, Cumulative Charging* (Decision) STL-11-01/1 (16 February 2011) paras 237–39.

[28] *Prosecutor v Dusko Tadić* (Judgment) ICTY-94-1-A (15 July 1999) para 228; *Prosecutor v Milorad Krnojelac* (Judgment) ICTY-97-25-A (17 September 2003) para 84; *Prosecutor v Kvocka, et al* (Judgment) ICTY-98-30/1-A (28 February 2005) para 82; *Prosecutor v Mitar Vasiljevic* (Judgment) ICTY-98-32-A (25 February 2004) para 97; *Prosecutor v Milomir Stakić* (Judgment) ICTY-97-24-A (22 March 2006) para 65; *Prosecutor v Radoslav Brđanin* (Judgment) ICTY-99-36-A (3 April 2007) para 365; *Prosecutor v Blagoje Simic, et al* (Judgment) ICTY-95-9-T (17 October 2003) para 157; *Prosecutor v Momcilo Krajišnik* (Judgment) ICTY-00-39-T (27 September 2006) para 79. See also A Bogdan, 'Individual Criminal Responsibility in the Execution of a "Joint Criminal Enterprise" in the Jurisprudence of the *Ad hoc* International Tribunal for the Former Yugoslavia' (2006) 6 *International Criminal Law Review* 63, 82; Farrell, 'Attributing Criminal Liability' (above n 16) at 879.

[29] K Gustafson, 'The Requirements of an "Express Agreement" for Joint Criminal Enterprise Liability: A Critique of Brdanin' (2007) 5 *Journal of International Criminal Justice* 141. However, AM Danner and JS Martinez, 'Guilty Associations: Joint Criminal Enterprise, Command Responsibility and the Development of International Criminal Law' (2005) 93 *California Law Review* 150, 150–51 emphasise the need for the interpretation of the notion of joint criminal enterprise as requiring a significant level of contribution to the implementation of the common criminal plan. Likewise, JD Ohlin, 'Three Conceptual Problems with the Doctrine of Joint Criminal Enterprise' (2007) 5 *Journal of International Criminal Justice* 89 proposes a requirement for a 'substantial and indispensable contribution' before criminal liability is invoked for participation in a joint criminal enterprise under art 25 (3) (d) of the ICC Statute.

[30] This has been made particularly clear in the context of the distinction between the notions of joint criminal enterprise and aiding and abetting. See *Prosecutor v Dusko Tadić* (Judgment) ICTY-94-1-A (15 July 1999) para 229; *Prosecutor v Mitar Vasiljevic* (Judgment) ICTY-98-32-A (25 February 2004) para 102; *Prosecutor v Milan Milutinovic, et al* (Decision on Dragoljub Ojdanic's Motion Challenging Jurisdiction – Joint Criminal Enterprise) ICTY-99-37-AR72 (21 May 2003) para 20; *Prosecutor v Kvocka, et al* (Judgment) ICTY-98-30/1-A (28 February 2005) paras 89–90; *Prosecutor v Momcilo Krajišnik* (Judgment) ICTY-00-39-T (27 September 2006) para 885.

inal purpose.[31] When the crimes are committed within a system of ill treatment (systematic form of joint criminal enterprise), the shared intent to commit the core crimes carried out through such a system is inherent in the awareness of its nature and the intent to further it.[32] Criminal responsibility for the commission by other members of the criminal enterprise of foreseeable crimes, which are not part of the common criminal plan, only arises as long as there is a shared intent by all participants in the enterprise to have the core crimes of the enterprise committed.[33]

B The Notion of Joint Criminal Enterprise since the Decision of the ICTY Appeals Chamber of 21 May 2003: Turning a Notion of Partnership in Crime or Accomplice Liability into a Notion of Co-Perpetration

The Charters and case law of the International Military Tribunal and the International Military Tribunal for the Far East embraced a unitary ('monistic') model, which did not distinguish between the perpetration of a crime (which gives rise to principal liability) and participation in a crime committed by a third person (which gives rise to accessorial or derivative liability).[34] Furthermore, although article II(2) of Allied Control Council Law No 10 introduced, for the first time, the distinction between principal and accessorial liability in international criminal

[31] *The Prosecutor v Milan Milutinovic, et al* (Decision on Dragoljub Ojdanic's Motion Challenging Jurisdiction – Joint Criminal Enterprise) ICTY-99-37-AR72 (21 May 2003) para 20.

[32] As E Van Sliedregt, 'Joint Criminal Enterprise as a Pathway to Convicting Individuals for Genocide' (2007) 5 *Journal of International Criminal Justice* 186 has pointed out: 'With regard to the *mens rea*, the First and Second Category of JCE require "an intention to participate in and further the criminal activity or purpose of the group", thus suggesting that all participants possess the same intent'. See *Prosecutor v Dusko Tadić* (Judgment) ICTY-94-1-A (15 July 1999) para 228; *Prosecutor v Milorad Krnojelac* (Judgment) ICTY-97-25-A (17 Sep 2003) paras 93-4; *Prosecutor v Kvocka, et al* (Judgment) ICTY-98-30/1-A (28 Feb 2005) para 82; *Prosecutor v Radoslav Brđanin* (Judgment) ICTY-99-36-A (3 Apr 2007) para 365; *Prosecutor v Vlastimir Djordjevic* (Judgment) IT-05-87/1-T (23 February 2011) para 1864.

[33] *Prosecutor v Dusko Tadić* (Judgment) ICTY-94-1-A (15 July 1999) para 228; *Prosecutor v Mitar Vasiljevic* (Judgment) ICTY-98-32-A (25 February 2004) para 101; *Prosecutor v Tihomir Blaskic* (Judgment) ICTY-95-14-A (29 July 2004) para 33; *Prosecutor v Popovic, et al* (Judgment) ICTY-05-88-T (10 June 2010) para 1030; *Prosecutor v Gotovina, et al* (Judgment) IT-06-90-T (15 April 2011) para 1953; *Prosecutor v Sesay, Kallon and Gbao* (Judgment) SCSL-04-15-A (26 October 2009) para 475; *Decision on the Applicable Law: Terrorism, Conspiracy, Homicide, Perpetration, Cumulative Charging* (Decision) STL-11-01/1 (16 February 2011) paras 239–41. See also H Van der Wilt, 'Joint Criminal Enterprise: Possibilities and Limitations' (2007) 5 *Journal of International Criminal Justice* 91, 96; and Van Sliedregt, 'Joint Criminal Enterprise' (above n 32) at 186.

[34] Cassese, *Amicus Curiae* Brief (above n 10) para 39. See also G Werle, *Tratado de Derecho Penal Internacional* (Valencia, Tirant lo Blanch, 2005) 211, fn 636; K Ambos, *La Parte General del Derecho Penal Internacional: Bases para una Elaboración Dogmática* (Uruguay, Konrad- Adenauer-Stiftung, 2005) 75.

law,[35] military tribunals acting under Allied Control Council Law No 10 also embraced the unitary model.[36]

As a result, the application of any notion of criminal liability somewhat akin to joint criminal enterprise in Second World War related cases was made under the following premise: such notion constituted a theory of partnership in crime which gave rise to criminal liability that was not *per se* qualified as principal or accessorial. This approach is consistent with the fact that in those common law jurisdictions where the notion of joint criminal enterprise originated, participation in a joint criminal enterprise gives rise to principal liability if the accused physically commits the crime, and to accessorial liability if this is not the case – and this is applicable to both the foundational crimes of the enterprise and any foreseeable incidental crime committed in the execution of the common criminal plan.[37]

In 1999, the *Tadić* Case Appeals Judgment, after stating that the notion of joint criminal enterprise was included in article 7(1) of the ICTY Statute, addressed the following issue: whether joint criminal enterprise was part of any of the five modes of criminal liability explicitly referred to in article 7(1) of the ICTY Statute (planning, instigating, ordering, committing or aiding and abetting) or whether it constituted an additional mode of liability falling within the general scope of application of article 7(1) of the ICTY Statute.[38] As a result, the question arose as to the exact nature of the notion of joint criminal enterprise. In particular, whether it constituted a theory of (i) co-perpetration giving rise to principal liability (and thus falling under the heading 'committing' in article 7(1) of the ICTY Statute); (ii) accessorial or derivative liability; or (iii) partnership in crime or accomplice liability in a common law sense (which could give rise to principal or accessorial liability depending on the defendant's contribution and state of mind).

[35] Art II(2) of Allied Control Council Law No 10, which followed the provisions on the definition of the crimes, established that: 'Any person without regard to nationality or the capacity in which he acted, is deemed to have committed a crime as defined in paragraph 1 of this Article, if he was (a) a principal or (b) was an accessory to the commission of any such crime or ordered or abetted the same or (c) took a consenting part therein or (d) was connected with plans or enterprises involving its commission or (e) was a member of any organization or group connected with the commission of any such crime or (f) with reference to paragraph 1 (a) if he held a high political, civil or military (including General Staff) position in Germany or in one of its Allies, co-belligerents or satellites or held high position in the financial, industrial or economic life of any such country'.

[36] Werle, *Tratado* (above n 34) at 211, fn 636; Ambos, *La Parte General* (above n 34) at 75.

[37] As Gillies has pointed out, at 173, in common law jurisdictions 'pursuant to the doctrine of common purpose, a person becomes liable as an accessory to any crime committed by another person in that circumstance where the two of them are currently party to an agreement for the commission of this crime'; and hence this doctrine 'does not represent a substantive addition to, or supplanting of, the general principles of accessorial liability': P Gillies, *Criminal Law* 4th edn (North Ryde, LBC Information Services, 1997). According to Smith and Hogan, the main exception to this general approach is Australia where all participants in a joint criminal enterprise or all persons acting with a common criminal purpose are considered as principals. However, as Smith and Hogan have pointed out, this approach 'is contrary to all English authority'. See JC Smith and B Hogan, *Criminal Law* 11th edn (London, Butterworths, 2005) 169. See also K Hamdorf, 'The Concept of a Joint Criminal Enterprise and Domestic Modes of Liability for Parties to a Crime: A Comparison of German and English Law' (2007) 1 *Journal of International Criminal Justice* 208, 221–23; Van Sliedregt, 'Joint Criminal Enterprise' (above n 32) at 197.

[38] *Prosecutor v Dusko Tadić* (Judgment) ICTY-94-1-A (15 July 1999) para 220.

As Van Sliedregt has pointed out, the *Tadić* Case Appeals Judgment did not provide a clear answer to this question, as it simultaneously used the expressions 'accomplice liability'[39] and 'co-perpetration'[40] to refer to the notion of joint criminal enterprise.[41]

Only if the ICTY Appeals Chamber understood at the time it issued the *Tadić* Case Appeals Judgement that the notion of joint criminal enterprise constituted a theory of partnership in crime (or accomplice liability in a common law sense), would the simultaneous use of both expressions be consistent.[42] Such an interpretation would also be consistent with the application of any notion of criminal liability somewhat akin to joint criminal enterprise in Second World War related cases, and the nature of joint criminal enterprise in those common law jurisdictions where it originated. Moreover, one should keep in mind that, at the time the *Tadić* Case Appeals Judgement was issued, the ICTY case law had not yet clearly adopted a dualist system of criminal liability based on the distinction between principal and accessorial liability.

As a result, the ICTY Appeals Chamber Decision on Joint Criminal Enterprise of 21 May 2003 would constitute the first ICTY Appeals Chamber's decision stating unambiguously that under customary international law – as well as under article 7 of the ICTY Statute – there is a distinction between principal and accessorial liability and the notion of joint criminal enterprise is not a notion of partnership in crime (accomplice liability in a common law sense) insofar as it constitutes a notion of co-perpetration (principal liability) which falls under the heading 'committing' in article 7 (1) of the ICTY Statute.[43]

Subsequently, this approach has been followed by the ICTY case law in the *Krnojelac*,[44] *Vasiljevic*,[45] *Blaskic*,[46] *Krstic*,[47] *Kvocka*,[48] *Simic*,[49] *Brđanin*,[50] and

[39] ibid at para 192.

[40] ibid at para 220.

[41] Van Sliedregt, 'Joint Criminal Enterprise' (above n 32) at 189.

[42] The conclusions on the foundation of the notion of joint criminal enterprise reached at paras 64–66 of the Cassese, *Amicus Curiae* Brief (above n 10) appear to also support this interpretation. Indeed, even if the notion of joint criminal enterprise is understood as a general theory of partnership in crime, one has problem understanding how its existence is supported by notions as diverse as: (i) the doctrine of 'joint unlawful enterprise' and 'joint enterprise liability'; (ii) the doctrines on conspiracy and complicity in the United States; (iii) the notions of criminal association and complicity in countries such as France, Italy, Korea, Switzerland and the former Socialist Federal Republic of Yugoslavia; and (iv) the notions of co-perpetration and complicity in countries such as Belgium and Germany.

[43] *The Prosecutor v Milan Milutinovic, et al* (Decision on Dragoljub Ojdanic's Motion Challenging Jurisdiction – Joint Criminal Enterprise) ICTY-99-37-AR72 (21 May 2003) paras 20, 31.

[44] *Prosecutor v Milorad Krnojelac* (Judgment) ICTY-97-25-A (17 September 2003) paras 30, 73.

[45] *Prosecutor v Mitar Vasiljevic* (Judgment) ICTY-98-32-A (25 February 2004) paras 95, 102.

[46] *Prosecutor v Tihomir Blaskic* (Judgment) ICTY-95-14-A (29 July 2004) para 33.

[47] *Prosecutor v Radislav Krstic* (Judgment) ICTY-98-33-A (19 April 2004) paras 134, 137, 266–69.

[48] *Prosecutor v Kvocka, et al* (Judgment) ICTY-98-30/1-A (28 February 2005) at para 79.

[49] Implicitly in *Prosecutor v Blagoje Simic* (Judgment) ICTY-95-9-A (28 November 2006) para 243, fn 265.

[50] Implicitly in the *Prosecutor v Radoslav Brđanin* (Judgment) ICTY-99-36-A (3 April 2007) paras 431, 434, 444–50.

Krajišnik[51] Appeal Judgments. Likewise, the International Criminal Tribunal for Rwanda (ICTR) Appeals Chamber has also embraced this approach, in particular, in the *Ntakirutimana*,[52] *Gacumbitsi*[53] and *Nahimana*[54] cases. As a result, after the ICTY Appeals Chamber Decision on Joint Criminal Enterprise of 21 May 2003, *Ad hoc* Tribunals Appeals Chambers case law has embraced a subjective approach to the distinction between principal and accessorial liability based on the notion of joint criminal enterprise.

According to this approach, where crimes are committed by a plurality of persons acting together, the distinction between principals and accessories to the crimes is grounded in a subjective criterion consisting of the sharing of the common criminal purpose of the enterprise. Those who make relevant – in the sense of significant – contributions with the aim to have the core crimes of the enterprise committed are automatically principals to the crimes, regardless of the specific level of their contribution (notable, substantial, essential).[55] In turn, those others who carry out substantial, or even essential contributions with knowledge of the common criminal purpose but without sharing it, are not members of the joint criminal enterprise, and therefore can only be accessories to the crimes pursuant to other modes of liability provided for in articles 6 and 7 of the ICTR and ICTY Statutes (in particular aiding and abetting).[56]

The ICTY Appeals Chamber Decision on Joint Criminal Enterprise, and the subsequent *Ad hoc* Tribunals Appeals Chambers case law, have also upheld the customary status of the above-mentioned subjective criterion to distinguish between principal and accessorial liability and the configuration of the notion of joint criminal enterprise as a theory of co-perpetration.[57]

The author has explained in detail elsewhere why he cannot share this conclusion.[58] For the purpose of this chapter, it suffices to highlight that, since 2003, the *Ad hoc* Tribunals Appeals Chambers case law has exclusively relied in support of the said conclusion on the analysis made by the *Tadić* Case Appeals Judgement in 1999. In this regard, the ICTY Appeals Judgement in the *Martić* case (8 October 2008) on the matter has highlighted:

> With regard to the contention that JCE had no basis in international customary law at the time relevant to Martić's case, the Appeals Chamber recalls that it is well established in the Tribunal's jurisprudence that JCE existed in customary international law at the time relevant to the charges against Martić. In Tadić, the Appeals Chamber conducted a thorough analysis of pre-1991 international criminal case-law and concluded that 'the

[51] *Prosecutor v Momcilo Krajišnik* (Judgment) ICTY-00-39-A (17 March 2009) para 662.

[52] *Prosecutor v Elizaphan Ntakirutimana and Gerard Ntakirutimana* (Judgment) ICTR-96-10-A and ICTR-96-17-A (13 December 2004) para 462.

[53] *Sylvestre Gacumbitsi v The Prosecutor* (Judgment) ICTR-2001-64-A (7 July 2006) para 158.

[54] The Prosecutor v Ferdinand Nahimana, Jean-Bosco Barayagwiza, Hassan Ngeze (Judgment) ICTR-99-52-A (28 November 2007) para 478.

[55] *The Prosecutor v Milan Milutinovic, et al* (Decision on Dragoljub Ojdanic's Motion Challenging Jurisdiction – Joint Criminal Enterprise) ICTY-99-37-AR72 (21 May 2003) para 20.

[56] ibid.

[57] See above (nn 43–55).

[58] Olasolo, *Criminal Responsibility* (above n 8) at ch 2 VII.

> notion of common design as a form of accomplice liability is firmly established in customary international law'.[59]

Similarly, the latest relevant ICTY Appeals Judgement, issued on 17 March 2009 in the *Krajišnik* case, also dealt with the issue of the customary nature of joint criminal enterprise by referring to the findings in the *Tadić* Case Appeals Judgement.[60]

However, little support can be provided by this analysis in light of the fact that it was carried out at a time in which the *Ad hoc* Tribunals case law had not clearly adopted the distinction between principal and accessorial liability and understood the notion of joint criminal enterprise as a theory of partnership in crime or accomplice liability in a common law sense. In this regard, the author is of the view that article 25(3) of the ICC Statute is more in line with the treatment of the notion of joint criminal enterprise in Second World War related case law and in the *Tadić* Case Appeals Judgement, than the ICTY Appeals Chamber Decision on Joint Criminal Enterprise and the subsequent *Ad hoc* Tribunals Appeals Chamber case law.

Article 25(3) of the ICC Statute affirms the distinction between principal and accessorial liability[61] (just as the ICTY Appeals Chamber Decision on Joint Criminal Enterprise does). However, instead of altering the nature of the notion of joint criminal enterprise so as to portray it as a theory of co-perpetration and affirming the customary status of this new concept, the drafters of the ICC Statute:

1. Provided in paragraph 3(a) of article 25 of the ICC Statute for a material-objective criterion (the notion of control over the crime) to distinguish between principals and accessories to the crime.[62]
2. Included in paragraph 3(d) of article 25 of the ICC Statute a notion somewhat akin to that of joint criminal enterprise, with full respect for its traditional nature as a theory of partnership in crime or accomplice liability.[63]

[59] *Prosecutor v Milan Martić* (Judgment) ICTY-95-11-A (8 October 2008) para 80, citing *Prosecutor v Dusko Tadić* (Judgment) ICTY-94-1-A (15 July 1999) paras 194–220.

[60] *Prosecutor v Momcilo Krajišnik* (Judgment) ICTY-00-39-A (17 March 2009) paras 657–59.

[61] *Prosecutor v Thomas Lubanga Dyilo* (Decision concerning Pre-Trial Chamber's I Decision of 10 February 2006 and the Incorporation of Documents into the Record of the Case against Mr Thomas Lubanga Dyilo) ICC-01/04-01/06-8-Corr (24 February 2006) Annex I, para 78; *Prosecutor v Thomas Lubanga Dyilo* (Decision on the Confirmation of Charges) ICC-01/04-01/06-803-tEN (29 January 2007) para 320; *Prosecutor v Germain Katanga and Mathieu Ngudjolo Chui* (Decision on the Confirmation of Charges) ICC-01/04-01/07-717 (30 September 2008) paras 466, 467.

[62] *Prosecutor v Thomas Lubanga Dyilo* (Decision on the Confirmation of Charges) ICC-01/04-01/06-803-tEN (29 January 2007) paras 333–41; *Prosecutor v Germain Katanga and Mathieu Ngudjolo Chui* (Decision on the Confirmation of Charges) ICC-01/04-01/07-717 (30 September 2008) para 488(a), 520, 521; *Prosecutor v Jean-Pierre Bemba Gombo* (Decision on the Confirmation of Charges) ICC-01/05-01/08 (15 June 2009) paras 348, 350. See also, inter alia, JM Gómez Benítez, 'Elementos Comunes de los Crímenes contra la Humanidad en el Estatuto de la Corte Penal Internacional' (2002) 42 *Actualidad Penal* 1121; K Ambos, 'Article 25. Individual Criminal Responsibility' in O Triffterer (ed), *Commentary on the Rome Statute of the International Criminal Court* 2nd edn (Oxford, Munich, Hart Publishing and Verlag CH Beck, 2008); A Eser, 'Individual Criminal Responsibility' in A Cassese, P Gaeta, and JRWD Jones (eds), *The Rome Statute of the International Criminal Court: A Commentary* (Oxford, Oxford University Press, 2002) 791; Manacorda and Meloni, 'Joint Perpetration *versus* JCE' (above n 14) at 168–69.

[63] *Prosecutor v Thomas Lubanga Dyilo* (Decision on the Confirmation of Charges) ICC-01/04-01/06-803-tEN (29 January 2007) para 33; *Prosecutor v Germain Katanga and Mathieu Ngudjolo Chui* (Decision on the Confirmation of Charges) ICC-01/04-01/07-717 (30 September 2008) para 483.

As a result, whenever a crime is committed by a plurality of persons acting together in pursuance of a common criminal purpose, one will analyse whether the defendant is a principal to the crime in light of the different manifestations of the notion of control over the crime (direct perpetration, indirect perpetration, co-perpetration based on joint control or indirect co-perpetration).[64] In this regard, Ambos has underscored in his *Amicus Curiae Brief* that:

> If one construes JCE I as containing objective and subjective elements, in the sense of the functional control concept, it can be considered as a form of co-perpetration within the meaning of art 25 (3) (a) alt 2 ICC Statute and as such as a form of commission pursuant to art 7 (1) ICTY/art 6 (1) ICTR Statutes.[65]

If the defendant cannot be regarded as a principal to the crime pursuant to article 25(3)(a) of the ICC Statute, one will analyse whether he can be considered an accessory pursuant to: (i) the traditional notions of accessorial liability provided for in article 25(3)(b) and (c) of the ICC Statute (ordering, soliciting, inducing and aiding and abetting); or (ii) the theory of partnership in crime somewhat akin to the notion of joint criminal enterprise provided for in article 25(3)(d) of the ICC Statute.[66]

As a result, the main difference between article 25(3) of the ICC Statute on the one hand, and the analysis made in Second World War related case law and the *Tadić* Case Appeals Judgment on the other, appears to be the exclusion of the extended category of joint criminal enterprise.[67]

IV Extended Form of Joint Criminal Enterprise

The case law of the *Ad hoc* Tribunals has distinguished three variants of the notion of joint criminal enterprise, usually referred to as 'the basic form of JCE, the sys-

[64] *Prosecutor v Thomas Lubanga Dyilo* (Decision on the Confirmation of Charges) ICC-01/04-01/06-803-tEN (29 January 2007) paras 333–41; *Prosecutor v Germain Katanga and Mathieu Ngudjolo Chui* (Decision on the Confirmation of Charges) ICC-01/04-01/07-717 (30 September 2008) paras 488–93.

[65] K Ambos (*Prosecutor v Kaing Guek Eav, alias 'Duch' Case Amicus Curiae* Concerning Criminal Case File No 001/18-07-2007-ECCC/OCIJ (PTC 02)) 001/18-07-2007-ECCC/OCIJ (PTC 02)-D99-3-27 (27 October 2008) at 19.

[66] *Prosecutor v Thomas Lubanga Dyilo* (Decision on the Confirmation of Charges) ICC-01/04-01/06-803-tEN (29 January 2007) para 337; *Prosecutor v Germain Katanga and Mathieu Ngudjolo Chui* (Decision on the Confirmation of Charges) ICC-01/04-01/07-717 (30 September 2008) para 483. See also *Prosecutor v Dusko Tadić* (Judgment) ICTY-94-1-A (15 July 1999) paras 222–23, where it was held that that JCE is a 'substantially similar notion' to what is described in Art 25(3)(d) of the Rome Statute. See also Werle, *Tratado* (above n 34) at 212–13; A Cassese, 'The Proper Limits of Individual Responsibility under the Doctrine of Joint Criminal Enterprise' (2007) 5 *Journal of International Criminal Justice* 109. Nevertheless, in his more recent book, Cassese sees Art 25(3)(d) of the ICC Statute and joint criminal enterprise as two different notions (A Cassese, *International Criminal Law* 2nd edn (Oxford, Oxford University Press, 2008) 213).

[67] GP Fletcher and D Ohlin, 'Reclaiming Fundamental Principles of Criminal Law in the Darfur Case' (2005) 3 *Journal of International Criminal Justice* 539, 549.

temic form of JCE and the extended form of JCE'.[68] The basic and systemic forms of joint criminal enterprise are applicable to the so-called 'core crimes' of the enterprise, which are those that are an integral part of the common criminal plan because their commission is its ultimate goal or the means to achieve it.[69] The systemic form of joint criminal enterprise is a sub-category of the basic form, and is only applicable when the common criminal plan consists of setting up and/or furthering an organised system of ill-treatment (such as a concentration camp or a detention camp) to commit the crimes.[70]

The extended form of joint criminal enterprise is only applicable to the so-called 'foreseeable' crimes, that is to say, those crimes committed beyond the scope of the common criminal plan because they are not an integral part of it, but are nevertheless a natural and foreseeable consequence of its implementation.[71]

[68] *Prosecutor v Dusko Tadić* (Judgment) ICTY-94-1-A (15 July 1999) paras 227–28; *Prosecutor v Kvocka, et al* (Judgment) ICTY-98-30/1-A (28 February 2005) paras 79–83; *Prosecutor v Milorad Krnojelac* (Judgment) ICTY-97-25-A (17 September 2003) paras 83-84; *Prosecutor v Mitar Vasiljevic* (Judgment) ICTY-98-32-A (25 February 2004) para 96; *Prosecutor v Milomir Staki´c* (Judgment) ICTY-97-24-A (22 March 2006) para 64; *Prosecutor v Radoslav Brđanin* (Judgment) ICTY-99-36-A (3 April 2007) para 364; *Prosecutor v Milan Martić* (Judgment) ICTY-95-11-A (8 October 2008) paras 80–84; *Prosecutor v Momcilo Krajišnik* (Judgment) ICTY-00-39-A (17 March 2009) paras 167–69; *Prosecutor v Vlastimir Djordjevic* (Judgment) IT-05-87/1-T (23 February 2011) paras 1860, 1864; *Prosecutor v Gotovina, et al* (Judgment) IT-06-90-T (15 April 2011) para 1950; *Prosecutor v Elizaphan Ntakirutimana and Gerard Ntakirutimana* (Judgment) ICTR-96-10-A and ICTR-96-17-A (13 December 2004) para 463; *Sylvestre Gacumbitsi v The Prosecutor* (Judgment) ICTR-2001-64-A (7 July 2006) para 158; *Prosecutor v Kanyarukiga* (Judgment) ICTR-02-78-T (1 November 2010) para 623; *Prosecutor v Jean-Baptiste Gatete* (Judgment) ICTR-00-61-T (31 March 2011) para 576 . See also McGill University (*Prosecutor v Kaing Guek Eav, alias 'Duch' Amicus Curiae* Brief submitted by the Center for Human Rights and Legal Pluralism, McGill University Montreal (Quebec) Canada), 001/18-07-2007-ECCC/OCIJ (PTC 02)-D99-3-25 (27 October 2008) paras 15–24; Cassese, *Amicus Curiae* Brief (above n 10) paras 23–29; Ambos, *Amicus Curiae* Brief (above n 65) at 8–15. See also V Haan, 'The Development of the Concept of Joint Criminal Enterprise at the International Criminal Tribunal for the Former Yugoslavia' (2005) 5 *International Criminal Law Review* 167, 170; Manacorda and Meloni, 'Joint Perpetration *versus* JCE' (above n 14) at 162.

[69] *Prosecutor v Momcilo Krajišnik* (Judgment) ICTY-00-39-T (27 September 2006) para 1096; *Prosecutor v Momcilo Krajišnik* (Judgment) ICTY-00-39-A (17 March 2009) para 167.

[70] As *Prosecutor v Milorad Krnojelac* (Judgment) ICTY-97-25-T (15 March 2002) para 78 affirmed: 'The Trial Chamber is satisfied that the only basis for the distinction between these two categories made by the *Tadić* Appeals Chamber is the subject matter with which those cases dealt, namely concentration camps during World War II'. See also *Prosecutor v Dusko Tadić* (Judgment) ICTY-94-1-A (15 July 1999) paras 202, 203, 228; *Prosecutor v Milorad Krnojelac* (Judgment) ICTY-97-25-A (17 September 2003) para 89; *Prosecutor v Mitar Vasiljevic* (Judgment) ICTY-98-32-A (25 February 2004) para 98; *Prosecutor v Kvocka, et al* (Judgment) ICTY-98-30/1-A (28 February 2005) para 82; *Prosecutor v Momcilo Krajišnik* (Judgment) ICTY-00-39-T (27 September 2006) para 80; *Prosecutor v Popovic, et al* (Judgment) ICTY-05-88-T (10 June 2010) para 1021; *Prosecutor v Vlastimir Djordjevic* (Judgment) IT-05-87/1-T (23 February 2011) para 1864; *Prosecutor v Gotovina, et al* (Judgment) IT-06-90-T (15 April 2011) para 1951. See also Haan, 'The Development' (above n 68) at 170.

[71] Its application has been considered particularly apposite to cases in which the common criminal plan is to forcibly remove at gunpoint members of one ethnicity from their town, village or region (to effect 'ethnic cleansing') with the consequence that, in the course of doing so, one or more of the victims is shot and killed. While murder may not have been explicitly acknowledged to be part of the common plan, it was nevertheless foreseeable that the forcible removal of civilians at gunpoint could very well result in the deaths of one or more of those civilians. See in particular, *Prosecutor v Dusko Tadić* (Judgment) ICTY-94-1-A (15 July 1999) paras 204, 228; *Prosecutor v Mitar Vasiljevic* (Judgment) ICTY-98-32-A (25 February 2004) para 99. See also *Prosecutor v Mitar Vasiljevic* (Judgment) ICTY-98-32-A (25 February 2004) paras 220, 228; *Prosecutor v Milorad Krnojelac* (Judgment) ICTY-97-25-A (17 September 2003) para 32; *Prosecutor v Tihomir Blaskic* (Judgment) ICTY-95-14-A (29 July 2004)

There is no extended form of joint criminal enterprise without the existence of a basic or systemic form of joint criminal enterprise in which the defendant participates.[72] As a result, only if the defendant is found to be a co-perpetrator of the core crimes of a basic or systemic enterprise, can one proceed to analyse whether the defendant might also be a co-perpetrator of those other crimes which, despite falling outside the common criminal plan, are natural and foreseeable consequences of its implementation.

From a subjective perspective, the extended form of joint criminal enterprise requires the defendant to be aware that the commission of the foreseeable crimes is a possible consequence of the implementation of the common criminal plan, and to voluntarily take the risk by joining or continuing to participate in the enterprise.[73] As a result, it embraces an advertent recklessness standard because the defendant need not be aware that there is a 'likelihood' or a 'substantial likelihood' (high level of risk) that the foreseeable crimes will be committed as a result of implementing the common criminal plan. He needs only to be aware that the commission of the foreseeable crimes is just a 'possible consequence' (low level of risk) of effecting the common criminal plan.[74] Moreover, in spite of the fact that the defendant only needs to be aware of the existence of a low level of risk, he is not required to 'clearly or expressly' accept the commission of the foreseeable crimes. On the contrary, it is sufficient that he takes the risk by joining or continuing to participate in the joint criminal enterprise.[75] This marks a critical

para 33; *Prosecutor v Kvocka, et al (*Judgment) ICTY-98-30/1-A (28 February 2005) para 83; *Prosecutor v Milomir Stakić* (Judgment) ICTY-97-24-A (22 March 2006) para 65; *Prosecutor v Milan Martić* (Judgment) ICTY-95-11-A (8 October 2008) paras 83–84; *Prosecutor v Momcilo Krajišnik* (Judgment) ICTY-00-39-T (27 September 2006) para 81; *Prosecutor v Momcilo Krajišnik* (Judgment) ICTY-00-39-A (17 March 2009) paras 166–69; *Prosecutor v Vlastimir Djordjevic* (Judgment) IT-05-87/1-T (23 February 2011) para 1865; *Prosecutor v Gotovina, et al* (Judgment) IT-06-90-T (15 April 2011) para 1952. See also Haan, 'The Development' (above n 68) at 191–92.

[72] ibid.

[73] ibid.

[74] ibid.

[75] In this regard, the ICTY Appeals Judgment in *Prosecutor v Tihomir Blaskic* (Judgment) ICTY-95-14-A (29 July 2004) para 33, made the following comments on the subjective elements required by the extended form of joint criminal enterprise: 'In relation to the responsibility for a crime other than that which was part of the common design, the lower standard of foreseeability – that is, an awareness that such a crime was a possible consequence of the execution of the enterprise – was applied by the Appeals Chamber. However, the extended form of joint criminal enterprise is a situation where the actor already possesses the intent to participate and further the common criminal purpose of a group. Hence, criminal responsibility may be imposed upon an actor for a crime falling outside the originally contemplated enterprise, even where he only knew that the perpetration of such a crime was merely a possible consequence, rather than substantially likely to occur, and nevertheless participated in the enterprise'. The same clear language has been recently used in *Prosecutor v Ramush Haradinaj, et al* (Judgment) ICTY-04-84-T (3 April 2008) para 139: 'The objective element does not depend upon the accused's state of mind. This is the requirement that the resulting crime was a natural and foreseeable consequence of the JCE's execution. It is to be distinguished from the subjective state of mind, namely that the accused was aware that the resulting crime was a possible consequence of the execution of the JCE, and participated with that awareness'. This interpretation is supported by a number of authors, such as S Powles, 'Joint Criminal Enterprise: Criminal Liability by Prosecutorial Ingenuity and Judicial Creativity?' (2004) 2 *Journal of International Criminal Justice* 606, 609; Van der Wilt, 'Joint Criminal Enterprise' (above n 33) at 96; Ambos, *Amicus Curiae* Brief (above n 65) at 18.

distinction from the notion of *dolus eventualis* which, according to ICC PTC I, constitutes the lowest level of intention.[76]

Nevertheless, for some authors, the extended form of joint criminal enterprise could also be applied in situations in which the defendant is not aware that the commission of the foreseeable crimes is a possible consequence of the implementation of the common criminal plan.[77] As long as the defendant is, objectively, in a position to foresee that possibility, it is irrelevant whether he actually foresees it.[78] Accordingly, the extended form of joint criminal enterprise would be applicable as long as it can be shown that a 'man of reasonable prudence' in the same position as the defendant would predict that the commission of the foreseeable crimes is a possible consequence of the implementation of the common criminal plan.[79]

The adoption of this approach would amount to introduce a negligence standard insofar as the defendant would be convicted for breaching his duty to conduct himself with due diligence in analysing the possible consequences of the implementation of the common criminal plan prior to joining it.[80] Although its

[76] According to ICC PTC I, the cumulative reference to 'intent' and 'knowledge' in art 30 of the ICC Statute requires the existence of a volitional element on the part of the suspect. This would, inter alia, include 'situations in which the suspect (a) is aware of the risk that the objective elements of the crime may result from his actions or omissions, and (b) accepts such an outcome by reconciling himself or herself with it or consenting to it (also known as *dolus eventualis*)'. Moreover, according to ICC PTC I, in situations of *dolus eventualis* one can distinguish two types of scenarios: 'First, if the risk of bringing about the objective elements of the crime is substantial (that is, there is a risk of the substantial likelihood that "it will occur in the ordinary course of events") the fact that the suspect accepts the idea of bringing about the objective elements of the crime can be inferred from: (i) the awareness by the suspect of the substantial likelihood that his or her actions or omissions would result in the realisation of the objective elements of the crime; and (ii) the decision by the suspect to carry out his or her actions or omissions despite such awareness. Secondly, if the risk of bringing about the objective elements of the crime is low, the suspect must have clearly or expressly accepted the idea that such objective elements may results from his or her actions or omissions'. See *Prosecutor v Thomas Lubanga Dyilo* (Decision on the Confirmation of Charges) ICC-01/04-01/06-803-tEN (29 January 2007) paras 350–53. See also the concurring definition of *dolus eventualis* provided for in the *Prosecutor v Milomir Stakić* (Judgment) ICTY-97-24-T (31 July 2003) para 587.

ICC PTC I has also underscored in the *Lubanga* case that *dolus eventualis* and advertent recklessness are different notions insofar as (advertent) recklessness: '[r]equires only that the perpetrator be aware of the existence of a risk that the objective elements of the crime may result from his or her actions or omissions, but does not require that he or she reconcile himself or herself with the result. In so far as recklessness does not require the suspect to reconcile himself or herself with the causation of the objective elements of the crime as a result of his or her actions or omissions, it is not part of the concept of intention. According to Fletcher, 'Recklessness is a form of *culpa* – equivalent to what German Scholars call "conscious negligence". The problem of distinguishing "intention" and "recklessness" arises because in both cases the actor is aware that his conduct may generate a specific result'. (*Prosecutor v Thomas Lubanga Dyilo* (Decision on the Confirmation of Charges) ICC-01/04-01/06-803-tEN (29 January 2007) para 355, fn 438). See also GP Fletcher, *Rethinking Criminal Law* 2nd edn (Oxford, Oxford University Press, 2000) 443.

[77] Cassese, *Amicus Curiae* Brief (above n 10) paras 26–27.

[78] ibid.

[79] ibid.

[80] The standard proposed by the Cassese, *Amicus Curiae* Brief (above n 10) paras 26–27, does not even reach the level of inadvertent recklessness, which resembles to the civil law category of 'gross negligence', insofar as it is based on a 'man of reasonable prudence' or 'average man' standard. See the distinction between inadvertent recklessness (gross negligence) and mere negligence in *Prosecutor v Thomas Lubanga Dyilo* (Decision on the Confirmation of Charges) ICC-01/04-01/06-803-tEN (29 January 2007) para 358.

supporters justify it in light of the need to require particular care from those who enter into common criminal plans,[81] the case law of the *Ad hoc* Tribunals has consistently rejected the introduction of any negligence standard.[82]

According to the ICTY Appeals Chamber, the extended form of joint criminal enterprise is applicable to crimes whose definition requires a more stringent general subjective element, such as *dolus directus* in the first degree (specifically aiming at causing the objective elements of the crime), *dolus directus* in the second degree (acceptance of the occurrence of the objective elements of the crime as a necessary consequence of the achievement of one's main purpose) or even *dolus eventualis*.[83] It is also applicable to crimes, such as genocide, which in addition to the general subjective element, require an additional ulterior intent or *dolus specialis* (ie, the intent to destroy in whole or in part a national, ethnical, racial or religious group).[84] As a result, a defendant can be convicted for genocide pursuant

[81] The Cassese, *Amicus Curiae* Brief (above n 10) para 82, gives the following justification: '(i) With regard to the degree of culpability, though the necessary offender did not have the intention (*dolus directus*) to commit the unconcerted crime, he was part to a criminal enterprise to commit an agreed upon crime, and the extra-crime was rendered possible both by his participation in the criminal enterprise and by his failure to drop out, or to stop the crime, once he was able to foresee the extra crime. Thus, there was a causal link between the concerted crime, the secondary offender's mental attitude, and the extra crime perpetrated by the primary offender. [. . .] It is the JCE 1 that normally creates the platform for which the perpetrators are able to commit JCE 3 crimes. Particularly when one deals with government/officially sanctioned criminality at the JCE 1 level, this official support for the "first set of crimes" can open the door to the next set of crimes. This risk is heightened when one is involved with massive JCE's involving many people sharing a broad common purpose and implementing such common purpose by using the institutions under their control to commit the crimes (sometimes using the principal perpetrators)'.

[82] See, inter alia, *Prosecutor v Milomir Stakić* (Judgment) ICTY-97-24-T (31 July 2003) para 587; *Prosecutor v Stanislav Galic* (Judgment and Opinion) ICTY-98-29-T (5 December 2003) paras 54–55; *Prosecutor v Radoslav Brđanin* (Judgment) ICTY-99-36-T (1 September 2004) para 386; *Prosecutor v Naser Oric* (Judgment) ICTY-03-68-T (30 June 2006) para 348; *Prosecutor v Milan Marti* (Judgment) ICTY-95-11-T (12 June 2007) para 60. Moreover, in the context of command responsibility, the 'should have known' standard introduced by *Prosecutor v Tihomir Blaskic* (Judgment) ICTY-95-14-T (3 March 2000) para 332 has been systematically rejected by the Appeals Chambers of the *Ad hoc* Tribunals because, according to them, art 7(3) of the ICTY Statute and 6(3) of the ICTR Statute do not criminalise the superiors' mere lack of due diligence in complying with their duty to be informed of their subordinates' activities. See in this regard, *Prosecutor v Ignace Bagilishema* (Judgment) ICTR-95-1A-A (3 July 2002) paras 35–42; *Prosecutor v Zejnil Delalic, et al* (Judgment) ICTY-96-21-A (20 February 2001) para 241; *Prosecutor v Milorad Krnojelac* (Judgment) ICTY-97-25-A (17 September 2003) para 151; *Prosecutor v Tihomir Blaskic* (Judgment) ICTY-95-14-A (29 July 2004) para 62; *Prosecutor v Stanislav Galic* (Judgment) ICTY-98-29-A (30 November 2006) para 184; *Prosecutor v Enver Hadzihasanovic and Amir Kubura* (Judgment) ICTY-01-47-A (22 April 2008) paras 26–29; *Prosecutor v Naser Oric* (Judgment) ICTY-03-68-A (3 July 2008) 51; *Prosecutor v Pavle Strugar* (Judgment) ICTY-01-42-A (17 July 2008) para 297.

[83] In the *Stakić* case, the Defence argued on appeal that the notion of joint criminal enterprise could not be used to 'impermissibly enlarge' the general subjective element provided for in the definition of such crimes and that would constitute a violation of the principle of legality. The *Prosecutor v Milomir Stakić* (Judgment) ICTY-97-24-A (22 March 2006) paras 100–01, rejected the Defence claim by merely stating that, insofar as the notion of joint criminal enterprise does not violate the principle of legality because it has been found to be part of customary international law since 1992, its individual components (including the subjective element of the extended form of joint criminal enterprise) do not violate the legality principle either.

[84] See the explanation of the notion of ulterior intent given by Smith and Hogan, *Criminal Law* (above n 37) at 112–13. Particular attention must be paid not to confuse the common law notions of

to the extended form of joint criminal enterprise, even though he did not act with the requisite genocidal intent.[85]

The case law of the *Ad hoc* Tribunals has made no distinction concerning the nature of the three forms of joint criminal enterprise. As a result, after the ICTY Appeals Chamber Decision on Joint Criminal Enterprise of 21 May 2003, all three forms of joint criminal enterprise have been consistently considered theories of co-perpetration that give rise to principal liability. Nevertheless, as the *Amicus Curiae* Briefs presented by Ambos and McGill University in the ECCC Case 002 case have pointed out, this presents unique problems in relation to the extended form of joint criminal enterprise.[86]

In this regard, it is important to highlight that, under the notion of co-perpetration, an individual can be held criminally liable as a principal to a crime despite the fact that he has not carried out all the objective elements of the crime. This is only possible because he is attributed the actions or omissions of other individuals due to the fact that they all acted in a coordinated manner pursuant to a common plan and that they all shared the intention to have the relevant crime committed.[87]

'specific intent' (which refers to the general subjective element and its equivalent to the civil law notion of *dolus directus* in the first degree) and 'ulterior intent' (which refers to an additional subjective element consisting of a specific purpose that must motivate the commission of the crime and its equivalent to the civil law notion of *dolus specialis*). See also *Prosecutor v Popovic, et al* (Judgment) ICTY-05-88-T (10 June 2010) paras 808, 1031.

[85] *Prosecutor v Radoslav Brđanin* (Decision on Interlocutory Appeal) ICTY-99-36-A (19 March 2004) paras 5–10. This argument has been also recently upheld by Trial Chamber II in the *Popovic et al* case. Even though none of the defendants were found guilty of *committing* the Srebrenica genocide *based on the extended JCE*, it held: 'For third category JCE liability, the accused does not need to possess the requisite intent for the extended crime – the crime falling outside the common purpose. This also applies to specific intent crimes' (*Prosecutor v Popovic, et al* (Judgment) ICTY-05-88-T (10 June 2010) para 1031). At the ICTR, the *Prosecutor v Andre Rwamakuba* (Decision on Interlocutory Appeal Regarding Application of Joint Criminal Enterprise to the Crime of Genocide) ICTR-98-44-AR72.4 (22 October 2004) did not explicitly deal with the question of whether the extended form of joint criminal enterprise can be applied to genocide. On the contrary, it dealt with the general issue of whether 'international customary law supports the application of joint criminal enterprise to the crime of genocide', and, in its analysis, the ICTR Appeals Chamber did not distinguish between the basic, the systemic and the extended forms of joint criminal enterprise. Hence, by answering the question in the affirmative, the ICTR Appeals Chamber, at best, implicitly endorsed the conclusion reached by the ICTY Appeals Chamber in the *Brdanin* case, that the extended form of joint criminal enterprise is also applicable to genocide. See *Prosecutor v Andre Rwamakuba* (Decision on Interlocutory Appeal Regarding Application of Joint Criminal Enterprise to the Crime of Genocide) ICTR-98-44-AR72.4 (22 October 2004) paras 10, 14, 31.

[86] Ambos, *Amicus Curiae* Brief (above n 65) at 15–17; McGill, *Amicus Curiae* Brief (above n 68) at paras 42 *et seq*. See also generally the problems identified by A Zahar and G Sluiter, *International Criminal Law: A Critical Introduction* (Oxford, Oxford University Press, 2007) 221–57; M Boot, *Genocide, Crimes against Humanity and War Crimes: Nullum Crimen Sine Lege and Subject Matter Jurisdiction of the International Criminal Court* (Antwerpen, Intersentia, 2002) 288–304; Ohlin, 'Three Conceptual Problems' (above n 29) at 69 *et seq*; Van Sliedregt, 'Joint Criminal Enterprise' (above n 32) at 184 *et seq*. This has prompted some strong supporters of the notion of joint criminal enterprise to caution against its overbroad application. See Cassese, 'The Proper Limits' (above n 66) at 109.

[87] *Prosecutor v Thomas Lubanga Dyilo* (Decision on the Confirmation of Charges) ICC-01/04-01/06-803-tEN (29 January 2007) para 326; *Prosecutor v Germain Katanga and Mathieu Ngudjolo Chui* (Decision on the Confirmation of Charges) ICC-01/04-01/07-717 (30 September 2008) para 520.

The situation in an extended form of joint criminal enterprise is different because, in spite of the existence of a common criminal plan, the foreseeable crimes are not part of such plan, as they are only natural and foreseeable consequences of its implementation, and there is no shared intention among the members of the joint criminal enterprise to have the incidental crimes committed. All that is required is that the defendant himself (and nobody else) perceives the commission of the said crimes by one of the members of the joint criminal enterprise as a 'possible consequence' of implementing the common criminal plan. Whether the other members of the enterprise also foresee such possibility and jointly take the risk is irrelevant.

As a result, the defendant should not be attributed the actions or omissions of those other members of the enterprise who complete the objective elements of the foreseeable crimes. In this regard, Ambos has explained in his *Amicus Curiae* Brief that

> [t]he conflict of JCE III with the principle of culpability is obvious. If, according to JCE III, *all* members of a criminal enterprise incur criminal responsibility even for criminal acts by *some* members which have not been agreed upon by all members before the actual commission but are, nonetheless, attributed to all of them on the basis of foreseeability, the previous agreement or plan of the participants as the basis of reciprocal attribution and, thus, a general principle in the law of co-perpetration is abolished. The existence of causality between the initial agreement or plan and the criminal excess does not overcome the deficit of culpability.[88]

Portraying the extended form of joint criminal enterprise as a theory of co-perpetration that gives rise to principal liability, as the case law of the *Ad hoc* Tribunals has done since 2003, poses some additional problems if one intends to apply it to crimes whose definition requires a more stringent general subjective element, and crimes requiring an additional ulterior intent or *dolus specialis*.[89]

[88] Ambos, *Amicus Curiae* Brief (above n 65) at s I.5, p 16.

[89] In this regard, McGill, *Amicus Curiae* Brief (above n 68) at para 49, has highlighted: 'The lower standard of *mens rea* in JCE 3 is controversial because defendants are held liable for having specific intent to perpetrate the crime in question, when they may only have been reckless. JCE to specific-intent crimes lowers the *mens rea* standard in a way that conflicts with the additional mental requirements particular to those crimes. JCE tests the elasticity of intent as an element of criminal responsibility for the worst crimes. As a result, "extended" JCE makes it easier to convict secondary participants than perpetrators. On this basis, several domestic criminal systems including Germany, The Netherlands and Switzerland "rejected" extended JCE as a mode of participation. Even in jurisdictions where it is accepted, such as Canada, the US and the United Kingdom, the doctrine is highly criticized'.

Likewise, Ambos, *Amicus Curiae* Brief (above n 65) at s I.5, p 16, has underscored: '[t]he foreseeability standard is neither precise nor reliable. Quite ironically, one may say that the foreseeability standard applied in this way makes the punishability for the accused unforeseeable. For this very reason – the insecurity of the foreseeability standard – one cannot blame the member of the JCE for not having withdrawn from the criminal enterprise: how and why should he do so if he does not even foresee the criminal result with certainty? Ultimately, the doctrine introduces a form of strict liability with this standard. While this may just be the reason for the attractiveness of the doctrine for the prosecution, ie, the possibility of elegantly overcoming the typical evidentiary problems in international criminal law crime scenarios, especially where proof of direct participation is lacking, it turns out to be its main disadvantage from the defense perspective'.

In particular, in relation to the crime of genocide, Van Sliedregt has pointed out that, where the defendant does not act with a genocidal intent, but is aware of the possibility that some of the other participants in the enterprise may do it, he cannot be considered a principal (co-perpetrator) to the crime. More recently, the Special Tribunal for Lebanon Appeals Chamber also stated that 'the better approach under international criminal law is not to allow convictions under JCE III for special intent crimes like terrorism'.[90] It was held that a mode of accomplice liability would best describe the guilt of a person who foresees the possibility of such a crime being committed by another participant in the common plan and still willingly accepts that risk by continuing his participation in the enterprise.[91] As a result, only if the extended form of joint criminal enterprise is a theory of accessorial liability, can it be applicable to special intent crimes.[92]

In response to these concerns, those authors who support the development of the extended form of joint criminal enterprise as a theory of co-perpetration that gives rise to principal liability focus their discourse on 'policy arguments'. In this regard, Cassese has underscored in its *Amicus Curiae* Brief:

> As to the foundation as the very raison d'etre of JCE 3, it bears noting that this mode of responsibility is founded in considerations of public policy – the need to protect society against persons who band together to engage in criminal enterprises and who persist in their criminal conduct though they foresee that more serious crimes outside the common enterprise may be committed. [. . .] Finally, any fear of abuse in applying JCE liability is mitigated at the international level because (i) international trials are predicated on full respect of the rights of the accused; this entails that the defendant may bring elements to show that he could not possible foresee the extra crime (and he would thus not be culpable for it); (ii) international and hybrid tribunals, professional judges, capable of exercising care and prudence, determine whether the culpability of the offender is proved beyond a reasonable doubt.[93]

However, these policy arguments do not address any of the above-mentioned concerns based on the legality and culpability principles. Indeed, the relevance of these concerns is such, that the drafters of the ICC Statute excluded any form of criminal liability somewhat akin to the extended form of joint criminal enterprise from the realm of article 25(3)(d). This is the result of requiring under this

[90] Decision on the Applicable Law: Terrorism, Conspiracy, Homicide, Perpetration, Cumulative Charging (Decision) STL-11-01/1 (16 February 2011) para 249.

[91] ibid.

[92] Van Sliedregt, 'Joint Criminal Enterprise' (above n 32) at 281–85. In order to justify the application of the extended form of joint criminal enterprise to genocide, Van Sliedriegt has affirmed that it is a theory of accessorial liability to which the principles of derivative liability apply. She reaches her conclusion in light of the following two premises: (i) the notion of joint criminal enterprise as elaborated by the case law of the *Ad hoc* Tribunals is rooted in the common purpose doctrine applied in common law jurisdictions and in post Second World War cases; and (ii) common law jurisdictions and post Second World War cases have never regarded the common purpose doctrine as a theory of co-perpetration giving rise to principal liability; quite the contrary, they considered it as a theory of partnership in crime of accomplice liability. See ibid at 201–05. See also McGill, *Amicus Curiae* Brief (above n 68) paras 50–51; Ambos, *Amicus Curiae* Brief (above n 65) at s I.5, pp 17–18.

[93] Cassese, *Amicus Curiae* Brief (above n 10) paras 82–83.

provision that the relevant contribution be carried out, at the very least, 'in the knowledge of the intention of the group to commit the crime'.[94] As a consequence, no criminal liability arises under article 25(3)(d) of the ICC Statute in relation to those crimes which are not intended by the group, and are only a possible consequence of effecting the group's common plan.[95] Remarkably, this exclusion was made despite the fact that article 25(3)(d) of the ICC Statute only includes a 'residual form of accessorial liability' (as opposed to a theory of co-perpetration or of principal liability).[96]

V Conclusion

The nature and customary status of the notion of joint criminal enterprise in international criminal law is far from settled.

To a very important extent, this situation has contributed to the fact that the overall notion of joint criminal enterprise, which was originally conceived as a notion of partnership in crime or accomplice liability in a common law sense, has been turned into a theory of co-perpetration by the case law of the *Ad hoc* Tribunals since 2003. As a result, the situation existing in 1998, when the ICC Statute was approved, has been considerably altered, and the dichotomy between the ICC case law and the *Ad hoc* Tribunals case law is today manifest.

Moreover, several insurmountable problems arise from the fact that, since 2003, the case law of the *Ad hoc* Tribunals has portrayed the extended form of joint criminal enterprise as a theory of co-perpetration, and has upheld its application to crimes whose definition requires a more stringent general subjective element, as well as to ulterior intent or *dolus specialis* crimes.

[94] Concurring, Fletcher and Ohlin, 'Reclaiming Fundamental Principles' (above n 67) at 549.

[95] ibid.

[96] *Prosecutor v Thomas Lubanga Dyilo* (Decision on the Confirmation of Charges) ICC-01/04-01/06-803-tEN (29 January 2007) para 337; *Prosecutor v Germain Katanga and Mathieu Ngudjolo Chui* (Decision on the Confirmation of Charges) ICC-01/04-01/07-717 (30 September 2008) para 483. See also Werle, *Tratado* (above n 34) at 212–13.

8

Victims' Participation According to the Jurisprudence of the International Criminal Court*

I Introduction

The role conferred on victims pursuant to the Rome Statute of the International Criminal Court (ICC Statute) is unprecedented in international jurisdictions.[1] Literature has gone so far as to consider the role of these 'participants' in criminal proceedings as one of the most significant features of the ICC Statute.[2] During the negotiation of the Statute, the idea of victim participation was welcomed because of the trend in international human rights law and international humanitarian law towards increasing the role of victims.[3] The broad jurisprudence developed in

* Written with Alejandro Kiss (PhD and LLM, Westfälische Wilhelms Universität zu Münster. Legal Officer, Chambers ICC. Former Legal Advisor to Argentina's Attorney-General and former scientific assistant at the Institute for Criminal Law, Münster University). The present chapter is a revised and updated version of the piece entitled 'Role of Victims in Proceedings before the International Criminal Court' published in 2010 81(1) *Revue Internationale de Droit Pénal* 125–63. The authors thank the *Revue Internationale de Droit Pénal* for authorising printing of the present revised and updated version of the 2010 work. The views expressed herein are those of the authors alone and do not necessarily reflect the views of the ICC, the ICTY, the United Nations in general or the Spanish Government.

[1] G Bitti and H Friman, 'Participation of Victims in the Proceedings' in R Lee (ed), *The International Criminal Court, Elements of Crimes and Rules of Procedure and Evidence* (Ardsley, Transnational Publishers, 2001) 456, 471.

[2] See in this regard, SA Fernández de Gurmendi, 'Definition of Victims and General Principles' in R Lee (ed), *The International Criminal Court, Elements of Crimes and Rules of Procedure and Evidence* (Ardsley, Transnational Publishers, 2001); H Brady, 'Protective and Special Measures for Victims and Witnesses' in R Lee (ed), ibid; Bitti and Friman, 'Participation of Victims' (above n 1) at 459 *et seq*; JRWD Jones, 'Protection of Victims and Witnesses' in A Cassese, P Gaeta and JRWD Jones (eds), *The Rome Statute of the International Criminal Court: A Commentary* (Oxford, Oxford University Press, 2002) 1357 *et seq*; C Jorda and J De Hemptinne, 'The Status and Role of the Victim' in A Cassese, P Gaeta and JRWD Jones (eds), ibid, 1390 *et seq*; D Donat-Cattin, 'Article 68: Protection of Victims and Witnesses and their Participation in the Proceedings' in O Triffterer (ed), *Commentary on the Rome Statute of the International Criminal Court* 2nd edn (Oxford, Munich, Hart Publishing and Verlag CH Beck, 2008); C Stahn, H Olasolo and K Gibson, 'Participation of Victims in Pre-Trial Proceedings of the ICC' (2006) 4 *Journal of International Criminal Justice* 218, 219.

[3] WA Schabas, *An Introduction to the International Criminal Court* (Cambridge, Cambridge University Press, 2004) 172; Jorda and De Hemptinne, 'The Status and Role of the Victim' (above n 2) at 1389. See United Nations Commission on Human Rights (UNCHR), 'Basic Principles and Guidelines on the Right to a Remedy and Reparation for Victims of Violations of International Human Rights and

the context of the situations and the cases under the jurisdiction of the International Criminal Court (ICC) has established the basic aspects regarding the two most fundamental questions arising out of the participation of the victims at the ICC: *who* can become a participating victim and *what* can those victims procedurally carry out?

This chapter cannot deal with the axiological justification of conferring on victims procedural rights in criminal proceedings. It is broadly acknowledged that the prosecution is the organ primarily responsible for, and tasked with, ensuring that the interest of the society is protected. In addition, it is largely acknowledged that the interests of victims often differ from the interests of the Prosecution.[4] This discussion is not at all new and far less confined to international criminal law. To the contrary, it is well understood in debates about the history and justification of criminal sanctions that state punishment is meant to substitute its predecessor, private retaliation, and that the history of criminal law and criminal sanctions reflects the struggle to counteract private retaliation.[5]

Recent developments, especially in national jurisdictions, indicate that the dissatisfaction of victims has led to significant instances of penal power being 'returned' to victims (who originally delegated that power to the states 'in an effort to obtain peace') to offset states' inaction or insufficient action. Thus, the procedural standing of victims has been conceived as a tool to overcome state's inaction.[6]

However, these ideas cannot be transplanted into international criminal law without further analysis. States' inactivity is one of the enduring reasons advanced in support of the establishment of the ICC. The claim that the most serious crimes must not go unpunished has supported the delegation of one of the most fundamental components of state sovereignty to an international criminal court: the capacity to decide on the exercise (or non-exercise) of criminal prosecution.

Given that the establishment of the ICC was meant to ensure victims' protection in spite of potential inaction by the relevant states, was it reasonable to further confer on victims a procedural standing in the proceedings before the ICC? This question can be answered only with the benefit of hindsight, on scrutiny of what victims 'obtained' by exercising their participation rights. Although it may

Humanitarian Law' in UNCHR, 'Civil and Political Rights, including the Questions of Independence of the Judiciary, Administration of Justice, Impunity: The Right to Restitution, Compensation and Rehabilitation for Victims of Gross Violations of Human Rights and Fundamental Freedoms (Final Report of the Special Rapporteur Mr M Cherif Bassiouni submitted in accordance with Commission Resolution 1999/33)' (18 January 2000) UN Doc E/CN.4/2000/62, principle 12. See also MC Bassiouni, 'Proposed Guiding Principles for Combating Impunity for International Crimes' in MC Bassiouni (ed), *Post-Conflict Justice* (Ardsley, Transnational Publishers, 2002) 155.

[4] Schabas, *An Introduction* (above n 3) at 172–73; L Scomparain, 'Le Victime du Crime et la Jurisdiction Pénale Internationale' in M Delmas-Marty and A Cassese (eds), *Crimes Internationaux et Jurisdictions Internationales* (Paris, PUF, 2002) 335, underscores the symbolic dimension of victims' participation. See also Jorda and De Hemptinne, 'The Status and Role of the Victim' (above n 2) at 1388, 1394.

[5] L Ferrajoli, 'El derecho penal minimo' in JB Ramírez (ed), *Prevención y Teoría de la Pena* (Santiago, Editorial Jurídica Conosur Ltda, 1995) 37.

[6] That same inaction of states prompted the establishment of the International Criminal Court.

be too early for eliciting general conclusions, recent ICC decisions indicate a trend in this respect.

This aspect will be discussed after an analysis of the already abundant body of ICC case law in relation to *who* can become a participating victim, focusing on matters that have attracted special attention, such as: (i) whether deceased persons are included within the notion of natural persons; (ii) the necessary link between the victims and the charges; (iii) the relevant forms of victims' 'harm'; (iv) the distinction between 'direct' and 'indirect' victims; (v) the distinction between victims of the situation and victims of the case; and (vi) the reassessment of decisions by Pre-Trial Chambers (PTCs) on victims' status by Trial Chambers (TCs).

In relation to discussion of who can become a participating victim, this chapter focuses on *what* those victims procedurally can perform, with particular attention to: (i) the systematic versus the casuistic approach to the determination of the role of victims; (ii) the role of victims in the stage of investigation of a situation; (iii) the role of victims in the pre-trial proceedings; (iv) the role of victims in the trial; and (v) the role of victims in the recharacterisation of facts.

II *Who* can become a Participating Victim?

A definition of the notion of victim cannot be found in the ICC Statute but rather in rule 85 of the ICC Rules of Procedure and Evidence (RPE), which states as follows:

> For the purposes of the Statute and the Rules of Procedure and Evidence:
>
> (a) 'Victims' means natural persons who have suffered harm as a result of the commission of any crime within the jurisdiction of the Court;
> (b) Victims may include organizations or institutions that have sustained direct harm to any of their property which is dedicated to religion, education, art or science or charitable purposes, and to their historic monuments, hospitals and other places and objects for humanitarian purposes.

Several aspects of this definition have been interpreted by different Chambers of the Court. Their interpretations contain a number of common elements. First, the expression 'natural persons' has been considered as referring to human beings,[7] although it has been controversial whether a deceased person could participate in the proceedings through representatives. Secondly, the expression

[7] *Situation in the Democratic Republic of the Congo* (DRC) (Decision on the Applications for Participation in the Proceedings of VPRS 1, VPRS 2, VPRS 3, VPRS 4, VPRS 5 and VPRS 6) ICC-01/04-101-tEN-Corr (17 January 2006) para 80. See also *Situation in Uganda* (Decision on victims' applications for participation a/0010/06, a/0064/06 to a/0070/06, a/0081/06 to a/0104/06 and a/0111/06 to a/0127/06) ICC-02/04-101 (10 August 2007) para 105; *Prosecutor v Thomas Lubanga Dyilo* (Decision on victims' participation) ICC-01/04-01/06-1119 (18 January 2008) para 87.

'organizations or institutions' has been interpreted to include legal persons.[8] Thirdly, the notion of 'harm' has been interpreted as including physical harm, psychological harm, and material harm.[9] Fourthly, a causality link between the alleged harm and the commission of a crime within the jurisdiction of the Court has been consistently required.[10]

There are, however, certain aspects of the definition of victim provided for in rule 85 of the RPE that have been interpreted differently by ICC Chambers.

A Deceased Persons as Victims

According to rule 85, victims are 'natural persons' who have suffered harm. In view of the crimes under the jurisdictions of the Court, it is unsurprising that the Chambers were presented with applications for participation sent on behalf of deceased persons, who have died as a result of one of those crimes. The relevant provision of the RPE reads as follows:

> Rule 89(3) – An application referred to in this rule may also be made by a person acting with the consent of the victim, or a person acting on behalf of a victim, in the case of a victim who is a child or, when necessary, a victim who is disabled.

The jurisprudence has not been unanimous as to how to treat these applications. Pre-Trial Chamber I (PTC I) held that '[d]eceased persons do not fall within the meaning of "natural persons" under Rule 85(a) of the Rules'[11] and that '[a]pplications made on behalf of deceased persons will, in principle, be rejected'.[12] If an applicant alleges moral harm resulting from the death of his or her relatives,

[8] *Situation in the Democratic Republic of the Congo* (Décision sur les demandes de participation à la procédure déposées dans le cadre de l'enquête en République démocratique du Congo par a/0004/06 à a/0009/06, a/0016/06 à a/0063/06, a/0071/06 à a/0080/06 et a/0105/06 à a/0110/06, a/0188/06, a/0128/06 à a/0162/06, a/0199/06, a/0203/06, a/0209/06, a/0214/06, a/0220/06 à a/0222/06, a/0224/06, a/0227/06 à a/0230/06, a/0234/06 à a/0236/06, a/0240/06, a/0225/06, a/0226/06, a/0231/06 à a/0233/06, a/0237/06 à a/0239/06 et a/0241/06 à a/0250/06) ICC-01/04-423 (24 Dec 2007) paras 137–42. See also *Prosecutor v Thomas Lubanga Dyilo* (Decision on victims' participation) ICC-01/04-01/06-1119 (18 January 2008) para 87. A 'school' has been granted victim status as a legal person in the Decision on the applications by victims to participate in the proceedings, *Prosecutor v Thomas Lubanga Dyilo* (Annex 1 Decision on the applications by victims to participate in the proceedings) ICC-01/04-01/06-1556-Corr-Anx1 (15 December 2008) paras 105, 110–11.

[9] See subsection II.C below.

[10] *Situation in the Democratic Republic of the Congo* (Decision on the Applications for Participation in the Proceedings of VPRS 1, VPRS 2, VPRS 3, VPRS 4, VPRS 5 and VPRS 6) ICC-01/04-101-tEN-Corr (17 January 2006) paras 94, 115–17; *Situation in Uganda* (Decision on victims' applications for participation a/0010/06, a/0064/06 to a/0070/06, a/0081/06 to a/0104/06 and a/0111/06 to a/0127/06) ICC-02/04-101 (10 August 2007) para 12; *Prosecutor v Thomas Lubanga Dyilo* (Decision on victims' participation) ICC-01/04-01/06-1119 (18 January 2008) paras 90, 91.

[11] *Situation in Darfur, Sudan* (Corrigendum to Decision on the Applications for Participation in the Proceedings of Applicants a/0011/06 to a/0015/06, a/0021/07, a/0023/07 to a/0033/07 and a/0035/07 to a/0038/07) ICC-02/05-111-Corr (14 December 2007) para 36.

[12] *Prosecutor v Germain Katanga and Mathieu Ngudjolo Chui* (Public Redacted Version of the 'Decision on 97 Applications for Participation at the Pre-Trial Stage of the Case') ICC-01/04-01/07-579 (10 June 2008) para 63.

PTC I will analyse whether the applicant himself, as opposed to his deceased relatives, can be granted the procedural status of victim.

Pre-Trial Chamber III (PTC III) adopted a different position. In deciding that deceased persons can participate in the proceedings it has advanced that it is 'self-evident' and in conformity with 'internationally recognized human rights and related jurisprudence' that a victim does not cease to be a victim because of his or her death. Although the individual cannot personally participate in the proceedings (because he is deceased), his rights can be represented by his successors.[13] The Chamber highlighted that jurisprudence of the Inter-American Court of Human Rights indicates that the right to 'compensation' is transmitted to heirs by succession. Accordingly, it is argued, deceased victims' participation embodies an interpretation that accords to human rights standards (article 21(3)). The Chamber elicited from this finding that it is appropriate that those successors participate (in criminal proceedings, to prove that the accused is guilty) in order to safeguard potential reparations in the future.

Article 21(3), which holds that the application and interpretation of law must be consistent with internationally recognised human rights, has played a significant role in this discussion. PTC I appears to have answered in the negative the question as to whether participation 'on behalf of a deceased person' is a possible 'interpretation' of the ICC law given that, as set out above, it has maintained that no provision allows for applications to be made on behalf of deceased persons. Rule 89(3) authorises the submission of applications on behalf of others provided that those applications are made either on behalf of 'children' and 'disabled people' or with the consent of the victim.

In turn, the jurisprudence of the Trial Chambers so far is receptive to participation of deceased individuals in the specific situation of individuals deceased after having had submitted an application to the ICC. TC II concluded that the right to participate by individuals who passed away after having had personally submitted an application to the ICC can be taken over by their close relatives.[14]

The aforementioned jurisprudence of TC II could be said to correspond with the literal scope of rule 89(3) if it is assumed that, once an application for participation is filed by an individual claiming harm, or by a close relative with the consent of the said individual, it can be inferred that such individual consented to *post mortem* participation. According to such an understanding, rule 89(3) deals with two different case scenarios. First, an application may be made by a person acting with the consent of the victim. Secondly, an application may be made by a person acting on behalf of a child or a disabled person. This interpretation properly acknowledges the fact that children and (some) disabled persons cannot legally

[13] *Prosecutor v Jean-Pierre Bemba Gombo* (Fourth Decision on Victims' Participation) ICC-01/05-01/08-320 (12 December 2008) paras 39–52.

[14] *Prosecutor v Germain Katanga and Mathieu Ngudjolo Chui* (Decision on the treatment of applications for participation) ICC-01/04-01/07-933-tENG (26 February 2009) paras 40–42; *Prosecutor v Germain Katanga and Mathieu Ngudjolo Chui* (Motifs de la deuxième décision relative aux demandes de participation de victimes à la procedure) ICC-01/04-01/07-1737 (22 December 2009) paras 30–32.

'consent' to someone acting on their behalf in ICC proceedings. However, the limitation to 'children and disabled' provided for in the second case scenario does not apply to persons acting with the consent of the victim.

As a result, participation by a person 'acting on behalf' of a child or disabled person does not require those individuals' consent, whereas participation by someone acting 'with the consent' of the victim is not limited to children and disabled persons and can therefore support the participation by deceased individuals provided they had consented to such participation before passing away. In this last scenario, the relevant Chamber must be convinced that the deceased victims consented to *post mortem* participation.

B Victims Unrelated to the Charges

Pursuant to rule 85, victims are those who suffered harm as a result of 'any crime within the jurisdiction of the Court'. The majority of the judges of TC I, in a decision issued on 18 January 2008,[15] highlighted that rule 85 only requires that the alleged harm be the result, generally, 'of any crime within the jurisdiction of the Court' and thus it is not required that there is a link between the crimes alleged against the defendant and the harm suffered by those who apply for participation as victims.

Conceptually, this means that those providing sufficient evidence to show prima facie that they have been, for instance, harmed as a result of a crime against humanity allegedly committed in the territory of Colombia in 2003, could be recognised as victims in the proceedings relating to the situations in Democratic Republic of the Congo (DRC), Uganda, the Central African Republic and Darfur, as well as in the proceedings relating to, for instance, the case against Omar Al Bashir. Certainly, this does not mean that the Chamber attributed participatory rights to victims under that broad category. As will be further explained below, in order for victims to exercise any procedural right in a particular proceeding they would have to demonstrate that their personal interests may be engaged by those proceedings.[16] Hence, in TC I's jurisprudence, the potential number of participating victims would only be limited 'operatively', though not 'conceptually'.[17]

[15] *Prosecutor v Thomas Lubanga Dyilo* (Decision on victims' participation) ICC-01/04-01/06-1119 (18 January 2008) paras 93–95.

[16] ibid at para 86.

[17] Trial Chamber I, after defining the concept of victim in this broad manner, elaborates on the criteria to limit the material number of participating victims: 'However, self-evidently, it would not be meaningful or in the interests of justice for all such victims to be permitted to participate as victims in the case against Mr Thomas Lubanga Dyilo, given that the evidence and the issues falling for the examination of the case (which will be dependent on the charges he faces) will frequently be wholly unrelated to the crimes that caused harm to victims coming from this very wide category'. See ibid at para 95. As a result, out of the broad group of natural and legal persons that, according to Trial Chamber I, could potentially be recognised as victims of the case against Thomas Lubanga Dyilo, only those that have a connection with the evidence introduced by the parties or with the issues to be discussed during the trial could actually participate in such trial proceedings of the said case.

Even though the number of victims who participate effectively in the proceedings would not increase dramatically as a result of the aforementioned TC I jurisprudence, the Chamber, as outlined in the Dissenting Opinion to the decision of 18 January 2008, would be undertaking assessments outside the strict mandate of the charges brought against the accused in reviewing applications filed by this expanded pool of victims.[18] As pointed out in articles discussing this decision, the Chamber would be acting ultra vires.[19] Those determinations could include, for instance, that the Chamber finds that crimes under the jurisdiction of the Court have been prima facie committed in Colombia, Georgia or anywhere else with the sole requirement that someone sends a victim application to the Chamber.

PTC I has interpreted rule 85 in a different manner. According to PTC I, this rule provides for a definition of victim that can be applied to different stages of ICC proceedings.[20] In the view of PTC I, the group of natural and legal persons that can be granted victim status at a given stage of ICC proceedings is defined by the specific object of such a stage of the ICC proceedings. This leads to the distinction between 'victims of the situation' and 'victims of a case'.[21]

According to this distinction, in those proceedings conducted in relation to the investigations into the DRC, Uganda, Central African Republic and Darfur situations, victim status can only be granted to those natural and legal persons that show prima facie to have suffered harm as a result of a crime within the subject matter jurisdiction of the Court allegedly committed within the temporal, territorial and personal parameters that define the relevant situation.[22] As explained below, according to the jurisprudence of the Appeals Chamber, the participation of victims during the situation is narrowed to specific procedural acts.

[18] ibid at Judge Blattmann's Separate and Dissenting Opinion, para 11.

[19] H Friman, 'The International Criminal Court and Participation of Victims: A Third Party to the Proceedings?' (2009) 22 *Leiden Journal of International Law* 485, 491.

[20] *Situation in the Democratic Republic of the Congo* (Decision on the Applications for Participation in the Proceedings of VPRS 1, VPRS 2, VPRS 3, VPRS 4, VPRS 5 and VPRS 6) ICC-01/04-101-tEN-Corr (17 January 2006) para 65. *Situation in Uganda* (Decision on victims' applications for participation a/0010/06, a/0064/06 to a/0070/06, a/0081/06 to a/0104/06 and a/0111/06 to a/0127/06) ICC-02/04-101 (10 August 2007) paras 83–88. See also H Olasolo, *The Triggering Procedure of the International Criminal Court* (Leiden, Martinus Nijhoff Publishers, 2005).

[21] *Situation in the Democratic Republic of the Congo* (Decision on the Applications for Participation in the Proceedings of VPRS 1, VPRS 2, VPRS 3, VPRS 4, VPRS 5 and VPRS 6) ICC-01/04-101-tEN-Corr (17 January 2006) paras 65, 66; *Situation in Uganda* (Decision on victims' applications for participation a/0010/06, a/0064/06 to a/0070/06, a/0081/06 to a/0104/06 and a/0111/06 to a/0127/06) ICC-02/04-101 (10 August 2007) para 9. See also Olasolo, *Triggering Procedure* (above n 20) at 109.

[22] *Situation in Darfur, Sudan* (Corrigendum to Decision on the Applications for Participation in the Proceedings of Applicants a/0011/06 to a/0015/06, a/0021/07, a/0023/07 to a/0033/07 and a/0035/07 to a/0038/07) ICC-02/05-111-Corr (14 December 2007) para 49; *Situation in the Democratic Republic of the Congo* (Decision on the Applications for Participation in the Proceedings of VPRS 1, VPRS 2, VPRS 3, VPRS 4, VPRS 5 and VPRS 6) ICC-01/04-101-tEN-Corr (17 January 2006) para 68; *Situation in the Democratic Republic of the Congo* (Décision sur les demandes de participation à la procédure déposées dans le cadre de l'enquête en République démocratique du Congo par a/0004/06 à a/0009/06, a/0016/06 à a/0063/06, a/0071/06 à a/0080/06 et a/0105/06 à a/0110/06, a/0188/06, a/0128/06 à a/0162/06, a/0199/06, a/0203/06, a/0209/06, a/0214/06, a/0220/06 à a/0222/06, a/0224/06, a/0227/06 à a/0230/06, a/0234/06 à a/0236/06, a/0240/06, a/0225/06, a/0226/06, a/0231/06 à a/0233/06, a/0237/06 à a/0239/06 et a/0241/06 à a/0250/06) ICC-01/04-423 (24 December 2007) paras 4–5.

In turn, once, as a result of such investigations, a case arises through the issuance of a warrant of arrest or a summons to appear, victim status can only be granted to those natural and legal persons that show prima facie that they have suffered harm as a result of a crime included in the relevant arrest warrant or summons to appear (and, subsequently, the *charging document*).[23]

The Appeals Chamber, in its 11 July 2008 Decision, rejected the position adopted by the majority of the judges of TC I. In doing so, as discussed in the minority opinion attached to TC I's decision,[24] it has highlighted that the victims of a case are only those who can show prima facie that they have suffered harm as a result of a crime which is part of the charges in the relevant case.[25]

C Forms of Harm

One of the constituent elements in the definition of victims, included in rule 85, is that they have to have suffered 'harm'. The notion of harm is not defined in the statutory framework. There have been discussions within the jurisprudence as to the sources of interpretation for, and the definition of, the notion of 'harm'.

In particular, it has been argued that the United Nations (UN) Basic Principles and Guidelines on the Right to Remedy and Reparation for Victims of Gross Violations of International Humanitarian Law (UN Basic Principles) provide a legitimate source of interpretation. The Principles were adopted by the United Nations General Assembly, resolution 60/147, on 16 December 2005. Principle 8 reads as follows:

> 8. For purposes of the present document, victims are persons who individually or collectively suffered harm, including physical or mental injury, emotional suffering, economic loss or substantial impairment of their fundamental rights, through acts or omissions that constitute gross violations of international human rights law, or serious violations of international humanitarian law. Where appropriate, and in accordance

[23] It is for this reason that Pre-Trial Chamber I has only granted victim status in the pre-trial stage of the case of *Prosecutor v Germain Katanga and Mathieu Ngudjolo Chui* to those who could show prima facie to have suffered a harm as a result of the commission of any of the crimes included (i) in the arrest warrants issued on 2 and 6 July 2007 against Germain Katanga and Mathieu Ngudjolo Chui; and subsequently (ii) in the charging document filed by the Prosecution on 29 February 2008 – that is to say, those who could show prima facie to have been victimised during the joint attack carried out by *Front des Nationalistes et Intégrationnistes* (FNI) and the *Force de Résistance Patriotique en Ituri* (FRPI) against the village of Bogoro on 24 February 2003. See *Prosecutor v Germain Katanga and Mathieu Ngudjolo Chui* (Decision on the Applications for Participation in the Proceedings of Applicants a/0327/07 to a/0337/07 and a/0001/08) ICC-01/04-01/07-357 (2 April 2008). Pre-Trial Chamber I has followed the same approach in the case of *The Prosecutor v Thomas Lubanga Dyilo* (see *Prosecutor v Thomas Lubanga Dyilo* (Decision on the Applications for Participation in the Proceedings of a/0001/06, a/0002/06 and a/0003/06 in the case of the Prosecutor v Thomas Lubanga Dyilo and the investigation in the Democratic Republic of the Congo) ICC-01/04-01/06-228-tEN (28 July 2006)).

[24] *Prosecutor v Thomas Lubanga Dyilo* (Decision on victims' participation) ICC-01/04-01/06-1119 (18 January 2008) Judge Blattmann's Separate and Dissenting Opinion, para 7.

[25] *Prosecutor v Thomas Lubanga Dyilo* (Judgment on the appeals of The Prosecutor and The Defence against Trial Chamber I's Decision on Victims' Participation of 18 January 2008) ICC-01/04-01/06-1432-Anx (23 July 2008) paras 53–65.

with domestic law, the term 'victim' also includes the immediate family or dependants of the direct victim and persons who have suffered harm in intervening to assist victims in distress or to prevent victimization.

PTC I included the UN Basic Principles in its interpretation of the harm relevant for rule 85. However, it did not go so far as to establish that a *substantial impairment of the victim's fundamental rights* was a relevant form of harm. On the contrary, when discussing the forms of relevant harm, it has included 'emotional suffering', 'physical harm' and 'economic loss'.[26]

Also, in the *Lubanga* case, the UN Basic Principles were considered as a legitimate source of interpretation by the majority of the judges of TC I. They were introduced by way of resorting to article 21(3), which contains the principle that the application and interpretation of law must be consistent with internationally recognised human rights.[27] Departing from PTC I's jurisprudence, TC I interpreted, in its majority composition, that physical or mental injury, emotional suffering, economic loss or substantial impairment of fundamental rights were all forms of relevant harm.[28] The dissenting judge pointed out, in his Separate Opinion, that principle 8 of the UN Basic Principles was first inserted in a footnote to the draft Statute submitted to the Rome Conference and, due to lack of support, it was ultimately left out of the Statute.[29] Therefore, he considered that those principles hold no authority for the legal determination and definition of victims.[30]

In turn, the Appeals Chamber confirmed that reference to the UN Basic Principles of 2005 for the purpose of guidance is allowed.[31] However, when describing the relevant forms of harm it has referred to material, physical and psychological harm. The broader notion of 'substantial impairment of fundamental rights' has not been confirmed as a qualifying form of harm.[32]

[26] *Situation in the Democratic Republic of Congo* (Decision on the Applications for Participation in the Proceedings of VPRS 1, VPRS 2, VPRS 3, VPRS 4, VPRS 5 and VPRS 6) ICC-01/04-101-tEN-Corr (17 January 2006) para 172. Delegations considered that the inclusion of the phrase 'substantial impairment of their fundamental rights' in the Rules would result in a too broad definition: see Fernández de Gurmendi, 'Definition of Victims' (above n 2) at 432.

[27] *Prosecutor v Thomas Lubanga Dyilo* (Decision on victims' participation) ICC-01/04-01/06-1119 (18 January 2008) paras 35, 92. Scholars point out that the latter provision was one of the most contentious during the Rome Conference and that it was particularly directed at achieving a strict respect for the rights of the accused. They also warn that, although it was introduced with the intention to limit the judge's discretion in interpreting and applying the law, the provision bears a significant potential to broaden the Court's powers. M McAuliffe deGuzman, 'Article 21: Applicable Law' in O Triffterer (ed), *Commentary on the Rome Statute of the International Criminal Court* 2nd edn (Oxford and Munich, Hart Publishing and Verlag CH Beck, 2008) 711.

[28] *Prosecutor v Thomas Lubanga Dyilo* (Decision on victims' participation) ICC-01/04-01/06-1119 (18 January 2008) para 35.

[29] Fernández de Gurmendi, 'Definition of Victims' (above n 3) at 428.

[30] *Prosecutor v Thomas Lubanga Dyilo* (Decision on victims' participation) ICC-01/04-01/06-1119 (18 January 2008) Separate and Dissenting Opinion of Judge René Blattmann, paras 4–5.

[31] *Prosecutor v Thomas Lubanga Dyilo* (Judgment on the appeals of The Prosecutor and The Defence against Trial Chamber I's Decision on Victims' Participation of 18 January 2008) ICC-01/04-01/06-1432-Anx (23 July 2008) para 33.

[32] ibid at para 32.

D Indirect Victims

Another controversial element in the definition of victim provided for in rule 85 relates to whether the 'indirect harm' suffered by natural persons is included in the concept of 'harm' under rule 85. In its decision of 18 January 2008, TC I held that paragraph (b) of rule 85, which requires that the harm allegedly suffered be directly linked to the relevant crime, is only applicable to legal persons.[33] Hence, a *contrario*, such a requirement is not applicable to natural persons.

In a case such as *Lubanga*, in which the alleged crimes are those of enlistment, conscription and active use of children under the age of 15 in hostilities, the scope accorded to the notion of indirect victims could have significant consequences. Indeed, TC I heard submissions on this question of law after the Registrar consulted the Chamber regarding 200 applications it received from victims of crimes allegedly committed by children who had been conscripted, enlisted or used to participate actively in hostilities whilst under the age of 15.[34]

PTC I and PTC II have held that, even though the direct harm is only required in rule 85(2), natural persons should also have suffered a direct harm to qualify as victims.[35] Hence, whether the alleged victim is a natural or legal person does not make a difference.[36] The only exception would be those natural or legal persons who can show prima facie to have suffered harm when attempting to prevent the commission of the crime, put an end to such crime, or assist the direct victims of the crime.[37] As a result, it was not established that victims of any crimes allegedly committed by the child soldiers could participate in the proceedings held against those who enlisted, conscripted or used them to participate actively in hostilities.

In its decision of 11 July 2008, the Appeals Chamber decided as follows:

> The Appeals Chamber considers that the harm suffered by a natural person is harm to that person, ie personal harm. Material, physical, and psychological harm are all forms

[33] *Prosecutor v Thomas Lubanga Dyilo* (Decision on victims' participation) ICC-01/04-01/06-1119 (18 January 2008) para 91. See also *Prosecutor v Thomas Lubanga Dyilo* (Redacted Version of the'Decision on "indirect victims"') ICC-01/04-01/06-1813 (8 April 2009).

[34] As set out in the *Prosecutor v Thomas Lubanga Dyilo* (Redacted Version of the 'Decision on "indirect victims"') ICC-01/04-01/06-1813 (8 April 2009), the Registrar posed the question 'whether any of these applicants might be considered to be indirect victims in the case, if they were victims of crimes committed by persons who had been conscripted or enlisted whilst under the age of fifteen or used to participate actively in hostilities'.

[35] *Prosecutor v Thomas Lubanga Dyilo* (Decision on the Applications for Participation in the Proceedings of a/0001/06, a/0002/06 and a/0003/06 in the case of the Prosecutor v Thomas Lubanga Dyilo and of the investigation in the Democratic Republic of the Congo) ICC-01/04-01/06-228-tEN (28 July 2006) 8. See also *Prosecutor v Thomas Lubanga Dyilo* (Redacted Version of the 'Decision on "indirect victims"') ICC-01/04-01/06-1813 (8 April 2009).

[36] ibid.

[37] *Prosecutor v Thomas Lubanga Dyilo* (Decision on the Applications for Participation in the Proceedings of a/0001/06, a/0002/06 and a/0003/06 in the case of the Prosecutor v Thomas Lubanga Dyilo and the investigation in the Democratic Republic of the Congo) ICC-01/04-01/06-228-tEN (28 July 2006) 8. See also *Prosecutor v Germain Katanga and Mathieu Ngudjolo Chui* (Decision on the Applications for Participation in the Proceedings of Applicants a/0327/07 to a/0337/07 and a/0001/08) ICC-01/04-01/07-357 (2 April 2008).

> of harm that fall within the rule if they are suffered personally by the victim. Harm suffered by one victim as a result of the commission of a crime within the jurisdiction of the Court can give rise to harm suffered by other victims. This is evident for instance, when there is a close personal relationship between the victims such as the relationship between a child soldier and the parents of that child. The recruitment of a child soldier may result in personal suffering of both the child concerned and the parents of that child. It is in this sense that the Appeals Chamber understands the Trial Chamber's statement that 'people can be the direct or indirect victims of a crime within the jurisdiction of the Court'. The issue for determination is whether the harm suffered is personal to the individual. If it is, it can attach to both direct and indirect victims. Whether or not a person has suffered harm as the result of a crime within the jurisdiction of the Court and is therefore a victim before the Court would have to be determined in light of the particular circumstances.[38] [. . .] Accordingly, the Appeals Chamber confirms the finding of the Trial Chamber to the extent that the Trial Chamber determined that harm suffered by victims does not necessarily have to be direct and amends the decision to include that harm suffered by a victim applicant for the purposes of rule 85 (a) must be personal harm.[39]

Subsequently, in a recent decision issued on 8 April 2009, TC I made a refined interpretation of the Appeals Chamber Decision of 11 July 2008. According to this interpretation:

> Excluded from the category of 'indirect victims', however, are those who suffered harm as a result of the (later) conduct of direct victims. The purpose of trial proceedings at the ICC, as stated by the Appeals Chamber, 'is the determination of the guilt or innocence of the accused person of the crimes charged' and it is only victims 'of the crimes charged' who may participate in the trial proceedings pursuant to Article 68(3), when read together with Rules 85 and 89(1). The charges confirmed against the accused in this case are confined to the conscription, enlistment or use of children to participate actively in hostilities. Indirect victims, therefore, are restricted to those whose harm is linked to the harm of the affected children when the confirmed offences were committed, not those whose harm is linked to any subsequent conduct by the children, criminal or otherwise. Although a factual overlap may exist between the use of the child actively to participate in hostilities and an attack by the child on another, the person attacked by a child soldier is not an indirect victim for these purposes because his or her loss is not linked to the harm inflicted on the child when the offence was committed.

Thus, for TC I, 'indirect victims' are those who suffered harm as a result of the *harm* suffered by the direct victims (for example, the close relatives of the direct victims), along with those who suffered harm when attempting to prevent harm by direct victims. Conversely, those who suffered harm as a result of the subsequent

[38] *Prosecutor v Thomas Lubanga Dyilo* (Judgment on the appeals of The Prosecutor and The Defence against Trial Chamber I's Decision on Victims' Participation of 18 January 2008) ICC-01/04-01/06-1432-Anx (23 July 2008) para 32.

[39] ibid at para 39.

conduct by direct victims (a person injured by a conscripted child) cannot participate as indirect victims.[40]

E Reassessment of Pre-Trial Decisions on Victim's Status by the Trial Chambers?

A decision granting participation to a victim is binding regarding the stage of the proceedings within which that decision has been taken. If the PTC judges decide to concede participation on a victim, then the latter will be allowed to exercise his or her rights during the Pre-Trial stage. If such a decision is issued during the trial, the victim will be allowed to participate in trial proceedings.

One of the compelling questions in relation to 'who' can participate in the proceedings is that of whether the TCs need to reassess the decisions by the PTCs granting participating status. The jurisprudence of the different TCs differs on this point.

TC I decided to reassess all those applications granted during Pre-Trial.[41] Conversely, TC II decided that victims *authorised* to participate in the proceedings at the pre-trial stage must in principle automatically be authorised to participate in the proceedings at the trial stage, without the need for their applications to be assessed once again.[42] Exceptionally, those applications would be reassessed if

[40] One scholar has recently argued that child soldiers behave erratically and unpredictably, which makes them especially dangerous to persons other than the enemy forces. They are often provided with drugs and alcohol to make them more obedient; this results in the commission of crimes that they would not perpetrate under normal circumstances. Child soldiers suffer serious psychological harm from taking direct part in hostilities. It is thus argued that the loss, injury or damage suffered as a result of the conduct of child soldiers arises from the harm suffered by the child soldiers themselves, and is causally linked to the crime of using child soldiers to participate actively in hostilities. See V Spiga, 'Indirect Victims' Participation in the *Lubanga* Trial' (2010) 8 *Journal of International Criminal Justice* 183, 192. This interpretation is not persuasive. Recruiters may consider the likelihood by children to bold reactions as a decisive factor in order to incorporate them into the armed forces and subsequently use them to participate in hostilities. However, the unpredictable or particularly dangerous behaviour resulting from the use of drugs and alcohol is not a *consequence* of the use child soldiers but one of the reasons (*causes*) for their recruitment and subsequent use. Children may suffer harm as a result of their being used to participate in hostilities. But, it is the 'personal' portion of the harm, suffered by that child ('harm to that person') that qualifies as a relevant harm for the purposes of determining the 'direct' victim and, furthermore, for the determination of the indirect victims upon application of the causality rules. The use of child soldiers in armed hostilities can result in harm inflected on the children themselves and on third persons harmed by those children. However, this does not mean that the harm suffered by those third persons results from the harm suffered by the children. Such harm is connected with what the children have done and not with what the children have suffered. It follows that, under these circumstances, the link required by the jurisprudence of the Appeals Chamber would not be satisfied *Prosecutor v Thomas Lubanga Dyilo* (Judgment on the appeals of The Prosecutor and The Defence against Trial Chamber I's Decision on Victims' Participation of 18 January 2008) ICC-01/04-01/06-1432-Anx (23 July 2008).

[41] *Prosecutor v Thomas Lubanga Dyilo* (Decision on the applications by victims to participate in the proceedings) ICC-01/04-01/06-1556 (15 December 2008) paras 54–59, 137. According to the latter paragraph, those four victims have been 'granted' status to participate in the proceedings anew.

[42] *Prosecutor v Germain Katanga and Mathieu Ngudjolo Chui* (Decision on the treatment of applications for participation) ICC-01/04-01/07-933-tENG (26 February 2009) para 10.

the participating status had been granted as related to a charge which ended up not being confirmed, or if new evidence before the TC indicated that the previous decisions were based on invalid documentation.[43]

The language of regulation 86(8) of the Regulations of the Court supports the position held by TCII that once a Chamber decides that a victim has participation rights, that decision shall apply throughout the proceedings in the same case.[44] Moreover, this approach has permitted the Chamber to save significant time and resources by not reassessing 57 applications granted during pre-trial.[45]

Turning to the advantages of TC I's position, it is notable that it ensures that those victims participating at a particular stage would match the interpretation followed by the judges in charge of that stage of *who* can become a victim. Furthermore, it guarantees that no two equivalent applicants would receive a different treatment at the same stage of proceedings due to the differing approaches of the Pre-Trial and Trial Chambers.

The most appropriate system would merge the advantages of both positions. This could be achieved by way of introducing additional exceptions to those addressed by TC II. In the event that dissimilar criteria by the TCs would lead to denial of the authorisation to participate previously granted by the PTCs, reassessment should be authorised.

III *What* are Victims allowed to carry out in the Criminal Proceedings?

As set out above, the ICC Statute, in keeping with the modern trends in international human rights law, has provided victims with the procedural standing of *participants*. Certainly, this idea is well known in national legislations stemming from the Romano Germanic system. Frequently, they are even conferred the right to become a party in the criminal case. Conversely, the procedural

[43] ibid at paras 11–12. There, the Trial Chamber II develops some general caveats to this principle: 'The fact remains that the Chamber may see fit to rule on applications for participation which the Pre-Trial Chamber has already allowed, in particular where one or more victims have been authorised to participate in the proceedings at the pre-trial stage solely on the basis of the commission of a crime corresponding to a charge which was not confirmed by the Pre-Trial Chamber'. In paragraph 12 Trial Chamber II establishes that: 'The Chamber might also examine applications for participation already allowed if new information were to appear at the trial stage'.

[44] Reg 86(8) provides as follows: A decision taken by a Chamber under rule 89 [To grant or reject a victim application for participation] shall apply throughout the proceedings in the same case, subject to the powers of the relevant Chamber in accordance with rule 91, sub-rule 1 [A chamber may modify a previous ruling that a victim application is granted or rejected].

[45] *Prosecutor v Germain Katanga and Mathieu Ngudjolo Chui* (Decision on the treatment of applications for participation) ICC-01/04-01/07-933-tENG (26 February 2009) para 13. See the criticism relating to the time and energy expended in administering the victim participation system in CH Chung, 'Victims' Participation at the International Criminal Court: Are Concessions of the Court Clouding the Promise?' (Spring 2008) 6 *Northwestern Journal of International Human Rights* 459, 506.

status conferred on victims in common law legal systems tends to be much more limited.[46]

In the framework of international human rights law, the Inter-American Court of Human Rights[47] and the European Court of Human Rights[48] have paved the way in granting procedural rights to victims. However, this path was not followed by the international tribunals preceding the ICC, nor was it adopted in the statutes of the international tribunals subsequent to the ICC. The Statute for the International Criminal Tribunal for the former Yugoslavia and the Statute for the International Criminal Tribunal for Rwanda limited the role of victims during the proceedings to their appearance as witnesses. With regard to reparations, the authority of the ICTY and ICTR judges was confined to ordering the restitution of illegally seized property to the legitimate owners. In turn, the statutory framework of the Special Court for Sierra Leone neither provides for victims' participation nor reparations.

The ICC Statute establishes the participation of victims, though not as parties to the case (such as the prosecution and the defence). Victims' procedural stature, if compared with the parties' stature, is much more restrictive. For instance, victims do not have right to appeal decisions of the PTCs and the TCs.[49] Notably, the procedural stature of victims at the ICC is broader than the stature conferred by the common law legal systems, but it is more restrictive than that which is usually enjoyed by victims in the Romano-Germanic systems.

A Systematic versus Casuistic Approach to the Determination of the Role of Victims in Situations and Case Proceedings

The scope of victims' participation at the investigation stage of a situation and throughout case-related proceedings is today one of the critical issues before the ICC. Articles 15(3), 19(3) and 75 of the ICC Statute only refer to the participation of victims during the triggering procedure and in proceedings relating to jurisdiction, admissibility and reparations, and thus, they don't specify the role of victims during the investigation and throughout case-related proceedings. It follows that the key provision on such critical issues is article 68(3) of the ICC Statute, which states as follows:

[46] TM Funk, *Victims' Rights and Advocacy at the International Criminal Court* (Oxford, Oxford University Press, 2010) 19.

[47] The Inter-American Court of Human Rights (IACtHR) has decided that family members of victims have a right to know the truth about what happened to their relatives (which includes obtaining knowledge of the circumstances of the crime and the identification of those responsible) and that a denial of this right is equivalent to a state's denial of victims access to effective justice and procedural fairness (ie, *Bámaca Velásquez v Guatemala*, Case No 70, IACtHR, series C (25 November 2000) 201).

[48] The European Court of Human Rights (ECHR) found that Turkey violated art 2 of the Convention because it failed to inform victims or their closest relatives of the state's decision not to prosecute *Gulec v Turkey*, no 21593/93, ECHR 1998-IV.

[49] Victims have a right to present their views and concerns before the Appeals Chamber if – and only if – any of the *parties* have succeeded in opening the appeals stage of the proceedings.

> Where the personal interests of the victims are affected, the Court shall permit their views and concerns to be presented and considered at stages of the proceedings determined to be appropriate by the Court and in a manner which is not prejudicial to or inconsistent with the rights of the accused and a fair and impartial trial. Such views and concerns may be presented by the legal representatives of the victims where the Court considers it appropriate, in accordance with the Rules of Procedure and Evidence.

This article entrusts the Chambers with discretion with regard to the determination of when victims can participate in ICC proceedings and the specific manner in which such participation can take place.[50] Two general criteria govern the exercise of such discretion. First, victims are only entitled to participate at 'stages of the proceedings determined to be appropriate by the Court' when their 'personal interests' are affected. Secondly, they are only entitled to present 'their views and concerns' in a manner which is not 'prejudicial to or inconsistent with the rights of the accused and a fair and impartial trial'.

Rules 89–93 only provide limited guidance for the exercise of the aforementioned discretion.[51] Those rules establish that victims (through their legal representatives) may participate in hearings and put questions to witnesses and nothing else.

ICC Chambers have so far adopted different approaches to the interpretation of article 68(3). According to PTC I, PTC II and PTC III, the definition of victims' personal interests under article 68(3) includes interests that are common to all victims, such as verification of the events in which they were allegedly

[50] In this regard, Bitti and Friman, 'Participation of Victims' (above n 1) at 457, explains that the definition of the procedural role of victims in the proceedings before the ICC was left to the competent ICC Chambers. According to Bitti and Friman, this was the result of the fear by a number of delegations that victims' participation in ICC proceedings would be impracticable due to the high number of victims.

[51] Rules 89 and 90 of the RPE regulate the process of victims' applications for participation in ICC proceedings and the issues concerning victims' legal representation. Rule 91 of the RPE underscores that 'A legal representative of a victim shall be entitled to attend and participate in the proceedings in accordance with the terms of the ruling of the Chamber and any modification thereof given under rules 89 and 90. This shall include participation in hearings unless, in the circumstances of the case, the Chamber concerned is of the view that the representative's intervention should be confined to written observations or submissions. The Prosecutor and the defence shall be allowed to reply to any oral or written observation by the legal representative for victims'. Rule 91 of the RPE also regulates the procedure in which victims can request to question witnesses in those hearings in which they have been granted the right to attend and participate by the competent Chamber. Rule 92 of the RPE is concerned with notification of decisions and judicial proceedings to victims. Paras 2 and 3 provide for the notification to victims of (i) the Prosecution's decisions to not open an investigation and to not prosecute under article 53 of the ICC Statute, and (ii) the Pre-Trial Chamber's decision to hold a confirmation hearing. The *rationale* behind the notification of these decisions is 'to allow victims to apply for participation in the proceedings in accordance with rule 89'. Paras 5–8 provide for the notification to victims of those proceedings (including hearings and judicial decisions) in which they have been granted the right to participate by the competent Chamber. Finally, rule 93 of the RPE grants the ICC Chambers discretion to seek the views of victims in relation to any issue that may arise out of the proceedings. See Bitti and Friman, 'Participation of Victims' (above n 1) at 460–74.

harmed, identification and prosecution of the alleged perpetrators and securing reparations.[52]

The analysis of whether victims' personal interests have been affected must be carried out in relation to the *stage of the proceedings* – such as, for instance, the investigation stage of a situation, the confirmation hearing, the trial – and not in relation to *specific procedural activities* or items of evidence.[53] Therefore, if verified that the victims' personal interests are affected at a given stage of the proceedings, such a stage must be considered automatically as 'appropriate' for victims to present their views and concerns – that is to say, to participate.[54] 'Participation' means the exercise of the procedural rights with which victims are empowered which must be defined in a manner that 'is not prejudicial to or inconsistent with the rights of the accused and a fair and impartial trial'.[55] Thus, all those granted victim status are, except in cases of anonymity, entitled to the same role in the proceedings. In this chapter, this approach will be called the 'systematic approach' to victims' participation in ICC proceedings.[56]

In the decision of 18 January 2008, TC I considered that the finding that the 'general interests of victims' are affected at a particular stage of proceedings does not necessarily mean that those victims should be allowed to express their views and concerns in accordance with article 68(3).[57] For TC I, the mentioned provision requires an additional determination that the personal interests of victims

[52] *Situation in the Democratic Republic of the Congo* (Decision on the Applications for Participation in the Proceedings of VPRS 1, VPRS 2, VPRS 3, VPRS 4, VPRS 5 and VPRS 6) ICC-01/04-101-tEN-Corr (17 January 2006) paras 63, 72; *Prosecutor v Germain Katanga and Matthieu Ngudjolo Chui* (Decision on the Set of Procedural Rights Attached to Procedural Status of Victim at the Pre-Trial Stage of the Case) ICC-01/04-01/07-474 (13 May 2008) paras 31–44; *Situation in Uganda* (Decision on victims' applications for participation a/0010/06, a/0064/06 to a/0070/06, a/0081/06 to a/0104/06 and a/0111/06 to a/0127/06) ICC-02/04-101 (10 August 2007) paras 9–11; *Prosecutor v Jean-Pierre Bemba Gombo* (Fourth Decision on Victims' Participation) ICC-01/05-01/08-320 (12 December 2008) paras 90–91.

[53] *Situation in Darfur, Sudan* (Decision on the Requests for Leave to Appeal the Decision on the Application for Participation of Victims in the Proceedings in the Situation) ICC-02/05-121 (6 February 2008) 6; *Prosecutor v Jean-Pierre Bemba Gombo* (Third Decision on the Question of Victims' Participation Requesting Observations from the Parties) 01/05-01/08-253 (17 November 2008) paras 6–7; *Prosecutor v Jean-Pierre Bemba Gombo* (Fourth Decision on Victims' Participation) ICC-01/05-01/08-320 (12 December 2008) paras 84, 92–93.

[54] *Situation in Darfur, Sudan* (Decision on the Requests for Leave to Appeal the Decision on the Application for Participation of Victims in the Proceedings in the Situation) ICC-02/05-121 (6 February 2008) 6. A similar conclusion is implicitly reached in relation to the preliminary stage of case-related proceedings (also known as confirmation hearing stage) by *Prosecutor v Jean-Pierre Bemba Gombo* (Fourth Decision on Victims' Participation) ICC-01/05-01/08-320 (12 December 2008) paras 87–94.

[55] *Situation in Darfur, Sudan* (Decision on the Requests for Leave to Appeal the Decision on the Application for Participation of Victims in the Proceedings in the Situation) ICC-02/05-121 (6 February 2008) 9; *Prosecutor v Jean-Pierre Bemba Gombo* (Fourth Decision on Victims' Participation) ICC-01/05-01/08-320 (12 December 2008) paras 94–96.

[56] H Olasolo, 'Systematic and Casuistic Approaches to the Role of Victims in Criminal Proceedings before the International Criminal Court' (2009) 12 *New Criminal Law Review* 513, 520–24.

[57] *Prosecutor v Thomas Lubanga Dyilo* (Decision on Victims' Participation) ICC-01/04-01/06-1119 (18 January 2008) paras 97–98.

are engaged in the concrete issues or items of evidence on which they wish to express their views and concerns, case by case.[58]

Hence, securing 'participating status' does not mean that victims are entitled to exercise procedural rights in the trial proceedings. Quite the contrary, the second step towards the exercise of procedural rights is subject to individual applications by the victims, responses by the parties and participants and decisions by the Chamber throughout the relevant stage of the proceedings.[59] This approach can be qualified as a 'casuistic approach' to victims' participation.[60]

The casuistic approach has been put in place in association with a concept of victims defined in a manner that includes those who suffered harm as a result of a crime that, although under the jurisdiction of the Court in conceptual terms, has not been alleged against the accused.[61] With regard to victims coming from this very wide category, the issues falling under examination in the case would frequently be wholly unrelated to the crimes that caused harm to them, and, therefore, their personal interests would not be engaged in a real sense. The limitation to participation that is not achieved via the victims' definition is sought through reassessing – before any procedural activity – the question of personal interests.

The Appeals Chamber has ruled unambiguously in favour of the casuistic approach. This conclusion is suggested by a joint reading of its decisions of 2 February 2009,[62] 19 December 2008[63] and 13 June 2007.[64] In the outcome, the Appeals Chamber requires a 'charges' based definition of the victims and a case by case approach to victims' participation. Thus, the Appeals Chamber has adopted a double step approach to limiting the participation of victims – a construction that favours the accused.

B The Role of Victims in the Stage of Investigation of a Situation

In addition to embracing different approaches (systematic versus casuistic) to the determination of the role of victims, ICC Chambers have also differed on the

[58] ibid at para 95. In order to carry out this analysis, Trial Chamber I uses as its main reference tool the 'summary of evidence' that the Prosecution must file prior to the start of the trial. Ibid at para 102.

[59] ibid. This twofold application process has been the subject of a dissent in the minority opinion attached to that decision. It has been pointed out that it places too large a burden on victims.

[60] Olasolo, 'Systematic and Casuistic' (above n 56) at 524–27.

[61] *Prosecutor v Thomas Lubanga Dyilo* (Decision on victims' participation) ICC-01/04-01/06-1119 (18 January 2008) para 95.

[62] *Situation in Darfur* (Judgment on victim participation in the investigation stage of the proceedings in the appeal of the OPCD against the decision of Pre-Trial Chamber I of 3 December 2007 and in the appeals of the OPCD and the Prosecutor against the decision of Pre-Trial Chamber I of 6 December 2007) ICC-02/05-177 (2 February 2009) para 7.

[63] *Situation in the Democratic Republic of the Congo* (Judgment on victim participation in the investigation stage of the proceedings in the appeal of the OPCD against the decision of Pre-Trial Chamber I of 7 December 2007 and in the appeals of the OPCD and the Prosecutor against the decision of Pre-Trial Chamber 1 of 24 December 2007) ICC-01/04-556 (19 December 2008) paras 41–46.

[64] *Prosecutor v Thomas Lubanga Dyilo* (Decision of the Appeals Chamber on the Joint Application of Victims a/0001/06 to a/0003/06 and a/0105/06 concerning the 'Directions and Decision of the Appeals Chamber' of 2 February 2007) ICC-01/04-01/06-925 (13 June 2007) paras 26–29.

content of such role. In relation to the stage of investigation of a situation, PTC I, in its decision of 17 January 2006, explained that (i) the activities conducted during the stage of investigation of a situation constituted 'a stage of the proceedings' within the meaning of article 68(3) of the Statute,[65] (ii) the participation of victims was appropriate at this stage, and (iii) therefore, they were entitled to a procedural status during this stage.[66]

PTC II, in its decision of 10 August 2007, made clear that at the stage of investigation of a situation, victims could exercise participation in the procedures: (i) leading to the Prosecutor being authorised to exercise his *proprio motu* powers pursuant to article 15; (ii) related to the initiation of an investigation pursuant to article 53; (iii) related to the protection of the security and privacy of victims; and (iv) related to the preservation of evidence. As a general provision, they have also been allowed to participate in 'other issues' considered appropriate by the Chamber.[67]

Finally, the Appeals Chamber, in its decisions of 19 December 2008[68] and 2 February 2009,[69] held that that there is no procedural status for victims at the investigation stage as victims cannot participate outside the framework of 'judicial proceedings'. That participation of victims has to be done within 'judicial proceedings' means that there should be a case before the Chambers. The investigation of a situation cannot be understood as a 'judicial proceeding' given that it is a pre-procedural stage conducted by the Prosecution prior to the initiation of

[65] *Prosecutor v Germain Katanga and Matthieu Ngudjolo Chui* (Decision on the Set of Procedural Rights Attached to Procedural Status of Victim at the Pre-Trial Stage of the Case) ICC-01/04-01/07-474 (13 May 2008) paras 28–54.

[66] According to Pre-Trial Chamber I, this procedural status consisted of the right (a) to be heard, notwithstanding any specific proceedings being conducted in the framework of such an investigation, by the Chamber in order to present their views and concerns; (b) to file documents pertaining to the current investigation of the situation in the DRC; and (c) with regard to specific proceedings conducted before the Pre-Trial Chamber, and depending on the impact on victims' personal interests: (1) When specific proceedings are initiated *proprio motu* by the Pre-Trial Chamber under art 56(3) and art 57(3)(c) of the Statute, the Chamber decides at the time of their initiation whether victims may participate in them. (2) When specific proceedings are initiated by the Office of the Prosecutor or by counsel representing the general interests of the Defence, victims can participate in public proceedings and cannot participate in confidential/closed session proceedings, unless otherwise decided by the Pre-Trial Chamber. (3) Victims are also entitled to request the Pre-Trial Chamber, pursuant to art 68(3) of the Statute, to order specific proceedings, and the Chamber will decide on a case-by-case basis. *Prosecutor v Germain Katanga and Matthieu Ngudjolo Chui* (Decision on the Set of Procedural Rights Attached to Procedural Status of Victim at the Pre-Trial Stage of the Case) ICC-01/04-01/07-474 (13 May 2008) paras 55–74.

[67] *Situation in Uganda* (Decision on victims' applications for participation a/0010/06, a/0064/06 to a/0070/06, a/0081/06 to a/0104/06 and a/0111/06 to a/0127/06) ICC-02/04-101 (10 August 2007) paras 82–102.

[68] *Situation in the Democratic Republic of the Congo* (Judgment on victim participation in the investigation stage of the proceedings in the appeal of the OPCD against the decision of Pre-Trial Chamber I of 7 December 2007 and in the appeals of the OPCD and the Prosecutor against the decision of Pre-Trial Chamber I of 24 December 2007) ICC-01/04-556 (19 December 2008) paras 45–59.

[69] *Situation in Darfur* (Judgment on victim participation in the investigation stage of the proceedings in the appeal of the OPCD against the decision of Pre-Trial Chamber I of 3 December 2007 and in the appeals of the OPCD and the Prosecutor against the decision of Pre-Trial Chamber I of 6 December 2007) ICC-02/05-177 (2 February 2009) para 7.

the criminal procedure (a case) *stricto sensu*. On the basis of these reasons, the Appeals Chamber decided that victims do not generally have a right to participate during the investigation stage.

However, as acknowledged by the Appeals Chamber, some exceptional judicial proceedings may take place during the investigation of a situation. The PTCs will have to decide whether victims can participate in those specific judicial proceedings on a case by case basis.

C The Role of Victims in the Pre-Trial Proceedings of a Case

With regard to victims participation in case proceedings, there has been a significant difference between the approach of PTC I, on the one hand, and those of PTC III and TC I on the other.

PTC I has based its determination of the victims' role in the proceedings on the distinction between anonymous and non-anonymous victims. It was PTC I, which, for the first time, granted natural and legal persons who had come on a voluntary basis to the proceedings, the right to participate under the condition of anonymity. This protective measure is unknown in those criminal justice systems which provide for an ample role of victims in the proceedings, insofar as the Prosecution exercises the penal action, and participation in the proceedings against the accused person is fully voluntary. According to PTC I, granting anonymity was justified due to the following reasons:

> [T]he recent deterioration in the security situation in certain regions of Democratic Republic of the Congo (the DRC) has had repercussions on the range of protective measures currently available and which might be implemented to protect victims a/0001/06 to a/0003/06 who are particularly vulnerable and live in risk areas in the DRC; and that, in this context and following a meticulous examination of each case, non-disclosure of these victims' identities to the Defence for the purpose of the confirmation hearing, remains at present the only protective measure available and which might be implemented to duly protect them.[70]

For PTC I, the granting of anonymity to victims must have a restricting impact on the role that they can play in the proceedings. Based on the fundamental principle prohibiting anonymous accusations the Chamber decided that anonymous victims are not permitted, for instance, to add any point of fact or any evidence to those presented within the Prosecution's Charging Document and the list of evidence[71] and to question witnesses pursuant to rule 91(3).[72]

PTC III and TC I have departed from PTC's I distinction between the set of the procedural rights to which anonymous and non-anonymous victims are entitled.

[70] *Prosecutor v Thomas Luganga Dyilo* (Decision on the Arrangements for Participation of Victims a/0001/06, a/0002/06 and a/0003/06 at the Confirmation Hearing) ICC-01/04-01/06-462-tEN (22 September 2006) 6.

[71] ibid at 7.

[72] ibid at 8.

The approach taken by the TCs is discussed later. According to PTC III, victims should not be 'punished' as a result of being granted protective measures, such as the anonymity of their identities.[73] As a result, according to PTC III, anonymous and non-anonymous victims must both, at the very minimum, be entitled to the role granted by PTC I to anonymous victims[74] plus the possibility to extend those rights upon a case by case application.[75]

In turn, the Appeals Chamber has not yet decided on whether victims who voluntarily participate in the proceedings can be granted anonymity. Accordingly, it has not discussed whether anonymous and non-anonymous victims should have different participatory rights.

The procedural rights that anonymous victims could exercise in proceedings leading to the confirmation hearing, as well as in the confirmation hearing itself, were confined to the following: (i) notification of the public documents contained in the record; (ii) attendance at those status conferences, or the parts of those status conferences, which are to be held in public; (iii) making opening and closing statements at the confirmation hearing, in which they can, inter alia, address points of law, such as the legal characterisation of the facts, the modes of liability, the international or non-international character of a conflict; and (iv) requesting, during the status conferences and during the confirmation hearing, leave to intervene, in which case the Chamber would rule on a case by case basis.[76]

In exceptional circumstances, the aforementioned set of rights can be limited pursuant to the PTC I jurisprudence.[77] However, an extension of those rights can only be upheld if the victims agree to disclose their identities to the defence.[78]

In its decision of 13 May 2007 in the *Katanga and Ngudjolo* case, PTC I addressed the issue of the role of non-anonymous victims in the pre-trial proceedings of a case. In its decision, PTC I stated that, according to article 68 of the ICC Statute, the only criteria for the determination of this role is that it must not be prejudicial to or inconsistent with the rights of the accused and a fair and impartial trial.[79] In this regard, PTC I highlighted that the role of victims in criminal proceedings vary greatly in national jurisdictions; some national jurisdictions grant victims the role of private prosecutors, while others limit the role of victims to making impact statements at the sentencing stage.[80] PTC I also underscored that international and regional human rights bodies, such as the Human Rights

[73] *Prosecutor v Jean-Pierre Bemba Gombo* (Fourth decision on victims' participation) ICC-01/05-01/08-320 (12 December 2008) para 99.

[74] ibid at paras 101–10.

[75] ibid.

[76] ibid at 7–8.

[77] ibid at 7.

[78] ibid at 8.

[79] *Prosecutor v Germain Katanga and Matthieu Ngudjolo Chui* (Decision on the Set of Procedural Rights Attached to Procedural Status of Victim at the Pre-Trial Stage of the Case) ICC-01/04-01/07-474 (13 May 2008) paras 52–75.

[80] ibid.

Committee, the European Court of Human Rights or the Inter-American Court of Human Rights, had not yet found any of the aforementioned systems in violation of any of the fundamental rights of the accused, including the right to a fair and impartial trial, provided for in article 14 of the International Covenant on Civil and Political Rights, article 6 of the European Convention on Human Rights and article 8 of the Inter-American Convention on Human Rights. As a result, PTC I concluded that the internationally recognised human rights law provides no preference for any of the mentioned systems and thus the main criteria for the determination of the role of victims is the manner in which it systematically fits with the other core components of the ICC criminal procedure.[81]

On this basis, PTC I found that the role of non-anonymous victims includes up to six groups of procedural rights:[82]

1. The right to have access, prior to and during the confirmation hearing, to the record of the case kept by the Registry, including access to the evidence filed by the Prosecution and the Defence pursuant to rule 121 of the Rules.[83]
2. The right to make submissions on all issues relating to the admissibility and probative value of the evidence on which the Prosecution and the Defence intend to rely at the confirmation hearing; and the right to examine such evidence at the confirmation hearing.
3. The right to examine, at the confirmation hearing, any witness proposed by the Prosecution and the Defence.[84]

    i. The right to attend all public and closed session hearings convened in the proceedings leading to the confirmation hearing, as well as in all public and closed sessions of the confirmation hearing.[85]

[81] ibid at paras 79–89.

[82] ibid at paras 127–45.

[83] Which includes the rights to: (a) have access to all filings and decisions contained in the record of the case regardless of whether they are classified as public or as confidential (it does not, however, include the right to access those filings and decisions classified as 'ex parte' and only available to the Prosecution, the Defence, a different participant, the Registry or a combination thereof); (b) be notified on the same basis as the Prosecution and the Defence of all decisions, requests, motions, responses and other procedural documents which are filed in the record of the case and are not classified 'ex parte' and only available to the Prosecution, the Defence, a different participant, the Registry or a combination thereof; (c) have access to the transcripts of non ex parte hearings contained in the record of the case regardless of whether such hearings were held in public or in closed session; (d) be notified on the same basis as the Prosecution and the Defence of all proceedings before the Court, including public and closed session hearings (including those held ex parte) and any postponements thereof, and the date of delivery of decisions; and (e) the right to have access to the evidence proposed by the Prosecution and the Defence and contained in the record of the case in the format (unredacted versions, redacted versions or summaries, as well as electronic versions with the data required by the e-Court Protocol) in which the evidence is made available to the party which has not proposed it.

[84] This is considered part of the evidentiary debate that takes place at the confirmation hearing – examination of witnesses by victims takes place after their examination by the Prosecution, and victims like the Prosecution and the Defence, do not have to file the list of questions that they intend to pose to the relevant witnesses prior to the examination of the witnesses.

[85] It does not include the right to attend those hearings held on an ex parte basis with the Prosecution, the Defence, a different participant, the Registry or a combination thereof.

ii. The right to participate by way of oral motions, responses and submissions.[86]
iii. The right to file written motions, responses and replies in accordance with regulation 24 of the Regulations, in relation to all matters other than those in which the victim's intervention has been excluded by the Statute and the Rules.[87]

The right of victims to access the record of the case and to participate in the evidentiary debate at the confirmation hearing can be, according to PTC I, limited for reasons relating, inter alia, to 'national security, protection of witnesses and victims, and Prosecution's investigations'.[88] Nevertheless, preventing non-anonymous victims from accessing confidential materials is the exception and not the general rule at the pre-trial stage of a case (where the record of the case is certainly limited).[89] Otherwise, as the bulk of the evidence filed by the Prosecution and the Defence in the record of the respective cases is usually classified as confidential, victims would essentially be prevented from effectively participating in the evidentiary debate held at the confirmation hearing.[90]

PTC I has also highlighted that the statutory framework provided for by the Statute and the Rules for the pre-trial stage of a case leaves no room for: (i) victims' independent investigative powers;[91] (ii) victims' access to Prosecution situation and case files;[92] (iii) victims' extension of the facts and charges contained in the Prosecution Charging Document;[93] (iv) victims' presentation of additional

[86] This was considered relevant (a) with regard to all those hearings in which participating victims have the right to attend; and (b) in relation to all matters other than those in which their intervention has been excluded by the ICC Statute and the Rules (for instance, matters relating to the *inter partes* disclosure process or any discussion of the evidence which aims at extending the factual basis contained in the Prosecution [Amended] Charging Document).

[87] This also includes the right to: (a) file, in accordance with rule 121(7) of the Rules, written submissions with the Pre-Trial Chamber on evidentiary and legal issues to be discussed at the confirmation hearing; (b) make opening and closing statements at the confirmation hearing as provided for in rule 89(1) of the Rules; and (c) raise objections or make observations concerning issues related to the proper conduct of the proceedings prior to the confirmation hearing in accordance with rule 122(3) of the Rules. Nevertheless, it does not include the right to resort to certain procedural remedies that, according to the ICC Statute and the Rules, can only be exercised by Prosecution, Defence and/or other participants (such as challenges to jurisdiction or admissibility).

[88] *Prosecutor v Germain Katanga and Matthieu Ngudjolo Chui* (Decision on the Set of Procedural Rights Attached to Procedural Status of Victim at the Pre-Trial Stage of the Case) ICC-01/04-01/07-474 (13 May 2008) para 149.

[89] ibid at para 150.

[90] ibid at para 151. Furthermore, according to Pre-Trial Chamber I, 'those filings, decisions and transcripts included in the record of the case that could contain information affecting, inter alia, national security, the protection of witnesses and victims and the Prosecution's investigations (such as rules 81(2) and (4) requests for redactions, reports on the status of requests for admission into the Court's Witness Protection Programme or unredacted versions of statements which are only disclosed to the Defence in a redacted format) are classified ex parte, and therefore they cannot be accessible to victims'. See ibid at para 152.

[91] ibid at paras 80–84.

[92] ibid at paras 85–89.

[93] ibid at paras 115–23.

evidence;[94] and (v) victims' participation in the process of disclosing evidence between the Prosecution and the Defence.[95]

PTC I supported its conclusion that victims are not entitled to present additional evidence at this stage of the proceedings on the following four arguments.[96] First, according to PTC I, granting such a right would distort the object and purpose, as well as the limited scope of the confirmation hearing, which 'by no means can be seen as an end in itself, but it must be seen as a means to distinguish those cases that should go to trial from those that should not go to trial'. Secondly, it would inevitably delay the commencement of the confirmation hearing. Thirdly, it would infringe upon the Defence's right not to rely at the confirmation hearing on any of the materials disclosed by the Prosecution pursuant to its disclosure obligation under article 67(2) and rule 77. Finally, it would require the PTC to act ultra vires as the Pre-Trial Chamber does not have the power, pursuant to article 61(7) of the ICC Statute, to request that the Prosecution should submit additional evidence nor to authorise victims to present such additional evidence.

Moreover, according to PTC I, as victims are not entitled to present additional evidence at this stage of the proceedings, they cannot have, in principle, any disclosure obligations, and therefore there is no reason to depart from the traditional configuration of the disclosure process as an *inter partes* process between the Prosecution and the Defence.[97] Victims' access to the evidence on which Prosecution and Defence intend to rely at the confirmation hearing shall take place in the same manner in which the Chamber gets access to it, that is to say through the Registry once the relevant party has filed the evidence after having disclosed it to the other party in the proceedings.[98]

[94] In particular, PTC I highlighted that a number of arguments supported its conclusion that victims are not entitled to present additional evidence at this stage of the proceedings. First, according to PTC I, granting such a right would distort the object and purpose, as well as the limited scope of the confirmation hearing, which 'by no means can be seen as an end in itself, but it must be seen as a means to distinguish those cases that should go to trial from those that should not go to trial'. Secondly, it would inevitably delay the commencement of the confirmation hearing. Thirdly, it would infringe on the Defence's right not to rely at the confirmation hearing on any of the materials disclosed by the Prosecution pursuant to its disclosure obligation under art 67(2) and rule 77. Finally, it would require the PTC to act ultra vires as the Pre-Trial Chamber does not have the power, pursuant to art 61(7) of the ICC Statute, to request the Prosecution to submit additional evidence nor to authorise victims to present such additional evidence. Ibid at paras 90–114, in particular paras 101–04.

[95] ibid. As victims are not entitled to present additional evidence at this stage of the proceedings, they cannot have, in principle, any disclosure obligations, and therefore there is no reason to depart from the traditional configuration of the disclosure process as an *inter partes* process between the Prosecution and the Defence. Victims' access to the evidence on which Prosecution and Defence intend to rely at the confirmation hearing shall take place in the same manner in which the Chamber gets access to it, that is to say through the Registry once the relevant party has filed the evidence after having disclosed it to the other party in the proceedings.

[96] *Prosecutor v Germain Katanga and Matthieu Ngudjolo Chui* (Decision on the Set of Procedural Rights Attached to Procedural Status of Victim at the Pre-Trial Stage of the Case) ICC-01/04-01/07-474 (13 May 2008) paras 90–114, in particular paras 101–04.

[97] ibid at para 113.

[98] ibid at para 127.

D The Role of Victims in the Trial Proceedings of a Case

As seen above, TC I has adopted a different approach from PTCs in determining the role of the victims in trial proceedings. According to TC I, victims' participatory rights are not to be pre-established prior to the commencement of the trial. On the contrary, they must be determined, as proceedings move forward, on a case by case basis (casuistic approach) in light of whether victims' personal interests are affected by the relevant procedural activity or piece of evidence, and their intervention is not prejudicial to or inconsistent with the rights of the accused and a fair and expeditious trial.[99]

So far, TC I has discussed the role of victims in trial proceedings in a number of rulings, the decision of 18 January 2008 being the most important one. Particularly relevant are the issues of: (i) victims' rights to tender evidence pertaining to guilt or innocence; (ii) victims' rights to question witnesses and the appropriate manner of questioning; (iii) victims' participation in the disclosure process; (iv) personal appearance of victims at trial; (v) evidence on reparations issues; and (vi) the role of victims in the legal recharacterisation of the facts.

i Victims' Rights to Tender Evidence pertaining to Guilt or Innocence

One of the most relevant findings of TC I was that victims' evidence pertaining to the guilt or innocence of the accused can be introduced via the judges' authority to request the submission of all evidence they consider necessary for the determination of the truth pursuant to article 69(3) of the ICC Statute, as long as the following criteria are met: '(i) a discrete application by victims to that effect; (ii) notice to the parties; (iii) demonstration of personal interests that are affected by the specific proceedings; (iv) compliance with disclosure obligations and protection orders; (v) a determination of appropriateness; and (vi) consistency with the rights of the accused and a fair trial'.[100]

This finding has been upheld by the Appeals Chamber in a 3:2 majority decision.[101] All five judges of the Appeals Chamber appear to agree on the fact that victims, in presenting their views and concerns, may warn the Chamber that available evidence would be relevant for the determination of the truth and that they might also offer reasons for or against the admissibility of evidence. Nevertheless, two out of the five judges of the Appeals Chamber did not agree with the majority's conclusion.[102]

[99] *Prosecutor v Thomas Lubanga Dyilo* (Decision on victims' participation) ICC-01/04-01/06-1119 (18 January 2008) paras 101–04.

[100] ibid at paras 108–11.

[101] *Prosecutor v Thomas Lubanga Dyilo* (Judgment on the appeals of The Prosecutor and The Defence against Trial Chamber I's Decision on Victims' Participation of 18 January 2008) ICC-01/04-01/06-1432-Anx (23 July 2008) paras 101–03.

[102] ibid at para 93.

For the two dissenting judges, the Statute does not permit the participation of anyone in the proof of the charges other than the Prosecutor and the accused. The participation of victims in the proceedings is confined to presenting their views and concerns. The defendant cannot have more than one accuser and that accuser, the Prosecution, is the one tasked to prove beyond reasonable doubt the charges alleged.[103] Moreover, the Statute is unambiguous in stating that the submission of evidence and the challenges on the admissibility of evidence is for the *parties* (articles 69(3) and 64(9)), excluding the participants.[104]

The majority, in reaching its conclusion, highlighted that the Trial Chamber must ensure the victims have a right to participate 'meaningfully', which may become ineffectual if victims were, under all circumstances, precluded from tendering evidence.[105]

Nevertheless, it is unclear whether the above-mentioned decisions by TC I and the Appeals Chamber mean that legal representatives have a 'right' to introduce evidence pertaining to the guilt or innocence of the accused. TC I's jurisprudence may advocate for an interpretation that the victims' rights are limited to proposing to the Chamber whether it considers the pieces of evidence to be of relevance for the determination of the truth, instead of possessing procedural standing to submit evidence.

In this regard, following a proposal by a legal representative of victims, three victims have been authorised to testify in the *Lubanga* case. Rather than simply analysing whether the criteria for the admissibility of evidence had been satisfied,[106] the Chamber has undertaken to explain in what manner those testimonies would contribute to the Chamber's determination of the truth.[107] Ultimately, it was the Chamber, and not the legal representatives, who 'requested' the evidence.[108] The same approach was consistently applied when analysing a request by victims' representatives to admit a document into evidence.[109]

In the decision of 11 July 2008, the Appeals Chamber affirmed that the participating victims should be allowed the possibility to *lead evidence* pertaining to the guilt or innocence of the accused.[110] In a more recent decision, however, the

[103] ibid at partially Dissenting Opinion of Judge Pikis, paras 6, 14, 15.

[104] ibid at partially Dissenting Opinion of Judge Kirsh, paras 19, 33.

[105] ibid at para 97.

[106] Those criteria were developed by the Trial Chamber I in *Prosecutor v Thomas Lubanga Dyilo* (Decision on the admissibility of four documents) ICC-01/04-01/06-1399 (13 June 2008) paras 27–31.

[107] *Prosecutor v Thomas Lubanga Dyilo* (Decision on the request by victims a/ 0225/06, a/0229/06 and a/0270/07 to express their views and concerns in person and to present evidence during the trial) ICC-01/04-01/06-2032-Anx (26 June 2009).

[108] *Prosecutor v Thomas Lubanga Dyilo* (Decision on victims' participation) ICC-01/04-01/06-1119 (18 January 2008) para 108.

[109] *Prosecutor v Thomas Lubanga Dyilo* (Decision on the request by the legal representative of victims a/0001/06, a/0002/06, a/0003/06, a/0049/06, a/0007/08, a/0149/08, a/0155/07, a/0156/07, a/0404/08, a/0405/08, a/0406/08, a/0407/08, a/0409/08, a0149/07 and a/0162/07 for admission of the final report of the Panel of Experts on the illegal exploitation of natural resources and other forms of wealth of the Democratic Republic of the Congo as evidence) ICC-01/04-01/06-2135 (22 Sep 2009) paras 21–22.

[110] *Prosecutor v Thomas Lubanga Dyilo* (Judgment on the appeals of The Prosecutor and The Defence against Trial Chamber I's Decision on Victims' Participation of 18 January 2008) ICC-01/04-01/06-1432-Anx (23 July 2008) para 105.

Appeals Chamber changed (or at least clarified) its previous jurisprudence by stating that, rather than a right by victims to lead evidence pertaining to the guilt of the accused, participating victims have a right to make submissions aimed at persuading the judges that it is necessary for the determination of the truth that *the Chamber* requests the submission of evidence in the possession of those victims.[111]

ii Victims' Right to Question Witnesses and the Appropriate Manner of Questioning

With regard to the questioning of witnesses, TC I has not recognised, as did PTC I, a victim's general right to question all witnesses called by the Prosecution and Defence. Following its casuistic approach, TC I has required victims to make a 'discrete written application' whenever they want to question a witness. Such application must be filed seven days prior to the appearance of the witness and may be subject to litigation by the parties. The applications must contain the questions that the victims intend to ask and an allegation as to how the personal interest of the requesting victim is engaged. Victims are only granted authorisation under the condition that the questions have not previously been posed by the Prosecution, that they affect their personal interests and that they are not contrary to the accused's rights.

In regards to the manner of questioning, the Chamber ruled that for the *party* calling a witness, it is appropriate to follow 'neutral' questioning. Closed, leading and challenging questions have been considered, in principle, appropriate for the parties' not calling the witnesses only (cross-examination).[112] The victims, who are not parties, are authorised to ask neutral questions. This interpretation considers that, under the scheme of the Statute, questioning by the victims' legal representatives is linked to the broad purpose of assisting the bench in its pursuit of the truth.[113]

[111] See the recent *Prosecutor v Germain Katanga and Mathieu Ngudjolo Chui* (Judgment on the Appeal of Mr Katanga Against the Decision of Trial Chamber II of 22 January 2010 Entitled 'Decision on the Modalities of Victim Participation at Trial') ICC-01/04-01/07-2288 (16 July 2010) para 40. 'It is only if the Trial Chamber is persuaded that the requirements of article 68(3) have been met, and, in particular, that it has been established that the personal interests of the victims are affected, that the Chamber may decide whether to exercise its discretionary powers under the second sentence of article 69(3) of the Statute "to request the submission of all evidence that it considers necessary for the determination of the truth"'. See also *Prosecutor v Germain Katanga and Mathieu Ngudjolo Chui* (Directions for the conduct of the proceedings and testimony in accordance with Rule 140) ICC-01/04-01/07-1665-Corr (1 December 2009) paras 45–48.

[112] *Prosecutor v Thomas Lubanga Dyilo* (Decision on the Manner of Questioning Witnesses by the Legal Representatives of Victims) ICC-01/04-01/06-2127 (16 September 2009) para 23.

[113] This link (as approved by the Appeals Chamber) between the questioning of witnesses by the victims participating in proceedings and the power of the Chamber to determine the truth tends to support a presumption in favour of a neutral approach to questioning on behalf of victims. Ibid at para 28.

iii Victims' Participation in the Disclosure Process

The effectiveness of victims' participation is shaped by the information the participants are given to prepare for the hearings. Victims have not been attributed a general right to access the non-public record of the proceedings. In the event, confidential material is of relevance to the personal interests of the victims, that information may be given to the interested victims so long as appropriate protective measures have been put in place.[114]

TC I has insisted that '[i]t is for the victims to establish their interest in the area of evidence or issue prior to disclosure to them of non-public material'.[115] However, the parties are entrusted, provided the victims' personal interests may be engaged by any particular confidential filings or documents, with assisting by disclosing the relevant material to the victims' legal representatives.[116]

This principle has been developed in the discussions on the disclosure obligations by the Prosecution,[117] and thereafter maintained in respect of disclosure by the Defence:

In order to ensure that the proceedings do not become bedevilled by applications to adjourn, because it is only revealed when the witnesses are giving evidence that the personal interests of particular victims are involved, the Defence are to consider the position of each of the participating victims and to disclose the relevant material if there is a prima facie basis for concluding that any of them may be granted leave to question one or more witnesses. The Chamber will then be in a position to grant or refuse applications to put questions to witnesses and to make any necessary additional disclosure orders.[118]

[114] *Prosecutor v Thomas Lubanga Dyilo* (Decision on victims' participation) ICC-01/04-01/06-1119 (18 January 2008) para 106.

[115] *Prosecutor v Thomas Lubanga Dyilo* (Trial Chamber I Transcript) ICC-01/04-01/06-T-220-Red-ENG (9 December 2009) p 24; this ruling was consistent with the previous *Prosecutor v Thomas Lubanga Dyilo* (Decision on victims' participation) ICC-01/04-01/06-1119 (18 January 2008) para 107.

[116] ibid at paras 101–07.

[117] ibid at para 108.

[118] *Prosecutor v Thomas Lubanga Dyilo* (Trial Chamber I Transcript) ICC-01/04-01/06-T-220-Red-ENG (9 December 2009) pp 28, 29. The governing principles for Defence's disclosure to legal representatives have recently been set out, as follows: (i) The Defence is to provide the Chamber, the Prosecution and the participating victims with a list of the witnesses to be called seven days in advance of their testimony, together with their anticipated order (19 November 2009, document 2192, para 64). (Subject to (iii), (iv), (v) below). (ii) Simultaneously (with (i) above), the Defence shall provide the Chamber, the Prosecution and the participating victims with a list of the documents and other tangible objects that are going to arise during the course of the evidence of the witnesses who are to be called, together with a list of any relevant materials that the Defence seeks to introduce from the Bar table. (Therefore, also, at least seven days' in advance) (19 November 2009, document 2192, para 64). (iii) However, it is for the victims to establish their interest in the area of evidence or the issue prior to disclosure to them of non-public material and not the other way around. And accordingly, the essential prerequisite of disclosure of confidential evidence or other material, or notification of non public filings to victims, is that the evidence or the issue relates to the interests of a particular individual who seeks to participate (8 April 2009, transcript 167, p 13). (iv) It follows that disclosure of the Defence list of witnesses and summaries of their evidence, or their statements, will depend on a decision by the Chamber, first, that the relevant victims' personal interests are affected and second, that it is appropriate to impose these disclosure obligations against the backdrop of the rights of the accused (9 December

Recently, the Appeals Chamber has decided on the question as to whether victims have a duty to disclose to the Defence exculpatory material in their possession. The Appeals Chamber ruled that it is inappropriate to impose such a duty on victims. That the Prosecution shall disclose to the Defence all the exculpatory evidence that it has gathered in the course of the investigations is closely linked to its obligation to impartially collect both incriminating and exculpatory evidence. The latter obligation, and its consequences, is not transmissible to victims.[119]

iv Personal Appearance of Victims at Trial

The personal appearance of a large number of victims invited to give their views and concerns in person may frustrate the Chamber's duty to ensure that the trial is fair and expeditious. It has been established that, in principle, those acting during the hearings would have to be lawyers rather than individual victims because 'people without legal training coming to talk about very difficult things that have happened to them could have a real capacity for destabilising these court proceedings'.[120] To limit complications in this respect, the Chamber has determined that those victims will be in principle represented by common counsel.[121]

However, the possibility of admitting the victims' submissions in person during the trial has not been ruled out. On a request by a legal representative that

2009, transcript 222, p 28). The Defence is to consider the position of each of the participating victims and to disclose the relevant material if there is a prima facie basis for concluding that any of them may be granted leave to question one or more witnesses. The Chamber will then be in a position to grant or refuse applications to put questions to witnesses and to make any necessary additional disclosure orders (9 December 2009, transcript 222, pp 28-9). (v) The Chamber today emphasises that for victims who prima facie may be granted leave to question one or more witnesses (in accordance with (iv)) if the Defence considers that disclosure of non public material should not be affected, it is to notify the Chamber so that the matter can be resolved. (vi) The parties and the participants have an obligation to provide the Registry with the electronic version whenever possible of any evidence they intend to use at a hearing at least three full working days in advance of its introduction (29 January 2008, document 1140, para 34; 19 November 2009, document 2192, para 64). (vii) [...] (viii) Advance notice to victims of the materials on which the Defence intends to rely ordinarily should be effected by the Court's electronic database but on occasion, for instance, if an issue has arisen late, it may be provided in some other electronic form or by way of paper copies. [...] (8 April 2009, transcript 167, pp 10–11). (ix) For victims who have not been granted leave to participate as regards a particular area of evidence or issue, common courtesy should encourage the Prosecution and the Defence to provide non-sensitive information whenever this does not raise any significant security or confidentiality issues, and it is not unduly onerous to the lawyers who are in court on a daily basis following these proceedings on behalf of the victims (8 April 2009, transcript 167). *Prosecutor v Thomas Lubanga Dyilo* (Trial Chamber I Transcript) ICC 01/04-01/06-T-236-Red-ENG (27 January 2010).

[119] *Prosecutor v Germain Katanga and Mathieu Ngudjolo Chui* (Judgment on the Appeal of Mr Katanga Against the Decision of Trial Chamber II of 22 January 2010 Entitled 'Decision on the Modalities of Victim Participation at Trial') ICC-01/04-01/07-2288 (16 July 2010) para 87.

[120] See *Prosecutor v Thomas Lubanga Dyilo* (Trial Chamber I Transcript) ICC-01/04-01/06-T-101-ENG ET WT (12 January 2009) 43.

[121] Detailed criteria on common legal representation have not been set out by the Chamber. Instead, consideration of the language spoken by the victims, the links between them provided by time, place and circumstance and the specific crimes of which they are alleged to be victims has been deemed of potential relevance, in the case of *Prosecutor v Thomas Lubanga Dyilo* (Decision on victims' participation) ICC-01/04-01/06-1119 (18 January 2008) para 124.

three victims are authorised to testify at trial (to tender their personal witnesses' account as evidence) and, subsequently, to present their views and concerns in person during the hearings, the Chamber decided to adjourn the decision on the latter request until having heard the victims' testimonies. The guiding principle was the aim of avoiding unnecessary repetition:

> [T]he Chamber will need to ensure that issues and facts are not unnecessarily repeated (eg first in a victims' personal presentation of his or her views and concerns, then repeated by them in evidence and finally addressed on a third occasion by the legal representatives in submissions).[122]

TC II has expressly ruled on the possibility for victims authorised to participate in the proceedings to provide evidence as witnesses in the case. In particular, TC II considered that such an authorisation can be granted only if the accused's right to be tried without undue delay is observed; the victims are not transformed into auxiliary prosecutors; and the victims are not anonymous vis-à-vis the Defence.[123] TC II stressed that in these circumstances special attention shall be given to the need for the accused to be provided with adequate time and facilities for the preparation of his defence and that victims' appearance is appropriate, in any event, directly after the Prosecution has presented its case.[124]

The requests – to be presented in written form by the legal representative of the victim who wishes to testify – will be granted if the testimony relates to matters that were not addressed by the Prosecution already (to avoid unnecessary repetition); the topics on which the victim proposes to testify are sufficiently closely related to issues which the Chamber must consider; the proposed testimony is typical of a larger group of participating victims, who have had similar experiences as the victim who wishes to testify, or whether the victim is uniquely apt to give evidence about a particular matter; and the testimony will likely bring to light new information that is substantial and relevant.[125]

v Evidence on Reparations Issues

A critical discussion took place in the *Lubanga* trial on whether the Chamber would hear, during the trial, evidence for the purposes of reparations, pursuant to regulation 56. The Defence opposed such a course on the basis that, given that reparations proceedings require a 'conviction', discussion during the trial of evidence for the purposes of reparations would infringe on the presumption of innocence.

[122] *Prosecutor v Thomas Lubanga Dyilo* (Decision on the request by victims a/ 0225/06, a/0229/06 and a/0270/07 to express their views and concerns in person and to present evidence during the trial) ICC-01/04-01/06-2032-Anx (26 June 2009) para 26.

[123] *Prosecutor v Germain Katanga and Mathieu Ngudjolo Chui* (Directions for the conduct of the proceedings and testimony in accordance with rule 140) ICC-01/04-01/07-1665-Corr (1 December 2009) para 22.

[124] ibid at paras 23 and 24.

[125] ibid at para 30.

TC I rejected the Defence's challenge. In so doing, the judges have avoided burdening witnesses with giving evidence twice. Moreover, the Chamber gave weight to the argument that, at a later stage of the proceedings, the evidence relevant to reparations may be unavailable.[126] It was pointed out that the ICC is composed of professional judges as opposed to jurors. These judges will be able to isolate and rely on those pieces of evidence if and when the reparations' stage of the proceedings is reached.

vi The Role of Victims in the Recharacterisation of Facts

In the Lubanga trial the question arouse as to the role of the victims in the (re) characterisation of the facts attributed to the accused in accordance with the documents containing the charges and the decision on the confirmation of the charges. Indeed, in this trial, victims' participation led to a number of decisions, first setting out the powers of the TC to define the factual basis of the trial and second analysing whether that factual basis can accord to a different legal characterisation.

As to PTC I's 29 January 2007 Decision on the Confirmation of the Charges, the *Lubanga* case proceeded to trial on the basis of six charges: enlistment, conscription and use to actively participate in hostilities of children under the age of fifteen in the context of an international armed conflict and in the context of a non-international armed conflict. Nevertheless, the legal representatives of the victims, in a joint filing, requested TC I to consider a legal re-characterisation of the facts as, respectively, sexual slavery pursuant to articles 7(l)(g) or 8(2)(b)(xxii) or 8(2)(e)(vi) of the ICC Statute, and inhuman and/or cruel treatment pursuant to articles 8(2)(a)(ii) or 8(2)(c)(i) of the Statute.[127]

In a divided ruling, the Chamber decided that it was allowed by regulation 55(2) to add new facts to those contained in PTC I's Decision on the Confirmation of the Charges[128] provided those 'additional facts' have come to light during the trial and conform, from the procedural point of view, with the course of events described in the charges.[129]

[126] *Prosecutor v Thomas Lubanga Dyilo* (Decision on victims' participation) ICC-01/04-01/06-1119 (18 January 2008) paras 120, 122.

[127] *Prosecutor v Thomas Lubanga Dyilo* (Demande conjointe des représentants légaux des victimes aux fins de mise en oeuvre de la procédure en vertu de la norme 55 du Règlement de la Cour) ICC-01/04-01/06-1891 (22 May 2009).

[128] *Prosecutor v Thomas Lubanga Dyilo* (Decision giving notice to the parties and participants that the legal characterisation of the facts may be subject to change in accordance with Regulation 55(2) of the Regulations of the Court) ICC-01/04-01/06-2049 (14 July 2009) para 28.

[129] Clarification and further guidance to parties and participants in relation to ibid at para 8. It is of note that the legal consequences of this discussion are far reaching. The TC ruled that those new facts formed a 'procedural unity' with the factual allegations confirmed against the accused. If in addition to constituting a procedural unity, 'the former' and 'the new' facts actually integrate 'the same conduct', then any trial before the ICC or another Court involving 'the former' or 'the new' facts would have to constitute double jeopardy, either if the accused is convicted or acquitted by the ICC on the basis of any of those facts. (*Ne bis in idem*, art 20 of the ICC Statute).

According to the majority of the Chamber, it had heard evidence at trial concerning, inter alia, the sexual practices to which girls under the age of 15 were subjected while being members of the organised armed group of which the accused was allegedly the commander-in-chief. This, in the view of the majority, justified – as submitted by the victims' legal representatives – the inclusion of additional facts that may be subsumed under the crimes of sexual slavery. Moreover, by reference to the legal representatives' submissions, the Chamber concluded that the training practices child soldiers were subjected to may constitute inhuman and/or cruel treatment. Consequently, notice was given to parties and participants that the legal characterisation of facts may be subject to the changes proposed by the legal representatives.

The Appeals Chamber overturned the TC's decision. In so doing, it found that regulation 55 shall not be used to exceed the facts and circumstances described in the charges or any amendments thereto.[130] One of the most significant legal findings within this decision is the definition of, or further guidance on, what is the scope and meaning of the term 'facts'. This discussion was included in a footnote, as follows:

> In the view of the Appeals Chamber, the term 'facts' refers to the factual allegations which support each of the legal elements of the crime charged. These factual allegations must be distinguished from the evidence put forward by the Prosecutor at the confirmation hearing to support a charge (article 61 (5) of the Statute), as well as from background or other information that, although contained in the document containing the charges or the confirmation decision, does not support the legal elements of the crime charged.[131]

Elaborating on the criteria set by the Appeals Chamber, the legal representatives submitted that the term 'circumstances described in the charges' should be interpreted as covering all the 'circumstances of the crime', which according to rule 145(l)(b) and (c), are relevant to the determination of the sentence, including 'the circumstances of manner, time and location'. In the legal representatives' view, although the said circumstances were included in the charging documents as circumstances of manner (that is to say, the way the crime of enlisting and conscripting children under the age of 15 was committed), they constituted, considered in isolation, crimes under the jurisdiction of the Court.[132] Hence, the legal representatives argued that the requested modification of the legal characterisation of the facts was permitted, even in light of the Appeals Chamber judgment.[133]

[130] *Prosecutor v Thomas Lubanga Dyilo* (Judgment on the appeals of Mr Lubanga Dyilo and the Prosecutor against the Decision of Trial Chamber I of 14 July 2009 entitled 'Decision giving notice to the parties and participants that the legal characterisation of the facts may be subject to change in accordance with Regulation 55(2) of the Regulations of the Court') ICC-01/04-01/06-2205 (8 December 2009) para 88.

[131] ibid at fn 163.

[132] *Prosecutor v Thomas Lubanga Dyilo* (Observations conjointes des Représentants Légaux des Victimes quant aux conséquences de l'arrêt de la Chambre d'appel du 8 décembre 2009) ICC-01/04-01/06-2211 (15 December 2009) para 21.

[133] ibid at para 26.

However, the TC rejected the legal representatives' submissions with the understanding that, pursuant to the Appeals Chamber decision, it is necessary to analyse:

> Whether the requested modification of the legal characterisation of facts arises (i) from factual allegations included in the Decision on the Confirmation of Charges, which (ii) support each of the legal elements of the crimes with which the accused is charged.[134]

The TC was not persuaded that those factual allegations mentioned in the Decision on the Confirmation of the Charges with the purpose of describing the way a charged crime was committed (ie, included either as a circumstances of manner or as aggravating circumstances) could be 'upgraded' to factual allegations supporting the legal elements of crimes not included in the Confirmation Decision. Such a position would inevitably conflict with the interpretation rendered by the Appeals Chamber,[135] and thus, the legal representatives' motion was rejected.

Although, as discussed, the legal representatives' motion was rejected, their participation led to a crucial determination as to the factual basis of the trial. For the first time, the extent to which the TC is bound by the Decision on the Confirmation of the Charges – which in turn is bound by the Document Containing the Charges – was established. The TC cannot go beyond the 'facts' contained in that decision; the 'facts' of the trial are frozen.[136] Additional facts referred to by witnesses at trial cannot be introduced and then legally qualified by the TCs. It was also established that 'factual allegations', if proven during trial, are not all the facts referred to in the decision on the confirmation of the charges but rather those 'which support each of the legal elements of the crimes with which the accused is charged'.[137]

In any event, the role of the victims' legal representative in the recharacterisation of factual allegations in the *Lubanga* trial shows how victims' participation makes available to the Trial Chamber useful information to appraise the Prosecution's use of its inherent powers, and permits victims to express what their

[134] Because those factual allegations would not have been described to 'support each of the legal elements of the crimes with which the accused is charged'. *Prosecutor v Thomas Lubanga Dyilo* (Decision on the Legal Representatives' Joint Submissions concerning the Appeals Chamber's Decision on 8 December 2009 on Regulation 55 of the Regulations of the Court) ICC-01/04-01/06-2223 (8 January 2010) para 28.

[135] *Prosecutor v Thomas Lubanga Dyilo* (Judgment on the appeals of Mr Lubanga Dyilo and the Prosecutor against the Decision of Trial Chamber I of 14 July 2009 entitled 'Decision giving notice to the parties and participants that the legal characterisation of the facts may be subject to change in accordance with Regulation 55(2) of the Regulations of the Court') ICC-01/04-01/06-2205 (8 Dec 2009) n 163.

[136] C Stahn, 'Modification of the Legal Characterization of Facts in the ICC System; A Portrayal of Regulation 55' (2005) 1 *Criminal Law Forum* 1, 16; K Ambos and D Miller, 'Structure and Function of the Confirmation Procedure before the ICC from a Comparative Perspective' (2007) 7 *International Criminal Law Review* 335, 360.

[137] This interpretation leaves little room for any modification of the legal characterisation of facts pursuant to reg 55. Although the Appeals judgment ruled out reg 55 expressly (textually) stipulating what modifications are permissible, the chance that cases different than those involving 'lesser included offences' (containing the same elements as the original offence) could comply with this second requirement would be, in the outcome, at the very least quite exceptional.

interests are and, if applicable, how they are different from those of the Prosecution (in this case by having an opportunity to question before TC I the Prosecution's decision to limit the first ICC trial to offences related to enlistment, conscription and use of child soldiers).

IV Conclusion

The role accorded to victims in the ICC proceedings is considered the most significant feature of the ICC Statute. It is therefore unsurprising that extensive jurisprudence, ruling on several controversial areas which are of utmost relevance for shaping such a role, has emerged.

However, various aspects related to the definition of victims and the activities they are allowed to undertake have been the subject of controversy between different Chambers. Even though the case law of the Appeals Chamber is contributing, to a certain extent, to homogenising the different approaches, the need for legal certainty in this area is far from being achieved and the work that lies ahead for the ICC Chambers will be arduous. Victims need to be certain as to whether they are eligible for participation and how they can participate in proceedings. Likewise, it is crucial for the Prosecution and the Defence to know the scope of victims' participation.

As said in the introductory section, whether and to what extent, the role accorded to victims in the ICC Statute is beneficial in terms of justice will only become apparent in the long term after scrutinising what victims have 'obtained' by exercising their participation rights. Although it may be too early for eliciting general conclusions, the participation of victims has already shown that victims' interests at the ICC can differ from those of the Prosecution and has provided those victims with an opportunity to bring their own distinct interests before the Chambers. Victim participation counterbalances the inherent powers of the Prosecution, as it is permitted to question the decision by the Prosecution to investigate some facts and leave others behind.

9

Legal Clinics in Continental Western Europe: The Approach of the Utrecht Legal Clinic*

I would like to thank Rick Wilson, Elizabeth Andersen and the American Society of International Law for giving me the opportunity to talk about something on which Leo Zwaak and I have spent most of our time since my appointment as the Chair of International Criminal Law and Procedure at the University of Utrecht: the newly established Utrecht Law Faculty Clinical Programme on Conflict, Human Rights and International Justice (the Utrecht Legal Clinic).

In continental Western Europe, legal education has been traditionally divided into two different stages. Students were first provided with a basic theoretical framework during their bachelor-in-law education. They were subsequently given an opportunity to apply such a framework in actual cases through traditional apprenticeships. This was accompanied with the institutionalisation at the bachelor's level of the so-called *magister* or *ex cathedra* lessons, which are based on a teaching technique that lacks interaction and consists of a law professor explaining general principles of law and students listening to the professor's explanations. As a result, a gap was created between law schools, where students were taught the core legal principles of a plurality of legal disciplines, and judicial institutions, law firms and non-governmental organisations where apprenticeships were subsequently carried out. This, in turn, led to a situation in which, during several years, law students were not exposed to those problems posed by the application in real cases of the principles that they were taught at the university.

Nevertheless, in the last decade, we have experienced in continental Western Europe a slow, but steady, movement towards other forms of legal education which combine theoretical teaching of basic legal principles with awareness of the main problems posed by the actual application of such principles in real cases. Case studies, moot court competitions, and, in the last few years, clinical and externship programmes are forms of legal education that are being increasingly resorted to in continental Europe (although most of these new educational techniques are still limited, to an important extent, to master-in-law programmes, which, unlike bachelor-in-law programmes, are usually designed to bring students

* Published in American Society of International Law, proceedings of the 104th annual meeting (2010). The Author thanks the American Society of International Law for granting its authorisation to reprint the present work. The views expressed herein are those of the author alone and do not necessarily reflect the views of the ICC, the ICTY, the United Nations in general or the Spanish Government.

into contact with judicial institutions, law firms and non-governmental organisations). However, whereas case studies and moot court competitions currently enjoy a wide acceptance in continental Western Europe, one can only count as of today, a few legal clinics in Western Europe, including three located in the Netherlands (Utrecht, Maastricht and Amsterdam Universities) and two in Spain (University Carlos III in Madrid and University Rovira I Virgili in Tarragona).

The Utrecht Legal Clinic was established in the year 2009 and, following the tradition of human rights clinics in the United States, has been included in the curriculum of the LLM programme on the International Law of Human Rights and International Criminal Justice. It is comprised of three groups of six students: two of them provide pro bono legal services on issues relating to international justice to Hague-based international courts and tribunals, whereas the third group provides legal advice on international human rights matters to the Inter-American Court of Human Rights. Students work under the close supervision of individuals who have practised law for several years in the partner institutions and have extensive publications in the relevant areas. A skills training series is a core component of the Utrecht Legal Clinic and includes seminars on respecting legal ethics, conducting legal research, drafting legal memoranda, party-motions and judicial decisions, and analysing strategy and oral advocacy in pre-trial, trial and appeal proceedings from the perspectives of the prosecution, defence and victims is a core component of the Utrecht Legal Clinic. This skills training is organised in cooperation with the Hague-based TMC Asser Institute, and consists of monthly sessions which take place both in Utrecht and The Hague and are taught by Hague-based international judges, prosecutors, defence counsels and legal representatives of victims.[1]

In the introduction to this panel, Professor Wilson referred to five features of a paradigmatic human rights law clinic in the United States. The Utrecht Legal Clinic shares most of them, such as the fact that it is: (i) within the Utrecht Law School LLM curriculum and offered for credit; (ii) students provide actual legal services to individual or institutional clients with real legal problems; (iii) students are closely supervised by experienced practitioners; and (iv) practical case work is often accompanied by a classroom component focusing on both skills and substance.

Clinical education is developed to provide students with an opportunity to apply their knowledge in ongoing real cases. By placing them under the close supervision of experienced (former) practitioners, they can provide legal services to individual or institutional clients.

Nevertheless, the Utrecht Legal Clinic, as other law clinics in Western Europe, differ from a paradigmatic US human rights clinic as defined by Professor Wilson in at least two key aspects: (i) the types of clients to whom they provide legal

[1] Further information about the Utrecht Law Faculty Clinical Programme on Conflict, Human Rights and International Justice can be found in the section on the official website of the Utrecht Legal Clinic: www.uu.nl/legalclinic.

services; and (ii) the level of student autonomy and supervisors' involvement in the development of the legal work which is to be delivered to the clinic's clients. Both aspects appear to be interrelated as the level of student autonomy and supervisor's involvement in the development of the final 'product' varies depending on who the clinic's clients are, and the nature of their requirements.

There exists a consensus on the understanding that human rights clinics ought to play a social role within their communities. For this reason, most US human rights clinics focus on clients who are indigent or otherwise unable to gain access to justice due to poverty or another marginal status. This is also the case with some continental Western Europe law clinics, such as that at the University of Maastricht, which works with indigent clients in that area of the Netherlands.

Nevertheless, other legal clinics in continental Western Europe – including the Utrecht Legal Clinic – are somewhat different. For instance, the clinic set up at the University of Amsterdam provides legal services to Amsterdam-based law firms and non-governmental organisations, which are neither indigent nor unable to gain access to justice due to poverty or other marginal status. Moreover, the two existing Spanish law clinics also provide legal advice to institutions and non-governmental organisations which are not necessarily located in Spain and work on those areas in which the clinics have particular expertise (the clinic set up at the Rovira I Virgili University in Tarragona specialises in environmental law, whereas the Carlos III Law Clinic in Madrid works primarily with the Inter-American Commission of Human Rights).

The Utrecht Legal Clinic constitutes a unique model because it focuses its work on international organisations which have a strong judicial component, and also because it combines the provision of pro bono legal services to international judicial institutions located in nearby areas, such as The Hague as well as the Inter-American Court of Human Rights located thousands of kilometres away in San Jose, Costa Rica. As a result, the social impact of the Utrecht Law Clinic takes place at both a macro-level and a local level as its activities are directed at strengthening the application of international justice and furthering respect for international human rights all while working with organisations that, despite their international nature, are located in and form part of nearby communities.

The uniqueness of the Utrecht Law Clinic's institutional clients, and their particular demands concerning the work product coming out of the clinic, require certain adjustments to the way in which a paradigmatic US human rights clinic operates. First, by choosing to serve different organs of international judicial institutions, the Utrecht Law Clinic made a conscious decision not to litigate cases before such international courts and tribunals in order to avoid conflicts of interest. As a result, for those who feel more attracted by the litigation side of international justice and human rights, an externship programme was also set up in the year 2009 at the Utrecht Law Faculty to place LLM students with Hague-based international lawyers representing defendants or victims before in international criminal proceedings. Students in the externship programme, which is also part of the Utrecht Law Faculty LLM curriculum and offered for credit, are supervised by those international lawyers with whom they are placed, and must sign confidentiality agreements prohibiting disclosure to the Utrecht Law Faculty staff the details of the work performed.[2]

Secondly, staff members of international judicial institutions require from the Utrecht Legal Clinic a highly detailed work product that makes it worthy of their time to review it carefully and subsequently to discuss it with the students and supervisors of the clinic. Hence, the clinical work of the Utrecht Law School cannot simply comprise of exhaustive legal research. Research must be translated into legal memoranda containing a thorough analysis of the relevant legal issues. As a result, the method of analysis and the format in which the relevant information is presented constitute key elements of the clinical work. This, along with the specialised area of the work of the Utrecht Law Clinic, and the many years of experience of the clinic's clients, results in closer supervision of the students' work and a higher level of supervisors' involvement in the final stages of the clinic's work product before delivery to international courts and tribunals.

As a consequence, students and supervisors together form a joint legal team that is tasked with providing pro bono consultancy work. In this setting, the need for experimental learning is fulfilled through intensive practical interaction with supervisors who have worked for several years in the partner international judicial institutions. It is from this perspective that the Utrecht Legal Clinic, due to the specific characteristics of its clients and the demands place on the clinic by them, constitutes an innovative model of approaching clinical education, which to a considerable extent departs from the model traditionally embraced by US human rights clinics.

Nevertheless, as seen above, the Utrecht Legal Clinic, despite its singularness, follows the core features that characterise clinical education, insofar as it shares the main goal of providing students with an opportunity to apply their knowledge in ongoing real cases by placing them in a situation in which, with the close supervision of experienced (former) practitioners, they can provide legal services to institutional clients.

[2] Further information about the Utrecht Law Faculty Externship Programme on Conflict, Human Rights and International Justice can be found in the section on the Externship Programme of the website: www.uu.nl/legalclinic.

Reflections on Complementarity and Cooperation in Early Practice under the Rome Statute

I Introduction

The International Criminal Court (ICC) was created in order to respond to a historic necessity. The preamble of the Rome Statute reminds us that 'millions of children, women and men have been victims of unimaginable atrocities that deeply shock the conscience of humanity'. These atrocities have often had grave consequences for peace and security at the national, regional and international levels. While responsibility for the prosecution of these crimes lies, first and foremost, with national courts, history has demonstrated that in the face of the worst atrocities and when the national systems of government collapse or are corrupted as a consequence of armed conflicts or states of emergency, national courts are often unable to act or unwilling to do so. It is precisely in order to overcome this impunity gap that international judicial enforcement mechanisms like the ICC were created.

Long before the ICC, the international community and individual states had ventured, sometimes tentatively, to make use of judicial enforcement mechanisms to fill the impunity gap and to address what we would now refer to as international crimes. These efforts have been manifested in a variety of forms. One usually finds references in the legal literature to the medieval examples of the trial of Conradin von Hohenstaufen in 1268 at Naples by international judges for 'waging an unjust war', what we might now refer to as the international crime of aggression, and the trial of Peter von Hagenbach in 1474 by an ad hoc tribunal comprised of 27 judges from different parts of the Holy Roman Empire for what we would now call war crimes. One also finds references to the Treaty of Versailles, which provided for the establishment of an ad hoc international tribunal in order to prosecute Kaiser Wilhelm II for his responsibility in having initiated the First World War, and the international military tribunals at Nuremberg and Tokyo established by the Allies at the end of the Second World War. Some 50 years later, the United Nations Security Council created the International Criminal Tribunals for Rwanda and the former Yugoslavia, which constitute the most recent predecessors to the ICC.

These precedents have achieved a venerable place in the legal literature and, for this reason, it is not necessary to look at them in detail in this work.

Often forgotten, there is another antecedent to the ICC, another initiative to address the impunity gap through the establishment of a judicial enforcement mechanism, which is also fitting of consideration. I am referring to the international courts for the abolition of the slave trade. These courts were established through bilateral treaty agreements between states in the nineteenth century with the aim of ending impunity for a particular manifestation of what we would now refer to as the international crime of enslavement. Although these international courts were not criminal courts, the history of these courts is an attestation to the salience of two of the key pillars of the Rome Statute regime. That is, essential to fulfilling the goal of stamping out the international slave trade through these international courts was the evolution of complementary and cooperative relations between the courts' efforts and those of individual states. So too are 'complementarity' and 'cooperation' pillars of the Rome Statute regime.

Complementarity and cooperation are mechanisms through which the drafters of the Statute endeavoured to ensure that a process of cross-fertilisation took place such that, not only would the ICC be strengthened and enriched by the diversity of national criminal justice systems, but that, in turn, national criminal justice systems would also evolve. In this way, as the preamble of the Rome Statute underscores, the drafters affirmed their commitment to 'lasting respect for and the enforcement of international justice'. It is this forward momentum resulting from the implementation of complementarity and cooperation to which I would like to devote my thoughts. To this end, this contribution is divided into four parts. First, with a view towards a comparative perspective on the role of complementarity and cooperation, I will briefly describe the regime of the international courts for the suppression of the slave trade. Secondly, and by way of context, I will describe the statutory framework for complementarity through the thresholds of 'jurisdiction' and 'admissibility' and the interpretation of the latter by the Appeals Chamber. Thirdly, I will highlight some examples of complementarity in action in relation to the situations and cases presently under consideration by the ICC. Fourthly, I will briefly describe the statutory framework for cooperation and highlight a few examples of cooperation in action at the national level.

II Complementarity and Cooperation under the Regime of the International Courts for the Abolition of the Slave Trade

The international courts for the suppression of the slave trade were created at the initiative of Great Britain and were established through bilateral treaty arrangements between Britain and other countries that were involved in the international slave trade during the period 1817–71.[1] The first bilateral treaties of the kind were set up between Britain and, respectively, the Netherlands, Portugal and Spain.[2] While there were some jurisdictional caveats unique to the individual treaties, broadly speaking, they provided for mutual rights of search and seizure of suspected slave ships and the establishment of courts to condemn captured ships.[3] The courts were established in Freetown, Sierra Leone; Havana, Cuba; Rio de Janeiro, Brazil; and Suriname, which were, respectively, in British, Spanish, Portuguese and Dutch possession.[4] A second wave of treaties was concluded between 1826 and 1862 between Britain and Brazil, Chile, the Argentine Confederation, Uruguay, Bolivia, Ecuador and, late in the game, the United States of America, resulting in the creation of a number of additional courts for the suppression of the slave trade in Luanda, Boa Vista, Spanish Town, Cape Town, Sierra Leone and New York.[5] The judges of these courts were of the nationalities of the signatory state and they applied international law and the rules of procedure annexed to the relevant treaties.[6]

It is estimated that during their period of existence, these courts tried over 600 cases and freed some 80,000 slaves who were on board slave ships at the time of the ships' capture.[7] Thus, these courts are a remarkable example of courts established as an international enforcement mechanism for what would today be characterised as the international crime of enslavement. I am indebted, in particular, to Jenny Martinez for her insightful article in the *Yale Law Journal* on the genesis and evolution of these courts.

Historical records indicate that for some the progress of the courts in stamping out the slave trade was frustratingly slow.[8] This led to policy questions concerning the efficiency and effectiveness of the courts as an enforcement mechanism for achieving the desired goal. For example, by the 1840s some officials in Britain questioned the deterrent effect of such a regime.[9] At the same time, even those who supported their continued operation found it troubling that after decades of struggle and throwing vast resources behind the operation of the courts, the transatlantic slave trade was still in existence.[10] Despite the ICC's few years in operation, such questions today linger in the minds of both its proponents and its detractors.

Success, however, is not only a function of time. Like the ICC, the effectiveness of these courts was impeded by non-participation of countries in the courts regime and treaty-based limitations on its jurisdiction. However, one of the most significant impediments to the effectiveness of these courts was the paucity of

[1] JS Martinez, 'Anti-Slavery Courts and the Dawn of International Human Rights Law' (2008) 17(4) *Yale Law Journal* 552.
[2] ibid at 576.
[3] ibid.
[4] ibid at 579.
[5] ibid at 595.
[6] ibid at 579.
[7] ibid at 553.
[8] ibid at 599–602.
[9] ibid at 601–02.
[10] ibid at 602.

complementary and cooperative actions on the domestic front by certain of the states who *were* party to the bilateral treaty regimes. For example, at the beginning of the nineteenth century Spain, Portugal and Brazil were not strictly enforcing the ban on the slave trade which was already in place under their respective domestic laws.[11] The sought after complementary and cooperative action meant, for example, taking enforcement action not on the high seas, but at the point of sale in the Americas, which required criminal prosecutions at the national level and compliance with decisions of the international courts set up under the bilateral regimes.[12] While other geo-political and economic factors played a role in the final vanquishing of the international slave trade, the complementary and cooperative action between the courts and states, even if not expressed in explicit terms, was a key element in the eventual achievement of this goal.[13]

III Complementarity in the ICC Context

The goals of the Rome Statute are threefold: (i) to put an end to the impunity of the perpetrators of the gravest crimes that threaten the peace, security and welfare of the world; (ii) to contribute to the prevention of those crimes; and (iii) to guarantee that international justice is respected and implemented in a sustainable manner. The principle of complementarity is at the heart of the Court's powers to achieve these goals and it is given form in the Statute through two notions which, while related, remain distinguished: 'jurisdiction' and 'admissibility'.

A Jurisdiction

The ICC is the first permanent and truly international tribunal. The jurisdiction *ratione materie* of the Court is comprised of the gravest crimes of concern to the international community as a whole. These have been enumerated as four categories of crimes: genocide, crimes against humanity, war crimes and, although not yet operational, the crime of aggression. The ICC has jurisdiction in situations where these crimes are committed in the territory of a State Party, with respect to people accused of crimes who are nationals of a State Party, and where these crimes have been committed and the situation is referred to the Court by the United Nations Security Council. Unlike the *Ad hoc* Tribunals, its jurisdiction is prospective and not limited to a specific period of time or events that have occurred prior to the entry into force of the Statute. The Court does not act retroactively, and in this sense, it has jurisdiction only over events that occurred after the entry into force of the Statute on 1 July 2002.

[11] ibid at 615.
[12] ibid at 615–17.
[13] ibid at 615.

B Admissibility

With the creation of the ICC, the international community acknowledged the necessity of establishing a permanent international jurisdiction with potentially global reach. However, even where the Court has jurisdiction with respect to an alleged crime, this does not mean that it has an inescapable obligation to act. On the contrary, the drafters of the Statute acknowledged that the institution created should act *only* in those situations in which national criminal justice systems are unwilling or unable to act. That investigation and prosecution of the crimes within the jurisdiction of the court remains first and foremost the dominion of national jurisdictions is affirmed in the preamble of the Statute. The preamble recalls that 'it is the duty of every State to exercise its criminal jurisdiction over those responsible for international crimes'.

However, there may be situations where the criminal justice system of a state collapses completely or fails to function effectively. Such circumstances in which the suitability of a national criminal justice system is called into question may be due to an ongoing armed conflict or a state of emergency. Other cases may occur where the government of a country acquiesces to the atrocities or participates in them. Cases may also occur where the government shields those who are responsible from bearing individual criminal responsibility through criminal investigations or prosecutions conducted in bad faith or by refusing to investigate or prosecute altogether. Bearing in mind the potential for such scenarios, the preamble declares that effective prosecution of the most serious crimes of concern to the international community as a whole 'must be ensured by taking measures at the national level and by enhancing international cooperation'. Further, the preamble notes that the ICC 'shall be complementary to national criminal jurisdictions'.

Thus, when there is no longer any prospect of justice by other means, the ICC may intervene, and in this sense it is 'a court of last resort'. In order for the Court to assert its jurisdiction over an alleged crime in such circumstances, certain criteria must be satisfied. These requirements are set out under the carefully worded parameters of article 17 of the Rome Statute under the designation 'admissibility'. Under article 17, it is the ICC and not the States Parties to the Rome Statute that determines when there is no longer a prospect of justice by other means. How does the Court determine this? Otherwise put, how does the Court determine if a case is 'admissible'?

There are three admissibility criteria, and they are cumulative. If any of them is not satisfied, the Court will declare a case inadmissible. I will only touch on the first two here. First, article 17 provides that a case is inadmissible if the concerned individual has already been tried for the same conduct that has been the subject of a complaint before the ICC.[14] This is an expression of the *ne bis in idem* principle which has been long established under national criminal law. It also constitutes an internationally recognised fundamental human right. However, this principle has

[14] Art 17(1)(c) Rome Statute.

been adapted by the drafters to properly reflect the purposes of the ICC, including ending impunity for the perpetrators of international crimes. As such, a caveat was attached to article 17, read in conjunction with article 20, entitled '*ne bis in idem*'. Under the terms of the two articles, a case that would otherwise be inadmissible in respect of the *ne bis in idem* principle would be admissible where either the trial took place for the purpose of shielding the concerned individual from criminal responsibility or the trial was not conducted independently or impartially or was otherwise conducted in a manner consistent with an intent to bring the concerned individual to justice.[15] The second admissibility criteria – which I will not delve into for the purposes of this contribution – is that the case should be of 'sufficient gravity' to justify action by the Court.[16]

The third and final criteria is that a case is inadmissible before the ICC where it is the object of an investigation or prosecution in a state that has jurisdiction over it, or the matter has been investigated by a state that has jurisdiction over it and that state has decided not to institute criminal proceedings against the person concerned.[17] However, notwithstanding the existence of a prior or contemporaneous investigation or prosecution, a case may become admissible if the state that exercises jurisdiction is 'unwilling' or 'unable genuinely' to carry out the investigation or prosecution of those alleged to be responsible for the crimes within the jurisdiction of the Court, or if the decision to not institute criminal proceedings following an investigation resulted from the 'unwillingness' or 'inability genuinely' to prosecute.[18]

Article 17 provides guidance to judges on how they should interpret 'unwilling' and 'unable'. A state is unwilling where the following criteria are met:

> (a) The proceedings were or are being undertaken or the national decision was made for the purpose of shielding the person concerned from criminal responsibility for crimes within the jurisdiction of the Court referred to in article 5;
> (b) There has been an unjustified delay in the proceedings which in the circumstances is inconsistent with an intent to bring the person concerned to justice;
> (c) The proceedings were not or are not being conducted independently or impartially, and they were or are being conducted in a manner which, in the circumstances, is inconsistent with an intent to bring the person concerned to justice.[19]

Thus, 'unwillingness' is linked to the purpose for which the process is or was conducted, or to the state's intention when putting the accused to trial. The analysis requires an evaluation of the state's subjective motivations in light of its national regime, including its laws, proceedings, practices and norms, combined with the presence of certain empirical factors particular to each case.

With respect to 'inability', article 17 provides that the Court shall consider the following:

[15] Art 17(1)(c) read together with Art 20(3) Rome Statute.
[16] Art 17(1)(d) Rome Statute.
[17] Art 17(1)(a) and (b) Rome Statute.
[18] ibid.
[19] Art 17(2) Rome Statute.

> [W]hether, due to a total or substantial collapse or unavailability of its national judicial system, the State is unable to obtain the accused or the necessary evidence and testimony or otherwise unable to carry out its proceedings.[20]

The determination that a state is truly 'unable' to carry out an investigation will be made in those situations in which the conditions in the state are not conducive to conducting national proceedings. This may be a consequence of, for example, the collapse of the national criminal justice system, the inexistence of such a system or the inability to obtain the accused. The 'total collapse' of the national criminal justice system may encompass situations of a total non-existence of a prosecution service or courts of justice. The situation of Rwanda in 1994, ravaged by armed conflict and genocide following the assassination of the president, is a historical example of 'total collapse'. 'Substantial collapse' requires an evaluation of quantitative elements, including the part of the criminal justice system affected by the crisis, in addition to an assessment of qualitative elements related to those types of institutions or personnel affected by the crisis. These criteria are objective and are determined by the facts. Where these facts are manifest, despite a state's willingness to investigate and, where indicated, to prosecute, the state is not able to fulfil its duties under the Rome Statute. Under these circumstances and where the other two admissibility criteria are satisfied, prima facie, such a case would be admissible.

C Clarification on Parameters of Admissibility by the Appeals Chamber

The Appeals Chamber interpreted the parameters of admissibility provided for in the *Katanga* case. First, the Appeals Chamber established that the admissibility of a case must be judged solely on the basis of the situation that exists at the moment in which the Court is seized of the question of admissibility.[21] However, the Appeals Chamber clarified that where a case has been deemed admissible for the reason that the State Party with an obligation to investigate has not proceeded with an investigation, it can become *inadmissible* if, thereafter, the state begins to investigate the crimes.[22] In this sense, admissibility is 'not necessarily static, but ambulatory'.[23] I will revisit the notion of the admissibility's 'ambulatory' character below when I discuss the Court's progress with respect to the situation in the Republic of Kenya.

Secondly, the Appeals Chamber affirmed that when a state fails to act, that is, it does not commence investigation or prosecution, the case is admissible. This is so

[20] Art 17(3) Rome Statute.

[21] Judgment on the Appeal of Mr Germain Katanga against the Oral Decision of Trial Chamber II of 12 June 2009 on the Admissibility of the Case, *Prosecutor v Germain Katanga and Mathieu Ngudjolo Chui*, ICC-01/04-01/07, Appeals Chamber, 25 September 2009, § 56.

[22] ibid.

[23] ibid.

regardless of the unwillingness or inability to investigate. Hence, the Appeals Chamber clarified that when the domestic jurisdiction remains 'inactive', the case is admissible and the question of the unwillingness or inability to prosecute is irrelevant.[24]

Finally, the Appeals Chamber clarified the notion of a 'decision not to prosecute' by national authorities under the terms of article 17(1)(b). The Appeals Chamber held that a decision by domestic authorities engaged in a domestic investigation into a case, to close domestic investigations and to surrender the concerned individual to the Court, is not a 'decision not to prosecute' within the meaning of article 17(1)(b). On the contrary, the Appeals Chamber asserted that such a course of action is a decision *to* prosecute, although through the ICC rather than the domestic jurisdiction. In these circumstances, article 17(1)(b) does not render a case inadmissible.[25]

IV Complementarity in Action in Situations and Cases before the ICC

Through the statutory thresholds of jurisdiction and admissibility, the drafters of the Rome Statute have codified their commitment to the principle of complementarity. Having made this outline of the requirements of the complementarity regime, I would now like to provide a brief overview of some of the situations and cases before the Court where we can observe complementarity in action.

Before canvassing the Court's work thus far, it is important to highlight that any interpretation of the provisions of the Rome Statute requires ICC judges to undertake a thorough analysis of international and comparative law. The Statute was the result of legal, political and diplomatic negotiations, and it is now being put into practice by a court comprised of judges specialised in criminal or international law and who have been trained in legal systems from all over the world. Thus, the interpretation of a statute of a hybrid nature by a court of a hybrid, ecumenical nature, relying neither purely on the common law nor purely on the Romano-Germanic traditions, requires a new approach to legal analysis ensuring deference to different legal traditions and fairness and equality for all the participants.

The principle of complementarity under the Rome Statute regime allows for a number of channels through which a situation may appear before the Court. At present, there are three States Parties to the Rome Statute that have themselves referred situations occurring in their territories to the Court: Uganda, the Democratic Republic of the Congo and the Central African Republic. In addition, the United Nations Security Council has twice referred situations to the Court acting in exercise of its Chapter VII powers to maintain and restore international

[24] ibid at §§ 78–79.
[25] ibid at § 82.

peace and security. The first referral was in 2005, when the situation in Darfur (Sudan) was referred to the Court. Notably, the permanent members of the Security Council, who are not States Parties to the Rome Statute did not use their veto power to block the passage of a resolution referring the situation to the Court. More recently, in February 2011, the Security Council referred the situation in Libya to the ICC by a unanimous decision of all members of the Security Council with voting power. Finally, in 2009, with respect to the situation in the Republic of Kenya, the Prosecutor has for the first time exercised his *proprio motu* powers under article 15 of the Statute whereby he may, on his own initiative, seek to initiate an investigation on the basis of information on crimes within the jurisdiction of the Court. We will now touch on some of these situations in more detail in relation to the principle of complementarity.

The ICC began its first trial in early 2009 in the *Lubanga* case. The accused in this case is presently being tried for war crimes consisting of conscripting and enlisting children under the age of 15 and using them to participate actively in hostilities. When referring this matter to the Court, the President of the Democratic Republic of the Congo, Joseph Kabila, presented a letter stating that, due to the particular situation within his country, the competent authorities could not carry out the investigation and prosecution of these crimes without the involvement of the ICC.[26]

The complementarity regime between the ICC and the Democratic Republic of the Congo was the subject of careful analysis by Pre-Trial Chamber I. The accused was then detained in Kinshasa and had been charged by national courts with crimes within the jurisdiction of the ICC. In assessing admissibility, the Chamber declared that for the case to be inadmissible, it was a '*conditio sine qua non* [. . .] that national proceedings encompass both the person and the conduct which is the subject of the case before the Court.'[27] The Chamber observed that the arrest warrant issued against Lubanga by the Democratic Republic of the Congo did not contain any reference to his alleged criminal responsibility for the crimes charged in the Prosecutor's application, namely enlisting and conscription children under the age of 15 and using them to participate actively in hostilities. The other limbs of the admissibility test having been satisfied, the case was declared admissible before the Court on the grounds that the Congolese national judicial system was not undertaking any action with respect to the specific case brought before the ICC.

The situation in Uganda was referred to the Court by the government of that country in January 2004. Arrest warrants were issued against five members of the Lord's Resistance Army, including its leader, Joseph Kony. Among the crimes enumerated in the arrest warrants were the crime against humanity of sexual enslavement, rape, murder and inhumane acts and the war crimes of enlisting

[26] See Letter from Mr Joseph Kabila to the ICC by the President of the Democratic Republic of the Congo, ICC-01/04-01/06-32-AnxA1, 21 March 2004.

[27] Decision concerning Pre-Trial Chamber's I Decision of 10 February 2006 and the Incorporation of Documents into the Record of the Case against Mr Thomas Lubanga Dyilo, *Prosecutor v Thomas Lubanga Dyilo*, ICC-01/04-01/06, Pre-Trial Chamber I, 24 February 2006, § 31.

children to participate actively in hostilities, attack against the civilian population, cruel treatment and pillaging. On issuing arrest warrants, Pre-Trial Chamber II noted in its May 2004 'Letter of Jurisdiction' to the Court, the Government of Uganda declared that it 'has not conducted and does not intend to conduct national proceedings in relation to the persons most responsible'.[28] Thus, the Chamber found, on the basis of the Prosecutor's application, the evidence and other information submitted by the Prosecutor, and without prejudice to subsequent determination, that the case appeared to be admissible.[29]

The situation in Darfur, Sudan, was referred to the ICC by the United Nations Security Council on the basis of a recommendation by the International Commission of Inquiry on Darfur which had been dispatched by the UN Secretary-General and which had concluded that crimes against humanity and war crimes within the jurisdiction of the ICC had been committed in the territory of Sudan. With respect to the question of complementarity, the Commission indicated the following in its report to the United Nations:

> The normal and ideal response to atrocities is to bring the alleged perpetrators to justice in the courts of the State where the crimes were perpetrated or of the State of nationality of the alleged perpetrators. [. . .] Considering the nature of the crimes committed in Darfur and the shortcomings of the Sudanese criminal justice system, which have led to effective impunity for the alleged perpetrators, the Commission is of the opinion that the Sudanese courts are unable and unwilling to prosecute and try the alleged offenders.[30]

Two out of the four cases initiated by the Prosecutor which have arisen from the situation in Darfur have reached the confirmation of charges stage of the proceedings. While in the *Abu Garda* case, Pre-Trial Chamber I declined to confirm the charges, the Chamber did make a finding on admissibility. The Chamber found that 'according to the information provided by the Prosecution, no State with jurisdiction over the case against Mr Abu Garda is acting, or has acted [. . .] in relation to the facts alleged in this case'.[31] Thus, in keeping with the Appeals Chamber's jurisprudence, the Chamber found that 'in the absence of any State action, it is not necessary to address any issues related to the unwillingness or inability of any given State to investigate or prosecute the Case'.[32] On 7 March 2011, in the absence of additional submissions by the parties or participants, Pre-Trial Chamber I relied, inter alia, on its admissibility finding in the *Abu Garda* case, in order to confirm the charges in the *Banda and Jerbo* case.[33]

[28] Warrant of Arrest for Joseph Kony issued on 8 July 2005 as amended on 27 September 2005, Situation in Uganda, ICC-02/04-01/05, Pre-Trial Chamber II, 27 September 2005, § 37.

[29] ibid at § 38.

[30] *Report of the International Commission of Inquiry on Darfur to the Secretary-General*, UN Doc S/2005/60, 1 February 2005, § 568.

[31] Decision on the Confirmation of Charges, *Prosecutor v Bahar Idriss Abu Garda*, ICC-01/05-02/09, Pre-Trial Chamber I, 8 February 2010, § 29.

[32] ibid at § 29.

[33] Corrigendum of the 'Decision on the Confirmation of Charges', *Prosecutor v Abdallah Banda Abakaer Nourain and Saleh Mohammed Jerbo Jamus*, ICC-02/05-03/09, Pre-Trial Chamber I, 7 March 2011, §§ 27 and 28.

Finally, I would like to raise the novel issue which is presently before Pre-Trial Chamber II concerning what the Appeals Chamber called the 'ambulatory' character of admissibility. On 26 November 2009, pursuant to his *proprio motu* powers under article 15 of the Statute, the Prosecutor of the ICC filed a request for authorisation to open and investigate the situation in the Republic of Kenya in relation to the post-election violence of 2007–08.[34] On 31 March 2010, Pre-Trial Chamber II authorised the commencement of an investigation.[35] The Chamber determined that 'the available information indicates that there is a situation of inactivity with respect to the elements that are likely to shape the potential case'.[36] The Chamber therefore found – the other limbs of the test having been met – that the case was admissible.[37]

Exactly one year after Pre-Trial Chamber II authorised the investigation, and some three weeks after the Chamber issued summonses to appear for six specific individuals (divided into two cases), the Republic of Kenya filed an application requesting that the Chamber determine that both cases were inadmissible before the ICC.[38] In its application, the Government of Kenya acknowledged 'all the criticisms and shortcomings that have been raised [. . .] of its judicial and investigative organs, many of which were relied upon by the Prosecutor in his request to open an investigation'.[39] Moreover, the Government of Kenya accepted without reservation that 'it was not possible to seek to have the ICC Prosecutor's investigation deferred to the Kenyan authorities before the adoption of the new Constitution and the legislative and other reforms that have followed as a consequence [of the ICC investigation]'.[40] Thus, the Pre-Trial Chamber now has the opportunity to further interpret the notion of what the Appeals Chamber termed the 'ambulatory' character of admissibility under the Rome Statute.

V Cooperation in Action at the National Level

Irrespective of the decision taken by Pre-Trial II in the Kenya cases, it is fair to say that the evolution now underway in the Kenyan criminal justice system is an example of the forward momentum of the principle of complementarity and the linked principle of cooperation. While Kenya is perhaps the most high-profile example,

[34] Request for authorisation of an investigation pursuant to Article 15, Situation in the Republic of Kenya, ICC-01/09, Office of the Prosecutor, 26 November 2009.

[35] Decision Pursuant to Article 15 of the Rome Statute on the Authorization of an Investigation into the Situation in the Republic of Kenya (Judge Hans-Peter Kaul dissenting), Situation in the Republic of Kenya, ICC-01/09, Pre-Trial Chamber II, 31 March 2010, at 83.

[36] ibid at § 54.

[37] ibid at §§ 187 and 200.

[38] Application on behalf of the Government of the Republic of Kenya Pursuant to Article 19 of the ICC Statute, *Prosecutor v William Samoei Ruto et al, and Prosecutor v. Francis Kirimi Muthaura at el*, ICC-01/09-01/11 and ICC-01/09-02/11, 31 March 2011, § 1.

[39] ibid at § 4.

[40] ibid.

there are many others. Complementarity – and by extension cooperation – have had a positive, rapid and significant impact on the domestic criminal laws of numerous States Parties. Before turning to a snapshot of cooperation in action at the national level, I will briefly set out the cooperation framework under the ICC.

Again, we must recall that the preamble of the Statute affirms that it is the 'duty of every State to exercise criminal jurisdiction over those most responsible for international crimes' and affirms that 'effective prosecution must be ensured by taking measures at the national level and by enhancing international cooperation'. Part IX of the Rome Statute, entitled 'International Cooperation and Judicial Assistance', sets out a range of specific obligations that States Parties assume to this end. The enumerated obligations range from providing assistance to the Court in identifying the whereabouts of persons, in servicing judicial documents, the identification, tracing and freezing or seizure of assets and with respect to enforcing sentences of imprisonment.

In regulation of such specific obligations, article 86 of the Part, provides that 'States Parties shall [. . .] cooperate fully with the Court in its investigation and prosecution of crimes within the jurisdiction of the Court'.[41] Further, article 88 provides that 'States Parties shall ensure that there are procedures available under their national law for all of the forms of cooperation which are specified under this Part'.[42] It is State cooperation through changes to national legislation which facilitates investigation and prosecution to which I would now like to turn.

A State Cooperation with the ICC through Changes in National Legislation

Following the ratification of the Statute and its entrance into force, many States Parties have reviewed their domestic legislation on genocide, crimes against humanity and war crimes in order to ensure compliance with their obligations under the Statute. Given that such initiatives have assumed a variety of forms, I will only attempt to provide a snapshot.

In some states, this review resulted in the enactment of new laws in order to ensure that its authorities could apply international criminal law. In the case of Germany, for example, the implementation of its obligation under the Statute was carried out through two laws: the Law on Implementation of the Rome Statute (*IStGH-AusführungsG*) and the International Criminal Code (*Völkerstrafgesetzbuch, VStGB*). In other states, the review has given rise to amendments to existing national laws in order to fill any gaps. In Switzerland, for example, the review resulted in modifications to the criminal code, the criminal procedure law as well as the military penal law.[43] Similarly, in Australia, the International Criminal

[41] Art 86 Rome Statute.

[42] Art 88 Rome Statute.

[43] Loi fédérale portant modification de lois fédérales en vue de la mise en oeuvre du Statut de Rome de la Cour pénale internationale, 18 juin 2010, available at : www.iccnow.org/documents/Loi_mise_en_oeuvre_18_Juin_2010.pdf.

Court Act was adopted in 2002 as a way of amending the relevant existing legal framework, including with respect to the existing criminal code and, for example, the existing law that addresses Australia's obligations under the Geneva Conventions of 1949. The same Act sets out an extensive framework for cooperation, in particular, in relation to the specific obligations enumerated under Part IX of the Rome Statute.

In a different sort of initiative to foster compliance with the Rome Statute's cooperation regime, British Commonwealth countries adopted a model law in 2005 with a view to assisting the 34 Commonwealth countries who are States Parties to the ICC to implement their obligations under the Statute through changes in their domestic legislation. In February 2011, a group of experts met in London in order to revise this model law with the aim of recommending modifications that reflect recent practices and new legal developments. The results of this meeting will be presented during the next meeting of the Ministers of the Commonwealth to be held in Sydney in July 2011.

This is just a glimpse at the efforts undertaken by States Parties to the Rome Statute in order to meet their obligations under the ICC's cooperation regime. Through such efforts these States are now in a better position to comply with any request for cooperation originating from ICC. At the same time, through revision of their respective domestic legal frameworks, these national criminal justice systems, should, in theory, be better equipped to investigate and prosecute the crimes under the jurisdiction of the Court themselves. As such, through compliance with the cooperation pillar of the Rome Statute, States are at the same time reinforcing the complementarity pillar of the Rome Statute such that the circumstances where there can be no justice by any other means are fewer and fewer and the ICC will remain, as it should be, a court of last resort.

VI Conclusion

The creation of the ICC was an achievement of historic significance and represents the culmination of a protracted effort over centuries by the international community and individual states to close the impunity gap – for what we now refer to as international crimes – through judicial enforcement mechanisms. The legal regimes buttressing these attempts were a function of the political and legal realities of the time such that we find a great deal of variation among these regimes with respect to the powers of these judicial mechanisms, and the relationship between these judicial mechanisms and states.

Like the international courts for the abolition of the slave trade, the success of the ICC in achieving its goal to end impunity will depend upon the fortitude of a process of cross-fertilisation between the Court and domestic enforcement mechanisms. Certainly, we are only at the beginning of this process under the Rome Statute regime and the judges must ever be mindful that the integrity of such a process, as we move forward, will also depend upon judicial development of buttressing procedural rules which must guarantee the full rights of the accused.

The early practice of the ICC demonstrates that momentum is building in this regard under the Rome Statute regime. The Court is fulfilling its role to step in as a court of last resort when justice is not possible by other means at the national level. At the same time, the complementarity and cooperation regime has had important positive effects on national criminal justice systems, including with respect to the ability of national authorities to respond to cooperation requests from the Court. But especially important, is the improved capacity of domestic criminal justice systems to themselves investigate and prosecute the crimes within the jurisdiction of the Court.

René Blattmann
Judge and former Vice-President, International Criminal Court
Carl Bertelsmann Prize
Dr.h.c. University of Basel (Switzerland) and Dr.h.c. Humboldt University of Berlin

The Hague, 27 May 2011

Final Reflections: The Challenges of the International Criminal Court

The creation of the International Criminal Court (ICC) by the Rome Statute marked a culminating point in the surge of idealist cosmopolitan doctrines in the 1990s, a decade which favoured questions of human security over state security, and considered justice and the rule of law as indispensible conditions for achieving peace.

However, in its functioning, the Court is forced to operate within an international system that is dominated by states and depends on their cooperation in order to investigate and prosecute. This cooperation cannot be taken for granted. The same states that created the Court may be reluctant to provide support if they feel that the institution is not effective or affects essential national or international interests.

In order to consolidate itself as an institution and assert itself as a relevant actor on the international scene, the Court must not only respect the legal framework defined by the states, it must demonstrate its legitimacy to act on concrete situations and cases, and show its ability to fulfil its mandate of investigating and prosecuting with impartiality and efficiency. Without prejudice to its objectives, the institution will need to maintain and expand external cooperation in order to operate efficiently. For this reason, legality, legitimacy, efficiency and cooperation are key concepts in understanding the main challenges facing the International Criminal Court in the years to come.

I Legality

The process of negotiating the Rome Statute and its main supplementary instruments – that is the Elements of the Crimes and the Rules of Procedure and Evidence – reflected, in the first place, the classic tension between internationalism and national sovereignty that opposes concerns for human rights with the principle of non-interference in internal affairs. This tension underlies many of the controversies during the negotiating process and explains some of the restrictions imposed on the system of jurisdiction and the regime of cooperation of the International Criminal Court.

But this tension – while important – does not suffice as a valid explanation for all the discrepancies. Equally important was the tension between the aspirations of justice with concerns for peace. This tension generated controversies about the role of the International Criminal Court in the system of international relations, particularly with regard to the articulation of its relationship with the United Nations Security Council.

As a consequence of these tensions, the states finished designing a mandate bound by restrictions based on three fundamental principles: legality, gravity and complementarity. Thus, the Court only has jurisdiction over the gravest international crimes of concern to the international community as a whole, namely genocide, crimes against humanity, war crimes and, in a programmatic form, the crime of aggression. This selection of the gravest crimes was followed by an effort to define the appropriate threshold of gravity for each of them, in order to narrow the universe of the acts covered.

Central among the restrictions of the Court's mandate, is the definition of an unprecedented system of 'complementarity' which is of paramount importance to the Court's effectiveness and is used as a last resort only in a genuine absence of state action.

The regulatory framework to be applied by the Court was defined in great detail by those states that, departing from all the precedents in the area, wrote in detail the rules of substantive and procedural law and embraced a strict approach to the interpretation of the principle of legality. The states considered it necessary to retain the design of these rules rather than leave the interpretation of the elements of the crimes and elaboration of the rules of procedure in the hands of the judges, as was reflected in the model used in the Statutes of the International Criminal Tribunals for the former Yugoslavia and for Rwanda. It was concluded that this model was not appropriate for an International Criminal Court of general and permanent character.

II Legitimacy

The strict respect for the pre-established regulatory framework is a necessary condition, but is not sufficient to ensure support for the Court's operation. The Court's operation must also be perceived as legitimate in the international community.

Legitimacy is an essential condition of judicial institutions in general, and of the legal mechanisms applied in situations of crisis in particular. Domestic tribunals are closer to the populations affected and better equipped to understand the context in which the crimes occurred. In contrast, international tribunals, separated from the relevant national systems, must permanently fight to obtain legitimacy and cooperation from the societies involved and the community in general.

The notion of legitimacy is understood to be a general perception that the International Criminal Court is justified to act, and that its actions are desirable, correct and appropriate in a particular context.[1]

The International Criminal Court's legitimacy is based on its democratic origins and the design of a substantive and procedural legal framework – representative of diverse systems of values, traditions and beliefs – through a process of multilateral negotiation open to all states and non-governmental organisations of the world. This legitimacy will be strengthened as an increasing number of ratifications and accessions to the Court will fulfil its universal aspiration.

However, this original legitimacy may not be sufficient to justify the Court's selection of a particular situation and to further provide the Court with sufficient integration into the national society concerned.

The Statute provides a system of guidance for this selection which combines the principle of independence of the international Prosecutor with the participation of state and non-state actors equipped with the power to refer situations to the Court and provide information. The States, the Security Council and civil society have the capacity to increase the legitimacy of the selection by referring situations or providing information about crimes to the Court. However, it is the Prosecutor who decides the situations and cases to be investigated and prosecuted, through a process of independent decision making, taking into account the factors established by the Statute.

The negotiators of the Rome Statute assumed that the states would be a natural source of legitimacy for the Court's operation in any given situation. They accepted without question that a State Party may request the intervention of the International Criminal Court regardless of its level of involvement in the situation, based on their belief that the state remains the entity with the greater legitimacy to act in the international system.

Therefore, it is not surprising that in the initial stage of the Court's legal proceeding, the Prosecutor also has privileged state referrals as a mechanism for triggering the Court's jurisdiction. The first two investigations, in the Democratic Republic of the Congo and in Uganda, and subsequently in the Central African Republic, were opened on the basis of referrals from the states on whose territory the crimes were committed. Engaging the Court through these state referrals eliminated an eventual tension between sovereignty and internationalism.

Voluntary referral of situations to the Court by the states directly affected was an early expression of confidence which gave the Court the opportunity to demonstrate its viability in the initial phase. However, the controversy that started over these 'self-referrals' demonstrated that there are no simple solutions to increase legitimacy. Whether it is the state, the Security Council or the Prosecutor acting on his own initiative based on information provided from any source, sup-

[1] Mark Suchman defines legitimacy as a premise or generalised perception that the actions of a entity are desirable, correct, or appropriate in the sense of a system of social norms, values, beliefs and definitions. See M Suchman, 'Managing Legitimacy: Strategic and Institutional Approaches' (1995) 20 *The Academy of Management Review* 571, 574.

port for the Court will not depend so much on the initial impulse, but on the specific circumstances of each situation. It will also depend on the quality and efficiency of the subsequent action of the Court in each of the stages of the procedure, including its strategy concerning communications and outreach.

III Efficiency

In the first years of the Court's operation, its supporters focused their attention on the opening of investigations. The selection of specific cases for investigation and prosecution was considered synonymous with the Court's setting into motion an imperative condition of its success. With the course of time, expectations became more diverse. Because of anxiety pertaining to judicial activity, new concerns were added to improve the institutional and judicial quality of the Court.

Both inside and out of the Court, it is now recognised that a priority concern is necessary to accelerate the judicial proceedings. Nevertheless, a clear answer does not exist about the concrete measures that should be adopted to achieve this. The main challenge of the years to come will not consist of establishing the existence of the problem, but capturing the underlying causes and agreeing on courses of action in order to resolve them.

The practice already developed by the institution in its first cases permits it to begin a critical analysis of the normative design as established by the states in the creation process with a view to identifying, and where necessary, amending those rules of procedure which might be obstacles to the smooth development of criminal proceedings. Although states themselves developed the legal framework currently applied by the Court, it will be vital for the success of any resulting amendment process to consult with and take sufficient account of the work and experience of those who have had the responsibility to apply such legal framework in practice.

IV Cooperation

The Court depends absolutely on external cooperation in order to comply with its mandate. The Court's need for cooperation in order to investigate and detain people in specific situations is exacerbated in the context of violence in which it is called to operate. The Court can only effectively and efficiently carry out its judicial activities if it has sufficient cooperation from the international community.

To ensure cooperation, it is necessary to strengthen the will of states and organisations to provide information and other modes of assistance to the Court and to detain and surrender accused persons. Beyond the principal support for justice, the initial experience of the Court demonstrates the difficulties it faces in obtaining cooperation for its activities.

Expanding universal support for the Court by increasing the number of ratifications and accessions will also strengthen cooperation. The Court is not yet a universal institution and the system in which it bases its jurisdiction has not entirely displaced the requirement of state consent in certain situations. In the absence of a referral by the United Nations Security Council, the acceptance of the Court's jurisdiction by the state where the crimes were committed or the state of the nationality of the alleged responsible persons is required. This limits the Court's ability to protect the values shared by humanity as a whole, and thereby undermines the global ideal it is called to embody. Therefore, in order to consolidate itself as a relevant international institution, the Court must achieve universal participation.

Silvia A Fernández de Gurmendi
Judge, International Criminal Court

The Hague, 10 May 2011

Epilogue: Building the Proceedings Before the Pre-Trial Chamber of the International Criminal Court

When Hector asked me to write an epilogue for his book of studies in international criminal justice to mark the occasion of his inaugural lecture as professor at Utrecht University, I accepted with a mixture of happiness and nostalgia. This is a work that represents the end of a stage in which Hector and I had the opportunity to work closely in the first proceedings before the International Criminal Court, and the beginning of a new stage of his professional life at the university.

I met Hector for the first time at the beginning of 1999, when he was a young PhD candidate at Columbia University and formed part of the Spanish delegation to the Preparatory Commission for the International Criminal Court (at that time I was part of the Brazilian delegation).

In addition to his knowledge of criminal law and international and comparative criminal procedure, what always caught more of my attention was Hector's belief that international criminal justice, and the International Criminal Court in particular, could help make the world more just.

What I never could have expected at that moment, is that years later I would be appointed as a judge of the International Criminal Court, and in August 2004 Hector would be named legal officer for the Pre-Trial Division and I would then request that he be assigned to my supervision (at that time in the structure of the Chambers of the Court, each judge exercised supervision over a lawyer). Nor could I foresee at the time that I would be appointed single judge over the issues relating to the Democratic Republic of the Congo and Darfur, including the first proceedings in the cases against Thomas Lubanga Dyilo, Germain Katanga and Mathieu Ngudjolo Chui and Omar Al Bashir.

Although there were situations that raised questions every step of the way – particularly in the preparation of the first confirmation of the charges hearing in the case of Thomas Lubanga Dyilo – what is certain is that we were able to count on Hector to always be very supportive. He always had the virtue of providing several possible alternatives from his experience of comparative and international law and was not limited to analysing the solution to the specific problem, but could analyse the advantages and disadvantages of the different alternatives within the penal and procedural system in which we were operating as a whole. His observations always had in mind that the answers of today should not only be valid for the case we were facing, but should serve as a guide for us to solve similar problems that may arise in future cases.

In this sense, one must highlight that it was our task at that moment to establish the first case law of the first permanent International Criminal Court on pre-trial issues, in relation to which we soon discovered that there was no precedent from other international tribunals to serve us as a guide.

I suppose it had to be that profound belief in international criminal justice, and embedded humanistic spirit, which I already saw when I met him in 1999, that must have motivated Hector to spend so many tireless nights at the office helping to advance those first proceedings which led to the International Criminal Court. Otherwise, it is difficult to understand the extraordinary commitment that, over more than six years spent working together, he showed with this Court and me as well.

It is for this reason that I write these lines, along with the happiness of the moments spent, also with a certain nostalgia because the appointment of Hector as a professor at Utrecht University marks the beginning of a new – and I am sure, brilliant – stage, this time a little further away from the writer of this Epilogue. While, in view of the numerous books, articles, supervision of doctoral theses, participation in master programmes, law clinics, inter-university competitions, training activities for judges, prosecutors, defence counsels and other legal actors, consultancies, international cooperation programmes and many other activities that Hector has been involved in in recent years, Hector's new appointment was not surprising; it always seems that it arrives too soon.

In any case, with these words I want to express to Hector publicly once again my appreciation for the work he has done by my side during the first six years of the existence of the International Criminal Court. I also want to encourage the reader to continue working towards strengthening international criminal justice after reading this magnificent work. Finally, I want to congratulate Richard Hart and Hart Publishing for having the wisdom to publish an author truly unique in his professional career as Professor Hector Olasolo.

Sylvia H Steiner
Judge and President of the Pre-Trial Division, International Criminal Court

The Hague, 1 May 2011

BIBLIOGRAPHY

Aguirre X, 'Gravity of Crimes and Responsibility of the Suspect' in M Bergsmo (ed), *Criteria for Prioritizing and Selecting Core International Crimes Cases* (Oslo, Forum for International Criminal and Humanitarian Law Publications, 2009).

Akehurst M, 'Humanitarian Intervention' in H Bull (ed), *World Politics* (Oxford, Clarendon Press, 1984).

Alcaide Fernández J, 'La Complementariedad de la Corte Penal Internacional y de los Tribunales Nacionales: ¿Tiempos de "Ingeniería Jurisdiccional"?' in JA Carrillo Salcedo (ed), *La Criminalización de la Barbarie: La Corte Penal Internacional* (Madrid, Consejo General del Poder Judicial, 2000).

Ambos K, 'Superior Responsibility' in A Cassese, P Gaeta and JRWD Jones (eds), *The Rome Statute of the International Criminal Court: A Commentary* (Oxford, Oxford University Press, 2002).

—— *La Parte General del Derecho Penal Internacional: Bases para una Elaboración Dogmática* (Uruguay, Konrad-Adenauer-Stiftung, 2005).

—— 'Joint Criminal Enterprise and Command Responsibility' (2007) 5 *Journal of International Criminal Justice* 159.

—— *El Marco Jurídico de la Justicia de Transición. Especial Referencia al Caso Colombiano* (Bogotá, Temis, 2008).

—— *Prosecutor v Kaing Guek Eav, alias 'Duch' Case Amicus Curiae* Concerning Criminal Case File No 001/18-07-2007-ECCC/OCIJ (PTC 02)) 001/18-07-2007-ECCC/OCIJ (PTC 02)-D99-3-27 (27 October 2008).

—— 'Epilogue: Future Developments of International Criminal Law in Relation to the Responsibility of Superiors for International Crimes' in H Olasolo, *The Criminal Responsibility of Senior Political and Military Leaders as Principals to International Crimes* (Oxford, Hart Publishing, 2009).

—— *Procedimiento de La Ley de Justicia y Paz (Ley de 2005) y Derecho Penal Internacional* (Bogotá, GTZ, Universidad de Göttingen, 2010).

—— 'The *Fujimori* Judgment: A President's Responsibility for Crimes Against Humanity as Indirect Perpetrator by Virtue of an Organised Power Apparatus' (2011) 9 *Journal of International Criminal Justice* 137.

Ambos K and Grammer C, 'Dominio del Hecho por Organizacion. La Responsabilidad de la Conduccion Militar Argentina por la Muerte de Elisabeth Kasemann' (2003) 12 *Revista Penal* 28.

Ambos K and Miller D, 'Structure and Function of the Confirmation Procedure before the ICC from a Comparative Perspective' (2007) 7 *International Criminal Law Review* 335.

Arbour L and Bergsmo M, 'Conspicuous Absence of Jurisdictional Overreach' in H Von Hebel, JG Lammers and J Schukking (eds), *Reflections on the International Criminal Court. Essays in Honour of Adriaan Bos* (The Hague, TMC Asser Press, 1999).

Arvelo JE, 'International Law and Conflict Resolution in Colombia: Balancing Peace and Justice in the Paramilitary Demobilization Process' (Winter 2006) 77 *Georgetown Journal of International Law* 411.

Bassiouni MC, 'International Crimes: Ius Cogens and Obligatio Erga Omnes' (1996) 59 *Law and Contemporary Problems* 63.
—— 'Proposed Guiding Principles for Combating Impunity for International Crimes' in MC Bassiouni (ed), *Post-Conflict Justice* (Ardsley, Transnational Publishers, 2002).
—— *Introduction to International Criminal Law* (Ardsley, Transnational Publishers, 2003).
—— 'The Making of the International Criminal Court' in MC Bassiouni (ed), *International Criminal Law* vol 3 3rd edn (Leiden, Martinus Nijhoff Publishers, 2008).
Bethell L, 'The Mixed Commissions for the Suppression of the Transatlantic Slave Trade in the Nineteenth Century' (1966) 7 *Journal of African History* 79.
Bellamy A, *A Responsibility to Protect: The Global Effort to End Mass Atrocities* (Cambridge, Polity Press, 2009).
Bergsmo M and Pejic J, 'Article 15' in O Triffterer (ed), *Commentary on the Rome Statute of the International Criminal Court* 2nd edn (Oxford, Munich, Hart Publishing and Verlag CH Beck, 2008).
Bitti G and Friman H, 'Participation of Victims in the Proceedings' in R Lee (ed), *The International Criminal Court, Elements of Crimes and Rules of Procedure and Evidence* (Ardsley, Transnational Publishers, 2001).
Bogdan A, 'Individual Criminal Responsibility in the Execution of a "Joint Criminal Enterprise" in the Jurisprudence of the *Ad hoc* International Tribunal for the Former Yugoslavia' (2006) 6 *International Criminal Law Review* 63.
Boot M, Genocide, *Crimes against Humanity and War Crimes: Nullum Crimen Sine Lege and Subject Matter Jurisdiction of the International Criminal Court* (Antwerpen, Intersentia, 2002).
Boraine A, *A Country Unmasked: Inside South Africa's Truth and Reconciliation Commission* (Oxford, Oxford University Press, 2001).
Brading DA, *The First America: The Spanish Monarchy, Creole Patriots, and the Liberal State 1492–1867* (Cambridge, Cambridge University Press, 1991).
Brady H, 'Protective and Special Measures for Victims and Witnesses' in R Lee (ed), *The International Criminal Court, Elements of Crimes and Rules of Procedure and Evidence* (Ardsley, Transnational Publishers, 2001).
—— 'Australia' in C Kress, B Broomhall, F Lattanzi and V Santori (eds) *The Rome Statute and Domestic Legal Orders Vol II: Constitutional Issues, Cooperation and Enforcement* (Baden-Baden, Nomos/Il Sirente, 2005).
Broomhall B, 'The International Criminal Court: A Checklist for National Implementation' in MC Bassiouni (ed), *ICC Ratification and National Implementing Legislation, Nouvelles Études Pénales* vol 13 (Érès, Nouvelles Études Pénales, 1999).
Brownlie I, *International Law and the Use of Force by States* (Oxford, Clarendon Press, 1963).
—— 'Humanitarian Intervention' in J Moore (ed), *Law and Civil War in the Modern World* (Baltimore, Johns Hopkins University Press, 1974).
—— 'The Principle of Non-Use of Force in Contemporary International Law' in W Butler (ed), *The Non-Use of Force in International Law* (Dordrecht, Martinus Nijhoff, 1989).
Bujosa Vadell L, *La Cooperación Procesal de los Estados con la Corte Penal Internacional* (Barcelona, Atelier, 2006).
Burbridge P, 'Justice and Peace? – The Role of Law in Resolving Colombia's Civil Conflict' (2008) 8 *International Criminal Law Review* 557.
Burke-White W, 'Complementarity in Practice: The International Criminal Court as Part of a System of Multi-level Global Governance in the Democratic Republic of Congo' (2005) 18 *Leiden Journal of International Law* 557.

—— 'Implementing a Policy of Positive Complementarity in the Rome System of Justice' (2008) 19 *Criminal Law Forum* 59.

Burmester BF, 'On Humanitarian Intervention: The New World Order and Wars to Preserve Human Rights' (1994) 1 *Utah Law Review* 269.

Cárdenas C, 'The Admissibility Test before the ICC under Special Considerations of Amnesties and Truth Commissions' in JK Kleffner and G Kor (eds), *Complementary Views on Complementarity* (The Hague, TMC Asser Press, 2006).

Cassese A, 'From Nuremberg to Rome: International Military Tribunals to the International Criminal Court' in A Cassese, P Gaeta and JRWD Jones (eds), *The Rome Statute of the International Criminal Court: A Commentary* vol I (Oxford, Oxford University Press, 2002).

—— 'Jurisdiction *ratione materiae* – Genocide' in A Cassese, P Gaeta and JRWD Jones (eds), *The Rome Statute of the International Criminal Court: A Commentary* (Oxford, Oxford University Press, 2002).

—— 'The Rome Statute: A Tentative Assessment' in A Cassese, P Gaeta and JRWD Jones (eds), *The Rome Statute of the International Criminal Court: A Commentary* (Oxford, Oxford University Press, 2002).

—— 'Is the ICC Still Having Teething Problems' (2006) 4 *Journal of International Criminal Justice* 434.

—— 'The Proper Limits of Individual Responsibility under the Doctrine of Joint Criminal Enterprise' (2007) 5 *Journal of International Criminal Justice* 109.

—— *International Criminal Law* 2nd edn (Oxford, Oxford University Press, 2008).

—— *Prosecutor v Kaing Guek Eav, alias 'Duch', Amicus Curiae* Brief of Professor Antonio Cassese and Members of the Journal of International Criminal Justice on Joint Criminal Enterprise Doctrine, 001/18-07-2007-ECCC/OCIJ (PTC 02) - D99-3-24 (27 October 2008).

Chrétien JP, *Rwanda: Les Médias du Génocide* 2nd edn (Paris, Karthala/Reporters sans Frontiers, 2002).

Chung CH, 'Victims' Participation at the International Criminal Court: Are Concessions of the Court Clouding the Promise?' (Spring 2008) 6 *Northwestern Journal of International Human Rights* 459.

Cross ME and Williams S, 'Recent Developments at the ICC: Prosecutor v Germain Katanga and Mathieu Ngudjolo Chui: A Boost for Co-operative Complementarity?' (2010) 10 *Human Rights Law Review* 336.

Crow J, *The Epic of Latin America* 4th edn (Berkeley, University of California Press, 1992).

Cryer R, Friman H, Robinson D and Wilmshurst E, *An Introduction to International Criminal Law and Procedure* 2nd edn (Cambridge, Cambridge University Press, 2010).

Danner AM and Martinez JS, 'Guilty Associations: Joint Criminal Enterprise, Command Responsibility and the Development of International Criminal Law' (2005) 93 *California Law Review* 150.

De las Casas B and Griffin N (tr), Brevísima Relación de la Destrucción de las Indias (*A Short Account of the Destruction of the Indies*) (London, Penguin Classics, 1999).

De Vitoria F and Scott JB (ed), *Relectiones Theologicae* (New York, London, Oceana Publications, 1917).

Delbruck J, 'A Fresh Look at Humanitarian Intervention under the Authority of the United Nations' (1992) 67 *Indiana Law Journal* 887.

Donat-Cattin D, 'Article 68: Protection of Victims and Witnesses and their Participation in the Proceedings' in O Triffterer (ed), *Commentary on the Rome Statute of the International Criminal Court* 2nd edn (Oxford, Munich, Hart Publishing and Verlag CH Beck, 2008).

Dugard J, 'Dealing with Crimes of a Past Regime. Is Amnesty an Option?' (1999) 12 *Leiden Journal of International Law* 1001.

El Zeidy MM, 'The Principle of Complementarity: A New Machinery to Implement International Criminal Law' (2002) 32 *Michigan Journal of International Law* 869.

—— 'The Ugandan Government Triggers the First Test of the Complementarity Principle: An Assessment of the First State's Party Referral to the ICC' (2005) 5 *International Criminal Law Review* 83.

—— 'Some Remarks on the Question of the Admissibility of a Case during Arrest Warrant Proceedings before the International Criminal Court' (2006) 19 *Leiden Journal of International Law* 741.

—— *The Principle of Complementarity in International Criminal Law: Origin, Development and Practice* (Leiden, Boston, Martinus Nijhoff, 2008).

Escobar Hernandez C, 'La Progresiva Institucionalización de la Jurisdicción Penal Internacional' in M Garcia Aran and D Lopez Garrido (eds), *Crimen Internacional y Jurisdicción Universal (el Caso Pinochet)* (Valencia, Tirant lo Blanch, 2000).

Eser A, 'Individual Criminal Responsibility' in A Cassese, P Gaeta and JRWD Jones (eds), *The Rome Statute of the International Criminal Court: A Commentary* (Oxford, Oxford University Press, 2002).

—— 'Mental Elements – Mistakes of Fact and Law' in A Cassese, P Gaeta and JRWD Jones (eds), *The Rome Statute of the International Criminal Court: A Commentary* (Oxford, Oxford University Press, 2002).

Evans G, *The Responsibility to Protect: Ending Mass Atrocity Crimes Once and for All* (Washington, DC, Brookings Institution Press, 2008).

Farrell N, 'Attributing Criminal Liability to Corporate Actors: Some Lessons from the International Tribunals' (2010) 8 *Journal of International Criminal Justice* 880.

Fernández de Gurmendi SA, 'The Role of the International Prosecutor' in R Lee (ed), *The International Criminal Court: The Making of the Rome Statute – Issues, Negotiations, Results* (The Hague, Kluwer Law International, 1999).

—— 'Definition of Victims and General Principles' in R Lee (ed), *The International Criminal Court, Elements of Crimes and Rules of Procedure and Evidence* (Ardsley, Transnational Publishers, 2001).

Ferrajoli L, 'El Derecho Penal Minimo' in JB Ramírez (ed), *Prevención y Teoría de la Pena* (Santiago, Editorial Jurídica Conosur Ltda, 1995).

Ferré Olivé J and Anarte Borrallo E (eds), *Problemas de Autoría y Participación en la Criminalidad Organizada* (Huelva, Universidad de Huelva, 1999).

Fierens J, '*Gacaca* Courts: Between Fantasy and Reality' (2005) 3 *Journal of International Criminal Justice* 896.

Fife RE, 'Article 80. Non-Prejudice to National Application of Penalties and National Laws' in O Triffterer (ed), *Commentary on the Rome Statute of the International Criminal Court: Observers' Notes, Article by Article* (Baden Baden, Nomos, 1999).

Fisse B, *Howard's Criminal Law* 5th edn (Sydney, Law Book Company, 1990).

Fletcher GP, *Rethinking Criminal Law* (New York, Oxford University Press, 2000).

—— 'Amicus Curiae Brief of Specialists in Conspiracy and International Law in Support of Petitioner' 2006 *West Law* 53979, filed in *Hamdan v Rumsfeld*, 548 US 557 (2006).

—— *Rethinking Criminal Law* 2nd edn (Oxford, Oxford University Press, 2008).

Fletcher GP and Ohlin J, 'Reclaiming Fundamental Principles of Criminal Law in the Darfur Case' (2005) 3 *Journal of International Criminal Justice* 539.

Fontán Balestra C, *Tratado de Derecho Penal: Parte General* (Albany, Lexis Publishing, 1995).

Franck T, 'Legality and Legitimacy in Humanitarian Intervention' in T Nardin and MS Williams (eds), *Humanitarian Intervention* (New York, New York University Press, 2006).

Friman H, 'The International Criminal Court and Participation of Victims: A Third Party to the Proceedings?' (2009) 22 *Leiden Journal of International Law* 485.

Funk TM, *Victims' Rights and Advocacy at the International Criminal Court* (Oxford, Oxford University Press, 2010).

Gallón Giraldo G, Reed Hurtado M and Lleras Cruz C (eds), *Anotaciones sobre la Ley de Justicia y Paz. Una Mirada desde los Derechos de las Víctimas* (Bogotá, Comisión Colombiana de Juristas, 2007).

Gillies P, *Criminal Law* 4th edn (North Ryde, LBC Information Services, 1997).

Gimbernat Ordeig A, *Autor y Cómplice en Derecho Penal* (Madrid, Universidad de Madrid, 1966).

Gioia F, 'State Sovereignty, Jurisdiction, and "Modern" International Law: The Principle of Complementarity in the International Criminal Court' (2006) 19 *Leiden Journal of International Law* 1095.

Gómez Benítez JM, 'Elementos Comunes de los Crímenes contra la Humanidad en el Estatuto de la Corte Penal Internacional' (2002) 42 *Actualidad Penal* 1121.

Gonzalez Rus J, 'Autoría Única Inmediata, Autoría Mediata y Coautoría' in Consejo General del Poder Judicial (ed), *Cuadernos de Derecho Judicial No XXXIX* (Madrid, 1994).

Gordon R, 'Humanitarian Intervention by the United Nations: Iraq, Somalia, and Haiti' (1996) 31 *Texas International Law Journal* 43.

Grotius H, *De Mare Liberum* (1609) trans R Magoffin (New York, Oxford University Press 1916).

—— *Dejure Belli AC Pacis* book II (1625) trans F Kelsey (Gloucestershire, Clarendon Press 1925).

Guariglia F, 'The Selection of Cases by the Office of the Prosecutor of the International Criminal Court' in C Stahn and G Sluiter (eds), *The Emerging Practice of the International Criminal Court* (The Hague, Martinus Nijhoff, Brill, 2009).

Gustafson K, 'The Requirements of an "Express Agreement" for Joint Criminal Enterprise Liability: A Critique of Brđanin' (2007) 5 *Journal of International Criminal Justice* 141.

—— 'ECCC Tackles JCE: An Appraisal of Recent Decisions' (2010) 8 *Journal of International Criminal Justice* 1323.

Haan V, 'The Development of the Concept of Joint Criminal Enterprise at the International Criminal Tribunal for the Former Yugoslavia' (2005) 5 *International Criminal Law Review* 167.

Hall CK, 'Article 19. Challenges to the Jurisdiction of the Court or the Admissibility of a Case' in O Triffterer (ed), *Commentary on the Rome Statute of the International Criminal Court: Observers' Notes, Article by Article* (Baden Baden, Nomos, 1999).

—— 'Developing and Implementing an Effective Positive Complementarity Prosecution Strategy' in C Stahn and G Sluiter, *The Emerging Practice of the International Criminal Court* (Leiden, Brill, 2009).

Hamdorf K, 'The Concept of a Joint Criminal Enterprise and Domestic Modes of Liability for Parties to a Crime: A Comparison of German and English Law' (2007) 1 *Journal of International Criminal Justice* 208.

Haslam E, 'Victim Participation at the International Criminal Court: A Triumph of Hope over Experience?' in R Lee (ed), *The International Criminal Court: Elements of Crimes and Rules of Procedure and Evidence* (New York, Transnational Publishers, 2001).

Hehir A, *Humanitarian Intervention: An Introduction* (London, Palgrave Macmillan, 2010).

Heller KJ, 'Situational Gravity under the Rome Statute' in C Stahn and L van den Herik (eds), *Future Directions in International Criminal Justice* (The Hague, TMC Asser/ Cambridge University Press, 2009).

Henrad K, 'The Viability of National Amnesties in View of the Increasing Recognition of Individual Criminal Responsibility at International Law' (1999) 8 *Michigan State University-DCL Journal of International Law* 595.

Holmes JT, 'The Principle of Complementarity' in R Lee (ed), *The International Criminal Court: The Making of the Rome Statute – Issues, Negotiations, Results* (The Hague, Kluwer Law International, 1999).

—— 'Complementarity: National Courts versus the ICC' in A Cassese, P Gaeta and JRWD Jones (eds), *The Rome Statute of the International Criminal Court: A Commentary* (Oxford, Oxford University Press, 2002).

International Commission on Intervention and State Sovereignty (ICISS), *The Responsibility to Protect* (Ottawa, International Development Research Centre, 2001).

Jain N, 'A Separate Law for Peacekeepers: The Clash between the Security Council and the International Criminal Court' (2005) 16 *European Journal of International Law* 239.

Jayawickrama N, *The Judicial Application of Human Rights Law: National, Regional and International Jurisprudence* (Cambridge, Cambridge University Press, 2003).

Jenkins C, 'A Truth Commission for East Timor: Lessons from South Africa?' (2002) 7 *Journal of Conflict and Security Law* 233.

Jessup P, *A Modern Law of Nations* (New York, The Macmillan Company, 1948).

Jiménez García F, 'Hacia una Jurisdicción Internacional Obligatoria en el Siglo XXI: El Estatuto del Tribunal Penal Internacional Adoptado en Roma el 17 de Julio de 1998' (1999) 3 *Studia Carande* 103.

Jones JRWD, *The Practice of the International Criminal Tribunals for the Former Yugoslavia and Rwanda* (Irvington-on-Hudson, Transnational Publishers, 2000).

—— 'Protection of Victims and Witnesses' in A Cassese, P Gaeta and JRWD Jones (eds), *The Rome Statute of the International Criminal Court: A Commentary* (Oxford, Oxford University Press, 2002).

Jorda C and De Hemptinne J, 'The Status and Role of the Victim' in A Cassese, P Gaeta and JRWD Jones (eds), *The Rome Statute of the International Criminal Court: A Commentary* (Oxford, Oxford University Press, 2002).

Joyner C, 'The Responsibility to Protect: Humanitarian Concern and the Lawfulness of Armed Intervention' (2007) 47 *Virginia Journal of International Law* 693.

Kalmanovitz P, 'Introduction: Law and Politics in the Colombian Negotiations with Paramilitary Groups' in M Bergsmo and P Kalmanovitz, (eds), *Law in Peace Negotiations* (Oslo, Forum for International Criminal and Humanitarian Law Publications, 2009).

Keen B, *The Legacy of Bartolomé de Las Casas* (Boulder, Westview Press, 1998).

Kress C, '"Self-Referrals" and "Waivers of Complementarity": Some Considerations in Law and Policy' (2004) 2 *Journal of International Criminal Justice* 944.

Kress C and Grover L, 'International Criminal Law Restraints in Peace Talks to End Armed Conflicts of a Non-International Character' in M Bergsmo and P Kalmanovitz (eds), *Law in Peace Negotiations* (Oslo, Forum for International Criminal and Humanitarian Law Publications, 2009).

Lattanzi F, 'Compétence de la Cour Pénale Internationale et consentement des états' (1999) *Revue Générale de Droit International Public* 425.

Lauterpacht H, 'The Grotian Tradition in International Law' in *British Yearbook of International Law* (London, Oxford University Press, 1946).
—— (ed), *Oppenheim's International Law: A Treatise* 6th edn (London, Longmans Green and Company, 1947).
Lewis P, 'The United Kingdom' in C Kress, B Broomhall, F Lattanzi and V Santori (eds), *The Rome Statute and Domestic Legal Orders Vol II: Constitutional Issues, Cooperation and Enforcement* (Baden-Baden, Nomos/Il Sirente, 2005).
Lillich R, 'Forcible Self-Help by States to Protect Human Rights' (1967) 53 *Iowa Law Review* 325.
—— 'Intervention to Protect Human Rights' (1969) 15 *McGill Law Journal* 205.
—— 'Humanitarian Intervention: A Reply to Ian Brownlie and a Plea for Constructive Alternatives' in JN Moore (ed), *Law and Civil War in the Modern World* (Baltimore, Johns Hopkins University Press, 1974).
—— 'Forcible Self Help Under International Law' (1980) 62 *Readings in International Law from the Naval War College Review* 129.
Lirola Delgado I and Martín Martínez M, *La Corte Penal Internacional. Justicia versus Impunidad* (Barcelona, Ariel Derecho, 2001).
Locke J, 'The Second Treatise of Government' (1690) in P Laslet (ed), *Two Treatises of Government* 3rd edn (Cambridge, Cambridge University Press, 1988).
Losada A, *The Controversy between Sepúlveda and Las Casas in the Junta of Valladolid* (DeKalb, Northern Illinois University Press, 1971).
Luzón Peña DM, *Curso de Derecho Penal. Parte General* (Madrid, Editorial Universitas SA, 1999).
Manacorda S and Meloni C, 'Joint Perpetration *versus* Joint Criminal Enterprise: Concurring Approaches in the Practice of International Criminal Law?' (2011) 9 *Journal of International Criminal Justice* 161.
Martinez JS, 'Anti-Slavery Courts and the Dawn of International Human Rights Law' (2008) 117(4) *Yale Law Journal* 550.
McAuliffe deGuzman M, 'Article 21: Applicable Law' in O Triffterer (ed), *Commentary on the Rome Statute of the International Criminal Court* 2nd edn (Oxford and Munich, Hart Publishing and Verlag CH Beck, 2008).
McGill University (*Prosecutor v Kaing Guek Eav, alias 'Duch', Amicus Curiae* Brief Submitted by the Center for Human Rights and Legal Pluralism, McGill University Montreal (Quebec) Canada), 001/18-07-2007-ECCC/OCIJ (PTC 02)-D99-3-25 (27 October 2008).
Moore JN, 'Toward an Applied Theory for the Regulation of Intervention' in JN Moore (ed), *Law and Civil War in the Modern World* (Baltimore, Johns Hopkins University Press, 1974).
Morris M, 'High Crimes and Misconceptions: The ICC and Non-Party States' (2000) 64 *Law and Contemporary Problems* 13.
Morris V and Scharf M, *An Insider's Guide to the International Criminal Tribunal for the Former Yugoslavia* vol I (Irvington-on-Hudson, Transnational Publishers, 1995).
Muñoz Conde F and García Arán M, *Derecho Penal. Parte General* (Valencia, Tirant lo Blanch, 1998).
—— *Derecho Penal: Parte General* 5th edn (Valencia, Tirant lo Blanch, 2002).
Muñoz Conde F and Olasolo H, 'The Application of the Notion of Indirect Perpetration through Organised Structures of Power in Latin America and Spain' (2011) 9 *Journal of International Criminal Justice* 113.

Murphy S, *Humanitarian Intervention: The United Nations in an Evolving World Order* (Washington, DC, PAIL Institute, 1996).

Nafziger J, 'Self-Determination and Humanitarian Intervention in a Community of Power' (1991) 20 *Denver Journal of International Law and Policy* 9.

Nerlich V, 'Lessons for the International Criminal Court: The Impact of Criminal Proceedings on the South African Amnesty Process' in G Werle (ed), *Justice in Transition: Prosecution and Amnesty in Germany and South Africa* (Berlin, Berliner WissenschaftsVerlag, 2006).

Ntanda Nsereko DD, 'Article 18: Preliminary Rulings Regarding Admissibility' in O Triffterer (ed), *Commentary on the Rome Statute of the International Criminal Court* 2nd edn (Oxford and Munich, Hart Publishing and Verlag CH Beck, 2008).

Ohlin JD, 'Three Conceptual Problems with the Doctrine of Joint Criminal Enterprise' (2007) 5 *Journal of International Criminal Justice* 89.

—— 'Attempt to Commit Genocide' in P Gaeta (ed), *The UN Genocide Convention: A Commentary* (Oxford, Oxford University Press, 2009).

—— 'Incitement and Conspiracy to Commit Genocide' in P Gaeta (ed), *The UN Genocide Convention: A Commentary* (Oxford, Oxford University Press, 2009).

Olasolo H, *Corte Penal Internacional: Dónde Investigar? Especial Referencia a la Fiscalía en el Proceso de Activación* (Valencia, Tirant lo Blanch, 2003).

—— 'Reflexiones sobre el Principio de Complementariedad en el Estatuto de Roma' (2003) 82 *Revista Española de Derecho Militar* 47.

—— 'Apuntes Prácticos sobre el Tratamiento de los Crímenes de Guerra en el Estatuto de Roma de la Corte Penal Internacional' (2005) 86 *Revista Española de Derecho Militar* 107.

—— *The Triggering Procedure of the International Criminal Court* (Leiden, Martinus Nijhoff Publishers, 2005).

—— 'The Triggering Procedure of the International Criminal Court, Procedural Treatment of Complementarity and the Role of the Office of the Prosecutor' (2005) 5 *International Criminal Law Review* 121.

—— 'The Lack of Attention to the Distinction between Situations and Cases in National Laws on Cooperation with the ICC: Special Attention to the Spanish Case' (2007) 20 *Leiden Journal of International Law* 193.

—— 'Reflections on the Treatment of the Notions of Control of the Crime and Joint Criminal Enterprise in the *Stakić* Appeal Judgment' (2007) 7 *International Criminal Law Review* 143.

—— 'Admisibilidad de situaciones y casos objeto de procesos de justicia de transición ante la Corte Penal Internacional' in J Almqvist and C Espósito (eds), *El papel de los tribunales en contextos de justicia transicional: oportunidades y desafíos actuales en la región Iberoamericana* (Madrid, Centro de Estudios Constitucionales y Políticos, AECID, 2009); reprinted in H Olasolo (ed), *Ensayos sobre la Corte Penal Internacional* (Universidad Javeriana/Dyke, Bogotá, 2009).

—— 'El Desarrollo de la Coautoria Mediata en Derecho Penal Internacional' (2009) 7 *Iter Criminis* 121.

—— 'Systematic and Casuistic Approaches to the Role of Victims in Criminal Proceedings before the International Criminal Court' (2009) 12 *New Criminal Law Review* 513.

—— *The Criminal Responsibility of Senior Political and Military Leaders as Principals to International Crimes* (Oxford, Hart Publishing, 2009).

Olasolo H and Pérez Cepeda A, 'The Notion of Control of the Crime and its Application by the ICTY in the Stakić Case' (2004) 4 *International Criminal Law Review* 475.

Olasolo H and Carnero-Rojo E, 'The Application of the Principle of Complementarity to Decide where to Open an Investigation: The Admissibility of *Situations*' in C Stahn and MM El Zeidy (eds), *The International Criminal Court and Complementarity: From Theory to Practice* (Cambridge, Cambridge University Press, 2011).

Osiel M, 'The Banality of the Good: Aligning Incentives against Mass Atrocity' (2005) 105 *Columbia Law Review* 1751.

Padgen A, *The Fall of Natural Man: The American Indian and the Origins of Comparative Ethnology* (Cambridge, Cambridge University Press, 1982).

Pérez Cepeda A, *La Responsabilidad de los Administradores de Sociedades: Criterios de Atribución* (Barcelona, Cedecs Editorial, 1997).

Petersen R and Zukerman S, 'Revenge or Reconciliation: Theory and Method of Emotions in the Context of Colombia's Peace Process' in M Bergsmo and P Kalmanovitz (eds), *Law in Peace Negotiations* (Oslo, Forum for International Criminal and Humanitarian Law Publications, 2009).

Piacente N, 'Importance of the JCE Doctrine for the ICTY Prosecutorial Policy' (2004) 2 *Journal of International Criminal Justice* 446.

Pignatelly y Meca F, *La Sanción de los Crímenes de Guerra en el Derecho Español*, (Madrid, Ministerio de Defensa, 2002).

Piragoff DK, 'Article 30. Mental Element' in O Triffterer (ed), *Commentary on the Rome Statute of the International Criminal Court: Observers' Notes, Article by Article* (Baden Baden, Nomos, 1999).

Powles S, 'Joint Criminal Enterprise: Criminal Liability by Prosecutorial Ingenuity and Judicial Creativity?' (2004) 2 *Journal of International Criminal Justice* 606.

Pozo Serrano MP, 'Medidas Nacionales Adoptadas para la Ratificación y la Aplicación del Estatuto de la Corte Penal Internacional: Un balance provisional' (2003) 18 *Anuario de Derecho Internacional* 299.

Pueyo Losa J, 'Un Nuevo Modelo de Cooperación Internacional en Materia Penal: entre la Justicia Universal y la Jurisdicción Internacional' in S Álvarez González and JR Remacha y Tejada (eds), *Cooperación jurídica internacional* (Madrid, Colección Escuela Diplomática, 2001).

Quintero Olivares M, *Manual de Derecho Penal. Parte General* (Cizur Menor (Navarra), Aranzadi, 2002).

Ramcharan B, 'The National Responsibility to Protect Human Rights' (2009) 39 *Hong Kong Law Journal* 361.

Ramsbotham O and Woodhouse T, *Humanitarian Intervention in Contemporary Conflict: A Reconceptualization* (Cambridge, Polity Press, 1991).

Rastan R, 'What is a "Case" for the Purpose of the Rome Statute?' (2008) 19 *Criminal Law Forum* 435.

Reisman W, 'Sovereignty and Human Rights in Contemporary International Law' (1990) 84 *American Journal of International Law* 866.

Richemond D, 'Normativity in International Law: The Case of Unilateral Humanitarian Intervention' (2003) 6 *Yale Human Rights and Development Law Journal* 45.

Robinson D, 'Serving the Interests of Justice: Amnesties, Truth Commissions and the International Criminal Court' (2003) 14 *European Journal of International Law* 481.

—— 'Comments on Chapter 4 of Claudia Cárdenas Aravena' in JK Kleffner and G Kor (eds), *Complementary Views on Complementarity* (The Hague, TMC Asser Press, 2006).

Rodriguez-Villasante y Prieto JL, 'Análisis del Estatuto del Tribunal Penal Internacional' in Miño and Dávila (eds), *Jornadas 'Fuerrzas Armadas y Derechos Humanos: Es Posible Alcanzar el Equilibrio?' (1999: Sevilla, Spain)* (Madrid, Miño and Dávila, 2000).
——'Los Principios Generales del Derecho Penal en el Estatuto de Roma' (2000) 75 *Revista Española de Derecho Militar* 381.
Ronzitti B, *Rescuing Nationals Abroad through Military Coercion and Intervention on Grounds of Humanity* (Dordrecht, Martinus Nijhoff Publishing, 1985).
Roxin C, 'Straftaten im Rahmen organisatorischer Machtapparate' (1963) *Goldtdammers' Archiv für Strafrecht* 193.
—— *Täterschaft und Tatherrschaft* 1st edn (Berlin, De Gruyter, 1963).
——*Autoria y Dominio del Hecho en Derecho Penal* 6th edn (Madrid, Marcial Pons, 1998).
——'Probleme von Täterschaft und Teilnahme bei der organisierten Kriminalität' in E Samson, F Dencker, P Frisch, H Frister and W Reiss (eds), *Festschrift für Grünwald* (Baden Baden, Nomos, 1999).
Rush P and Yeah S, *Criminal Law Sourcebook* (Sydney, Butterworths, 2000).
Sadat L, 'The Legacy of the ICTY: The International Criminal Court' (2003) 37 *New England Law Review* 1073.
——'Commentary on *Prosecutor v Kvocka*' in A Klip and G Sluiter (eds), *Annotated Leading Cases of International Criminal Tribunals* (Antwerp, Intersentia, 2005).
——'El dominio de la organización como forma independiente de autoría mediata' (2006) 7 *Revista de Estudios de la Justicia* 11.
——(ed), *Forging a Convention for Crimes Against Humanity* (Cambridge, Cambridge University Press, 2011).
Sadat L and Scharf M (eds), *The Theory and Practice of International Criminal Law: Essays in Honor of M Cherif Bassiouni* (Leiden, Martinus Nijhoff, 2008).
Sánchez Legido A, *Jurisdicción Universal Penal y Derecho Internacional* (Valencia, Tirant lo Blanch, 2004).
Sancinetti MA, *Derechos Humanos en la Argentina Postdictatorial* (Buenos Aires, Lerner, 1988).
Sarkin J, *Carrots and Sticks: TRC and the South African Amnesty Process* (Oxford/Antwerp, Intersentia, 2004).
Schabas WA, *Genocide in International Law* (Cambridge, Cambridge University Press, 2000).
——*An Introduction to the International Criminal Court* (Cambridge, Cambridge University Press, 2004).
——'Genocide Trials and *Gacaca* Courts' (2005) 3 *Journal of International Criminal Justice* 879.
Scheffer D, 'Genocide and Atrocity Crimes' (2006) 1 *Genocide Studies and Prevention* 229.
——'Atrocity Crimes Framing the Responsibility to Protect' (2007–08) 40 *Case Western Reserve Journal of International Law* 111.
Scheffer D and Cox A, 'The Constitutionality of the Rome Statute of the International Criminal Court' (2008) 98 *Journal of Criminal Law and Criminology* 983.
Scomparain L, 'Le Victime du Crime et la Jurisdiction Pénale Internationale' in M Delmas-Marty and A Cassese (eds), *Crimes Internationaux et Jurisdictions Internationales* (Paris, PUF, 2002).
Seibert Fohr A, 'The Relevance of the Rome Statute of the ICC for Amnesties and Truth Commissions' (2003) 7 *Max Planck Yearbook of United Nations Law* 553.
Seils P, 'The Selection and Prioritization of Cases by the Office of the Prosecutor of the International Criminal Court' in M Bergsmo (ed) *Criteria for Prioritizing and Selecting*

Core International Crimes Cases (Oslo, Forum for International Criminal and Humanitarian Law Publications, 2009).
Simons KW, 'Rethinking Mental States' (1992) 72 *Boston University Law Review* 463.
Smith JC and Hogan B, *Criminal Law* 11th edn (London, Butterworths, 2005).
Snyman CR, *Criminal Law* (Oxford, Butterworths, 1995).
Spiga V, 'Indirect Victims' Participation in the *Lubanga* Trial' (2010) 8 *Journal of International Criminal Justice* 183.
Stahn C, 'Complementarity, Amnesties and Alternative Forms of Justice: Some Interpretative Guidelines for the International Criminal Court' (2005) 3 *Journal of International Criminal Justice* 695.
—— 'Modification of the Legal Characterization of Facts in the ICC System; A Portrayal of Regulation 55' (2005) 1 *Criminal Law Forum* 1, 16.
—— 'The Geometry of Transitional Justice: Choices of Institutional Design' (2005) 18 *Leiden Journal of International Law* 425.
—— 'Responsibility to Protect: Political Rhetoric or Emerging Legal Norm?' (2007) 101 *American Journal of International Law* 99.
Stahn C, Olasolo H and Gibson K, 'Participation of Victims in Pre-Trial Proceedings of the ICC' (2006) 4 *Journal of International Criminal Justice* 219.
Suárez F, 'Defensio Fidei Catholicae adversus Anglicanae sectae errores (The Defence of the Catholic Faith against the Errors of the Anglican)' (1613) in F Suárez, *Selections from Three Works of Francisco Suárez, S.J.: De legibus, ac deo legislatore, 1612; Defensio fidei catholicae, et apostolicae adversus anglicanae sectae errores, 1613; De triplici virtute theologica, fide, spe, et charitate, 1621*, trans GL Williams and H Davis (London, Clarendon Press, 1944).
Suchman M, 'Managing Legitimacy: Strategic and Institutional Approaches' (1995) 20 *The Academy of Management Review* 571.
Tallgreen I, 'Article 20. Ne Bis in Idem' in O Triffterer (ed), *Commentary on the Rome Statute of the International Criminal Court: Observers' Notes, Article by Article* (Baden Baden, Nomos, 1999).
Teson F, *Humanitarian Intervention: An Inquiry into Law and Morality* 3rd edn (Ardsley, Transnational Publishers, 2005).
Thakur R, 'Outlook: Intervention, Sovereignty and the Responsibility to Protect: Experience from ICISS' (2002) 33 *Security Dialogue* 323.
—— *The United Nations, Peace and Security: From Collective Security to the Responsibility to Protect* (Cambridge, Cambridge University Press, 2006).
Thompson B, *The Criminal Law of Sierra Leone* (Lanham, University Press of America, 1999).
Tully LD, 'Human Rights Compliance and the Gacaca Jurisdictions in Rwanda' (2003) 26 *Boston College International and Comparative Law Review* 385.
United Nations Commission on Human Rights (UNCHR), 'Basic Principles and Guidelines on the Right to a Remedy and Reparation for Victims of Violations of International Human Rights and Humanitarian Law' in UNCHR, 'Civil and Political Rights, including the Questions of Independence of the Judiciary, Administration of Justice, Impunity: The Right to Restitution, Compensation and Rehabilitation for Victims of Gross Violations of Human Rights and Fundamental Freedoms (Final Report of the Special Rapporteur Mr M Cherif Bassiouni submitted in accordance with Commission Resolution 1999/33)' (18 January 2000) UN Doc E/CN.4/2000/62.
United Nations Commission on Human Rights (UNCHR), 'Report of the Special Rapporteur on Extrajudicial, Arbitrary or Summary Executions, Mr BW Ndiaye, on his Mission to Rwanda from 8 to 17 April 1993' (11 August 1993) E/CN.4/1994/7/Add.1.

United Nations General Assembly (UNGA), 'Report of the Preparatory Committee on the Establishment of an International Criminal Court' (1996) UN Doc A/51/22.
UNGA and UNSC, 'Report of the Panel on United Nations Peace Operations' (21 August 2000) UN Doc A/55/305-S/2000/809.
—— '2005 World Summit Outcome' (24 October 2005) UN Doc Res A/Res/60/1.
—— 'Implementing the Responsibility to Protect: Report of the Secretary-General' (12 January 2009) UN Doc A/63/677.
United Nations Security Council (UNSC), 'An Agenda for Peace-Preventative Diplomacy, Peacemaking, and Peace-Keeping' (17 June 1992) UN Doc A/47/277-S/24111.
—— 'Report of the Secretary-General Pursuant to Paragraph 2 of the Security Council Resolution 808 (1993)' (3 May 1993) UN Doc S/25704.
—— 'Report of the Secretary-General on the Situation in Rwanda' (31 May 1994) UN Doc S/1994/640.
—— 'Report of the Secretary-General Pursuant to Paragraph 5 of Security Council Resolution 955 (1994)' (13 February 1995) UN Doc S/1995/134.
—— 'No Exit without Strategy: Security Council Decision-making and the Closure or Transition of United Nations Peacekeeping Operations' (20 April 2001) UN Doc. S/2001/394.
—— High-Level Panel on Threats, Challenges and Change, 'A More Secure World: Our Shared Responsibility' (2 December 2004) UN Doc A/59/565.
—— 'Report of the International Commission of Inquiry on Darfur to the Secretary-General' (1 February 2005) UN Doc S/2005/60.
Van der Wilt H, 'Joint Criminal Enterprise Possibilities and Limitations' (2007) 5 *Journal of International Criminal Justice* 91.
—— 'The Continuous Quest for Proper Modes of Criminal Responsibility' (2009) 7 *Journal of International Criminal Justice* 311.
Van Sliedregt E, 'Joint Criminal Enterprise as a Pathway to Convicting Individuals for Genocide' (2007) 5 *Journal of International Criminal Justice* 184.
Van Zyl P, 'Unfinished Business: The Truth and Reconciliation Commission's Contribution to Justice in Post-Apartheid South Africa' in MC Bassiouni (ed), *Post-Conflict Justice* (Ardsley, Transnational Publishers, 2002).
Von Hebel H and Robinson D, 'Crimes within the Jurisdiction of the Court' in R Lee (ed), *The International Criminal Court: The Making of the Rome Statute – Issues, Negotiations, Results* (The Hague, Kluwer Law International, 1999).
Waller L and Williams C, *Criminal Law Text and Cases* (Sydney, Butterworths, 2001).
Weigend T, 'Intent, Mistake of Law and Co-Perpetration in the *Lubanga* Decision on Confirmation of Charges' (2008) 6 *Journal of International Criminal Justice* 471.
Weiss T and Hubert D, *The Responsibility to Protect: Research, Bibliography and Background* (Ottawa, International Development Research Centre, 2001).
Werle G, *Principles of International Criminal Law* (The Hague, TMC Asser Institute, 2005).
—— *Tratado de Derecho Penal Internacional* (Valencia, Tirant lo Blanch, 2005).
—— 'Individual Criminal Responsibility in Article 25 ICC Statute' (2007) 5 *Journal of International Criminal Justice* 953.
Williams S, 'Article 17: Issues of Admissibility' in O Triffterer (ed), *Commentary on the Rome Statute of the International Criminal Court: Observers' Notes, Article by Article* (Baden Baden, Nomos, 1999).

Wilmshurst E, 'Jurisdiction of the Court' in R Lee (ed), *The International Criminal Court: The Making of the Rome Statute – Issues, Negotiations, Results* (The Hague, Kluwer Law International, 1999).

Yee L, 'The International Criminal Court and the Security Council' in R Lee (ed), *The International Criminal Court: The Making of the Rome Statute – Issues, Negotiations, Results* (The Hague, Kluwer Law International, 1999).

Zacklin R, 'Beyond Kosovo: The United Nations and Humanitarian Intervention' in LC Vorah, F Pocar, Y Fetherstone, O Fourney, C Graham, J Hocking and N Robson (eds), *Man's Inhumanity to Man* (The Hague, Kluwer Law International, 2003).

Zahar A and Sluiter G, *International Criminal Law: A Critical Introduction* (Oxford, Oxford University Press, 2007).

Zimmermann A, 'Article 5. Crimes within the Jurisdiction of the Court' in O Triffterer (ed), *Commentary on the Rome Statute of the International Criminal Court: Observers' Notes, Article by Article* (Baden Baden, Nomos, 1999).

Zugaldia Espinar JM (ed), *Derecho Penal: Parte General* (Valencia, Tirant lo Blanch, 2002).